T0306000

Enhancing Public Innovation by Transforming Public Governance

Rising and changing citizen expectations, dire fiscal constraints, unfulfilled political aspirations, high professional ambitions and a growing number of stubborn societal problems have generated an increasing demand for innovation of public policies and services. Drawing on the latest research, this book examines how current systems of public governance can be transformed in order to enhance public innovation. It scrutinizes the need for new roles and public sector reforms and analyses how the gradual transition towards New Public Governance can stimulate the exploration and exploitation of new and bold ideas in the public sector. It argues that the key to public innovation lies in combining and balancing elements from Classic Public Administration, New Public Management and New Public Governance, and theorizes how it can be enhanced by multi-actor collaboration for the benefit of public officials, private stakeholders, citizens and society at large.

Jacob Torfing is Professor of Politics and Institutions at Roskilde University. He is also Research Director of the Roskilde School of Governance. His research interests include network governance, public administration reforms, public innovation and public leadership and management. He has published more than 200 articles and book chapters and more than 25 books. He is the author of *Collaborative Innovation in the Public Sector* (2016).

Peter Triantafillou is Professor in Public Policy and Performance Management at Roskilde University. His research interests are with governance and power relations in public policy and performance management in the public sector. His research has been published in numerous academic articles, edited volumes and the monograph *New Forms of Governing: A Foucauldian Inspired Analysis* (2012).

Enhancing Public Innovation by Transforming Public Governance

Jacob Torfing

Roskilde University, Denmark

Peter Triantafillou

Roskilde University, Denmark

CAMBRIDGE
UNIVERSITY PRESS

University Printing House, Cambridge CB2 8BS, United Kingdom

Cambridge University Press is part of the University of Cambridge.

It furthers the University's mission by disseminating knowledge in the pursuit of
education, learning, and research at the highest international levels of excellence.

www.cambridge.org
Information on this title: www.cambridge.org/9781107088986

© Jacob Torfing and Peter Triantafillou 2016

First published 2016

A catalogue record for this publication is available from the British Library.

Library of Congress Cataloging-in-Publication Data
Torfing, Jacob, editor. | Triantafillou, Peter, editor.
Enhancing public innovation by transforming public governance / edited by
Jacob Torfing, Roskilde University, Denmark and Peter Triantafillou,
Roskilde University, Denmark.
Cambridge, United Kingdom ; New York : Cambridge University Press,
2016. | Includes bibliographical references and index
LCCN 2016018125 | ISBN 9781107088986
LCSH: Organizational change. | Organizational effectiveness. | Public
administration. | Administrative agencies – Management.
LCC JF1525.O73 E65 2016 | DDC 352.3/67–dc23
LC record available at https://lccn.loc.gov/2016018125

ISBN 978-1-107-08898-6 Hardback

Contents

Figures

Tables

Contributors

ROBERT ÅGREN is a researcher at Lund University. His interests are innovation, public–private partnerships and public procurement. His research has appeared in an extensive range of academic journals and book chapters. He is the assistant editor of *Upphandlingsrättslig Tidskrift* [The Procurement Law Journal].

CHRISTOPHER K. ANSELL is professor of political science at UC Berkeley. His current research focuses on the collaboration of public and private institutions to manage risks and to govern unruly public problems. Ansell has a strong substantive interest in public health and environmental policy. His research has been published in numerous academic journals. He recently co-authored *Public Innovation through Collaboration and Design* (2014).

VICTOR BEKKERS is professor of public administration at Erasmus University Rotterdam and is currently the head of department of public administration and sociology. He is coordinator of the European FP7 research programme on social innovation in the public sector (LIPSE). He is interested in how public sector innovation and new technologies change the course and content of public policy, governance and service delivery processes. He has published extensively on these issues in academic journals and recently co-authored *Visual Culture and Public Policy. Towards a Visual Polity?* (2015).

LOTTE BØGH ANDERSEN is a professor at Aarhus University. Her main interests are with public leadership and public service motivation. She has published extensively on these topics in a score of prestigious academic journals.

TONY BOVAIRD is emeritus professor of public management and policy at University of Birmingham and a director of Governance International. His main interests are in public governance, user and community co-production of public outcomes and the strategic commissioning of public services. He has undertaken research projects for OECD, the

European Commission and governments throughout Europe. He is co-editor of *Public Management and Governance* (3rd ed., 2015).

TOM CHRISTENSEN is professor in political science at University of Oslo. His key interests are in public organizations, public sector reforms and public policy. His research has appeared in a large number of journal articles and books. He co-edited *The Ashgate Research Companion to New Public Management* (2011).

JEAN HARTLEY is professor of public leadership at the Open University. Her main research interests are in public leadership, notably leadership with political astuteness, and in innovation and organizational change in public services. She has published extensively on these issues in academic journals. She has published *Leadership for Healthcare* (with John Benington, 2010) and is the co-editor of *The Routledge Companion to Leadership* (2016).

MADS LETH FELSAGER JAKOBSEN is an associate professor at Aarhus University. His interests are in public organizations, public regulations, public service motivation and performance management. His research has appeared in numerous academic journals. He recently co-authored *Regelstaten: Væksten i danske love og bekendtgørelser 1989–2011* (2014).

PER LÆGREID is a professor at the University of Bergen. His interests include public sector reforms, comparative public administration, institutional change and democratic governance. His research has been published in a large number of academic journals and books. He co-authored *Government Agencies: Practices and Lessons from 30 Countries* (2012) and *Organizing for Coordination in the Public Sector* (2014).

VEIKO LEMBER is a senior research fellow at the Tallinn University of Technology and the director of the Ragnar Nurkse School of Innovation and Governance. His main research interests are in public–private cooperation, public services delivery and innovation policy. His research has appeared in several academic journals. Recently, he co-authored *Public Procurement, Innovation and Policy: International Perspectives* (2014).

ELKE LOEFFLER is the Chief Executive of Governance International. Her expertise is in service improvement, quality and performance management, citizen involvement in the commissioning, design, delivery and evaluation of public services. Her research has been published in several journal articles and edited volumes. She co-edited *Public Management and Governance* (3rd ed., 2015).

MIRKO NOORDEGRAAF is professor of public management at Utrecht University and chair of the public governance and management faculty at the Utrecht School of Governance. He focuses on organization and management issues in public domains, with particular emphasis on public managers and public professionals. His research has been published in numerous academic journal articles. His most recent book is *Public Management. Performance, Professionalism and Politics* (2015).

STEPHEN P. OSBORNE is professor of international public management at the University of Edinburgh Business School and Director of the School's Centre for Service Excellence (CenSE). He is the editor of *Public Management Review*. His main interests are with partnerships and co-production, public management reforms, the role of the third sector, and public service innovation and management. He has published scores of articles on these topics and on the development of the Public Service-Dominant Logic for public services delivery. He recently co-edited *The Handbook of Innovation in Public Services* (2013).

B. GUY PETERS is a professor at the University of Pittsburgh, an honorary professor at several universities around the world and the recipient of several academic awards. He has a long-standing interest with comparative public administration and public policy, and US public administration. He has published on these issues in an astonishing number of academic journals and books. Some of his most recent books include *Strategies for Comparative Political Research* (2013) and *The Search for Coordination and Coherence: Managing Horizontal Government* (2015).

OLE HELBY PETERSEN is an associate professor at Roskilde University. His research interests are with public–private partnerships, contracting out, public procurement, public sector innovation and public policy in a comparative perspective. He was recently awarded the prestigious Tietgen prize for talented young researchers. His research has appeared in a score of academic journals and edited volumes.

ZOE RADNOR is professor of service management and Dean at the School of Management, University of Leicester. Her area of interest is in performance and process improvement and, service management in public sector organizations. She has published over 100 articles, book chapters and reports as well as presented widely on the topic to both academic and practitioner audiences. She recently was lead editor for *Public Service Operations Management* (2016).

WALTER SCHERRER is a professor at the University of Salzburg and academic director of the International Executive MBA and other post-graduate studies at the Business School of Salzburg University. His main interests are with the economic aspects of public–private partnerships, regional economics and innovation policy. His research has been published in numerous academic journals and edited volumes.

EVA SØRENSEN is a professor at Roskilde University. She has been the director of several large research programmes. Her main interests are with public governance, political leadership, democracy and public sector innovation. She has published extensively on these topics in academic journals. Recently she co-authored *Interactive Governance: Advancing the Paradigm* (2012).

CLAUS THRANE is an associate professor at Aarhus University. His interests are with entrepreneurship, innovation and marketing strategies. His research has appeared in several academic journals and book chapters.

JACOB TORFING is professor in politics and institutions at Roskilde University. He is also research director of the Roskilde School of Governance. His research interests include network governance, public administration reforms, public innovation and public leadership and management. He has published more than 200 articles and book chapters and more than 25 books. He is the author of *Collaborative Innovation in the Public Sector* (2016).

PETER TRIANTAFILLOU is professor in public policy and performance management at Roskilde University. His research interests are with governance and power relations in public policy and performance management in the public sector. His research has been published in numerous academic articles, edited volumes and the monograph *New Forms of Governing: A Foucauldian Inspired Analysis* (2012).

WOUTER VAN DOOREN is an associate professor at the University of Antwerp. His main research interest lies in performance, performance measurement and management in the public sector. He has published extensively on these issues in academic journals and books. He recently co-authored the second edition of *Performance Management in the Public Sector* (2015).

MONTGOMERY VAN WART is a professor at California State University San Bernadino. His research interests include administrative leadership, human resource management, training and development, administrative values and ethics, and organization behaviour. His research has appeared in a very large number of academic journals and books.

He recently co-edited *Leadership and Culture: Comparative Models of Top Civil Servant Training* (2015).

TOM WILLEMS is a postdoctoral researcher at University of Antwerp. His main interests are with democratic accountability in the public sector and public–private partnerships. His research has appeared in several academic journals.

1   Enhancing Public Innovation by Transforming Public Governance?

Jacob Torfing and Peter Triantafillou

1.1   Introduction

Innovation has recently moved to the top of the agenda in many public sectors around the world. Innovation may be regarded as a magic concept with a strong normative connotation (Pollitt and Hupe 2011). Thus, the innovation discourse in policy circles implicitly assumes that innovation equals improvement and that it is good to be a frontrunner, bad to be a laggard and even worse to forego the chance of innovating. You do not want to fall behind when it comes to innovation since it prevents you from saving money and delivering better results. A lot of high hopes and promises are ascribed to the notion of 'innovation', which is often considered as a silver bullet that can solve societal problems by producing new and smart solutions. Not surprisingly, the current quest for innovation is sometimes criticized for promising more than it delivers. However, the interesting thing about innovation is that it has the potential for delivering more than it promises because it is potentially a creative process that opens up for and embraces the emergence of the otherwise possible. Innovation often sends its participants to an uncharted territory where solutions are often encountered and results achieved that we could not even dream of because they are unknown or unthought of. Innovation is a heuristic and pragmatic search for and realization of new and emerging solutions that disrupt the current ways of thinking and doing things and, at least potentially, give us more than we hoped for. It is this potentiality that for better or worse has turned innovation into a magic concept.

Today, innovation challenges the narrow focus on administrative rationalization as the top priority of public organizations and public leaders. Political challenges such as demographic changes, increasing public health expenditure, unmet social demands, a growing number of wicked problems and the presence of numerous policy deadlocks cannot be solved by simply cutting public expenditures and making the public sector

The corresponding author for this chapter is Jacob Torfing.

leaner. After 30 years of cost-saving rationalization efforts, such as privatization, contracting out public services and eliminating slack in public
service organizations, we need to raise our ambitions by seeking to create
more and better public solutions for the same or less money, and innovation might be the tool for achieving exactly this.

At first, the growing interest in public innovation primarily led to
symbolic changes. From the 1990s onwards innovation was added to
the long list of strategic goals in public organizations. External experts
and consultants were hired to stimulate innovation, special development
and innovation units were established and some countries saw the creation of national innovation labs such as the American OPM Innovation
Lab, the British NESTA, the Danish MindLab and the Mexican
Laboratorio para la Ciudad. Later, the strategic and symbolic embrace
of the public innovation agenda has been followed by more practical and
operational attempts to spur innovation by means of training public
managers and employees and by encouraging them to develop and test
new ideas in practice. To support this endeavour, we have seen the
development of new methods for how to uncover user demands, stimulate knowledge exchange, generate innovative ideas, test prototypes and
manage the risks associated with innovation. In some countries the new
design thinking has played a key role in developing new methods for
stimulating innovation (Bason 2010). Gradually, the strategic and practical efforts to spur public innovation have come to fruition. An important
indication is that national innovation award schemes receive an increasing
number of applications, and a recent study of the American Government
Innovation Award programme shows that the innovation agenda has
expanded in every policy area from 1994 to 2010 (Borins 2014).
Another indicator is the growing number of surveys and measurement
programmes that report an increasing number of public innovations
(Arundel and Hollanders 2008; Arundel and Smith 2013; Kattel et al.
2014). One recent survey shows that two-thirds of public administration
institutions at the EU level have introduced a new or significantly
improved service in the last three years. Conversely, only 4 per cent of
the public managers who participated in the survey reported that no
positive effect had resulted from the innovation that had been implemented (European Commission 2011).

Innovation strategies and activities seem to be growing rapidly in the
public sector. Yet public innovation continues to be rather episodic and is
often triggered by accidental events such as economic crises and large-
scale budget cuts, scientific or technical breakthroughs, access to special
purpose funding, public criticism and negative evaluations, etc. There is
still quite some way to go before public innovation becomes a permanent

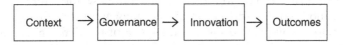

Figure 1.1 The connection between governance, innovation and public sector outcomes

and systematic activity pervading all aspects and levels of government. The key question today then is: How can we transform the institutional structure, the organizational designs and cultures, the steering systems, the management practices and more generally the entire system of public governance in order to further stimulate and enhance the production of innovative solutions to both deep-seated and emerging problems? This book is devoted to answering this pertinent question.

The overarching idea of this edited volume is that the way we shape the institutional forms of governance in the public sector affects its capacity for innovation. If we transform public governance in the right ways, public innovation may be boosted to the benefit of users, citizens, public employees, private stakeholders and society at large. How the system of public governance is reformed obviously depends on the context and varies between countries, levels and policy areas. Accordingly, we believe that context-sensitive governance reforms that change and adjust the balance between different governance paradigms will spur the production of public innovation and bring about new solutions that will outperform the existing ones. The analytical model informing our study of the link between governance and innovation is depicted in Figure 1.1.

Figure 1.1 indicates that the political, socio-economic and administrative context will affect the forms and content of governance reform, which in turn will help to spur innovation that may lead to better outcomes. These are the causalities that are further explored in this volume.

So far there have been few attempts to reflect on how the system of public governance affects the ability to innovate (see Eggers and Singh 2009; Hartley, Sørensen and Torfing 2013; Ansell and Torfing 2014). As a result the burgeoning literature on public governance and the expanding field of public innovation research remain largely unrelated. This book aims to close this gap in public management research and draw together these two strands of research by focusing on the attempts to transform governance in order to enhance innovation. Our hypothesis is that a further strengthening of governance practices associated with New Public Governance may help to further enhance public innovation. However, the existing governance paradigms (in terms of Classical Public Administration and New Public Management) are likely to continue playing an important role in the public sector. Moreover, they contain indispensable drivers of public innovation that in some cases might help to compensate some of the inherent problems in the governance practices associated with New Public Governance. Hence, the general argument pursued in this book is not that we are seeing or even need a wholesale transition to New Public Governance. Rather we are likely to see the addition of a new paradigmatic layer of governance on top of the existing ones that in some areas will continue to be predominant and contain important drivers of innovation. However, since New Public Governance is 'the new kid on the block' and tends to focus explicitly on innovation, we are particularly interested in how this way of thinking about public governance can stimulate public innovation.

With this book we take an important step in creating a scholarly *rapprochement* between governance and innovation theory. Our goal is both to contribute to the scholarly discussion about the effect of different governance paradigms on the innovation capacity of public organizations and to provide new inspiration to practitioners who are aiming to enhance public innovation by rethinking the way that that public sector is organized, governed and managed. Finally, we hope that this book will stir public debates about the future development and reform of the public sector. The stakes in these debates are high as there is much to gain in terms of efficiency, quality, effectiveness and perhaps even democracy from finding new ways of spurring innovation through reflexive and context-sensitive governance reforms.

The chapter is structured in the following way: Section 2 explains why we are witnessing a new focus on public innovation. Section 3 defines the concept of innovation and reflects on the key features of innovation in the public sector. Section 4 defines the notion of governance and analyses how different governance paradigms drive and hamper innovation respectively. Section 5 presents the theoretical framework that informs the studies presented in this book. Section 6 explains the structure of the book and briefly introduces the chapters.

1.2   A New Focus on Public Innovation

For more than a century innovation has been considered as the main source of economic growth and profitability in the private sector. According to the pioneering works of Schumpeter (1934), innovation is driven by cutthroat competition between private companies and propelled by individual entrepreneurs and large-scale research and development departments. When it comes to the public sector, the lack of competition and entrepreneurship seems to have nurtured the belief that innovation is both unnecessary and irrelevant. Many people perceive public innovation as a contradiction in terms since, unlike the dynamic private sector in which innovation is spurred by forward-looking and risk-taking entrepreneurs, the public sector is a large ossified bureaucracy based on hierarchical command and control and a growing number of rules and red tape.

This negative perception of public innovation has changed considerably over the last 30 years as public innovation has received steadily growing attention among both public administration researchers and practitioners (Damanpour 1991; Rogers 1995; Borins 1998, 2008; Hartley 2005; Eggers and Singh 2009; Steelman 2010; Mazzucato 2013). In the mid-1980s, there was a growing interest in publicly funded innovation in science and technology, which was seen as a vehicle for enhancing the competiveness of national economies in an increasingly globalized world market (Porter 1985). Public innovation can be spurred, it was argued, by creating national innovation systems that bring together relevant public and private actors in networks that facilitate coordination and knowledge exchange (Lundvall 1985). However, it should be noted that the purpose of stimulating public innovation in science and technology was not to improve the public sector itself but rather to enhance profitability of private firms. In short, public innovation was meant to create private rather than public value.

If public sector innovation was initially seen as a lever for enhancing the economic competiveness of private firms and national economies, private sector innovation in terms of new computer technology was increasingly seen as a driver of public sector innovation. As such, an expanding stream of research from the 1980s onwards focused on the conditions for introducing and exploiting new information and communicator technologies in the public sector (Perry and Danzinger 1980; Perry and Kraemer 1980; Kraemer and Perry 1989; Perry et al. 1993). Computers were considered as an instrument for the rationalization of administrative procedures, and the drivers and barriers to the diffusion of computer technology were a great concern.

From the 1990s onwards the US Reinventing Government Movement successfully promoted the idea that the efficiency of public service organizations could also be dramatically increased through an infusion of entrepreneurship and innovation and other core features of private firms (Osborne and Gaebler 1992). The Reinventing Government Movement, and its European counterpart the New Public Management reform programme (Hood 1991), criticized the rule-governed public bureaucracies for delivering poor and costly services and called for administrative reforms that would create a result-driven public sector in which public managers would enhance service innovation in response to competitive pressures from private contractors and incentives emanating for the systematic use of performance management and performance-related pay systems (Ansell and Torfing 2014).

However, as the administrative use of computer technology became more and more common in the public sector and the Reinventing Government Movement gradually reduced service improvement to rationalization efforts based on cost-reducing LEAN technologies, the innovation rhetoric almost died out. At least, the public innovation discourse seemed to have lost its momentum by the beginning of the new millennium. The recent revival and expansion of the public innovation discourse that has captured the mindset of many public leaders around the globe can be explained by several important factors. First, the economic and fiscal crisis, the growing pressures from the global market economy and the ageing populations in the Western world together put a squeeze on public budgets and seem to have generated a growing need for innovative solutions that can provide an intelligent alternative to across-the-board cuts. Second, there is a growing academic and political recognition of the increasingly complex and unruly character of public problems and challenges. Many of the problems that the public sector is supposed to solve are so complex and conflict ridden that they defy standard solutions, and if there are no adequate solutions, increased public spending will not solve the problems but only throw good money after bad money. Innovative solutions are needed in order to break policy deadlocks and political stalemate. Third, the attempt of politicians and professionally trained public employees to meet the calls for more individualized and personalized services, and the future challenges posed by ageing populations, climate change and other long-term systemic changes. With the growing wealth of Western societies the political and professional service ambitions seem to increase, while, simultaneously, the demand for individualized and tailor-made services enhances and the visibility of socio-economic problems and unmet social demands is increased. The combination of growing ambitions and expectations with austerity and scarce resources has stimulated the search for innovative solutions that can give us 'more for less'. Fourth, the emergence of a new generation of digital technologies has enabled novel forms of communication and interaction with users and citizens in the 'front office' and enabled the handling of huge amounts of behavioural and other data in the 'back office'. New breakthroughs in robotics have further stimulated the development of welfare technologies. As such, technological development is once again a driver of public innovation.

More studies are needed in order to pinpoint the relative impact and timing of the different factors that seem to have contributed to the current surge of interest in public innovation. Nevertheless, the combined effect of the economic, political, social and technological factors is that public innovation has become a strategic goal pursued by local, regional and national governments as well as by international organizations such as the EU, the OECD and the World Bank. A report from the European Commission indicates that there are still considerable obstacles to public innovation in terms of the lack of management support, staff resistance and a risk-averse culture (European Commission 2013). Nevertheless, the report also shows that there is a broad consensus about the conception of public innovation and the need to enhance it in the light of political ambitions, public demands and tightening resources.

1.3 Defining Public Innovation

Innovation involves the development and realization of new and creative ideas and practices. Innovation is often intentional and designed to significantly benefit a particular individual, group, organization or wider society (West and Farr 1990: 3). The innovation process is an open-ended and heuristic process that relies on imagination, intuition, chance discoveries and unacknowledged conditions that make it extremely difficult to plan and control and impossible to predict the result. Consequently, there is no guarantee that innovation leads to improvement. Innovation involves a break with established practices and conventional forms of knowledge, but whether it is deemed successful in producing additional public value depends on an ex post judgement that is based on subjective evaluations of relevant and affected actors. Therefore, the definition of innovation should not include any reference to successful outcomes and should not be defined as 'the successful exploitation of new ideas' (Bessant 2003). Hence, we shall here define innovation as *an intentional, yet inherently contingent, process that involves the development and realization of new and creative ideas that challenge conventional wisdoms and break with established practices in a particular context* (Sørensen and Torfing 2011). Innovation may ex post be considered as more or less successful and the successful innovations will tend to be consolidated, upscaled and diffused within and across organizations (Rogers 1995).

Innovation gives rise to a particular kind of discontinuous, or disruptive, change that is commonly referred to as 'step-change' (Hartley 2005). As such, innovation is more than a 'continuous improvement' of public services pursued in the day-to-day operation of public service organizations and less than a 'revolutionary transformation' that replaces an entire system of action with a new one (Hartley 2006; Osborne and Brown 2011). Innovative step-changes combine existing ideas and practices in new ways, while frequently adding new ones, and thereby amount to a change of the overall design, functionality, logic and impact. The steps can be small and incremental in the sense that they merely change the form and content of particular artefacts, practices and strategies, but they can also be large and radical and change the goals, character and operational logic of a particular organization or organizational field.

The more or less radical innovations might be a result of an invention of something entirely new that has never been seen on Earth, but they may also result from the diffusion and imitation of innovative solutions from elsewhere through complex processes of adoption and adaptation. Hence, it is not the source of innovation but rather the context of implementation that determines whether something is an innovation or not. If an artefact, practice or strategy is considered as new in a specific context, it is an innovation even if it can be found in a different context (Roberts and King 1996). As such, innovation is contextual and partly based on subjective perceptions of 'newness'.

Schumpeter (1934) distinguishes between technological innovations that include process and product innovation, organizational innovations that transform the structure, form and operation of private enterprises, and market innovations that either change the composition and use of raw materials or create new ways of marketing products. In the public sector there has been a lot of focus on process innovation and organizational innovation but less focus on product innovation and more focus on service and policy innovation (Polsby 1984; Roberts and King 1996; Albury 2005; Osborne and Brown 2013). There are also examples of democratic innovations aiming to create new arenas for active citizen participation (Smith 2009), governance innovations seeking to change the role and image of public authorities and the public sector at large (Hartley 2005) and discursive innovations aiming to transform the way that public problems and challenges are framed (Hajer 1995).

Public sector innovation not only seems to have a somehow different focus than private sector innovation but also seems to differ from private innovation in terms of the value that is produced through innovation. Whereas private sector innovation tends to produce private value in the sense of value that is created and appropriated by private firms and commercially protected by patents, public sector innovation aims to produce public value that is appropriated by society at large and bound by a political and moral obligation to spread new and better solutions throughout society enabling as many as possible to benefit (Moore and Hartley 2008; Hartley 2012). However, the distinction is not clear-cut since, for example, public universities also tend to patent scientific and technological innovations in order to control and benefit financially from their commercial exploitation.

The stubborn myth that public bureaucracies are virtually incapable of innovating due to the lack of market-based competition and the stifling effects of centralized control, red-tape rules and political stalemates is not correct. Empirical studies suggest that the public sector is much more innovative and dynamic than its reputation. Thus, a recent study that compares the contribution of public and private employees in the Scandinavian countries to the creation of service innovation in areas puts the public employees slightly ahead of the private employees (Bysted and Hansen 2015). More importantly, however, the study reveals that the real difference is not between the public and private sector but rather between different service areas. Hence, the employees in the technical and authoritative service areas tend to contribute less to the creation of innovation than the employees in the social service regardless of sector affiliation.

People who contrast the innovative private sector with the apparently ossified public sector often forget that public bureaucracies can actually stimulate innovation through the exercise of political and administrative leadership, the mobilization of public resources, the creation of rules and procedures for exploring and exploiting new ideas and fostering a supporting cultural environment (Jakobsen 2013). True, many public organizations – at least until the mid-1980s when the contracting out of public services became more frequent – lacked external competitive pressures that could help to spur innovation. However, it should be recalled that this deficiency is largely compensated by the presence of high political ambitions, strong public demands and fiscal constraints that together produce a strong impetus for innovation. We should also bear in mind that while competition may provide a strong incentive to pursue innovation in the private sector, it does not in itself provide any methods for actually creating innovation. When private firms recognize the need to innovate in order to maintain or improve their market position and begin to search for innovative solutions, they confront many of the same barriers that public organizations are facing since especially large firms are organized as bureaucracies in much the same ways as public organizations (Hartley, Sørensen and Torfing 2013). As such, big private corporations are hierarchically organized, contain organizational and mental silos and are bound by a large number of internal and external rules and regulations. In sum, we should be careful not to exaggerate the difference between the public and private sector in terms of their relative capacities to innovate.

In the wake of the current innovation hype, it is important to maintain that the enhancement of public innovation is not a goal in itself but rather a means to reach other important goals such as efficiency, effectiveness, quality improvement, removal of policy deadlocks, democratization, etc. (Bason 2010). We should not innovate for the sake of innovating but use innovation as a tool for enhancing public value production and achieving the many goals of the public sector.

It is also important to avoid the pro-innovation bias that readily asserts that public innovation is always called for, always successful and always leads to improvement (Abrahamson 1991). In countering this bias, we should, first and foremost, insist that innovation is not an all-purpose tool that should be used at all times and in all situations and contexts. Hence, well-functioning public programmes that produce and deliver desirable outcomes should not be innovated for the sake of innovating. Moreover, in the aftermath of large-scale policy reforms, there will typically only be a need for minor adjustments and small improvements while people are trying to learn and adapt to the new rules and procedures and are waiting for the expected effects to materialize. Stability is also in high demand among welfare recipients who want to be sure that they can rely on getting the same benefits and services the day after tomorrow, and among private contractors who need to be able to plan ahead knowing the conditions for their service delivery will not be drastically changed. Moreover, in some areas such as traffic regulation, control of nuclear power plants and the taxation of private pension schemes experimental change and radical innovations would even be considered as unwelcome and perhaps even dangerous (Mulgan 2007).

Second, it is important to remember that despite good intentions, brilliant ideas and many innovations born out of hard work often fail to consolidate step-change and achieve the stated objectives of the innovative endeavour. A review study suggests that as many as four out of five innovations result in failure (Van der Panne, Van Beers and Kleinknecht 2003). Iterative rounds of design, testing and re-design might help to turn an initial failure into subsequent success, but the positive effects of diligence and perseverance do not hide the fact that the failure rate in innovation is exceedingly high and success cannot be taken for granted.

Last but not least, it is well demonstrated that just as improvement might be a result of learning and small adjustments rather than innovation, innovation does not always lead to improvement (Hartley 2006). The implementation of new and innovative policies or services might not deliver the expected benefits, or the benefits might be overshadowed by some unintended negative effects. There might also be conflicting interpretations of the outcomes. What one actor perceives as a benefit might be perceived as a step in the wrong direction by other actors. As such, there is no way that we can equate innovation with improvement.

1.4 Governance Paradigms as Drivers of and Barriers to Public Innovation

Political science was originally preoccupied with studying formal political and administrative institutions and their role in governing society and the economy. The centre of attention in the study of government in Western democracies was and to a large extent still is the 'governmental chain' that connects voters with democratically elected assemblies, government officials, public bureaucracy and citizens, the latter conceived as recipients of benefits, service users or subjects of regulation. The relations in the circular chain of government are based on delegation and control and can be viewed as a series of Principal–Agent relations that have been carefully studied in election studies, research on political leadership, policy analysis and implementation studies. More recently, however, there has been a shift in political science and public administration theory from the original focus on 'government' to the study of 'governance' (Rhodes 1997). The shift has been prompted by the growing importance of more informal modes of governing and by the observation that governments have lost their alleged monopoly on governing society and the economy as public and private actors interact in numerous ways and to a growing extent in policy making, service production and public regulation. The focus on the formal institutions of government does not seem to fully capture the current processes of governing and the role of informal coordination and private actors herein. By contrast, the new focus on governance aims to grasp the formal as well as informal processes through which a plurality of actors interact in order to steer society and the economy in accordance with common objectives.

Talking about a shift from government to governance carries the danger of creating a simplistic image of the epochal change and the projection of a unified past and future by which governments used to control everything and now has become hollowed out and obsolete. Such an image is misleading for two reasons. First, there has always been governance in the sense of societal steering and policy making based on negotiations between a plethora of public and private actors that have been variously referred to as pluralism, corporatism or neo-corporatism. Second, the formal institutions of government continue to play a crucial role in the world of governance in which the exercise of power and the making of political decisions take place in decentred webs of formal and informal governing processes that cut through and blur the traditional demarcations between the public and private sphere, supranational, national and local jurisdictions, and policy makers and policy takers. Hence, instead of speaking of a shift from government to governance, we should rather see governance as a 'new perspective on an emerging reality' (Torfing et al. 2012). There has been a rise of joined-up government in response to the increasing fragmentation of the public sector and a proliferation of interactive and collaborative arenas for policy making, socio-economic regulation and service production that makes the traditional focus on government too constricted, but many governmental powers and capacities are still in place and new powers and capacities are being developed. In sum, the study of formal government institutions provides a very narrow lens for analysing the new and emerging reality. Conversely, the governance perspective must recognize the continued importance of governments and seek to understand how government is being transformed in the face of new and evolving forms of interactive governance.

While some people tend to define governance as a *Gegen Begriff* ('counter concept') that equates governance with the rise of networks, partnerships and collaborative steering mechanisms, we shall here define governance as an *Über Begriff* ('generic concept') that denotes the processes through which a plethora of public and private actors negotiate societal goals and deploy a variety of resources, mechanisms and strategies to steer society and the economy in accordance with these goals. The broad and generic definition of governance permits us to distinguish between different orders of governance (see Kooiman 2003). 'First-order' governance refers to the different modes of governance that produce particular governance outputs in terms of policies, plans, strategies, rules and procedures, standards, resource allocations, benefit schemes, etc. 'Second-order' governance refers to all those reflexive and strategic interventions that aim to improve the functioning of the different modes of governance so that they may contribute to goal attainment in terms of effective problem solving, efficient service production, democratic legitimacy, enhanced solidarity, etc. 'Third-order' governance refers to the normative, path-dependent and context-sensitive choice between different modes of governance or different combinations or mixes of governance modes that is based on particular hegemonic ideas about how to govern society and the economy. Foucault (1991) refers to this kind of third-order governance that defines a particular art of government that conditions the production of particular political practices with the neologism 'governmentality' (see also Dean 1999). Kooiman (2003) himself refers to second- and third-order governance as 'metagovernance' in order to capture the governance of governance (see also Jessop 2002). This book is particularly interested in how different modes of governance and the paradigms on which they are founded contribute to the production of innovative solutions that can help us to achieve some of the key goals of the public sector. However, we are not only interested in the effects of first-order governance but also in the various forms of second-order governance that aim to support and improve the different modes of governance and the third-order governance that regulates the choice between different modes of governance and thus may shift the balance between them in ways that are conducive to innovation.

In order to better understand the relation between governance and innovation we need to define the different and shifting modes of governance that are typically found in today's public sector. We shall here distinguish between three paradigmatic modes of governance that all seem to play a crucial role in structuring and defining roles and activities in public organizations. The first is Classical Public Administration (CPA), which is based on the defining traits of Weberian and Wilsonian bureaucracy. The second is New Public Management (NPM), which from the mid-1980s onwards has aimed to introduce market logics and strategic performance management into the public sector. The last is New Public Governance (NPG), which is a more recent phenomenon and tends to favour the development of collaborative forms of governance as well as a more integrative leadership and trust-based management (Salamon 2002; Osborne 2006, 2010; Crosby and Bryson 2010; Koppenjan 2012; Triantafillou and Torfing 2013; Ansell and Torfing 2014; Morgan and Cooke 2014). Since we are interested in the paradigmatic differences between the three modes of governance rather than their empirical forms and functions, we shall in the following refer to the three modes of governance as governance paradigms. Emphasizing the paradigmatic aspects of concrete modes of governance carries the risk of reification that wrongly gives the impression that the three governance paradigms exist in reality. However, the risk can be avoided by insisting that the three governance paradigms are merely analytical constructs that help us to make sense of and distinguish between different empirical forms of governance that are shaped by actors who have little if any knowledge of the paradigmatic forms of governance that are discussed here. An overview of the three governance paradigms is presented in Table 1.1.

The three governance paradigms emerged at different points in history, but rather than replacing each other in a chain of sequential substitution, the three paradigms and their associated practices have come to be layered on top of one another. Thus, just as the arrival of New Public Management did not eliminate the bureaucratic forms of governance associated with Classical Public Administration, the surge of New Public Governance has added a new layer on top of New Public

Table 1.1 *Stylized comparison of the three governance paradigms: CPA, NPM and NPG*

	Classical Public Administration	New Public Management	New Public Governance
Basic view of public organizations and employees	Public organizations are authorities and public employees are skilled full-time professionals who follow explicit rules and heed the call of public duty	Public organizations are service providers, and opportunistic behaviour of public employees must be curtailed through control-based performance management	Public organizations are arenas for co-production and the public service motivation of the employees must be enhanced through a more trust-based leadership and management
Problem diagnosis	Previous public systems have not delivered a stable, predictable and rights-based service	Public bureaucracies with monopoly status tend to produce services that are poor and costly	There is a growing number of problems which are seen as wicked and unruly and the fiscal constraints are dire
Solution	Public bureaucracies based on hierarchy, specialization, explicit rules and legal-rational authority	Deregulation, public–private competition and introduction of performance incentives	Public–private collaboration through networks, partnerships and relational contracting
Overall goal	Ensure legality, transparency and equity in public decision making and service provision	Enhance efficiency through persistent efforts to rationalize and cut slack	Enhance efficiency, quality and the capacity for public problem-solving through collaboration and innovation
Role of politicians	Sovereign decision makers who exercise authority and produce laws and rules	Board of directors steering the administration by defining overall goals, targets and budget frames	Political leaders of the political community who define problems and goals and develop new solutions
Role of managers	Administration of rules and resources, while focusing on legality and equity	Strategic management of their department or agency while focusing on inputs and outputs	Leaders of intra- and inter-organizational collaboration while focusing on processes and results

Table 1.1 (*cont.*)

	Classical Public Administration	New Public Management	New Public Governance
Role of employees	Incorruptible rule-followers who aim to treat citizens fairly and equally and are driven by a feeling of public duty	Service providers who aim to satisfy the needs of the customers and are predominantly driven by extrinsic motivation	Service facilitators who aim to discover and mobilize the citizens' resources and are predominantly driven by intrinsic motivation
Role of firms & NGOs	Pressure groups influencing government from the outside	Contracted providers of public services	Partners in negotiated co-creation of public solutions
Role of citizens	Bearers of legal rights, but subjected to public authority	Customers making rational choices between different service providers	Active citizens engaged in co-production, co-creation and co-governance of public services

Management. The more recently developed governance paradigms might be more fashionable and tend to dominate the thinking and action of opinion leaders, policy advisors, politicians, executive managers, researchers and newly educated public administration students. However, large parts of the public sector in Western industrialized countries will still be influenced by the previous and sedimented governance paradigms despite the apparent hegemony of the new ideas and practices. The thickness of the three layers of governance practices may vary across countries, levels and policy areas. Where the three paradigmatic modes of governance collide, it may either give rise to clashes and contradictions or result in the creation of hybrid forms of governance, as elements from different paradigms are merged and mutually modified with the production of unpredictable and unintended effects as a likely result.

Our key concern is not the empirical prevalence and hybridity of the modes of governance associated with the three paradigms, but rather their impact on the creation of public innovation. We believe that all three paradigms contain important drivers for and barriers to public innovation. Table 1.2 lists some of the most important drivers and barriers that are commonly ascribed to the three governance paradigms (Zaltman, Duncan and Holbek 1973; Mintzberg 1980; Jacobsen and Thorsvik

Table 1.2 *Key innovation drivers and innovation barriers ascribed to the three governance paradigms*

	Innovation Drivers	Innovations Barriers
Classical public administration	• Public leaders can set the agenda, give direction to change and mobilize resources • Clear rules and job security may support the exploration and exploitation of new ideas • Administrative silos stimulate knowledge development among professionally trained employees	• Centralized control, fixed rules and standardization undermines creativity and entrepreneurship • The overall goal is stability and predictability, and change tends to be limited and incremental • Administrative silos hamper inter-organizational learning and knowledge-sharing
New public management	• Competition between public and private service providers stimulates innovation • Customer orientation and performance measurement create strong incentives for public managers to improve performance and thereby induce innovation • Devolution, deregulation and strategic management facilitate and spur change	• Competition hampers collaboration and knowledge-sharing • The strong performance and auditing regime produces risk aversion • Control-based performance management demotivates the public employees, and the transaction costs associated with documentation and measurement eliminate slack resources
New public governance	• Multi-actor collaboration facilitates mutual learning and creation of joint ownership to new and bold solutions • Trust-based management means that public employees have more room for using their skills and competences • The experiences, resources and ideas of citizens and civil society organizations are used in processes of co-production and co-creation	• Limited focus on competition may reduce the incentives to innovate • The focus on process may prevent a proper focus on outputs and outcomes • Consensus-based collaboration may produce a joint decision trap, and implementation of new and bold ideas in collaborative settings is hampered by unclear rules and procedures and the lack of a clear division of labour

2008; Eggers and O'Leary 2009; Osborne 2010; Coule and Patmore 2013; Mazzucato 2013; Ansell and Torfing 2014).

All three governance paradigms contain potent innovation drivers and unfortunate innovation barriers. However, since Classical Public

Administration and New Public Management have been with us for some time and New Public Governance is the 'new kid on the block', we shall pay special attention to the latter. The special focus on New Public Governance is motivated partly by the assumption that governance paradigms tend to produce a diminishing return to scale and thus may tend to exhaust themselves and partly by scientific curiosity to explore the special innovation promise of New Public Governance. Not only is New Public Governance praising innovation as an important tool for reinvigorating the public sector and enhancing efficiency, quality and effectiveness in public service production, but it also aims to tap into the resources, competences and ideas of public employees as well as citizens, private firms and NGOs while strengthening the political leadership of elected politicians. If the mobilization of resources and the prospect for collaboration is enhanced by organizational reforms aiming to strengthen vertical and horizontal integration (Christensen and Lægreid 2010) and cross-sector collaboration (Klijn and Koppenjan 2004), it seems plausible to expect that a strengthening of some of the key features of New Public Governance might help to spur public innovation.

However, as is clearly signalled in Table 1.2, New Public Governance also contains some potential barriers to innovation. Firstly, if all forms of competition are eliminated, the would-be innovators may have less incentive to innovative. Competition and rivalry between different networks and partnerships seem to be an important driver of collaborative innovation (Powell and Grodal 2004). Secondly, in the relative absence of hierarchical steering and control, New Public Governance creates a risk that public and private actors will spend all their energy and resources on seemingly endless processes of brainstorming, deliberation and collaboration without producing a clear and tangible result. As such, the lack of overall direction, goal setting and monitoring of results is fatal to the attempt to spur innovation. Last but not least, implementation of new and bold solutions might suffer from the lack of funding, the dispersion of responsibility and the absence of rule-based coordination in multi-actor settings. Hence, dismissing the virtues of bureaucracy may result in the accumulation of innovative ideas and solutions that are never properly implemented (O'Toole 1997).

The potential innovation barriers of New Public Governance call for deliberate attempts to preserve, and perhaps re-articulate, key elements of Classical Public Administration and New Public Management. Thus, New Public Management may infuse collaborative innovation processes with a healthy degree of competition and result orientation, and Classical Public Administration may provide the tools for securing the implementation of innovative solutions in multi-actor settings. In sum, a certain mix of governance paradigms is likely to prove helpful in order to optimize the processes, outputs and outcomes of collaborative innovation. Nevertheless, we believe that it is far too early to draw any steadfast conclusions about the relative impact of different forms of governance on capacity of the public sector to produce new and innovative solutions. What we need are further studies of how we can transform governance in order to enhance innovation, and in answering this question we are particularly curious about how new forms of governance can help us spur public innovation.

1.5   Theoretical Framing of the Book

The contributions to this book draw more or less explicitly upon insights from three broad theoretical fields that are rooted in different social science disciplines but have a cross-disciplinary relevance for studying how governance and innovation are linked.

The first theoretical field is *innovation theory*, which helps us understand what innovation is and what drives and impedes innovation processes (von Hippel 1988; Gray 1989; Teece 1992; Rogers 1995; Fagerberg, Mowery and Nelson 2004; Halvorsen et al. 2005; Van der Ven et al. 2008; Bason 2010; Osborne and Brown 2013; Torfing 2016). Innovation deals with important questions such as: What is the difference between innovation in the public and private sectors? How are processes of public innovation unfolding? Who are the innovators? How is innovation affected by organizational and cultural factors? Which forms of learning and knowledge diffusion can help to spur innovation? How are innovation and the associated risks managed and negotiated? What is the role of management and leadership in facilitating and driving innovation?

By applying a general social theory of evolutionary change to economics and private business, Schumpeter (1934) may be seen as a founding stone of innovation theory. Schumpeter emphasized the role of individual and collective entrepreneurs in developing and implementing new combinations that in some cases will spread throughout a given sector. The key focus was on the market-driven technological innovation in private firms, but it was duly noted that innovation could also take place in the public sector and that the public sector could play a role in enabling private sector innovation. Later on, innovation theory was expounded by organization theorists who were interested in the capacity of organizations to innovate (Thompson 1965; Mohr 1969) but failed to differentiate between public and private innovation. The focus was mostly on the role of managers and their call for organizational innovation as well as the obstacles they met or even produced themselves in the way. More recently, there has been an attempt by public administration researchers to dissociate public sector and private sector innovation, look for how innovation can benefit the public sector per se and analyse the drivers and barriers for innovation in the public sector (Halvorsen et al. 2005). Some scholars have also raised the question about the link between different forms of governance and the ability to enhance public innovation (Hartley 2005). However, the research on public innovation is still in its infancy, and more work needs to be done in this area.

The second theoretical field is *governance theory*, which helps us to understand the conditions for innovation in the public sector. Whereas innovation in the private sector tends to be linked to technology, public innovation is ultimately linked to authority and legitimacy (Kattel et al. 2014). However, authority cannot be reduced to the legal-rational authority of government. There are other forms of authority and legitimacy associated with social and democratic values – communicative reason, the accumulation of social and political capital and the ability to solve problems and deliver results. Public authority is ultimately about making authoritative decisions in the name of society through complex negotiations that involve a plethora of public and private actors. Hence, authority is essentially about pluricentric forms of governance rather than unicentric government.

Governance research has expanded dramatically in the last 30 years (Kooiman 1993; Mayntz 1993; March and Olsen 1995; Kickert, Klijn and Koppenjan 1997; Rhodes 1997; Jessop 1998; Scharpf 1999; Pierre and Peters 2000; Grote and Gbikpi 2002; Salamon 2002; Djelic and Sahlin-Andersson 2006; Agranoff 2007; Torfing et al. 2012). This is exactly the same period in which the new theories of public sector innovation emerged, but with a few exceptions, the two bodies of theory have remained largely unrelated (Ansell and Torfing 2014). This is regrettable since governance theory helps us answer a series of highly relevant questions such as: What are the key features of bureaucratic, market-driven and collaborative governance? What are the conditions and drivers for involving citizens and civil society organizations in participatory governance? How can governance contribute to the democratization of society? How can governance arrangement harness complexity? How can governance be governed and transformed in order to meet different and shifting political and normative goals? What is the role of experiments in transforming governance? What are the tools of governance and how are they evolving?

There is no unified theory about governance (Ansell and Torfing 2016), but it is possible to identify a number of theoretical strands that differ in terms of whether they see human action as driven by rational calculations or rule-following and in terms of whether they see governance as essentially conflict-ridden or more consensus-based (Sørensen and Torfing 2007).

Theories of governance provide competing definitions of governance, and there is a general lack of conceptual clarity, although most definitions tend to emphasize the complex and decentred processes through which different actors contribute to the governing of society and the economy. The conceptual and theoretical ambiguity is partly a result of the interdisciplinary character of the field of governance studies (Torfing et al. 2012), which can also be explained by the fact that governance theory is a relatively new field of study.

The third theoretical field is *institutional theory*, which helps us understand what drives and conditions the actions of institutionally situated actors, how governance arrangements are stabilized and how they can be changed through intentional reforms. The new institutionalism developed in opposition to the old institutionalism, which was mainly interested in the history of formal, constitutional institutions such as national elections, parliaments, ministries and courts and which suffered from a high degree of normativism (Rhodes 1995). By contrast, new institutionalism wanted to study the institutionalization of social, economic and political processes, and it was found that both formal and informal institutions mattered in the sense of constraining and enabling social and political action. These discoveries led neo-institutionalism to redefine and broaden the concept of institutions to include regulatory, normative, cognitive and ideational conditions of action. As such, institutions have been broadly defined as the rules, norms, procedures, rituals and scripts that facilitate, constrain and shape action and contribute to the reproduction of particular patterns of social and political interaction (March and Olsen 1989). In order to capture all these different aspects of institutions, a number of important subfields have emerged. Hence, today, we can identify at least four relevant subfields within the new institutionalism: rational choice institutionalism, historical institutionalism, sociological institutionalism and discourse institutionalism (see Peters 2012).

Governance arrangements cannot be defined as institutions in the strict sense of well-integrated systems of formal action that are firmly regulated by rules, norms, procedures, cognitive scripts and discourses, which are shared by all the actors and enforced by a legitimate authority. The interaction is formal as well as informal, and social and political actors tend to bring different norms, values, rules, resources and identities into the governance arena. However, over time, the social and political interactions in public governance arenas will tend to be stabilized through the formation of relatively sedimented patterns of exchange that are supported by formal and informal rules, norms, procedures and forms of knowledge that reduce the transaction costs of interacting and making joint decisions. As such, governance arrangements are subject to ongoing processes of institutionalization that result in increasing clarity, agreement and formalization of the content, explanation and justification of behavioural rules and the allocation, and access to and control over material and immaterial resources (Olsen 2009: 199). The bounded character of sovereign power and the periodic contestation of the form and functioning of governance arrangements foster an inherent ambiguity and openness of the institutional framework, which trigger ongoing processes of de-institutionalization that imply that existing rules and resource distributions are becoming more unclear, contested and uncertain (Torfing et al. 2012). The institutionalization of governance is a matter of degree, as some governance arrangements are highly institutionalized while other governance arrangements are not. As a rule of thumb, bureaucratic forms of governance tend to be more institutionalized than market-based and collaborative forms of governance.

Institutional theory helps answer important questions about whether human action is driven by self-interested calculations of costs and benefits; rules, norms and common ideas resulting from compromises obtained in the course of the more or less conflict-ridden interaction; interpretations of what constitutes appropriate action in a particular institutional context; or cognitive or ideational scripts that define the identity and world views of social and political actors (Peters 2012). The micro-level foundation of institutional theory is matched by particular macro-level views of how political institutions are changed. Rational choice institutionalists seem to have a firm belief in the 'efficiency of history' (March and Olsen 1995). Hence, they argue that changes in the external environment of public organizations will tend to change the preferences of rational, but institutionally situated actors who in turn will aim to redesign the institutional forms of governance so that they match the changing environment (Knight 1992).

Historical institutionalists are less optimistic about the prospects for intentional reforms of governance institutions since contingent events may create institutional paths that are difficult to change due to the existence of positive feedback mechanisms, increasing return to scale, and high transaction costs of reform that enable sub-optimal solutions to persist despite the existence of more efficient alternatives (Pierson 1994). In this perspective, change is only possible in critical junctures where crisis, war and other disruptive events destabilize the existing path and open a terrain for political struggles that may lead to the formation of a new path. However, later work in this field has pointed to the often quite substantive political changes generated by incremental layering of institutional changes (Mahoney and Thelen 2010).

Finally, both sociological and discursive institutionalism argue that change is not just taking place at breaking points in history where one

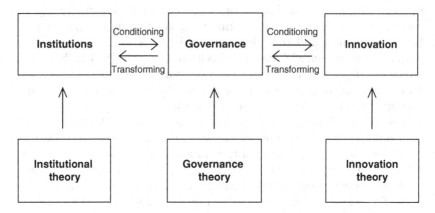

Figure 1.2 The relation between institutions, governance and innovation

institutional path replaces another. Social and political actors constantly aim to exploit the ambiguities in rules, norms, cognitive scripts and discourses in order to re-interpret and re-articulate the institutional framework. Hence, institutional settings are perceived as open-ended terrains for learning-based adaptation and political struggles over hegemony (March and Olsen 1995; Schmidt 2010).

The three theoretical fields have a joint focus on processes, but they tend to differ in terms of their assessment of the relative degree of stability and change in these processes. Hence, whereas innovation theory focuses on innovation processes, governance theory focuses on governance processes and institutional theory focuses on processes of institutionalization and de-institutionalization. Institutions are characterized by a relatively high degree of stability, and governance is predicated on the presence of a relatively stable set of rules, routines and procedures that facilitate interaction and give rise to particular modes of governance, while allowing for some degree of flexibility in the concrete acts of governing. By contrast, innovation involves a deliberate effort to disrupt stable ideas and practices and create new ones in the hope that these will outperform the previous ones. The conditioning and transformative relations between institutions, governance and innovation are shown in Figure 1.2. As the figure indicates, public governance is conditioned by the institutionalization of rules, norms and procedures that guide and channel the process of governance, which in turn condition the attempts to innovate. Successful innovation will sometimes transform the structures and forms of governance, which will in turn transform the institutional underpinning of public governance. The three theoretical fields enable us to understand different aspects of the processes that link institutions, governance and innovation.

Figure 1.2 charts the theoretical framework that the chapters in this edited volume draw upon. There is common theoretical thrust in book in the sense that the authors will eventually refer to different aspects and interpretations of the theories describe above. However, the theoretical framework is not meant to function as a straightjacket, and the chapters may stray beyond the theoretical fields discussed above in order to answer the fundamental questions about how governance may drive or impede innovation and how governance reform could possibly help to boost public innovation.

1.6 Structure and Content of the Book

The book is divided into three consecutive parts. The first part Linking Governance and Innovation aims to explore the relation between different forms of public governance and different forms and aspects of public innovation. Although both bureaucratic and market-based forms of governance are in focus, special attention is given to collaborative forms of governance and their ability to spur public innovation. Chapter 2 by Christopher K. Ansell examines the what, why and how of collaborative governance. The chapter distinguishes 'governance' from traditional forms of 'government'. It defines 'collaborative governance' and reflects on the recent surge of interest in collaborative forms of governance through the formation of networks and partnerships. Finally, it draws on pragmatist theory and a number of empirical case studies in order to analyse the capacity of collaborative forms of governance to solve wicked and unruly problems by means of promoting a creative and learning-based problem-solving.

Chapter 3 by Stephen Osborne and Zoe Radnor provides a systematic comparison of New Public Management and New Public Governance and explains why and how the latter can help enhance the innovation capacity of the public sector by strengthening the public service motivation of public employees, facilitating cross-organizational and cross-sectoral collaboration and expanding different kinds of co-production and co-creation. The chapter provides a new perspective on the public sector as an integrated service system that engages users and citizens in collaborative service production based on an active citizenship.

Chapter 4 by Jacob Torfing and Peter Triantafillou provides a thorough discussion of innovation and reflects on the specific forms of and conditions for innovation in the public sector. It critically examines the emerging discourses of public innovation that tend to construct innovation as a necessary tool for enhancing efficiency, before presenting and comparing seven empirical examples of public innovation from different parts of the world, including Asia and Latin America. The analysis focuses on the different, and sometimes conflicting, objectives and achievements of public innovation projects.

Chapter 5 by Jean Hartley examines the importance of diffusing public innovation. She argues that although the invention of new public policies and services that break with established practices and common wisdoms is crucial in the light of the economic crisis and the many unresolved societal problems, the public sector should improve its capacity for innovation diffusion. Some of the key findings from the emerging literature on innovation diffusion are cited and different ways of conceptualizing the process of innovation diffusion are explored, arguing that innovation diffusion is a complex and collaborative achievement that involves grafting and growing rather than a linear engineering exercise.

The second part of the book, Changing Roles of Public and Private Actors, reflects on how different social and political actors deal with the challenges they are facing when engaging in public innovation processes that might be more or less collaborative, market-based or bureaucratic. Chapter 6, by Eva Sørensen and Jacob Torfing, examines collaborative innovation in the public sector. It argues that while both hierarchy and competition can spur innovation, there is an unrealized potential for innovation through multi-actor collaboration. It presents and discusses different methods of collaborative innovation and analyses some of the typical drivers and barriers. It briefly presents and compares empirical case studies of collaborative innovation in Copenhagen and Oakland, before it concludes with some analytical and empirical reflections on how the role and identity of different public and private actors are challenged by collaborative innovation.

In Chapter 7, Viktor Bekkers and Mirko Noordegraaf discuss the challenges that collaborative innovation poses to public managers and professionals. While New Public Management calls upon public managers to play the role of strategic leaders who single-handedly turn around their organization and use their power to create in-house innovation, the demand for collaborative innovation places them in a new role as sponsors, conveners and facilitators of collaborative processes that develop and realize new ideas. The problem in relation to the professionals is a different one: it is an essential part of the identity of professional groups to focus on their own knowledge, methods and values, and this makes it difficult for them to engage with other professionals as well as with users and citizens. Hence, the attempt to spur collaborative innovation in the public sector requires a difficult and often painful reformulation of the roles of public managers and professionals.

Chapter 8, by Tony Bovaird and Elke Loeffler, examines what it takes to involve citizens and civil society actors in co-creation. They argue that it is crucial for public agencies to find ways of involving citizens and civil society organizations in processes of collaborative innovation because they bring valuable experiences, ideas, energies and resources into the innovation process. The chapter introduces the new design thinking as a new approach to collaborative innovation that inter alia uses an array of techniques in order to involve private actors not only as co-implementers of innovative solutions but also as co-initiators and co-designers.

In Chapter 9 Eva Sørensen discusses the role of elected politicians in collaborative policy innovation. While there has recently been a growing interest in public service innovation, policy innovation has only received scant regard. She argues that elected politicians can strengthen their political leadership by taking the lead in metagoverning processes of collaborative policy innovation. The chapter draws on empirical studies from Australia, Denmark and North America in order to examine the drivers of and barriers to political leadership of collaborative policy innovation that is particularly important in times of crisis.

Chapter 10, by Ole Helby Petersen, Veiko Lember, Walter Scherrer and Robert Ågren, examines how various forms of public–private collaboration may contribute to public innovation. They focus on three significant yet distinct market-based forms of public and private collaboration – namely contracting out and public–private partnership as examples of long-term and more innovation-focused forms of public–private collaboration, and finally public procurement as a distinct model for improving innovation. All three forms of public–private collaboration represent the main market-based policy tools that played a prominent role under the New Public Management era, which in spite of many shortcomings have remained firmly in governments' toolbox partly due to the ongoing economic troubles. The goal of the chapter is to examine how these specific, yet widely used, collaboration forms fit into the emerging New Public Governance paradigm and, most importantly, how these instruments can foster innovation and collaboration under the New Public Governance framework.

The final part of the book, Transforming Governance to Enhance Innovation, assesses how public organizations, management practices and steering systems can be changed in order to further enhance public innovation. In Chapter 11, Mads Leth Felsager Jakobsen and Claus Thrane examine the literature on the impact of organizational structures on organizational innovation and explore whether there is an optimal intra-organizational structure in an era of layered governance. While they do find that clear division of labour and specialization tend to correlate positively with innovation, they conclude there is not just one organizational structure that is optimal for innovation. They go on to argue that innovation arises as a nexus between entrepreneurial opportunities and entrepreneurial individuals. Therefore innovation is best spurred by paying attention both to organizational structures and to non-structural factors such as transformative leadership and dialogical processes around performance management systems.

Chapter 12, by Lotte Bøgh Andersen, examines whether command and incentive systems can enhance motivation and public innovation. After going through the available evidence, she argues that public managers can create an environment supportive of innovation through the use of financial incentives and command systems, but that this does not happen automatically. Considering the effects on public service motivation and intrinsic motivation might thus be an important part of facilitating innovation in the public sector.

In Chapter 13 Montgomery Van Wart discusses how administrative leadership may induce innovation in the public sector. He carefully examines the conventional wisdom regarding the pragmatic steps that increase the likelihood of success in implementing innovation and reform. After defining leadership and discussing the caveats about the role it plays with innovation, he provides an overview of the major theories of change related to leadership. He then puts forward a series of well-argued practical steps and concomitant competencies that practising leaders should strive to achieve.

Chapter 14, by Wouter Van Dooren and Tom Willems, discusses the need for reforming accountability systems to enhance innovation. They argue that New Public Management-flavoured accountability regimes have tended to stifle innovation rather than to foster it. Thus, in order to spur innovation, we need a reform of indicator-based accountability systems. The authors argue that performance indicators should be used for learning and innovation rather than for indicator-based accountability. Accountability can only enhance innovation when it allows for a meaningful performance dialogue with staff and stakeholders. In order to save results-based accountability from the unilateral focus on indicators, the authors propose a number of institutional changes.

In Chapter 15 Tom Christensen and Per Lægreid examine how organizational innovation impacts the relationship between multiple forms of public sector accountability. Based on studies of three organizational innovations of the welfare administration in Norway from 2001 onwards, they argue that a new form of local welfare office based on a partnership agreement between local and central government was introduced in 2005 and implemented during 2012. Second, a hospital reform introduced regional and local health enterprises based on a specific law. Third, in the field of immigration a new 'court-like' central agency, with extended autonomy from the ministry, was introduced in 2001 to handle complaints from immigrants and asylum seekers. They show that the political accountability is mostly constraining other types of accountability because of high political salience of the sectors.

In Chapter 16, Guy Peters draws on different strands of institutional theory in order to discuss the prospects and conditions for transforming public governance in order to enhance collaboration and innovation. He argues that although the public sector cannot be changed at will, policy makers, public managers, stakeholders and citizens are not completely powerless and merely stuck with the path that we are on. Hence, in times of crisis where the common wisdom and standard practices are problematized, it is possible to change the existing governance path and form new ones that shape the future choices. However, the transformation of public governance is often piecemeal, seldom a result of an overall master plan and frequently subject to political and bureaucratic struggles.

Finally, in Chapter 17, we summarize the key findings of the chapters and draw tentative conclusions regarding the innovative potentials of New Public Governance. We then outline how existing constellations of governance can be transformed and the challenges such changes pose to political and administrative leaders. Finally, we point to the types of research and research methods needed to further grasp and unravel the complex links between governance and public innovation.

References

Abrahamson, E. 1991. 'Managerial fads and fashions: The diffusion and rejection of innovations', *Academy of Management Review* 16(3): 586–612.

Agranoff, R. 2007. *Managing within Networks: Adding Value to Public Organizations*. Washington, DC: Georgetown University Press.

Albury, D. 2005. 'Fostering innovation in public services', *Public Money and Management* 25(1): 51–6.

Ansell, C. and Torfing, J. (eds.) 2014. *Public Innovation through Collaboration and Design*. Abingdon: Routledge.

  2016. *Handbook on Theories of Governance*. Cheltenham: Edward Elgar.

Arundel, A. and Hollanders, H. 2008. 'Innovation scoreboards: Indicators and policy use', in C. Nauwelaers and R. Wintjes (eds.), *Innovation Policy in Europe: Measurement and Strategy*. Cheltenham, UK: Edward Elgar, pp. 29–52.

Arundel, A. and Smith, K. H. 2013. 'History of the community innovation survey', in F. Gault (ed.), *Handbook of Innovation Indicators and Measurement.* Cheltenham, UK: Edward Elgar Publishing, pp. 60–87.

Bason, C. 2010. *Leading Public Sector Innovation.* Bristol: The Policy Press.

Bessant, J. 2003. 'Challenges in innovation management', in L. V. Shavinina (ed.), *The International Handbook on Innovation.* Oxford: Elsevier Science, pp. 761–74.

Borins, S. 1998. *Innovating with Integrity.* Washington, DC: Georgetown University Press.

(ed.) 2008. *Innovations in Government.* Washington, DC: Brookings Institution Press.

2014. *The Persistence of Innovation in Government: A Guide for Public Servants.* Washington, DC: IBM Center for the Business of Government.

Bysted, R. and Hansen, J. R. 2015. 'Comparing public and private sector employees' innovative behaviour', *Public Management Review* 17(5): 698–717.

Christensen, T. and Lægreid, P. 2010. 'Complexity and hybrid administration', *Public Organization Review* 11(4): 407–23.

Coule, T. and Patmore, B. 2013. 'Institutional logics, institutional work and service innovation in non-profit organizations', *Public Administration* 94(4): 980–97.

Crosby, B. C. and Bryson, J. M. 2010. 'Integrative leadership and the creation and maintenance of cross-sector collaboration', *Leadership Quarterly* 21(2): 211–30.

Damanpour, F. 1991. 'Organizational innovation: A meta-analysis of effects of determinants and moderators', *Academy of Management Journal* 34(3): 555–90.

Dean, M. 1999. *Governmentality: Power and Rule in Modern Society.* London: Sage.

Djelic, M.-L. and Sahlin-Andersson, K. (eds.) 2006. *Transnational Governance: Institutional Dynamics of Regulation.* Cambridge: Cambridge University Press.

Eggers, W. D. and O'Leary, J. 2009. *If We Can Put a Man on the Moon: Getting Big Things Done in Government.* Boston: Harvard Business Press.

Eggers, W. D. and Singh, S. 2009. *The Public Innovators Playbook.* Washington, DC: Harvard Kennedy School of Government.

European Commission. 2011. *Eurobarometer 2010: Innovation in Public Administration.* Brussels: EU.

2013. *European Public Sector Innovation Scoreboard.* Brussels: EU.

Fagerberg, J., Mowery, D. C. and Nelson, R. R. (eds.) 2004. *The Oxford Handbook of Innovation.* Oxford: Oxford University Press.

Foucault, M. 1991. 'Governmentality', in G. Burchell, C. Gordon and P. Miller (eds.), *The Foucault Effect.* Hertfordshire: Harvester Wheatsheaf, pp. 87–104.

Gray, B. 1989. *Collaborating: Finding Common Ground for Multiparty Problems.* San Francisco, CA: Jossey-Bass.

Grote, J. R. and Gbikpi, B. (eds.) 2002. *Participatory Governance.* Opladen: Leske and Budrich.

Hajer, M. 1995. *The Politics of Environmental Discourse: Ecological Modernization and the Policy Process.* Oxford: Clarendon Press.

Halvorsen, T., Hauknes, J., Miles, I. and Røste, R. 2005. 'On the Difference between Public and Private Sector Innovation'. PUBLIN Report no. D9. Oslo: NIFU STEP.

Hartley, J. 2005. 'Innovation in governance and public service: Past and present', *Public Money & Management* 25(1): 27–34.

2006. *Innovation and Its Contribution to Improvement.* London: Department for Communities and Local Government.

2012. 'Public value through innovation and improvement', in J. Benington and M. Moore (eds.), *Public Value: Theory and Practice.* Basingstoke: Palgrave Macmillan, pp. 171–84.

Hartley, J., Sørensen, E. and Torfing, J. 2013. 'Collaborative innovation: A viable alternative to market competition and organizational entrepreneurship', *Public Administration Review* 73(6): 821–30.

Hippel, E. von 1988. *The Sources of Innovation.* Oxford: Oxford University Press.

Hood, C. 1991. 'A public administration for all seasons?', *Public Administration* 69(1): 1–19.

Jacobsen, D. I. and Thorsvik, J. 2008. *Hvordan organisationer fungerer: Indføring i organisation og ledelse.* Copenhagen: Hans Reitzels Forlag.

Jakobsen, M. L. F. 2013. 'Bureaukrati: Ven eller fjende af (offentlig sektor) innovation?', *Politica* 45(3): 250–66.

Jessop, B. 1998. 'The rise of governance and the risks of failure: The case of economic development', *International Social Science Journal* 50(155): 29–45.

2002. *The Future of the Capitalist State.* Cambridge: Polity Press.

Kattel, R., Cepilovs, A., Drechsler, W., Kalvet, T., Lember, V. and Tonurist, P. 2014. 'Can we measure public sector innovation? A literature review', *LIPSE Working Paper Series* 3.

Kickert, W. J. M., Klijn, E.-H. and Koppenjan, J. F. M. (eds.) 1997. *Managing Complex Networks.* London: Sage.

Klijn, E.-H. and Koppenjan, J. F. M. 2004. *Managing Uncertainties in Networks.* London: Routledge.

Knight, J. 1992. *Institutions and Social Conflicts.* Cambridge: Cambridge University Press.

Kooiman, J. (ed.) 1993. *Modern Governance.* London: Sage.

Kooiman, J. 2003. *Governing as Governance.* London: Sage.

Koppenjan, J. F. M. 2012. *The New Public Governance in Public Service Delivery.* The Hague: Eleven International Publishing.

Kraemer, K. L. and Perry, J. L. 1989. 'Innovation and computing in the public sector: A review of research', *Knowledge in Society* 2(1): 72–87.

Lundvall, B. Å. 1985. *Product Innovation and User-producer Interaction.* Aalborg University Press.

Mahoney, J. and Thelen K. 2010. 'A Theory of Gradual Institutional Change', in J. Mahoney and K. Thelen (eds.), *Explaining Institutional Change: Ambiguity, Agency, and Power.* Cambridge: Cambridge University Press, pp. 1–37.

March, J. G. and Olsen, J. P. 1989. *Rediscovering Institutions.* New York: The Free Press.

1995. *Democratic Governance.* New York: The Free Press.

Mayntz, R. 1993. 'Modernization and the logic of interorganizational networks', in J. Child, M. Crozier, and R. Mayntz (eds.), *Societal Change between Markets and Organization*. Aldershot: Avebury, pp. 3–18.

Mazzucato, M. 2013. *The Entrepreneurial State: Debunking Public vs. Private Sector Myths*. London: Anthem Press.

Mintzberg, H. 1980. 'Structure in 5's: A synthesis of the research on organization design', *Management Science* 26(3): 322–41.

Mohr, L. B. 1969. 'Determinants of Innovation in Organizations', *American Political Science Review* 63(1): 111–26.

Moore, M. and Hartley, J. 2008. 'Innovations in governance', *Public Management Review* 10(1): 3–20.

Morgan, D. F. and Cook, B. J. (eds.) 2014. *New Public Governance: A Regime-Centered Perspective*. New York: Routledge.

Mulgan, G. 2007. *Ready or Not? Taking Innovation in the Public Sector Seriously*, NESTA, available at: www.nesta.org.uk/publications/ready-or-not-taking-in novation-public-sector-seriously.

Olsen, J. P. 2009. 'EU governance: Where do we go from here?', in B. Kohler-Koch and F. Larat (eds.), *European Multi-level Governance*. Cheltenham: Edward Elgar, 191–209.

Osborne, S. 2006. 'The New Public Governance?', *Public Management Review* 8(3): 377–88.

(ed.) 2010. *The New Public Governance?* London: Routledge.

Osborne, S. P. and Brown, L. 2011. 'Innovation, public policy and public services delivery in the UK: The word that would be King?', *Public Administration* 89(4): 1335–50.

(eds.) 2013. *Handbook on Innovation in Public Services*. Cheltenham: Edward Elgar.

Osborne, D. and Gaebler, T. 1992. *Reinventing Government: How the Entrepreneurial Spirit is Transforming the Public Sector*. Reading, MA: Addison-Wesley.

O'Toole, L. J. 1997. 'Implementing public innovations in network settings', *Administration and Society* 29(2): 115–38.

Perry, J. L. and Danzinger, J. N. 1980. 'The adoptability of innovations: An empirical assessment of computer applications in local governments', *Administration and Society* 11(4): 461–92.

Perry, J. L. and Kraemer, K. L. 1980. 'Chief executive support and innovation adoption', *Administration and Society* 12(2): 158–77.

Perry, J. L., Kraemer, K. L., Dunkle, D. and King, J. 1993. 'Motivations to innovate in public organizations', in B. Bozeman (ed.), *Public Management: The State of the Art*. San Francisco, CA: Jossey Bass, pp. 294–306.

Peters, B. G. 2012. *Institutional Theory in Political Science*. London: Continuum.

Pierre, J. and Peters, B. G. 2000. *Governance, Politics and the State*. Basingstoke: Macmillan.

Pierson, P. 1994. *Dismantling the Welfare State?* Cambridge: Cambridge University Press.

Pollitt, C. and Hupe, P. 2011. 'Talking about government: The role of magic concepts', *Public Management Review* 13(5): 641–58.

Polsby, N. W. 1984. *Political Innovation in America: The Politics of Policy Initiation.* New Haven, CT: Yale University Press.

Porter, M. 1985. *Competitive Advantage.* New York: Free Press.

Powell, W. W. and Grodal, S. 2004. 'Networks of innovators', in J. Fagerberg, D. C. Mowery and R. R. Nelson (eds.), *The Oxford Handbook of Innovation.* Oxford: Oxford University Press, pp. 56–85.

Rhodes, R. A. W. 1995. 'The institutionalist approach', in D. Marsh and G. Stoker (eds.), *Theories and Methods in Political Science.* London: Macmillan, pp. 42–57.

  1997. *Understanding Governance.* Buckingham: Open University Press.

Roberts, N. C. and King, P. J. 1996. *Transforming Public Policy: Dynamics of Policy Entrepreneurship and Innovation.* San Francisco: Jossey-Bass.

Rogers, E. M. 1995. *Diffusion of Innovations.* New York: The Free Press.

Salamon, L. M. (ed.) 2002. *The Tools of Government: A Guide to the New Governance.* New York: Oxford University Press.

Scharpf, F. W. 1999. *Governing in Europe: Effective and Democratic?* Oxford: Oxford University Press.

Schumpeter, J. 1934. *The Theory of Economic Development.* Cambridge, MA: Harvard University Press.

Schmidt, V. A. 2010. 'Taking ideas and discourse seriously: Explaining change through discursive institutionalism as the fourth new institutionalism', *European Political Science Review* 2(1): 1–15.

Smith, G. 2009. *Democratic Innovations.* Cambridge: Cambridge University Press.

Sørensen, E. and Torfing, J. (eds.) 2007. *Theories of Democratic Network Governance.* Basingstoke: Palgrave-Macmillan.

Sørensen, E. and Torfing, J. 2011. 'Enhancing collaborative innovation in the public sector', *Administration and Society,* 43(8): 842–868.

Steelman, T. A. 2010. *Implementing Innovation.* Washington, DC: Georgetown University Press.

Teece, D. J. 1992. 'Competition, cooperation and innovation', *Journal of Economic Behavior and Organization* 18(1): 1–25.

Thompson, V. A. 1965. 'Bureaucracy and Innovation', *Administrative Science Quarterly* 10(1): 1–20.

Torfing, J. 2016. *Collaborative Governance in the Public Sector.* Washington, DC: Georgetown University Press.

Torfing, J., Peters, B. G., Pierre, J. and Sørensen, E. 2012. *Interactive Governance: Advancing the Paradigm.* Oxford: Oxford University Press.

Triantafillou, P. and Torfing, J. 2013. 'What's in a name? Grasping New Public Governance as a political-administrative system', *International Review of Public Administration* 18(2): 9–25.

Van der Panne, G., Van Beers, C. and Kleinknecht, A. 2003. 'Success and failure of innovation: A literature Review', *International Journal of Innovation Management* 7(3): 1–30.

Van de Ven, A., Polley, D., Garud, R. and Venkataraman, S. 2008. *The Innovation Journey*. New York: Oxford University Press.

West, M. A. and Farr, J. L. (eds.) 1990. *Innovation and Creativity at Work: Psychological and Organizational Strategies*. Chichester: Wiley.

Zaltman, G., Duncan, R. and Holbek, J. 1973. *Innovations and Organizations*. New York: Wiley.

Part I

Linking Governance and Innovation

2   Collaborative Governance as Creative Problem-Solving

Christopher K. Ansell

2.1   Introduction

Recent calls to expand the agenda of public sector innovation have emphasized the potential for collaborative governance to serve as a key component of this agenda (Sørensen and Torfing 2011; Hartley, Sørensen and Torfing 2013; Ansell and Torfing 2014). The mechanisms that link collaborative governance to innovation, however, have not yet been fully or clearly stated. In this chapter, I argue that *creative problem-solving* is a key mechanism linking collaboration and innovation. Attention to *problems*, in general, builds on the finding that public sector innovation is often problem-driven (Borins 2000; Salge 2011) and illuminates the concrete matrix of incentives and constraints faced by collaborating stakeholders. Attention to *problem-solving* takes us inside the process of innovation and highlights the importance of common problem frames (Andrews, Pritchett and Woolcock 2013). Attention to the *creative* dimension of problem-solving orients us to the forward-looking, improvisational and transformative nature of successful collaborative innovation as it strives to generate unique or novel services, programmes or collective agreements in the face of political and institutional constraints (Hargadon and Beckhy 2006).

The view that collaborative governance itself is a strategy of problem-solving is a common one. However, it is useful to recognize at least three different images of this strategy at the outset, which in turn produce subtly different lenses for analysing problems, problem-solving and creativity:

(1) One image regards problems as complex or wicked. Their interdependent and multidimensional nature demands interdependent and multidimensional solutions. Collaborative governance is therefore a strategy for mobilizing complex solutions to complex problems. This might be called the *systems image* because a systems theory perspective

motivates the approach to collaborative problem-solving (e.g. Head and Alford 2015; Walker, Daniels and Emborg 2015).

(2) A slightly different image understands collaboration itself to be the chief problem. From this perspective, political polarization or the fragmented nature of public and private institutions undermines effective public policy. Collaborative governance is understood as a solution to this problem of polarization or fragmentation. This might be called the *political image* because it emphasizes the competing or conflicting interests and agendas of stakeholders (e.g. Ansell and Gash 2008).

(3) A third image understands problem-solving as a value-added strategy. From this perspective, collaborative governance synergistically brings together knowledge, resources, skills and perspectives to deliver improved public services and public goods (Lasker and Weiss 2003). This might be called the *public value image* because it points to the opportunities for the public sector to create value (e.g. Page et al. 2015).

These three images are often combined in practice and can be complementary. But it is useful to distinguish them because they imply somewhat different imperatives for relating collaboration to innovation via problem-solving. The systems image suggests that the chief problem-solving challenge for stakeholders is to recognize and adapt to the systemic nature of wicked problems. For the political image, the chief task is to overcome deep-seated political conflicts or to align or bridge conflicting institutional agendas. And the core challenge for the public value image is to discover where public value might be produced by finding synergies between dispersed knowledge, resources and skills.

These three images share the idea that collaborative innovation requires stakeholders to jointly achieve some kind of breakthrough or transformation. However, the breakthroughs or transformations they expect may differ in degree, if not in kind. The systems image expects breakthroughs to arise through a deeper understanding of the complex nature of problems; the political image expects breakthroughs to occur when stakeholders discover new ways of managing their differences or framing their shared interests; and the public value image expects breakthroughs to occur when stakeholders can imagine new ways of combining their resources or talents. Each of these tasks requires a creative process of exploration, discovery and invention; however, the demands on creativity may also be subtly different in each case. To solve wicked problems, stakeholders must find creative ways to investigate problems; to manage political differences, stakeholders must invent novel modes of stakeholder engagement; and to realize synergies, stakeholders must creatively imagine new combinations of agendas and capabilities.

The purpose of delineating these three images is not to oppose or reify the differences between them. Rather, appreciating these differences reminds us of the need for concreteness as we set about constructing a generic theoretical framework. Collaborative problem-solving is hard work, fraught with dangers and difficult to carry off. Locking stakeholders together in a room will not necessarily produce creative problem-solving. Collaborative problem-solving is a high-risk, high-reward endeavour, with many challenges lying between convening a forum and a breakthrough or transformative problem-solving innovation. Many such efforts will fail, and this is not a strategy for picking the low-hanging fruit of public sector innovation. However, it is a very desirable strategy for solving otherwise intractable problems, breaking through political stalemates and realizing major synergies in public services.

This chapter provides an analytical framework for thinking about collaborative governance as a creative problem-solving process. Section 2 provides an analysis of what collaborative governance means and the parameters that make it distinctive. Section 3 describes how the history and trajectory of problems might contextually shape the problem-solving process. Section 4 identifies some key components of collaborative governance as a problem-solving process, including a problem-solving orientation, problem definition, joint enquiry and reflexive reframing. Section 5 argues that these problem-solving components should be conceived as being nested in a wider social learning process that requires stakeholders to collectively overcome four social learning thresholds – willingness to participate, mutual recognition, commitment to collaboration and joint ownership of the collaborative process. As summarized in Figure 2.1, creative problem-solving is therefore understood to be a process within a process.

2.2   What Is Collaborative Problem-Solving?

To understand what collaborative problem-solving is, it is useful to begin with a broad definition of the concept of collaborative governance, which has been defined as

[a] governing arrangement where one or more public agencies directly engage non-state stakeholders in a collective decision-making process that is formal, consensus-oriented, and deliberative and that aims to make or implement public policy or manage public programs or assets. (Ansell and Gash 2008: 2)[1]

---

[1] Emerson, Nabatchi and Balogh provide an even more encompassing definition, which includes 'the processes and structures of public policy decisionmaking and management that engage people constructively across the boundaries of public agencies, levels of government, and/or the public, private and civic spheres in order to carry out a public purpose that could not otherwise be accomplished' (2012: 2).

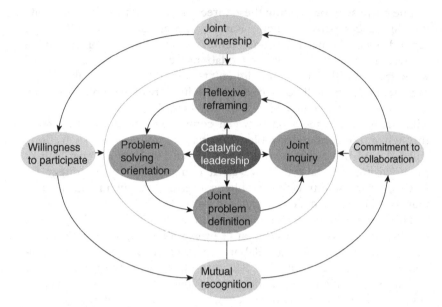

Figure 2.1 Creative problem-solving: a process within a process

At least six implicit or explicit features of this definition of collaborative governance establish the basic parameters of collaborative problem-solving: distributed action, jointness, self-production, consensus-orientation, deliberation and consequential decision making. Briefly considering each parameter helps us to set the stage for a deeper consideration of collaborative problem-solving in subsequent sections.

Collaborative problem-solving is based on *distributed action*. All accounts of collaborative governance assume that it brings together multiple stakeholders with relatively autonomous capacities – that is, stakeholders who enjoy their own authority, power or position. Although these capacities may vary considerably, the concept of collaborative governance makes little sense if the stakeholder does not have a considerable degree of autonomy.[2] This feature is fundamental for collaborative problem-solving in at least two senses. The first is that participation is understood to be, to a

[2] The emphasis on the distributed nature of action is important for distinguishing collaborative governance from routine forms of governance, such as the governing board of an organization. We would only refer to a board as a form of collaborative governance to the extent that the board members are engaged *qua* autonomous and independent stakeholders. When board members are paid or selected for what they contribute to the organization in question, they lose some degree of autonomy and independence.

significant degree, voluntary, which in turn means that the problem-solving process must be rooted in a process of mutual consent. The second is that the autonomy of stakeholders distinguishes collaborative governance from hierarchy, which brings stakeholders together under a common authority and coordinates them by command.[3] Collaborative problem-solving outcomes are not determined by fiat.

Although based on distributed action, a distinguishing feature of collaborative problem-solving is that it exhibits *jointness*. Jointness implies that stakeholders work together to produce a jointly determined framework for action or a joint product. Consider the definition of collaboration used by Thompson and Perry, which builds on Bardach's concept of jointness:

Collaboration is a process in which autonomous actors interact through formal and informal negotiation, jointly creating rules and structures governing their relationships and ways to act or decide on the issues that brought them together; it is a process involving shared norms and mutually beneficial interactions. (Thompson and Perry 2006: 23)[4]

Jointness implies both joint production and joint outcomes.[5] Note that crowdsourcing, an increasingly popular collective problem-solving strategy, may not embody either aspect of jointness.

Collaborative problem-solving also implies the stakeholders must be directly engaged in the problem-solving process. Problem-solving is *self-produced* as opposed to being delegated to experts or contracted out to consultants.[6] Therefore, collaborative problem-solving expects stakeholders to have a very substantial direct input into the conception of the joint framework or product (experts, consultants or contractors may be directly engaged as advisors or stakeholders). As a result, collaborative problem-solving places more stress on direct and inclusive participation than it does on formal mechanisms of representation.

Collaborative problem-solving processes also tend to be *consensus-oriented*. The point is not that collaborative governance is inherently cooperative, since it is quite often deployed as a technique in high-conflict

[3] Collaboration is sometimes mandated, which is a hybrid case. A mandate is a command and hence a species of hierarchy. However, mandated collaboration still respects the autonomy of stakeholders in the collaborative process itself.

[4] See Bardach (1998: 9).

[5] The criteria of jointness may also distinguish collaborative governance from network governance. Collaborative governance and network governance are sometimes used as near-synonyms. However, the term 'network' does not necessarily imply the same degree of jointness. For example, a policy network may refer to a distributed group of actors engaged in repeated exchange who do not jointly produce joint frameworks or products.

[6] Self-production is sometimes referred to as 'self-organization', a concept that comes from complexity theory. This is somewhat misleading, because the key issue is not whether distributed actors organize themselves but whether they contribute directly to jointness.

situations. But given the largely voluntary nature of participation, the lack of overarching authority, the limited role of representation and the desire to achieve joint outcomes, the collaborative problem-solving process leans heavily on consensus to move forward. Majoritarian voting rules are likely to be a last resort, since they may encourage losers to withdraw their support.

Due, in part, to this consensus-orientation, collaborative problem-solving tends to rely heavily on *deliberation* – that is, on intensive conversations to explore the creation of joint frameworks and products. Given the voluntary nature of collaborative governance, deliberation reflects the logic of 'voice' over 'exit' (Hirschman 1970). The deliberative process implies a multi-lateral, bi-directional mode of communication that is more or less formal (e.g. stakeholders are convened at an established time and place). This emphasis on formal, multilateral, bi-directional deliberation is important for distinguishing collaboration from consultation. Neither informal bilateral consultations between public agencies and stakeholders nor formal public comment procedures would be considered collaborative governance by this standard. Collaborative problem-solving therefore typically requires the creation of a distinct forum for problem-solving deliberation among stakeholders.

A final point is that the decisions made in these deliberative forums need to be *consequential*. The motivation of stakeholders to engage in a serious process of problem-solving is likely to be eroded if they sense that their input is symbolic or irrelevant. If a collaborative forum is regarded as a mere 'talking shop', stakeholders will have trouble having the tough conversations that effective collaboration often requires. In many cases, however, the decisions of a collaborative body are legally limited to being advisory. For stakeholders to engage seriously in collaborative problem-solving, they must believe that their advice will be taken seriously and may be consequential.[7]

For the purposes of further exploration of collaborative problem-solving process, distributed action, jointness, self-production, consensus-orientation, deliberation and consequential decision making are treated as parameters of collaborative governance.

2.3   The Push and Pull of Collaboration

To understand how collaborative governance can become a vehicle for creative problem-solving, it is useful to first consider how stakeholders

---

[7] The problem with the criteria 'significant consequences' is that it may be difficult to judge until the collaborative body has completed its work.

engage with problems in the first place. While problems come in many shapes and sizes, a useful distinction is between whether stakeholders are pushed by the problem to engage in collaboration versus being pulled by the possibility of achieving joint gains.

A *push factor* is a set of conditions or events that drive stakeholders towards collaboration. Often, stakeholders are pushed towards collaboration by the failure of other forms of governance (e.g. hierarchies, markets, networks of ad hoc bilateral exchange or adversarial, winner-take-all policy making) or by events that make collaborative governance look attractive relative to other governance strategies. In this case, failed governance shapes the understanding of the problem that must be solved and the conditions under which stakeholders engage one another. In extreme cases, a political stalemate has occurred that makes the situation suboptimal for stakeholders on different sides of the issue. In such situations, collaboration is itself understood to be a potential solution to prior governance failures. Such push factors therefore evoke a political image of collaborative problem-solving. Problem-solving becomes a search for ways that stakeholders might collaborate to escape a political stalemate or a suboptimal governance situation.

A similar push factor is the history of failure of stakeholders to successfully address problems unilaterally. Complex or wicked problems often evade unilateral strategies, gradually pushing stakeholders to explore more collaborative strategies. The failure to resolve problems unilaterally evokes the systems image of collaborative problem-solving. In such situations, the problem is to discover more systematic strategies of problem-solving that bring institutional jurisdictions together in order to respond to the interrelated dimensions of the problem. In this case, the past history of failed problem-solving may provide the reference point for collaborative problem-solving. Each stakeholder will bring different perspectives to the process, but there might be some initial agreement among stakeholders that they have a shared interest in addressing the complex dimensions of the problem.

Push factors do two important things that shape the subsequent process of collaborative problem-solving. First, they begin to illuminate the disadvantages of not working together. Failures illuminate the negative externalities that one actor's action produces for others or heighten actors' understanding of their interdependence. Second, they may illuminate the limitations of alternative strategies of problem-solving. The recognition that collaborative problem-solving is the 'only game in town' may enhance commitment to collaboration.

A *pull factor* is the perception of opportunities for the production of value through joint action. Pull factors tend to work by heightening awareness of positive opportunities and are thus associated with entrepreneurial energy. One important pull factor is the anticipation of synergies that might be realized through better alignment, coordination or exchange of knowledge and resources. Another important pull factor is the anticipation of win–win (positive sum) strategies that might be realized via joint action. Pull factors are framed in terms of the advantages of working together rather than in terms of the disadvantages of not working together. Positive relationships among stakeholders may themselves be a pull factor because they heighten the sense that synergies or win–win strategies are possible. The public value image tends to stress such pull factors.

Pull factors will shape the collaborative problem-solving process in different ways than push factors. For push factors, past failures frame the problem-solving process; for pull factors, aspirations are more likely to draw stakeholders to participate. In such cases, stakeholders will often have early agreement on common aspirations, but must discover modes of working together that actually result in synergies or produce value. As stakeholders begin to search for synergy or value, however, they may also have to confront the transaction costs of working together or may begin to discover the problems entailed by joint strategies. In a very broad sense, pull factors are the mirror image of push factors. Whereas past failures are likely to highlight the problem to solve, they may have also entrenched the different interests or strategies of different stakeholders. Stakeholders attracted to collaborative problem-solving to discover synergies or to produce public value may, by contrast, enjoy early agreement on general goals, but then unexpectedly begin to struggle as they begin to elaborate concrete agendas.

Push and pull factors shape how stakeholders define and engage with problems, and hence they exert an influence on the creative problem-solving process.

2.4   Collaborative Governance as Creative Problem-Solving

It is a common assumption that collaborative governance is a means of problem-solving and particularly for complex or wicked problems or for problems that require comprehensive solutions (Logsdon 1991; Lasker and Weiss 2003; Bryson, Crosby and Stone 2006). However, most work on collaboration has focused on the social process, institutional conditions and leadership imperatives for successful collaboration, rather than on problem-solving per se. Yet we cannot assume that collaboration leads to creative problem-solving, and hence to innovation. We must delve into the process of problem-solving itself (Hargadon and Beckhy 2006).

While problem-solving is still an underdeveloped area of collaborative governance research, it is possible to draw a preliminary model of creative problem-solving from the extant literature. This model has four key components that roughly flow in the following order: a problem-solving orientation, problem definition, joint problem-solving exploration and reflexive reframing.[8] However, as with other dimensions of the collaborative process, these components are best conceived not as discrete linear stages, but as activities that have recursive feedback effects on one another over time. Thus, they are best represented as a loop (see Figure 2.1).

A first step in the creative problem-solving process is that the stakeholders have to become oriented towards problem-solving in the first place. In many cases, a problem-solving orientation may precede the collaboration and be one of the motivations for stakeholders to collaborate in the first place. However, in situations of political conflict, orienting stakeholders towards problem-solving may be a critical step in more productive interaction. Negotiation theory distinguishes between a 'bargaining distributive' or 'positional' perspective on the one hand and a 'problem-solving' or 'integrative' perspective on the other (Trace and Peterson 1977; Fisher and Ury 1981; Hopmann 1995). Shifting from a more positional perspective to a problem-solving orientation is important because it triggers a more active search and communication process. Kim and Grunig (2011), for instance, find that as individuals become more invested or committed to problem-solving, they also become more active in searching for and communicating problem-relevant information.

Joint problem definition is often identified as a critical step in achieving deeper collaboration (Kelman 1996; Bryson, Crosby and Stone 2006; Van Buuren 2009). To proceed with problem-solving, stakeholders do not necessarily need to generate fundamental agreement or shared values. But they need to generate enough alignment or focus to engage in a deeper enquiry into the situation. Often this requires generating a collective sense of what the problem is that the collaborative is trying to solve. Basadur et al. (2000) argue that 'out of the box' problem definition is critical for creative problem-solving. Joint problem definition is not therefore a once-and-for-all step in the process, but an ongoing effort.

Joint problem definition requires stakeholders to explore their differences. De Wulf and Bouwen (2012) describe a range of ways that stakeholders deal with differences in framing, including pruning (eliminating more conflictual frames), polarization (escalating differences), mutual

---

[8] These elements are similar to the four elements of principled engagement identified by Emerson, Nabatchi and Balogh (2012) – discovery, definition, deliberation and determination. Another similar categorization is problem-setting, direction-setting and structuring (Selin and Chavez 1995).

adaptation (e.g. splitting the difference), reframing (to transcend differences) and interpenetration (embedding opposition in a wider framework). Quick and Feldman (2014) argue that collaborative work can manage differences by translating across, aligning among and decentring differences. Nowell (2010) finds support that problem frame-alignment is important to stakeholders' perceptions that the overall collaborative process is successful.

While the entire process of creative problem-solving can be said to require an enquiring attitude, joint enquiry may be a much more central, formal and explicit step during certain phases of the creative problem-solving process. In some cases, joint enquiry may require exchange of information among stakeholders, so that each stakeholder develops a deeper understanding of the position of other stakeholders (Findlater and Kelly 1999). Joint fact-finding is also an important way to cultivate a common base of knowledge among stakeholders with different perspectives and bases of knowledge (Karl, Susskind and Wallace 2007; Van Buuren 2009). This common knowledge can then become the basis for successful reframing processes. Collaborative monitoring has been found to enhance learning, community-building and trust (Fernandez-Gimenez, Ballard and Sturtevant 2008).

A final step in the creative problem-solving process is what Hargadon and Bechty (2006) have called 'reflexive reframing' or what Schön and Rein (1995) have called 'frame reflection'. It requires stakeholders to collectively reflect on the 'frames' that constitute disputes or that structure their perspectives.[9] This reflection can then help stakeholders to imagine alternative frames that may open up new perspectives on how to resolve disputes or open up new perspectives. Reframing is critical, they argue, for encouraging more distant search for solutions (Hargadon and Bechty 2006). If successful, reframing processes can lead to what have been called 'transformational moments' (Putnam, Burgess and Royer 2003; Putnam 2004). In high-conflict situations, however, reframing is far from an easy process (Gray 2004).

Putnam (2004) argues that 'transformational moments' occur when deliberation moves up levels of abstraction in order to articulate options from a common perspective. For example, Waage (2001) has found that stakeholders with conflicting perspectives successfully built consensus by starting with a shared place-based perspective. Van Buuren (2009) argues that framing processes in collaborative governance include frame reflection, converging images and enrichment or creativity. Frame reflection is

---

[9] Scholars have begun to distinguish between cognitive and interaction frames (Dewulf et al. 2009). Cognitive frames reside in the minds of stakeholders, typically as schemas, while interactional frames are co-constituted through the interaction of stakeholders.

the process of acknowledging and discussing normative frames of reference. Converging images refers to the process of searching for common perspectives. Enrichment or creativity refers to exploring the way common perspectives can transcend existing frames.

We should probably avoid thinking of reframing as a recipe. Rather reflexive reframing should be understood as being built up from positive collaborative interaction. Observational research suggests that the level of intensity or energy in collaborative interactions may be important, with reflexive reframing occurring as the flow of interaction intensifies (van Oortmerssen, van Woerkum and Aart 2015).

Research also suggests that facilitative leadership is likely to be important at each step in this creative problem-solving process (Reiter-Palmon and Illies 2004). Effective facilitation can aid stakeholders to shift from a positional to a problem-solving orientation, to explore options for aligning their problem frames, to plan and implement joint enquiry and to explore reflective reframing of problems and solutions. In a review of the literature on leadership and creativity, Mumford et al. (2002) not only identify many important support roles played by leaders, but also find that leadership goes beyond mere support. They argue that leadership of creativity requires an 'integrative style' that includes idea generation, structuring and promotion (2002: 738).

In the literature on collaborative governance, different facilitative leadership roles have been distinguished, including steward, mediator and catalytic roles (Ansell and Gash 2012). Catalytic leadership that helps stakeholders explore problem definition and reflexive reframing is likely to be particularly important for creative and integrative problem-solving (Mandell and Keast 2009; Morse 2010; Carmeli et al. 2014). Catalytic leadership might take the form of helping stakeholders to surface assumptions (Feyerherm 1994), redefine problem definitions (Luke and Luke 1997), integrate around common purposes and steer discussions towards opportunities (Morse 2010). Catalytic leaders might also make data available to the group (Ryan 2001), share knowledge (Carmeli, Gelbard and Reiter-Palmon 2013), communicate in a way that energizes stakeholders (Vangen and Huxham 2003) and prompt cognitive shifts (Ospina and Foldy 2010).

The problem-solving cycle of problem orientation, problem definition, joint enquiry and reflexive reframing may occur multiple times as stakeholders gradually adapt and refine their perspectives and agendas towards a joint framework of action. This is anything but a mechanical process of checking off steps in order to arrive at an innovation. It is much more likely to be an uneven process that will be contingent upon a larger set of factors that we can now discuss.

2.5   Collaborative Problem-Solving: A Process within a Process

It is useful to conceive of collaborative governance as a social learning process where stakeholders learn about their options, about each other and about their own level of commitment as they negotiate with each other. To be successful, stakeholders must develop some degree of trust in one another. However, trust between stakeholders is often lacking and often has to be built up through a positive process of deliberation and interaction. Stakeholders often come to a collaborative process not because they are committed to collaboration per se, but because they want to protect their interests. So part of the social learning process is to build that commitment. If this social learning process fails, collaborative governance is also likely to fail.

As a social learning process, collaborative governance can either positively or negatively reinforce the engagement of stakeholders with one another. Communication that engages stakeholders in intensive face-to-face dialogue is a fundamental feature of this process. Dialogue can reinforce antagonism and distrust, or it can become the vehicle for breaking down mutual stereotypes and exploring the constructive management of differences. 'Small wins' along the way can positively reinforce motivation, commitment and positive engagement, but it is equally possible that 'small losses' can weaken stakeholder investment and sour relations. Facilitative leadership can reassure stakeholders of the integrity of the process and help to mediate and explore differences, but it can sometimes polarize stakeholders further. Like creative problem-solving, the social learning process is best conceived as an iterative cycle with positive or negative feedbacks. A positive cycle may gradually build capacity for problem-solving (Page et al. 2015).[10]

Four learning thresholds must be achieved if the collaborative governance process is going to lead to the deep positive substantive engagement of stakeholders with one another (Ansell 2011):

(1) Stakeholders have to be willing to participate in the first place.
(2) Stakeholders must develop enough mutual respect to engage with each other in a constructive way.
(3) Stakeholders need to become committed to the collaborative process itself (Margerum 2001).
(4) And stakeholders must develop a sense of joint ownership over the collaborative process (Lachapelle and McCool 2005).

---

[10] Weber, Lovrich and Gaffney (2005) adopt a more structural approach to identifying problem-solving capacity, distinguishing vertical, horizontal and vertical–horizontal partnership capacities. The more process-oriented approach developed here is, however, close in spirit to what they call horizontal capacity.

In some cases, these thresholds may be trivial to overcome and implicit in the process itself. But in other cases, it may be difficult even to get stakeholders to show up in the first place, much less to engage each other with respect. These issues have already been extensively discussed in the collaborative governance literature. What has not been fully developed is how social learning might influence collaborative problem-solving per se.

The willingness of stakeholders to participate in the first place is often initially determined by motivational factors that precede or are external to the collaborative process. This willingness to participate is likely to shape stakeholders' orientation towards problem-solving. When stakeholders are mandated to collaborate or where they are only participating to protect their interests, they are likely to see collaboration as a process of positional or distributed bargaining. As a result, they may simply engage with other stakeholders in order to defend their interests and will be unwilling to more fully explore possibilities for more integrative outcomes. On the other hand, tense bargaining can itself create incentives for a shift to a problem-solving orientation. As McCool and Guthrie write: 'Where a balance of power exists, stalemates occur. Stalemates, however, often are incentives for creative solutions' (2001: 312).

Even when stakeholders are oriented towards problem-solving, it may be difficult for them to engage in the kind of quality communication necessary for creative problem-solving (Lasker and Weiss 2003). When stakeholders do not respect or trust one another, it will be difficult to give credence to the problem-solving strategies voiced by other stakeholders. To move forward, stakeholders do not have to agree with other stakeholders, but they must at least acknowledge that other stakeholders have a legitimate position. Mutual recognition can enhance the capacity for stakeholders to listen to each other and to move beyond a positional logic of interaction (McCool and Guthrie 2001). It is also important for fostering a sense of 'psychological safety' (a sense that it is ok to be yourself), which, research has found, is necessary for creative problem-solving (Carmeli et al. 2014). Note, however, that when steered in a productive direction, conflict may have a salutary effect on problem-solving (Laws, Hogendoorn and Karl 2014).

A fragile commitment to the collaborative process will undermine the investment of stakeholders in the kind of deep exploration of issues that creative problem-solving requires (Clark et al. 1993). Stakeholders may accord respect and recognition to one another, but discovery of win-win solutions may require a still deeper level of commitment to collaboration. Such solutions require commitment to discovering solutions that enhance the position of all parties, which requires stakeholders to see the issue from the perspective of other stakeholders.[11]

Joint ownership of the collaborative process means that stakeholders have come to appreciate that the process is 'theirs'. This sense of joint ownership goes beyond mutual recognition or commitment to the process itself. It implies that stakeholders feel that they have genuine input into joint decisions and a sense of collective responsibility for the outcome of the process. A dramatic example of this sense of joint ownership is offered by an observer of a collaborative process for protecting an endangered species: '[T]he most important achievement I saw was that a group of people walked into the room hating each other's guts and ready to slit each other's throats . . . and now if you were to come to visit a meeting and say something against the plan we've come up with, you're apt to get eaten by both sides' (Hoben 1999: 6). By overcoming this threshold of joint ownership, stakeholders achieve a sense of group empowerment that supports joint enquiry and reflexive reframing.

As this observation of the endangered species planning process suggests, the social learning process is often specific to the individual stakeholders who participate. Thus, it is not surprising that arrivals of new stakeholders or departures of established members can disrupt the psychological sense of collective empowerment. A case study of a problem-solving collaboration designed to overcome conflicts over the management of grizzly bears in Canada found that '[w]ith increasingly difficult issues to tackle, problem-solving skills and social capital declined with the entrance of new participants who had minimal integration and incongruent expectations. This fragmentation prevented the group from clarifying and sustaining the common interest' (Richie, Oppenheimer and Clark 2012: 280).

2.6   Conclusion

This chapter has conceived of innovation as a process of collaborative problem-solving and argued that this process poses not only high risks but also high rewards. It is a high-risk process because collaboration can entail significant transaction costs with uncertain success. Yet collaborative problem-solving also has the potential to create transformative innovations made possible by fundamental restructurings of relationships among issues, stakeholders and values. Collaborative problem-solving can help address wicked and otherwise intractable problems (the systems

---

[11] In a study of project teams and student collaboration, Li et al. (2007) found that procedural fairness and organizational commitment might be substitutes for one another in encouraging collaborative problem-solving.

image), breakthrough political stalemates (the political image) and create public value by leveraging synergies (the public value image).

Collaborative problem-solving operates within a distinctive context. This context is characterized by the distributed action of autonomous stakeholders who must engage in joint action to produce joint outcomes. The stakeholders themselves produce consequential outcomes through a deliberative and consensus-oriented process. This context sets the basic parameters for understanding problem-solving as a collaborative process. However, this process does not operate in isolation. The 'problems' that collaborative governance addresses have different histories and trajectories. Problems may essentially drive stakeholders to collaborate in the first place (push factors) or stakeholders may be drawn to collaboration by the promise of innovation (pull factors).

As shown in Figure 2.1, collaborative problem-solving may be thought of as a process within a process. Within the inner problem-solving process, the chapter has identified four critical iterative steps: (1) the shift from positional bargaining to a problem-solving orientation, which allows stakeholders to begin to conceive of their joint activity as a problem-solving process; (2) the joint definition of the problem through a process of frame alignment, which allows (3) a deeper joint enquiry into the issues at stake in the problem-solving process, which in turn provides (4) the basis for a reflexive reframing of either problems, solutions, or both. Each step requires some degree of transformation that is 'catalysed' by facilitative leadership.

The chapter further argued that this collaborative problem-solving process can be conceived as being nested within a broader social learning process that, like facilitative leadership, supports each transformative step. This chapter has presented this in terms of four process thresholds that must be overcome in order to orient and commit stakeholders to a deep and authentic exploration of issues. These thresholds are conceived as building upon one another. The first threshold that must be overcome is simply the willingness to participate in the collaborative process; the second threshold is for stakeholders to achieve a mutual recognition of one another, according each other enough respect to listen to what others have to say; the third threshold requires stakeholders to become committed to a process of collaboration; and finally, these stakeholders must develop a joint sense that they 'own' the collaborative problem-solving process.

This model suggests why innovation via collaborative problem-solving can be of both high risk and high reward. Collaborative problem-solving can lead to a deep and broad-ranging transformation of how stakeholders engage with each other. However, there is no guarantee that this process will produce creative solutions to challenging problems. The outcome depends, in a sense, on a collective transformation of the stakeholders themselves.

References

Andrews, M., Pritchett, L. and Woolcock, M. 2013. 'Escaping capability traps through problem driven iterative adaptation (PDIA)', *World Development* 51: 234–44.

Ansell, C. 2011. *Pragmatist Democracy: Evolutionary Learning as Public Philosophy.* New York: Oxford University Press.

Ansell, C. and Gash, A. 2008. 'Collaborative governance in theory and practice', *Journal of Public Administration Research and Theory* 18(4): 543–71.

2012. 'Stewards, mediators, and catalysts: Toward a model of collaborative leadership', *The Innovation Journal* 17(1): 2.

Ansell, C. and Torfing, J. (eds.) 2014. *Public Innovation through Collaboration and Design* (Vol. 19). New York: Routledge.

Bardach, E. 1998. *Getting Agencies to Work Together: The Practice and Theory of Managerial Craftsmanship.* Washington, DC: Brookings Institution Press.

Basadur, M., Pringle, P., Speranzini, G. and Bacot, M. 2000. 'Collaborative problem solving through creativity in problem definition: Expanding the pie', *Creativity and Innovation Management* 9(1): 54–76.

Borins, S. 2000. 'What border? Public management innovation in the United States and Canada', *Journal of Policy Analysis and Management* 19(1): 46–74.

Bryson, J. M., Crosby, B. C. and Stone, M. M. 2006. 'The design and implementation of cross-sector collaborations: Propositions from the literature', *Public Administration Review* 66(s1): 44–55.

Carmeli, A., Sheaffer, Z., Binyamin, G., Reiter-Palmon, R. and Shimoni, T. 2014. 'Transformational leadership and creative problem-solving: The mediating role of psychological safety and reflexivity', *The Journal of Creative Behavior* 48(2): 115–35.

Carmeli, A., Gelbard, R. and Reiter-Palmon, R. 2013. 'Leadership, creative problem-solving capacity, and creative performance: The importance of knowledge sharing', *Human Resource Management* 52(1): 95–121.

Clark, N. M., Baker, E. A., Chawla, A. and Maru, M. 1993. 'Sustaining collaborative problem solving: Strategies from a study in six Asian countries', *Health Education Research* 8(3): 385–402.

Dewulf, A. and Bouwen, R. 2012. 'Issue framing in conversations for change: Discursive interaction strategies for "doing differences"', *The Journal of Applied Behavioral Science* 48(2): 168–93.

Dewulf, A., Gray, B., Putnam, L., Lewicki, R., Aarts, N., Bouwen, R. and Van Woerkum, C. 2009. 'Disentangling approaches to framing in conflict and negotiation research: A meta-paradigmatic perspective', *Human Relations* 62(2): 155–93.

Emerson, K., Nabatchi, T. and Balogh, S. 2012. 'An integrative framework for collaborative governance', *Journal of Public Administration Research and Theory* 22(1): 1–29.

Fernandez-Gimenez, M. E., Ballard, H. L. and Sturtevant, V. E. 2008. 'Adaptive management and social learning in collaborative and community-based monitoring: A study of five community-based forestry organizations in the western USA', *Ecology and Society* 13(2): 4.

Feyerherm, A. E. 1994. 'Leadership in collaboration: A longitudinal study of two interorganizational rule-making groups', *The Leadership Quarterly* 5(3): 253–70.

Findlater, J. E. and Kelly, S. 1999. 'Reframing child safety in Michigan: Building collaboration among domestic violence, family preservation, and child protection services', *Child Maltreatment* 4(2): 167–74.

Fisher, R. U. and Ury, W. W. 1981. *Getting to Yes: Negotiating Agreement without Giving In*. London: Penguin.

Gray, B. 2004. 'Strong opposition: Frame-based resistance to collaboration', *Journal of Community & Applied Social Psychology* 14(3): 166–76.

Hargadon, A. B. and Bechky, B. A. 2006. 'When collections of creatives become creative collectives: A field study of problem solving at work', *Organization Science* 17(4): 484–500.

Hartley, J., Sørensen, E. and Torfing, J. 2013. 'Collaborative innovation: A viable alternative to market competition and organizational entrepreneurship', *Public Administration Review* 73(6): 821–30.

Head, B. W. and Alford, J. 2015. 'Wicked problems: Implications for public policy and management', *Administration & Society* 47(6): 711–39.

Hirschman, A. O. 1970. *Exit, Voice, and Loyalty: Responses to Decline in Firms, Organizations, and States* (Vol. 25). Cambridge, MA: Harvard University Press.

Hoben, M. L. 1999. 'Clark County habitat conservation planning process', in C. W. Coughlin, M. L. Hoben, D. W. Manskopf and S. W. Quesada, *A Systematic Assessment of Collaborative Resource Management Partnerships*. Masters Thesis. Ann Arbor: University of Michigan.

Hopmann, P. T. 1995. 'Two paradigms of negotiation: Bargaining and problem solving', *The Annals of the American Academy of Political and Social Science* 542(1): 24–47.

Karl, H. A., Susskind, L. E. and Wallace, K. H. 2007. 'A dialogue, not a diatribe: Effective integration of science and policy through joint fact finding', *Environment: Science and Policy for Sustainable Development* 49(1): 20–34.

Kelman, H. C. 1996. 'Negotiation as interactive problem solving', *International Negotiation* 1(1): 99–123.

Kim, J. N. and Grunig, J. E. 2011. 'Problem solving and communicative action: A situational theory of problem solving', *Journal of Communication* 61(1): 120–49.

Lachapelle, P. R. and McCool, S. F. 2005. 'Exploring the concept of "ownership" in natural resource planning', *Society and Natural Resources* 18(3): 279–85.

Lasker, R. D. and Weiss, E. S. 2003. 'Broadening participation in community problem solving: A multidisciplinary model to support collaborative practice and research', *Journal of Urban Health* 80(1): 14–47.

52   *Christopher K. Ansell*

Laws, D., Hogendoorn, D. and Karl, H. 2014. 'Hot adaptation: What conflict can contribute to collaborative natural resource management', *Ecology and Society* 19(2): 39.

Li, H., Bingham, J. B. and Umphress, E. E. 2007. 'Fairness from the top: Perceived procedural justice and collaborative problem solving in new product development', *Organization Science* 18(2): 200–16.

Logsdon, J. M. 1991. 'Interests and interdependence in the formation of social problem-solving collaborations', *The Journal of Applied Behavioral Science* 27(1): 23–37.

Luke, J. S. and Luke, J. S. 1997. *Catalytic Leadership*. San Francisco: Jossey-Bass.

Mandell, M. P. and Keast, R. 2009. 'A new look at leadership in collaborative networks: Process catalysts', in J. A. Raffel, P. Leisink and A. E. Middlebrooks (eds.), *Public Sector Leadership: International Challenges and Perspectives*. Northampton, MA: Edward Elgar, pp. 163–78.

Margerum, R. D. 2001. 'Organizational commitment to integrated and collaborative management: Matching strategies to constraints', *Environmental Management* 28(4): 421–31.

McCool, S. F. and Guthrie, K. 2001. 'Mapping the dimensions of successful public participation in messy natural resources management situations', *Society & Natural Resources* 14(4): 309–23.

Morse, R. S. 2010. 'Integrative public leadership: Catalyzing collaboration to create public value', *The Leadership Quarterly* 21(2): 231–45.

Mumford, M. D., Scott, G. M., Gaddis, B. and Strange, J. M. 2002. 'Leading creative people: Orchestrating expertise and relationships', *The Leadership Quarterly* 13(6): 705–50.

Nowell, B. 2010. 'Out of sync and unaware? Exploring the effects of problem frame alignment and discordance in community collaboratives', *Journal of Public Administration Research and Theory* 20(1): 91–116.

Ospina, S. and Foldy, E. 2010. 'Building bridges from the margins: The work of leadership in social change organizations', *The Leadership Quarterly* 21(2): 292–307.

Page, S. B., Stone, M. M., Bryson, J. M. and Crosby, B. C. 2015. 'Public value creation by cross sector collaborations: A framework and challenges of assessment', *Public Administration* 93(3): 715–32.

Putnam, L. L. 2004. 'Transformations and critical moments in negotiations', *Negotiation Journal* 20(2): 275–95.

Putnam, L. L., Burgess, G. and Royer, R. 2003. 'We can't go on like this: Frame changes in intractable conflicts', *Environmental Practice* 5(3): 247–55.

Quick, K. S. and Feldman, M. S. 2014. 'Boundaries as junctures: Collaborative boundary work for building efficient resilience', *Journal of Public Administration Research and Theory* 24(3): 673–95.

Reiter-Palmon, R. and Illies, J. J. 2004. 'Leadership and creativity: Understanding leadership from a creative problem-solving perspective', *The Leadership Quarterly* 15(1): 55–77.

Richie, L., Oppenheimer, J. D. and Clark, S. G. 2012. 'Social process in grizzly bear management: Lessons for collaborative governance and natural resource policy', *Policy Sciences* 45(3): 265–91.

Ryan, C. M. 2001. 'Leadership in collaborative policy-making: An analysis of agency roles in regulatory negotiations', *Policy Sciences* 34(3–4): 221–45.

Salge, T. O. 2011. 'A behavioral model of innovative search: Evidence from public hospital services', *Journal of Public Administration Research and Theory* 21(1): 181–210.

Schön, D. A. and Rein, M. 1995. *Frame Reflection: Toward the Resolution of Intractable Policy Controversies.* New York: Basic Books.

Selin, S. and Chevez, D. 1995. 'Developing a collaborative model for environmental planning and management', *Environmental Management* 19(2): 189–95.

Sørensen, E. and Torfing, J. 2011. 'Enhancing collaborative innovation in the public sector', *Administration & Society* 43(8): 842–68.

Thomson, A. M. and Perry, J. L. 2006. 'Collaboration processes: Inside the black box', *Public Administration Review* 66(s1): 20–32.

Tracy, L. and Peterson, R. B. 1977. 'Differences in reactions of union and management negotiators to the problem solving process', *Industrial Relations Journal* 8(4): 43–53.

Van Buuren, A. 2009. 'Knowledge for governance, governance of knowledge: Inclusive knowledge management in collaborative governance processes', *International Public Management Journal* 12(2): 208–35.

Vangen, S. and Huxham, C. 2003. 'Enacting leadership for collaborative advantage: Dilemmas of ideology and pragmatism in the activities of partnership managers', *British Journal of Management* 14(s1): S61–76.

Van Oortmerssen, L. A., van Woerkum, C. M. and Aarts, N. 2015. 'When interaction flows: An exploration of collective creative processes on a collaborative governance board', *Group & Organization Management* 40(4): 500–28.

Waage, S. A. 2001. '(Re)claiming space and place through collaborative planning in rural Oregon', *Political Geography* 20(7): 839–57.

Walker, G. B., Daniels, S. E. and Emborg, J. 2015. 'Public participation in environmental policy decisionmaking: Insights from twenty years of collaborative learning fieldwork', in Anders Hansen and Robert Cox (eds.), *The Routledge Handbook of Environment and Communication.* Abingdon, UK: Routledge, pp. 111–30.

Weber, E. P., Lovrich, N. P. and Gaffney, M. 2005. 'Collaboration, enforcement, and endangered species: A framework for assessing collaborative problem-solving capacity', *Society and Natural Resources* 18(8): 677–98.

3 The New Public Governance and Innovation in Public Services
A Public Service-Dominant Approach

Stephen P. Osborne and Zoe Radnor

3.1 Introduction[1]

In his previous works, the lead author of this chapter (Osborne 2006, 2009, 2010) has argued that the increasingly fragmented and inter-organizational context of public service delivery (Haveri 2007) necessitates asking new questions about public service delivery. It is now no longer possible to continue with a focus solely either upon administrative processes or upon intra-organizational management – the central pre-occupations of public administration and (new) public management, respectively. However, these foci must be integrated with a broader paradigm that emphasizes both the governance of inter-organizational (and cross-sectoral[2]) relationships and the efficacy of public service delivery *systems* rather than discrete Public Service Organizations (PSOs). This broader framework has subsequently been termed the New Public Governance (NPG) (Osborne 2010). This framework does not replace the previous foci, of course, but rather embeds them in a new context. A similar argument has been made by Thomas (2012).

This chapter will evaluate the consequences of this evolution, in relation to the topic of innovation in public services. Specifically, it explores the contingencies and challenges of innovation within the context of the NPG. In this context, 'innovation' is not simply another or an alternative word for 'change'. Rather it is a subset of change that carries its own distinctiveness, opportunities and challenges. Put simply, innovation is a form of change that involves discontinuity. It is not incremental improvement but rather involves genuine 'newness'. In the context of public services and their delivery, this implies a discontinuity in the needs

The corresponding author for this chapter is Stephen P. Osborne.

[1] The introductory section of this chapter is adapted from Osborne et al. (2013).

[2] 'Cross-sectoral relationships' here refers to relationships between public service organizations in the public, private and third (non-profit) sectors.

being addressed by a public service and/or the skills and capacities located within public service organizations (Osborne and Brown 2011).

This discussion in this chapter is divided into three parts. First, it outlines briefly the development of the prevailing paradigm of public management and develops our critique of its fatal flaw (in its product-dominant bias) and its increasing irrelevance to the contemporary world of public policy and public service delivery. Second, it explores the potential of the NPG to generate new theoretical insights and frameworks for public management that are more 'fit for purpose' for contemporary public service delivery. At the heart of this will be an articulation of the *public service-dominant logic* that is at the core of the NPG. Finally, it considers the implications of this for the facilitation and sustenance of innovation in public services. In this context, we would emphasize that we are not taking a normative stance that perceives innovation as some sort of normative good. We are indeed exploring its potential to contribute to public service reform – but in the context of recognition of its challenges and limitations. Indeed, sometimes innovation may be the wrong response to changing societal and economic needs – incremental change may be a more appropriate response. This is one of the challenges for public service reform.

3.2   The Theoretical Basis of Public Management: A Flawed Approach?

Contemporary public management theory is broadly encapsulated within the New Public Management (NPM) paradigm. The genesis of this body of theory and practice and its limitations have been well analysed elsewhere (for example, McLaughlin et al. 2009; Thomas 2012; Osborne et al. 2013). It arose as a response to significant critiques of the traditional public administration premise of the 'politics–administration dichotomy' (Svara 2008). While it resolved some of these issues, the NPM produced its own problems – not least the development of a 'silo' mentality to public service delivery, an obsession with internal efficiency and unit costs rather than external effectiveness and public value creation and an absorption with imposing a goods-dominant logic on the delivery of public *services*. A good example of this has been the implementation of Lean reforms within public services in the United Kingdom (Radnor and Osborne 2013).

To an extent, this debate about the legitimacy, or otherwise, of the NPM model has been overtaken by events. While the issues of efficient and effective utilization of public resources have never gone – and will never go – away, they have become subsumed increasingly within a post-modern societal reality (Haveri 2007). This reality has meant that the *intra-organizational* focus of the NPM and previous, paradigms does not reflect the *inter-organizational and interactive* nature of contemporary public service provision. Nor have they embraced either the increasingly *processual and systemic* (as opposed to *discrete and transactional*) nature of the public service delivery process or the way in which they have become knowledge-driven within the digital economy. Subsequently, therefore, novel approaches have developed that have attempted to respond to this new reality – including public value (Moore 2002), digital governance (Dunleavy et al. 2006), and the *NPG* (Bingham et al. 2005; Osborne 2010; see also Alford and Hughes 2008).

3.3   The New Public Governance

Public governance has often been broken down into five distinct strands: socio-political governance (Kooiman 1999), public policy governance (Hanf and Sharpf 1978; Börzel 1997), administrative governance (Lynn et al. 2001; Salamon 2002), contract governance (Kettl 1993, 2000) and network governance (Rhodes 1997; Denters and Rose 2005). All of these theoretical perspectives make an important contribution to our understanding of public policy implementation and public service delivery. The intention here though is to argue that, from being an element within the Public Adminisration (PA) and NPM regimes of public policy implementation and public service delivery, public governance has become a distinctive regime in its own right – the NPG. This posits both *a plural state*, where multiple interdependent actors contribute to the delivery of public services, and *a pluralist state*, where multiple systems and processes comprise public service delivery. The NPG is thus both a product of and a response to the increasingly complex, plural and fragmented nature of public policy implementation and service delivery in the twenty-first century (Osborne 2010).

What has been missing from this earlier 'public governance' work has been a genuine understanding of *process* and *system* with the NPG. 'Public governance' has articulated models of public service delivery that reflect the distributed nature of public service delivery across inter-organizational networks and reflect upon its implications. However, it has not embraced the central tenet of the NPG – that contemporary public service delivery is not simply dependent upon the governance of such inter-organizational networks. *Rather it requires an understanding of public services both as services and as the result of interactive public service systems which include not only PSOs themselves but also services users, their significant others, the community, other key stakeholders and hard and soft technology.* In order to develop a theoretical framework for the NPG that embraces this reality, it is necessary to look beyond the product-dominant models of the NPM that have been derived from the experience of manufacturing and industry – such as Porter's influential work on competitive advantage (Porter 1985). This latter body of theory assumes a range of core elements of the production process, but three are especially important: that production and consumption are discrete processes ruled by different logics; consequently, that the costs of production and consumption are distinguishable and separable; and that consumers are largely passive in these processes.

Over the past three decades, however, there has developed an alternative body of theory and research about the management of *services*. Originating in a discussion about the marketing of services (Gronroos 1978), this has now evolved into a substantive theory in its own right (e.g. Gronroos 2000; Normann 1991; Lusch and Vargo 2006). What is remarkable is that the debate about the management of public services has been conducted in almost total ignorance of this latter influential body of theory, despite its apparent relevance. Service management theory addresses the issue of the distinctiveness of the service experience, the often inter-organizational and systemic nature of public service delivery and the issue of the role of the consumer as the shaper, co-producer and evaluator of the service experience. The time is therefore long overdue to explore the potential and actual contribution of a service-dominant approach to public management and public service delivery. We denote this approach as *the public service-dominant logic* of public service delivery and management. We have outlined the elements of this approach and its implications for sustainable public services elsewhere (Osborne et al. 2013, 2015)[3] but provide a brief elucidation below.

3.4   The Public Service-Dominant Logic of the NPG

At its most basic level, manufacturing and product-dominant theory relates to activities that physically transform raw materials to produce saleable goods and include a transfer of ownership in this sale, whereas service-dominant theory relates to activities and processes concerned with the transaction of intangible benefits and where ownership of these activities is not transferred (Normann 1991). While there are numerous statements of the characteristics of such services, three core characteristics are traditionally referred to. First, that while a product is invariably concrete (such as a washing machine), a service is intangible – it is a process (staying at a hotel is not simply about the quality of the room that

---

[3] This formulation pays an explicit debt to the ground-breaking book by Lusch and Vargo (2006) and their concept of service-dominant logic.

you rent, it is also about the overall process/experience of your stay). This is not to say that the content of a service (its purpose) is irrelevant. This is nonsense. Of course, a service (whether a healthcare or lifestyle service) must deliver its intended benefits. However, research also consistently suggests that while service users expect a service to be 'fit for purpose', they base their judgement of its performance upon their expectations and experience of the process of service delivery rather than upon outcomes alone (Lovelock 1983). This means that influencing and understanding a user's expectations of a service is fundamental to their experience of, and satisfaction with, that service – and that this experience then affects quite profoundly the effectiveness and impact of that service. Gronroos has argued persuasively that a common failing of service management is attempting to provide a 'missing product' rather than concentrating upon the process of service delivery (Gronroos 1998). This is a failing that we would argue is endemic to public service management.

The second core concept of services theory is that there is a different production logic for manufactured products and services. For the former, production, selling and consumption occur separately (as with the above example of a washing machine). With services, however, production and consumption occur simultaneously (for example, the production of a sporting event takes place at exactly the same time as its consumption, as does the production and consumption of residential care). Because production and consumption are not separable for services, this implies entirely different business logic for them from manufactured products (Edvardsson and Loson 1996; Prahalad and Ramaswamy 2004). It is quite possible to reduce the unit costs of a manufactured product, for example, by reducing labour costs in order to increase the efficiency of production (perhaps through automation). To a great extent, changes to production staff do not affect the sale of that product in the market or the experience of it by its consumers. However, for a service, reducing its unit costs by changing staffing levels or qualifications directly affects the experience of that service by its users – and its subsequent effectiveness. The two processes are not separable.

This implies an entirely different logic to the management of manufacturing products, as opposed to services. Because the production and consumption of services take place contemporaneously, the production process directly affects consumption rather than having an articulated relationship to it. At an extreme, it matters little to users if the production staff making their washing machine are dressed only in their underpants, as long as the washing machine itself is fit for purpose. Yet this scenario would be wholly different in the case of business consultancy or residential care, for example.

Finally, the role of the user is qualitatively different for manufactured products and services. For the former, they are 'simply' their purchasers and consumers. However, for services, *the user is also a co-producer of the service.*[4] At the most extreme, no service is ever produced identically to two people – a meal in a restaurant is as much a product of the interaction between the customer and the waiter and the overall ambience of the restaurant and its customers, as it is of the quality of the food. The same is true for the interpersonal interaction in a consultancy intervention between the consultant and client, while the process of teaching is mediated by the needs, experiences and interactions of students as much as by the professional skills of the teacher. At a fundamental level, therefore, co-production is not an 'add-on' to public services but a core feature of them (Osborne and Strokosch 2013).

The implications of these three core characteristics for public services are myriad. However, one implication is especially significant. This is that the performance of a public service is not (solely) about its effectual design in relation to its purpose but is, at least, equally about the subjective experience of that service by its users. This is made up of the collision of their expectations of the service and their perceptions of the experience of the service delivery process – and this collision profoundly impacts upon the actual performance of that service. Thus, successful public service management is not exclusively about the effective design of public services – this is a necessary but not sufficient condition. Rather it also requires both governing and responding to the service expectations of service users and training and motivating the service delivery workforce to interact positively with these users. This is not simply about user satisfaction, as the consumerist movement would argue (Powell et al. 2010). Rather it concerns the iterative interactions between public service professionals and service users – which interactions directly influence upon public service outcomes. We have known this for some time in some specific public service domains (for example, in oncology – see Katz et al. 2005), but this knowledge has had little impact upon mainstream public management theory.

Three caveats must be added to this initial exposition. First, it is important not to reduce the array of service experiences to sophistry. The above characteristics are a continuum not a steady-state. There is a world of difference between hospitality services, the creative industries and financial services, for example – the latter may limit co-production

---

[4] Importantly, this does not imply any active willingness to co-produce on behalf of the user – simply that it is impossible to use a service without, in some way, contributing to its co-production (Korkman 2006).

purely to the completion of forms with personal data while the former may require far more interpersonal interaction (Maddern et al. 2007). Second, one has always to be careful when transferring lessons from the private to the public sector – whether from a manufacturing or service context. This needs to be framed within a critical view of the relationship between these sectors. Third, the increasing use of electronic and digital media to provide financial and retail services, in particular, has a whole logic and experience of its own that is challenging many of the hitherto assumptions about the process of service delivery (Bitner et al. 2000; Fassnacht and Koese 2006). This too has implications for public service delivery in the era of digital governance.

3.5   The NPG, Public Service-Dominant Logic and Innovation in Public Services Delivery

In this short chapter, we would highlight five significant implications of the NPG and a public service-dominant approach for innovation in public services (Osborne and Brown 2011). At the heart of these are five governance challenges for innovation in public services:
- the governance of public service systems,
- the governance of public service performance and its social construction,
- the governance of risk in public service innovation,
- the governance of co-production and
- the governance of inter-organizational collaboration and working.

Innovation and the Governance of Public Service Systems. First a great deal of the current literature in innovation in public services has concerned itself with the technical design of these services. The rational model of public service delivery has pre-supposed that effectiveness can be 'designed in' to public services in the same way that desirable characteristics are 'designed in' to manufactured products. Thus, processes of service planning have been privileged. Within a public service-dominant logic, however, the process is far more dynamic. On the one hand, one is not dealing with the design of 'stand-alone products' but rather addressing 'fail points' within service delivery processes and where innovation is enacted in the interaction of the multiple elements of public service systems – such as PSOs, public service professionals, service users and local communities. On the other hand, public service innovations themselves are inevitably process based (Osborne and Brown 2011). It is possible, of course, for an innovation to be a product used to support public service delivery (such as a new piece of medical equipment) to stimulate innovation in the public service – but this is a driver to public service innovation rather than the innovation itself. The implication of this is that the focus of public service innovation is not simply upon the discrete public services but rather upon the place that they occupy within the overall public service delivery system. This place and interaction are best revealed by the application of such service system technologies as service blueprinting (Radnor et al. 2013). These soft technologies both can make extant the systemic nature of public services and allow them to analyse in an integrative manner and can reveal 'fail points' in these systems that require innovative interventions to enhance the delivery of public services. They can also be instrumental in helping service professionals see service users at the heart of the service production process rather than as 'simple' recipients of public services.

Innovation and the Governance of Public Service Performance. Second, and deriving from this, the process of innovation in public services is a social one and is not easily evaluated by hard indicators. Such indicators can reveal part of the truth, of course (such as about the activities involved in an innovation, their costs and discrete viewpoints upon its impact). However, the true impact of an innovation will often be socially constructed by the range of actors interacting and involved in its enactment within a public service delivery system. To take just one example, an innovative teaching programme at a university will both be enacted by the interaction between students, academics and administrative staff in the university and be differentially evaluated by them in terms of its impact and outcomes (as well as by potential employers and families, of course). This is not a new observation. However, it is one that has been obscured by the subsequent years of the hegemony of the product and target-driven preoccupations of the NPM (see Chapter 15 by Christensen and Lægreid in this volume on multiple forms of accountability). The evaluation of public service innovation thus requires a sophisticated approach that can capture these differing perceptions and their impact upon both the innovation process and its effectiveness. Soft technologies adapted to this end do exist not least thanks to the influential work of Bryson on stakeholder engagement (2004).

Innovation and the Governance of Risk in Public Services. Third, and linked to this, how risk is responded to in innovation in public services is a product both of their processual nature and of their social construction and evaluation by their key actors. As a consequence, the current approach to risk 'management' in public service innovation is often deficient. This approach is invariably a technocratic one, based upon the 'objective' assessment of risk on scientific grounds by professional experts. Such an approach is not appropriate in areas where the nature of risks and their potential benefits are contested, as is often the case for public services. Two examples make this point. Consider first the implementation of community care services for adults with learning disabilities in the late twentieth century. These approaches have been proven to have had significant impact upon the quality of life of these individuals. At the time, however, the debate centred around whether it was right to put these vulnerable individuals at risk by taking them out of safe but constraining residential institutions and supporting them in an admittedly more risky, if arguable fulfilling, community setting. These risks and benefits were articulated and evaluated differently by a range of actors in the process (such as the individuals themselves, their families, service professionals and the community). However, implementation was primarily top-down by professionals who 'knew best'. This approach led to considerable resistance to the reforms that arguably slowed their implementation and effectiveness significantly. Second, the benefits and risks of caring for adults with serious mental health problems within the community are recurrently debated – how does one weigh the benefits to the individuals against the potential (if rare) risks to the community from challenging or dangerous behaviour resulting from mental illness?

One approach that does go beyond the technocratic approach is that of Renn (2008). He argues that both risk and acceptable levels of risk are socially constructed phenomena. Thus, risk management requires not just the application of scientific knowledge but also a political (in its broadest sense) process of negotiation. It requires social values to be integrated with evidence of risk levels and outcomes. As such risk governance (as opposed to management) requires an inclusive process with a premium upon broad political and stakeholder debate about acceptable levels of risk for identified innovations, interpersonal and inter-organizational negotiation and a commitment to ongoing communication about risk and comprehensive participation in its governance. The question at the core of these processes, he argues, is not 'how safe is safe', but rather 'how much uncertainty and ignorance [about real or potential risks of an innovation] are the main actors willing to accept in exchange for some given benefit' (Renn 2008: 277).

Such a negotiated approach to risk has much to offer to public policy concerned with innovation in public services. It lays bare the contested nature of innovation in public services and its outcomes and provides a framework for its governance and within which to negotiate levels of risk in such innovation – in societal, organizational, service user and workforce professional terms. It puts a premium upon communication and participation (remembering that much innovation in services comes precisely from service user co-production (Alam 2006)). As such, a framework for risk governance in innovation in public services is surely an essential prerequisite for the future and a step-change improvement from the mechanistic and technocratic approaches to risk management currently found in public policy. Such a framework has been developed in principle by Brown and Osborne (2013).

Innovation and the Governance of Co-Production. The fourth implication for public service innovation of the NPG and a public service-dominant logic goes to the very heart of the paradigm and deserves a more lengthy exposition. This is the role of the service user at the heart of public service delivery systems as the co-producers of public services. There is a substantial literature within the public administration and public management field concerned with 'co-production' in the implementation of public policy and the design and delivery of public services (inter alia, Ostrom 1972; Parks et al. 1981; Brudney and England 1983; Frederickson 1996; Alford 2009; Bason 2011; Pestoff et al. 2012). While this literature includes a continuum of perspectives on co-production, it has often set the co-production of public services apart as a variation on the 'usual' model of public service delivery where 'public officials are exclusively charged with responsibility for designing and providing services to citizens, who in turn *only* demand, consume and evaluate them' (Pestoff 2006: 506; emphasis added). Thus, it discusses the ways in which user involvement can be 'added into' the operational processes of service delivery (and as opposed to the up-stream, strategic level of policy making).

Such an understanding of co-production is derived from product-dominant logic where production and consumption are separated as discrete processes – thus, public services are conceptualized as products to be designed and produced by public policy makers and service professionals and consumed (relatively) passively by service users. Co-production can only occur at the behest of, and be controlled by, service professionals.

By contrast, a public service-dominant approach offers a very different perspective upon co-production. As our earlier discussion made explicit, co-production is a core element of the service delivery process – an essential and intrinsic process of interaction between any service organization and its service users at the point of delivery of a service (Gronroos 2000). From a public service-dominant approach, there is no way to avoid the co-production of public services because it is an *inalienable* (and oftentimes unconscious) element of such services. The question thus is not how to 'add-in' co-production to public services, but rather how to manage and work with its implications for effective public service delivery. Moreover, co-production is not always a normatively 'good' process. It can sometimes have deleterious effects if service users engage dysfunctionally in the service process.

As discussed above, Normann (1991) encapsulates such co-production as 'the moment of truth' of services delivery. Service organizations can only 'promise' a certain process or experience – the actuality is dependent upon such co-production. A classic example of this would be the co-produced experience of residential care by the interaction of staff and service users in a residential home for the elderly. The managers of this home may have a vision of what care they want to provide, but the actuality of it is enacted in the iterative interactions between service staff and service users (and other 'significant others'). In this debate, it is essential to articulate that co-production is not simply crass consumerism (Powell et al. 2010), where the views of the user hold hegemony above all others. Co-production is exactly what it says – the interaction of service users *and* service professionals (and perhaps others) within public service systems in order to enact public services – and in this context, stimulate public service innovation. Thus, it does not replace the public service professional by the public service user. Rather, it focuses attention on the governance of their interactions as a stimulus for public service innova-tion. This simple truth is often missed in much of the normative literature on co-production.

A core element of a public service-dominant approach to the co-production of innovation is that it seeks to unlock the tacit or 'sticky' knowledge that service users possess in order to stimulate innovation and service improvement (Von Hippel 1994, 2005). Here, the service organization proactively seeks to uncover, understand and satisfy 'latent (or future) needs', rather than simply reacting to existing or currently expressed needs – as has invariably been the case with public services. The services literature has highlighted a range of ways in which such co-production of innovation can be achieved (for example, Alam 2006; Kristensson et al. 2008) as well as highlighting some of its drawbacks and dangers (such as over-customization and its consequent financial implications). Such insights are a qualitative contribution to our under-standing of the nature and process of innovation in public services.

The challenge of unlocking this 'sticky knowledge' is a vital role for the public service professional within a NPG framework. Service users may not always be able to articulate clearly their experiences or be able to translate them into achievable goals for public service innovation. Hence, an NPG approach to innovation in public services reframes the roles of both the service user and the public service professional. The service user is no longer the passive recipient of a public service designed elsewhere and which is delivered to them. Rather, they are at the heart of the public service delivery process and the possessor of essential knowledge about the quality and performance of these services. The public service profes-sional is no longer the 'font of all knowledge' about a public service and its effective delivery (though they may possess specialist knowledge derived from long-term professional experience and research). A key task for them though is now to unlock the sticky knowledge of service users and combine it with their professional knowledge as a stimulus to public service improvement – including through innovation if appropriate. This relational governance is at the heart of a new public service professionalism rooted in the co-productive core of the NPG.

Innovation and the Governance of Inter-Organizational Working. Finally, it would be remiss to leave this discussion without considering the dimension of inter-organizational working for public service innovation. Within public service systems, as discussed above, public services are produced by a variety of public and private organizations among other parties – and with the role of third sector organizations (TSOs) being particularly important. In their seminal work, Berger and Neuhaus (1978) posit TSOs as mediating structures. Their argument starts with the presumption that people are the best experts on their own needs, but that mediating structures are necessary to enable the expression of these needs against the mega-institutions of society. Thus, TSOs can act as mediating structures to enable the inclusion of marginal groups in service delivery that do not have the necessary resources, capacity or power to be otherwise involved (Kearns 1995; Haugh and Kitson 2007).

Pestoff and Brandsen (2009) differentiate this inter-organizational role as *co-management*, where the TSO collaborates with public service planners in order to deliver a public service on behalf of its users, and as *co-governance*, where it delivers (either by itself or with other PSOs) both the planning and provision of a public service. However, not all agree that such roles are necessarily positive. There is an ongoing debate about whether they genuinely enhance the centrality of the service user to public service delivery, through the strength of collective action, or actually diminish it, by placing the TSO between the individual service users and their services – that is, it meets the needs of the TSO rather than the user (Brenton 1985; Pestoff et al. 2006). Finally, others have also argued that working under government contracts can dilute a TSO's role, original values and mission (as a mediating structure) to empower people, reconstructing its strategic purpose to that of the government agency funding it (Deakin 2001).

This latter issue is an important debate for the governance of public service innovation. Much government policy towards the third sector has been predicated upon the assumption of its inherent innovative capacity, though this has been challenged elsewhere (Osborne et al. 2010). There is a difficult edge to be balanced upon here. On the one hand it is true that different PSOs will bring different skill sets and knowledge to the reform of public services. Combining these approaches can lead to genuinely paradigm-changing and innovative forms of public service delivery. However, it also risks the dilution or destruction of unique organizational capacities where dominant organizations impose their logic through isomorphic pressures. Balancing these competing logics is a major governance challenge for public service innovation with the NPG.

3.6   Conclusions

This brief chapter has argued that NPG and the public service-dominant logic that is at its heart have profound implications at a theoretical and practical level for innovation in public services. It reveals the true nature of innovation in public services as being process based within service systems, with risk and co-production at its heart and where its impact is invariably contested and socially constructed by the range of parties to the service delivery process.

This chapter has then drawn out five areas of import for future study of the relationship between the NPG and innovation in public services. These are the appreciation of

- The implications of a systemic and processual approach to innovation in public services, rather than a focus on the discrete design of individual public service innovations,
- How public service innovation and its performance and impact is socially constructed within these systems,
- The need for sophisticated models and approaches to the governance of risk within public service innovation that recognize and mediate the multiple constituencies and perceptions of risk,
- The centrality of the governance of the relationship between public service professionals and service user in the co-production of public service innovation and
- The role that inter-organizational collaboration and working plays within the NPG as both a stimulant and challenge for public service innovation.

These five strands need to form the basis both of our theoretical debate and empirical research about a public service-dominant approach to innovation in public services. This is at the heart of the NPG and innovation in public service delivery. The key task is therefore not to ask how public services can be changed to enhance their innovative capacity. However, it is to recognize their true nature as services and to work with the actually existing reality of public service delivery and its governance rather than with the ideologically mistaken premises of the flawed and failed NPM.

References

Alam, I. 2006. 'Removing the fuzziness from the fuzzy front-end of service innovations through consumer interactions', *Industrial Marketing Management* 35(4): 468–80.

Alford, J. 2009. *Engaging Public Sector Clients: From Service-Delivery to Co-Production*. Basingstoke, UK: Palgrave.

Alford, J. and Hughes, O. 2008. 'Public value pragmatism as the next phase of public management', *American Review of Public Administration* 38(2): 130–48.

Bason, C. 2011. *Leading Public Sector Innovation. Co-Creating for a Better Society.* Bristol: Policy Press.

Berger, P. L. and Neuhaus, R. J. 1978. *To Empower People: The Role of Mediating Structures in Public Policy.* Washington DC: American Enterprise for Public Policy Research.

Bingham, L., Nabatchi, T. and O'Leary, R. 2005. 'The new governance: Practices and processes for stakeholder and citizen participation in the work of government', *Public Administration Review* 65(5): 547–58.

Bitner, M., Brown, S. and Meuter, M. 2000. 'Technology infusion in service encounters', *Journal of the Academy of Marketing Sciences* 28(1): 138–49.

Börzel, T. 1997 'What's so special about policy networks? An exploration of the concept and its usefulness in studying European governance', *European Integration online Papers (EIoP)* 1(16).

Brenton, M. 1985. *The Voluntary Sector in British Social Services.* London: Longman.

Brown, L. and Osborne, S. 2013. 'Innovation and risk in public services: Towards a new theoretical framework', *Public Management Review* 15(3): 186–208.

Brudney, J. L. and England, R. E. 1983. 'Toward a definition of the co-production concept', *Public Administration Review* 43(1): 59–65.

Bryson, J. 2004. 'What to do when stakeholders matter. Stakeholder identification and analysis techniques', *Public Management Review* 6(1): 21–53.

Deakin, N. 2001. 'Putting narrow-mindedness out of countenance: The UK voluntary sector in the new millennium', in A. Anheier and J. Kendall (eds.), *Third Sector Policy at the Crossroads.* London: Routledge, pp. 36–50.

Denters, D. and Rose, L. 2005. *Comparing Local Governance.* Basingstoke: Palgrave.

Dunleavy, P., Margetts, H., Bastow, S. and Tinkler, J. 2006. 'New public management is dead – Long live digital-era governance', *Journal of Public Administration Research and Theory* 16(3): 467–94.

Edvardsson, B. and Olson, J. 1996. 'Key concepts for new service development', *Service Industries Journal* 16(2): 140–64.

Fassnacht, M. and Koese, I. 2006. 'Quality of electronic services and testing a hierarchical model', *Journal of Service Research* 9(1): 19–37.

Frederickson, H. G. 1996. 'Comparing the reinventing government movement with the new public administration', *Public Administration Review* 56(3): 263–70.

Gronroos, C. 1978. 'A service oriented approach to the marketing of services', *European Journal of Marketing* 12(8): 588–601.

1998. 'Marketing services: The case of a missing product', *Journal of Business & Industrial Marketing* 13(4/5): 322–38.

2000. *Service Management and Marketing*. Chichester: John Wiley.

Hanf, K. and Scharpf, F. W. (eds.) 1978. *Interorganizational Policy Making*. London: Sage.

Haveri, A. 2007. 'Complexity in local government change', *Public Management Review* 8(1): 31–46.

Haugh, H. and Kitson, M. 2007. 'The third way and the third sector: New Labour's economic policy and the social economy', *Cambridge Journal of Economics* 31(6): 973–94.

Jung, T. 2010. 'Citizens, co-producers, customers, clients, captives? A critical review of consumerism and public services', *Public Management Review* 12(3): 439–46.

Katz, S., Lantz, P., Janz, N., Fagerlin, A., Schwartz, K., Liu, L. and Morrow, M. 2005. 'Patient involvement in surgery treatment decisions for breast cancer', *Journal of Clinical Oncology* 23: 5526–33.

Kearns, A. 1995. 'Active citizenship and local governance: Political and geographical dimensions', *Political Geography* 14(2): 155–75.

Kettl, D. 1993. *Sharing Power. Public Governance and Private Markets*. Washington, DC: Brookings Institution Press.

2000. *The Global Public Management Revolution*. Washington, DC: Brookings Institution Press.

Kooiman, Jan. 1999. 'Social-political governance: Overview, reflections and design', *Public Mangement Review* 1(1): 67–92.

Korkman, O. 2006. 'Customer value formation in practice: A practice-theoretical approach', Report A155, Hanken Swedish School of Economics, Helsinki, Finland.

Kristensson, P., Matthing, J. and Johansson, N. 2008. 'Key strategies for the successful involvement of customers in the co-creation of new technology-based services', *International Journal of Service Industry Management* 19(4): 474–91.

Lovelock, C. H. 1983. 'Classifying services to gain strategic marketing insights', *Journal of Marketing* 47(3): 9–20.

Lusch, R. and Vargo, S. (eds.) 2006. *The Service Dominant Logic of Marketing*. New York: M. E. Sharpe.

Lynn, L., Heinrich, C. and Hill, C. 2001. *Improving Governance. A New Logic for Empirical Research*. Washington, DC: Georgetown University Press.

Maddern, M., Maull, R., and Smart, A. 2007. 'Customer satisfaction and service quality in UK financial services', *International Journal of Production and Operations Management*, 27: 998–1019.

McLaughlin, K., Osborne, S. and Chew, C. 2009. 'Developing the marketing function in U.K. public service organizations: The contribution of theory and practice', *Public Money and Management* 29(1): 35–42.

Moore, M. 2002. *Recognizing Value in Policing*. Washington, DC: Police Executive Research Forum.

Normann, R. 1991. *Service Management: Strategy and Leadership in Service Business*. New York: Wiley.

Osborne, S. 2006. 'The New Public Governance?' *Public Management Review* 8(3): 377–88.

2009. 'Delivering public services: Are we asking the right questions?' *Public Money and Management* 29(1): 5–7.

2010. *The New Public Governance?* London: Routledge.

Osborne, S. and Brown, L. 2011. 'Innovation, public policy and public services: The word that would be king?' *Public Administration* 89(4): 1335–50.

Osborne, S., Radnor, Z. and Nasi, G. 2013. 'A new theory for public services management? Towards a (public) service-dominant approach', *American Review of Public Administration* 43(2): 135–58.

Osborne, S., Radnor, Z., Vidal, I. and Kinder, T. 2015. 'A sustainable business model for public services: the SERVICE framework', *British Journal of Management* http://onlinelibrary.wiley.com/doi/10.1111/1467–8551.12094/ abstract.

Osborne, S. and Strokosch, K. 2013. 'It takes two to tango? Understanding the co-production of public services by integrating the services management and public administration perspectives', *British Journal of Management* 24(S1): S31–47.

Ostrom, E. 1972. 'Metropolitan reform: Propositions derived from two traditions', *Social Science Quarterly* 53(3): 474–93.

Parks, R. B., Baker, P. C., Kiser, L., Oakerson, R., Ostrom, E., Ostrom, V. and Wilson, R. 1981. 'Consumers as co-producers of public services: Some economic and institutional considerations', *Policy Studies Journal* 9(7): 1001–11.

Pestoff, V. 2006. 'Citizens and co-production of welfare services: Childcare in eight European countries', *Public Management Review* 8(4): 503–19.

Pestoff, V. and Brandsen, T. 2009. 'The governance of co-production', Paper presented at the 13th Annual Conference of the International Research Society for Public Management, Copenhagen.

Pestoff, V., Osborne, S. P. and Brandsen, T. 2006. 'Patterns of co-production in public services', *Public Management Review* 8(4): 591–5.

Pestoff, V., Brandsen, T. and Verschuere, B. (eds.) 2012. *New Public Governance, the Third Sector and Co-Production*. London: Routledge.

Porter, M. 1985. *Competitive Advantage*. New York: Free Press.

Powell, M., Greener, I., Szmigin, I., Doheny, S. and Mills, N. 2010. 'Broadening the focus of public service consumerism', *Public Management Review* 12(3): 323–40.

Prahalad, C. and Ramaswamy, V. 2004. *The Future of Competition: Co-Creating Unique Value with Customers*. Boston: Harvard Business School Press.

Radnor, Z. and Osborne, S. 2013. 'Lean: A failed theory for public services?' *Public Management Review* 15(2): 265–87.

Radnor, Z., Osborne, S., Kinder, T. and Mutton, J. 2013. 'Operationalizing co-production in public services delivery: The contribution of service blueprinting', *Public Management Review* 16(3): 402–23.

Renn, O. 2008. *Risk Governance: Coping with Uncertainty in a Complex World*. London: Earthscan.

Rhodes, R. 1997. *Understanding Governance*. Buckingham: Open University Press.

Salamon, L. 2002. *The Tools of Government: A Guide to the New Governance*. New York: Oxford University Press.

Svara, J. 2008. 'Beyond dichotomy: Dwight Waldo and the intertwined politics–administration relationship', *Public Administration Review* 68(1): 46–52.

Thomas, J. C. 2012. *Citizen, Customer, Partner: Engaging the Public in Public Management*. New York: M. E. Sharpe.

Von Hippel, E. 1994. 'Sticky information and the locus of problem solving: Implications for innovation', *Management Science* 40(4): 429–39.

Von Hippel, E. 2005. *Democratizing Innovation*. Cambridge, MA: MIT Press.

4   Public Innovations around the World

Jacob Torfing and Peter Triantafillou

4.1   Introduction

This chapter aims to challenge the common understanding that innovation is something for the private sector only, is driven by competitive pressures and merely involves the invention, application and spread of new technology, marketing practices or product designs. This is done by demonstrating the importance, the multiple sources and the rich variety of public innovation in different parts of the world. If we compare the public sector of today with the public sector from the 1950s and 1960s, we clearly see that there have been numerous innovations in core policy fields such as health care, education, social policy and economic policy. Hence, public innovation is not a new phenomenon, despite the unfortunate neglect among practitioners who have talked about 'change', 'reform' and 'improvement' rather than 'innovation' and among academics who have failed to dissociate private and public innovation. Nevertheless, in the last decades there has been a growing focus on public innovation. The recent discovery of the distinctive character and particular conditions of public innovation has fostered a growing demand for innovation in public policy, public organizations and public service delivery among politicians who are facing dire fiscal constraints, policy experts who seek to solve intractable problems and citizens who have growing expectations for the quality and availability of public service. The attempt to spur public innovation has led to a strategic reorientation of the public sector, and the result is the proliferation of disruptive changes that aim to provide new and better public solutions.

The purpose of this chapter is, on the one hand, to illustrate the diversity of public innovations by highlighting different examples of public innovation. On the other hand, we want to explore the sources of public innovation and the role of leadership and management in supporting and driving innovation processes. It should be stressed that our aim is to provide a descriptive and exploratory rather than an explanatory account of empirical examples of public innovation. As such, our principal goal is to provide a

The corresponding author for this chapter is Jacob Torfing.

better understanding of what public innovation looks like and how it is brought about.

Accordingly, the chapter presents and compares seven examples of public innovation drawn from Africa, the Antipodes, Britain, continental Europe, Latin America and North America. In line with our dual objective, the empirical cases were selected to ensure diversity and allow us to understand the process of innovation and the role of leadership and management herein. We have pursued diversity in terms of geopolitical areas (including both developed countries in the North and developing countries in the South), policy areas (education, employment, housing, social care, waste management and crime prevention) and target groups (youth, families and older generations). While these cases do not pretend to constitute a representative sample of public innovations, they attest to the diversity of the forms of and conditions for innovation in the public sector. In order to allow us to examine the innovation processes and the role of leadership and management, we have picked cases in which we could find adequate data material. Our objective is not to demonstrate the uniformity of public innovation processes and the exercise of innovation management, but rather to reveal different sources of public innovation and show that no matter how public innovation is brought about, some kind of leadership and management is needed to initiate and drive the innovation process to fruition.

In the following sections, we first account for the descriptive variables used to analyse the seven cases. We then describe each of the seven cases. This is followed by an analysis of their differences and similarities in terms of the descriptive variables. Finally, we conclude by pointing out some of the core features of public innovations from around the world.

4.2   Descriptive Variables used to Examine the Cases

This chapter compares and analyses different cases of public innovation with regard to six basic parameters: the societal problem addressed, the solution provided, the initiation of and process through which innovation is fostered, the partners that were involved in the process, the role of leadership and management in supporting and facilitating the process, and the results of the innovation project.

First, to qualify as a case of public innovation, an innovation must produce public value by addressing a relevant societal problem or challenge. Wicked problems that are characterized by a high level of complexity (Head and Alford 2015) tend to defy standard solutions and thus call for creative problem-solving that aims to design and implement an innovative solution that breaks the trade-offs initially perceived by the relevant and affected actors. Accordingly, we briefly examine the nature and complexity of the societal problem or challenge addressed by the project that we are analysing.

Second, in order to understand how the project dealt with the particular problem or challenge at hand, we account for the content and character of the innovative solution. Innovations are step-changes in public policy, public organizations or public service provision that can be more or less incremental or radical depending on the size of the steps taken. We assess the innovativeness of the solution and examine whether it constitutes an invention created by first movers or rather an imitation of innovative solutions from elsewhere that have been adopted and adapted by second movers.

Third, as argued by leading scholars in the field of policy analysis and innovation theory (Kingdon 1995; Van der Ven et al. 2008), innovation processes are not linear processes, following neatly from a rational analysis of the problem or challenge at hand, but are complex, iterative and highly contingent processes. Nevertheless, we examine the constitutive phases of the innovation processes focusing on the initiation, design and implementation of new and creative solutions. Special attention is paid to whether political and social pressures and/or the availability of new technologies are driving the innovation process.

Fourth, since a key analytical focus of this book is on the impact of multi-actor collaboration on the production of public innovation, we account for the actors involved in the development and realization of the innovative solution. Hence, we assess the number actors (one or more) and their nature (public or private). We also describe their interaction and assess its more or less collaborative character (and if relevant account for other modes of interaction based on competition or the exercise of authority).

Fifth, based on the assumption that leadership and management play a crucial role in stimulating collaboration and enhancing innovation, we examine how the projects were led and managed. We account for the managerial strategies and instruments that are deployed as well as for the overall organization and design of the leadership and management function. With regard to the instruments, we distinguish between regulatory tools (laws, regulations, guidelines), financial incentives (economic subsidies, grants, bonuses) and administrative support (secretarial assistance, office space, technical advice). With regard to the organization and design of the system of network management, we draw on Provan and Kenis' well-known distinction between participant, lead organization and network administrative organization (Provan and Kenis 2008).

Finally, we want to emphasize that the relevance of public innovation hinges not only on finding new ways of addressing an urgent societal problem but also on its ability to produce actual results that politicians and the wider public find desirable and satisfying. Hence, we shall briefly account for the impact and results of innovative solutions. Here, we examine whether the results mainly pertain to process (a new way of producing and delivering services) or to product (a new kind of service), and whether they appear politically and financially sustainable.

4.3   Promoting Health Literacy in South Africa

Like in many other developing countries with low levels of literacy among substantial parts of the population, dissemination of health information is a major challenge in South Africa. Being unable to read in many cases constitutes a serious challenge to address and mitigate diseases and improve hygiene. People are dying not because of lack of medical staff or medicine, but because they cannot read and therefore have trouble learning how to prevent diseases and take care of and improve their health. Since the struggle against illiteracy will not be won any time soon, an innovative solution is needed.

The Speaking Book provides an innovative solution to the problem. The concept is fairly simple: the book has an electronic device powered by a small long-life battery that allows it to speak to the reader. In contrast to other awareness texts, a button – annotated on the page with a corresponding image – plays a soundtrack of the text when it is pressed. Therefore, no matter the reader's reading proficiency, the information contained within the book can be read, heard or both. In a 16-page, brightly coloured and simply worded format, each book deals with a particular health issue (Goldberg 2011). Topics range over a number of public and personal health concerns, including malaria, HIV and AIDS, hypertension and tuberculosis, as well as more socially focused aspects like how to apply for social benefits.

In 2004, a story appeared in the *Wall Street Journal* (*WSJ*) about a talking book being used for healthcare education in Afghanistan (SADAG 2014a). However, the price tag of $62.50 per book put it well out of reach of African and other developing countries. At the time, the South African Depression and Anxiety Group (SADAG) was working on a World Bank-financed rural project to combat teen suicide in South Africa, and it was facing problems with distributing health information to low-literacy communities. SADAG's founder, Zane Wilson, was inspired by the *WSJ* article to create an African solution for an African problem of low literacy that limited the effectiveness of all healthcare information. She found it necessary to produce a more affordable means of health dissemination and set out to create the Speaking Book. In 2005, the first two Speaking Books were launched at the Global Health Conference in Washington, DC. Since then SADAG has worked with both public and private health care institutions to provide health education to some of the poorest communities in the world. So far, hundreds of thousands of books have been produced and over 50 titles in 29 languages have been distributed in 30 countries.

Through its outreach work on education and empowerment in South African local communities, SADAG is collaborating with the South African Ministry of Health, local health institutions, lay counsellors, caregivers, teachers, churches, mothers and teenagers to design and disseminate Speaking Books that improve hygiene and combat diseases (SADAG 2014b). Since 2007, it has worked with Acumen Fund, a non-profit global venture fund (linked to the Rockefeller Foundation), which has provided financial support for the Speaking Books project. Moreover, the Brand Bridge Group, a branding and marketing consultancy firm, has helped Speaking Books redesign its brand and launch a new marketing platform. Finally, SADAG cooperates with a number of biomedical companies, health organizations and aid/charity organizations outside South Africa to promote the distribution of its books and adapt these to local needs. While some of these actors are for-profit market actors, they have become part of a strategic alliance based on collaboration.

Speaking Books have been adopted throughout large tracts of South Africa. They are also used in 30 other developing countries to create awareness of health and to enable citizens to take better care of themselves. So far, only relatively few studies have systematically assessed the effectiveness of the books to disseminate knowledge and spur health-improving conduct. Yet these studies do suggest a very positive impact. Both a pilot study in South Africa (Dhai, Etheredge and Cleaton-Jones 2010) and a more recent and through study in rural Uganda (Castelnuovo 2014) showed significant improvement in the target group's understanding of the health issues as compared to control groups (see also Engida and Simireta 2013).

4.4   Securing Housing and Employment for Young People in Australia

One in every 800 young persons – defined as a person in the age from 12 to 24 years – in Australia is homeless, and this rate is rising rapidly (Australia Bureau of Statistics 2012). Many of homeless youngsters are out of a job and do not have other forms of regular income (Considine and Hart 2008). Moreover, the lack of a permanent address makes it difficult for public agencies (and voluntary organizations) to assist these young people in finding a home and a job or other sources of income. Significantly, it is estimated that less than half of Australia's young homeless people are using homeless services.

The Young Homeless Jobseeker trial partnership known as YP4[1] is a three-year integrated service trial offered by a coalition of voluntary welfare organizations with a view to improve the actual availability of services to young homeless people and, ultimately, to reduce public costs in this area (Considine and Hart 2008: 162–3). With their close knowledge about and contact with local citizens, including the homeless, it was found that the voluntary organizations had a clear advantage over the traditional public services in addressing the complex issue of homelessness.

In two local communities and two metropolitan areas, YP4 worked to integrate the job services offered by three different government programmes and the housing services offered by three other government programmes. As many young homeless people were either unable or unwilling to navigate in this complex and compartmentalized service provision set-up, YP4 started with the needs of the individual homeless person with a view to provide an integrated case-management procedure that renders the relevant services more readily available to the homeless. This entailed having a flexible pool of money from the various programmes available to address the needs of the individual homeless person. In return for this 'free' sum of money, YP4 must account for its actions along a number of financial, process and outcome indicators. One of the challenges of the project is that it has to abide by three different sets of accountability systems in order to satisfy the three main government agencies supporting the programme (ibid.: 168). As the project's organizational innovation hinged on the formation of a new type of partnership in order to provide a more integrated and holistic service than the existing ones, it has proven difficult to satisfy all three accountability systems.

The idea for the YP4 project gradually evolved outside government and public service agencies. A group of voluntary welfare organizations formed a project on employment and homelessness in the mid-1990s (Considine and Hart 2008: 164–6). One of the experiences of this project was that the housing services offered to homeless people often neglected to integrate employment assistance. As lack of stable income is one of the key reasons for homelessness, the voluntary organizations found it obvious to try to work to better integrate these two types of services in homelessness interventions. After several discussions, project proposals

---

[1] The name 'YP4' refers to young people and the four key aspects of the trial: purpose (employment), place (accommodation), personal support and proof (research).

and dialogue – both internally between the voluntary organizations and externally with government agencies responsible for housing and employment policy – a project was approved for support in 2005.

The day-to-day operation of YP4 is conducted by an executive committee composed of the CEOs of the four voluntary welfare organizations. Thus, the government agencies are not immediately involved in the daily operation of the services offered under YP4 (ibid.: 166). Yet, public agencies play a crucial role in the project. Apart from funding YP4, the relevant housing and employment government agencies – from both state and federal level – are part of an Interagency Coordination Committee that monitors and guides the project. This includes a sub-committee in charge of systematic evaluation and tackling ethical questions. Moreover, in order to ensure the everyday functioning and delivery of services, the network of the four voluntary organizations had to further develop their collaboration with the relevant housing and employment public services. This entailed sharing data on services and individual clients, agreeing on the use of physical facilities and coming to terms with the timing and specific mix of services offered to the individual clients (Considine and Hart 2008: 170–1). In some instances, agreements were either difficult to reach or not reached at all, resulting in business-as-usual service delivery. Arriving at mutual agreements on service delivery in a fragmented organizational field has required sustained collaboration and a certain level of trust. The latter was challenged on several occasions and in particular in relation to the job component where the voluntary organizations were competing with each other for employment service contracts.

A systematic study of 222 young homeless people participating in YP4 over a two-year period showed improvements both in terms of reducing homelessness and the chance of getting a job (Grace and Gill 2014). However, a control group of 174 persons, who received standard services only, showed almost similar levels of improvement. The obvious explanation of the slight difference between the impacts of YP4 compared to the impacts of the standard services is that the former is simply not any better than the latter. It has been suggested that while the integrated case-management approach does provide an innovative service, it is simply too limited in its scope and in terms of resources allocated to implement it (Borland, Tseng and Wilkins 2013). Another possible explanation is that the high-level publicity around YP4 may have encouraged the standard service providers to improve their services. At least that would explain why outcomes improved in the control group as well. At any rate, YP4 may prove useful in the sense that the data generated by the project provides a baseline for future studies of the effects of homelessness interventions. Moreover, the project has also provided some valuable insights into the dynamics and difficulties in making voluntary and public sector organizations collaborate in an environment otherwise characterized by fragmentation and competition.

4.5   Open University in Britain

The Open University (OU) was established as a distance-learning institution in 1969 to meet a rising demand for university teaching in Britain. Rather than establishing a range of new universities all over the country including thinly populated rural areas, which would have been very costly, the OU was intended as a cost-effective institution that would make education come to the students rather than the other way around (Open University 2014a). While long-distance learning and open access to higher learning has existed in Britain since the mid-nineteenth century (Bell and Tight 1993), the advent of the OU clearly represents a significant technological and administrative innovation in British higher learning that today serves a broad range of students.

The key solution to meet the rapidly rising demand for academic education in a cost-effective manner was distance learning. The OU uses a variety of methods for distance learning, including written and audio materials, online lectures, disc-based software and television programmes on DVD. For most modules, students are supported by tutors who provide feedback on their work and are generally available to them at face-to-face tutorials, by telephone and via the Internet. Some modules have mandatory day schools. These are day-long sessions which a student must attend in order to pass the module. Similarly, many modules have traditionally offered week-long summer schools offering an opportunity for students to remove themselves from the general distractions of their life and focus on their study for a short time. The OU, which not only caters to learning but also research, is funded by a combination of student fees, contract income and allocations for teaching and research by the higher education funding bodies throughout the United Kingdom. It is notable for having an open-entry policy, i.e. students' previous academic achievements are not taken into account for entry to most undergraduate courses. The majority of its undergraduate students are based in the United Kingdom, but during the 1990s the OU undertook several initiatives to expand its international cooperation with universities in other countries and to attract foreign students (OU 2014b). Accordingly, today many of the OU's courses can be studied almost anywhere in the world.

Planning of the OU commenced in 1965 with the aim of widening access to higher education and involved setting up a planning committee consisting of university vice-chancellors, educationalists and the BBC. The collaboration with the BBC has since been sustained and developed. Even if radio and television broadcasting ceased as a mode of distance learning in 2006, the collaboration with BBC has continued in new ways in the shape of educational and documentary programmes produced jointly by the OU and the BBC (OU 2014c). Over the years, the OU has developed an extensive collaborative network not only with other academic institutions all over the world but also with British employers in order to ensure societal relevance of their studies. Staff members from private and public employers are teaching on a large number of OU courses. Employers are also participating in the design of several teaching programmes and societal relevance is ensured through accreditation schemes in which employers are also participating (ibid.). The network of collaborators around the OU helps to ensure its ability to compete with traditional universities in the expanding market of higher learning.

The structure of the OU is fairly traditional in that it holds a Council, a Senate and a General Assembly. The University's main governing body is the Council, supported by a number of sub-committees. The Council has a membership of 25 and includes representatives of academic and research staff, associate lecturer and non-academic staff, students and a number of external members that are appointed for their experience and expertise. It is significant that the external members hold the majority of Council places with a view to ensure the quality and societal relevance of OU learning and research. The Senate is the academic authority of the University, responsible for promoting the academic work of the University, both in teaching and research. It oversees academic management, including curriculum and all aspects of quality and standards associated with the University as a degree-awarding body. Finally, the General Assembly consists of elected representatives of the nations/ regions together with representatives appointed by the Senate. It may express an opinion to the Senate on any matter affecting the work and interests of the University, but it meets rarely, and only if convened by the Central Consultative Committee in consultation with the Vice-Chancellor.

With more than 250,000 students enrolled, including around 32,000 aged under 25 and more than 50,000 overseas students, it is the largest academic institution in the United Kingdom (and one of the largest in Europe) by number of students (Open University 2014d). Since it was founded, more than 1.5 million students have been enrolled. It was rated the top university in England and Wales for student satisfaction in the 2005, 2006 and 2012 national student satisfaction surveys, and it came second in the 2007 survey.

4.6   Cycling without Age in Denmark

Whereas in some countries it is customary to expect children to take care of their parents when they grow old and frail and can no longer take care of themselves, other countries rely on elderly people being placed in public or private elderly care facilities. In Denmark, local governments aim to help elderly people to stay as long as possible in the own home and their own life, and they provide training, technical solutions and free home care to make it possible. When elderly people can no longer stay in their own home, they are offered a place in an elderly care home with around-the-clock care. Here they have their own room, and if their health permits it, they participate in activities with other residents during the day. However, the combination of limited physical capacity of the elderly and the limited time and resources on the part of the professional staff means that the elderly do not come out of the care facility a lot. Their mobility is limited to walking around inside the care facility and perhaps using a walking frame to walk a few hundred metres down the road. The lack of mobility, wind in their hair and the separation from the local community where they used to live seriously reduce their quality of life, and the question has been how to enhance the mobility of elderly people and make them more outgoing?

An innovative project called 'Cycling without Age' provides a creative solution to the problem. The project draws on the Danish tradition for using bicycles as a common means of transportation and rides on a strong wave of voluntarism that is stimulated by a growing longing for community and purpose. The project is fairly simple. The municipality has purchased a fleet of rickshaws, and there is a network of volunteers who act as pilots and cycle elderly people around in their old neighbourhood in return for hearing their life story. The pilots typically do two to three cycle trips per week, but the number varies due to weather conditions and the time they have at their disposal. The rickshaw pilots run their own network, and locally appointed captains train new pilots who can also get instructions about how to drive the rickshaw on the networks webpage. In November 2014, there were about 150 volunteers in the 'Cycling without Age' network in Copenhagen that services 42 elderly care homes. Besides cycling one or two elderly people around in their old neighbourhood on a regular basis, the network also organizes large 'Cycling without Age' events in which rickshaw pilots drive a large group of elderly people through the city and are accompanied by friends, family, other cyclists and elderly people who are still capable of cycling. These small cycle demonstrations serve to show that people of all ages can benefit from cycling, and they typically end with coffee, cake and a small meal provided by restaurant chefs on a voluntary basis.

'Cycling without Age' began when a social entrepreneur named Ole Kassow showed up at the local elderly care home with a rented rickshaw and asked the social care assistant who greeted him whether there were any of the elderly who wanted to come for a ride. Contemplating the risks involved in letting a complete stranger driver away with an elderly resident, the social care assistant suggested that she would join Gertrud, at 86 years of age, for a ride. Over the following weeks, several other elderly residents went out on a rickshaw trip.

Today, the municipality of Copenhagen works closely together with the voluntary network of rickshaw pilots. The local government has now purchased 42 rickshaws. It also finances the efforts of social entrepreneurs to expand the project and spread it to other cities. The municipality is also represented on the board that has the overall responsibility for the local chapter of 'Cycling without Age'. A municipal innovation consultant shares management responsibilities with the project initiator. The project is truly collaborative and also involves local staff members at the elderly care homes as well as sponsors who support the special cycling events.

The 'Cycling without Age' project went on a campaign tour on rickshaws and bicycles from Odense to Hamburg to start 'Cycling without Age' projects in the cities they passed through. Together with massive and very positive media coverage, the trip has inspired more than 30 Danish cities to establish local 'Cycling without Age' projects. People from the original project in Copenhagen offer their help to start-ups, and on the project's website there are easy-to-follow instructions about how to form a local chapter of 'Cycling without Age'. After a recent TED Talk[2] about the project, chapters of 'Cycling without Age' have been established in 18 cities in ten different countries. Hence, the national and global diffusion of the innovation project is substantial.

As for the impact on the participating actors, the elderly people seem to benefit a lot from enhancing their mobility, getting fresh air and expanding their social contacts. Their quality of life is augmented as they get out more and can maintain a connection to their old neighbourhood. There are also unofficial reports that elderly people with dementia benefit from going back and seeing familiar streets and places. The rickshaw pilots not only get a lot of good physical exercise through a very meaningful communal activity but also engage in an inter-generational exchange that brings forth life stories that are easily overlooked and lost, and thus helps to give our busy city life a historical anchorage. The staff of the

---

[2] TED (Technology, Entertainment, Design) is a global set of conferences run by the Sapling Foundation, under the slogan 'Ideas Worth Spreading'.

elderly care homes benefit from the resources provided by the volunteers and from the elderly being more happy and cheerful when they return from a cycle trip and have interesting experiences to share with the other residents. Finally, it should be mentioned that the demand for rickshaws in Denmark has gone up, and new manufacturing companies have been established.

4.7   Neighbourhood Football Project to Reduce Youth Crime in the Netherlands

In 's-Hertogenbosch, a Dutch city with around 140,000 inhabitants, there are about 25 groups of young people that for some time have caused trouble and public annoyance and committed different criminal acts (Municipality of 's-Hertogenbosch 2011). Together these groups are responsible for a substantial share of common crime and even more serious misdemeanors, such as burglary, violence and drug dealing. Generally, the parents of these young people in 's-Hertogenbosch have relatively limited resources and many social and economic problems and therefore have not been very good at guiding the conduct of their children in societally desirable directions.

The football project *Wijksportproject Doelbewust* (literally: neighbourhood sports project goal directed) essentially involves the enrolment of at-risk youth with or without a criminal record in specially created soccer teams that in terms of culture, organization and management mirror professional football teams. The teenagers who become part of the new soccer teams become members of Den Bosch Football Club, a high-profile local football club, through a process that involves negotiating and signing contracts and enlisting sponsors. When the contract is signed, they participate in regular training sessions and play matches against other teams. While the teenagers do not have to have great football talents to get a contract, they must adhere to strict discipline, a code of mutual respect and agreed-upon rules. The rules apply not only to the activities in the football club but also to the teenagers' behaviour in school, to their spare time and their home life. The teenagers are not only supposed to behave as a professional football player but are also expected to play an active role as assistant trainers and referees and in enlisting sponsors and organizing soccer trips. Finally, they must participate in monthly thematic seminars on issues like health, drugs, sex, bullying and community politics.

The project was initiated in 2006 by the municipality of 's-Hertogenbosch with assistance from the voluntary welfare organization Divers in order to reduce youth crime and promote positive, social behaviour among teenagers. The project targets teenagers with a high-risk profile, such as school absenteeism and incidents of anti-social or criminal behaviour. In practice, this includes a relatively large number of first- and second-generation immigrant teenagers. By making the teenagers engage in a collective and physical activity, the project aims to advance and stimulate individual talent and instill a sense of social skills and team spirit in the teenagers. By 2010, seven teams with a total of 90 teenagers were established.

A number of diverse partners are involved in the project. The municipality of 's-Hertogenbosch initiates the project, contributes the bulk of its financing, appoints sports workers and is overall responsible for project implementation. The welfare organization Divers provides trained youth workers, maintains contact with and coordination between parents, police, schools, sports clubs and sponsors, and assists the teenagers in contract negotiations. The parents are involved in contract negotiations and home visits. The local police and probation officers organize thematic meetings and deliberate with community workers about specific teenagers, their problems and how to address them. The schools meet with community sports workers and the club about how the individual teenagers behave during and after school. Den Bosch FC supports the project and provides training. Two other organizations play a more distant though not unimportant role. First, the Dutch Institute for Sport and Exercise (NISB) served to inspire the project by way of its general 'communities on the move' approach that seeks to promote citizens' participation and social network creation by means of a variety of sports and physical exercise projects (Vroom 2006). Second, the W. J. H. Mullier Institute for social science has evaluated the project (Cevaal et al. 2010).

Overall project management is conducted jointly by the municipality and the voluntary organization Divers. They are responsible for project design, results and eventual modifications. However, the everyday coordination and execution of activities is mainly carried out by Divers and the organizations listed above. They are also the ones tackling everyday conflicts in the projects, in particular with enlisted teenagers not adhering to the rules or participating actively in the project.

The overall results of the project are very promising. Four years after project initiation, a project evaluation showed that the teenagers enlisted in the project had changed their conduct significantly. Their participation in anti-social and criminal acts had decreased significantly, their results in school had improved, their relations with other teenagers, fellow citizens and organizations had improved and so far no teenagers had been evicted from the project for breaching the rather strict behavioural rules. Police statistics corroborated that in 2010 less than 4 per cent of the youngsters in the project had contact with the police in relation to violence or crime as compared to 15 per cent of a comparable target group. However, an intermediary evaluation also showed that not all teenagers did equally well in the project. Some teenagers had left the project and the number of teams had been slightly reduced to cater for those teenagers actually willing to change their behaviour. Thus, an important learning from the project is that not all teenagers can be reached and that results take time. Notwithstanding these caveats, the project is very promising and was nominated for the European Crime Award in 2011 (European Crime Prevention Network 2011).

4.8   Electricity Supply and Waste Management in Brazil

The inhabitants of Santa Marta, a government-controlled favela (illegal urban habitation of mainly poor dwellers) in Rio de Janeiro, are facing the double problem of being unable to pay for electricity and lacking a system for collection and disposal of waste (Cipolla, Melo and Manzini 2013). Access to affordable electricity is a major problem in many low-income urban areas in Brazil. At the same time, electricity companies are reluctant to provide electricity because of low rates of profitability caused by a combination of low incomes and frequent incidents of electricity theft. Lack of garbage collection is a huge hygiene problem in many favelas and is difficult to solve not only because the inhabitants have few resources to pay for waste collection but also because many favelas are dangerous areas controlled by competing drug gangs that public and private refuse workers do not dare to enter.

The innovative solution, which seems to kill two problems with one stone, is to let the inhabitants pay for their electricity consumption by collecting garbage. At the collection point, the garbage is weighed and the discount determined by the amount of garbage that has been collected is recorded in the system and appears on the next electricity bill (Cipolla, Melo and Manzini 2013). It has been noted that some local citizens consider the fee for waste collection too low to generate a significant economic incentive. However, many of these citizens still participate because they think that the hygiene and environmental effects of garbage collection are considerable. As part of the project, the electricity company has installed a shielded network and telemetry that allows greater control over default and electricity theft. With this new model, if the consumer does not pay the bill, the power supply can be cut without sending a team to the site. These measures allow the company to operate with sustainable revenues.

Following a process of pacification whereby the police took control of the favela of Santa Marta, the Electricity Company of Rio de Janeiro launched the 'Light Recicla' project in 2011 with a view to reduce the electricity bill of the residents by exchanging garbage containing recyclable materials for energy credits. Inspired by previous experiments in the State of Ceará, the Light Recicla entails that electricity consumers collect garbage, wash it, separate it and bring it to the collection point to get it weighed.

In order to ensure proper implementation, Light Recicla has engaged in a partnership with other private companies: 3E Engenharia provides the Information and Communication Technology (ICT) system that records the credits and manages the infrastructure of the collection points; Doe Seu Lixo receives the garbage from customers and sends it for recycling and manages a permanent staff of waste transporters; the Coopama is responsible for the collection and recycling of cooking oil (Cipolla, Melo and Manzini 2013). These companies are all technically and economically involved in the project. Finally, the Government of Rio de Janeiro is granting the space and legal conditions for the project to function, but it does not provide financial subsidies as the project is supposed to be economically self-reliant.

The project does not have a formal management structure as leadership is distributed among companies in the partnership that also have a continued dialogue with local residents. There is no need for cooperation with public actors. Once the government and the police secured the safety of Santa Marta, the Light Recicla has mainly been driven on market conditions, although the involved companies collaborate rather than compete with each other. Market conditions are created by establishing a commercial relationship between the citizens of Santa Marta and the private companies according to which the citizens pay for what they get and have an economic incentive to collect garbage that is turned into profit by the private companies.

The project is still in a rather early phase, and it is therefore difficult to account for its results. However, in April 2013, less than three years after its inception, around 10,000 inhabitants were registered with the Light Recicla, and some 60 per cent of these were actively using it in the sense that they collected waste and used the income from this to access the electricity supply system (Light 2014). Prior to 2011, around 80 of the approximately 1,600 homes were officially connected to the network and received energy bills before pacification, but only 24 were actually paying them. By June 2013, with all the households officially connected to the power grid, overall bill payment is much higher (Cipolla, Melo and Manzini 2013). Accordingly, Light Recicla is planning to expand the electricity grid in Santa Marta because it believes that it may become a profitable business. Yet, the project has not been without problems.

Many inhabitants are not used to paying for electricity and remain wary of doing so. Also, some inhabitants have not been very committed to collecting, separating and cleaning renewable waste. This has, however, partly been compensated for by other citizens who have made it their business to purchase waste from non-participating citizens for a small sum, sort and clean it, and then sell it to Light Recicla.

4.9   Drug Courts in the United States

During the 1980s and 1990s, local courts in the United States experienced a dramatic increase in drug-related cases. New and tougher laws on drug trade and drug abuse made prison populations rise, and the costs of this went through the roof. Sending the drug abusers to jail did not seem to solve the drug problem, as the rate of recidivism was high. Accordingly, there was an urgent need to tackle a substantial societal problem with many negative effects in terms of deteriorating health conditions, an endless stream of robberies and violent assaults, and economic costs to the public coffers.

The innovative solution to the problem was the creation of a special kind of drug court. A drug court is essentially a court that seeks to reduce substance abuse and recidivism by early, continuous and intense judicial supervision, rehabilitation and sanction mechanisms (Hale 2011: 32). An interdisciplinary team of legal, law enforcement and health professionals works together to provide better treatment and to focus on health promotion, disease prevention and behavioural correction, rather than punishment (Nolan 2001). A key innovation of the drug court approach is that the judge now acts as a sort of hub for the ongoing interaction between the drug offender and the various authorities and voluntary organizations providing health and correctional assistance (Hale 2011: 113).

The first drug courts were introduced in 1989 as a handful of local programs established by local judges in response to the strain of drug-related caseloads in the criminal justice system (Hale 2011: 34). With federal financial support from the US Department of Justice, drug courts have gradually spread to all 50 states in the USA. The information produced, disseminated and shared by around 20 private non-profit organizations interested in various aspects of justice and drug policies was instrumental to the spread and development of drug courts throughout the USA (Hale 2011: 2–3). While these voluntary organizations had very different missions and ideologies on the topic of drug policies, the information network they created served to provide new ideas about how to deal with drug offenders. Some of these ideas were grabbed by local authorities and courts that saw a clear need for reforming existing drug policy approaches in the light of the increasing costs and the high rate of recidivism.

The development and spread of the drug courts involved a number of private and public actors that gradually came to an overall agreement on how to deal with drug offenders in other ways than through a purely punitive approach. Criminal courts both at local and state levels, the US Department of Justice, police at local and state levels, state administrators, and voluntary justice policy organizations shared information, discussed new justice and rehabilitation approaches, shared experiences and delegated funding (mainly from federal to state levels) that would gradually lead to the development of drug courts. Such information exchange took place through cross-organizational criminal justice boards, professional associations and numerous ad hoc statewide collaborative projects and working groups (Hale 2011: 72–83). The National Association of Drug Court Professionals proved particularly important for developing a set of best practice principles in 1997 that were flexible enough to allow for local adaptation. Local judges, prosecutors and defendants would interpret these to fit local circumstances and needs on the one hand but also ensure a less adversarial and more rehabilitation-oriented approach on the other (Hale 2011: 109–11).

The network of actors around the drug courts and their concrete actions are not governed by any central authority. As described above, it is a vast network cutting across several jurisdictions – both vertically and horizontally – and involving a large number of both public and private actors, often with diverse and conflicting interests. What unites this network is a more or less shared vision that incarceration of drug offenders in itself is insufficient, ineffective and too expensive. Therefore, incarceration needs to be supplemented with other approaches. Moreover, the gradual development of a set of voluntary and locally adaptable guidelines, the ongoing dialogue and experience sharing, combined with a certain element of federal support, have served to convince this diverse set of actors that drug courts are a viable contribution to solving drug-related problems.

Due to the substantial diversity of local drug court approaches and practices, it is notoriously difficult to make any general assessment of their results. Notwithstanding this qualification, a number of studies indicate that the drug courts significantly reduce recidivism among drug offenders as compared to similar groups going through the normal judicial process (e.g. Spohn et al. 2001; Gottfredson, Najaka and Kearley 2006; King and Pasquarella 2009). However, these studies also show that the (direct) financial costs of treating a drug offender through the drug courts are at least as high as those incurred by the normal judicial system. Moreover, research suggests that different groups of drug offenders fare differently within the drug court programmes and therefore may warrant differentiated approaches (Hale 2011: 84).

4.10   Cross-Case Analysis

In this section, we compare and analyse the cases of public innovation according to the six descriptive variables identified earlier in the chapter. The seven cases of public innovation mapped above display substantial diversity with regard to the solution, process initiation and management. Yet they also display some interesting similarities with regard to the nature of the social problem addressed, the collaborating actors and the results. In Table 4.1 below, we have summarized the main characteristics of the seven cases.

All the societal problems addressed in the examined innovation cases are fairly complex in the sense that they are tangled, difficult to define and have competing and changing goals. Moreover, they tend to cut across different sectors' boundaries and to be more or less politically disputed. In three cases, the problems appear to be urgent because they involve criminalized phenomena, namely theft, squatting and drug abuse. The other problems are deep-seated and long lasting but nevertheless call for innovative solutions. This finding is in line with the literature that suggests complex societal problems require innovative solutions fostered in and through collaborative forms of governance that bring together relevant and affected actors from the public and private sectors (Koppenjan and Klijn 2004; Head and Alford 2015).

The analysis of the character of the innovative solutions also reveals important similarities. Hence, active citizens in terms of users or volunteers play a key role in the design and realization of all the innovative solutions, which also tend to combine service innovation with some kind of organizational innovation that transforms the way that services are provided. However, the solutions vary in terms of how innovative they are. While all the solutions produce step-changes, the steps are of different size. Hence, the Australian social housing and employment and the British Open University are somewhat less radical than the other solutions. The innovation cases also differ in terms of how much they are diffused across jurisdictions. In particular, three cases have spread significantly: South African health literacy, Danish Cycling without Age and US drug courts. Whereas the market was an important driver of dissemination in the first case, networking has been the core driver of innovation diffusion in the last two cases.

Table 4.1 *Overview of case characteristics*

Characteristics	Cases
Societal problem or challenge	*Complex problems cutting across two or more policy sectors*: All cases *Problems involving some kind of illegality that gives them a sense of urgency*: Dutch football project; Brazilian electricity for waste collection; US drug courts *Problems that are deep-seated and long lasting*: South African health literacy; Australian social housing and employment; British Open University; Danish Cycling without Age
Solution	*Extensive involvement of users and volunteers in service innovation*: All cases *Combination of service innovation and organizational innovation*: All cases *Radical innovation*: All cases, except Australian social housing and employment and British Open University *Innovation diffusion*: South African health literacy; Danish Cycling without Age; US Drug Courts
Initiation and process	*Initiated by private actors*: South African health literacy; Australian social housing and employment; Danish Cycling without Age; Brazilian electricity for waste collection *Initiated by public actors*: British Open University; Dutch football project; US drug courts *Political and/or social pressures played a role*: Australian social housing and employment; British Open University; Dutch football project; Brazilian electricity for waste collection; US drug courts *New technology as a key driver*: South African health literacy; British Open University; Danish Cycling without Age; Brazilian electricity for waste collection
Collaboration	*Number of actors*: All projects involve multiple actors *Close collaboration between public and private actors involved in collaboration*: All cases, except Brazilian electricity for waste collection *Collaboration combined with elements of market and competition*: South African health literacy; Australian social housing and employment; British Open University; Brazilian electricity for waste collection
Management	Managerial instruments • *Regulatory*: Brazilian electricity for waste collection; US drug courts • *Financial*: Except for Brazilian electricity for waste collection, all innovations depend on external public and/or private funding • *Administrative support*: Australian social housing and employment; Danish Cycling without Age; Dutch football project; US drug courts Managerial structure • *Lead agency*: South African health literacy (private); British Open University (public); Danish Cycling without Age (private); Brazilian electricity for waste collection (private) • *Network Administrative* Organization: Australian housing and employment • *Participant governed*: Dutch football project; US drug courts
Results	*Political and financial viability of results*: All projects seem fairly viable, except the Australian social housing and employment project

With regard to the initiation of the innovation process, we find important differences again. Hence, four of the innovation projects were initiated by private actors and three by public actors. This is interesting because it reveals the relevance of the notion of 'social innovation', which refers to the ability of social actors to meet hitherto unmet social needs. The empirical analysis also reveals that political and social pressures can drive public innovation. At least this is the case in five out of the seven innovations that we have examined. This finding supports the idea that the relative absence of market pressures in the public sector by no means prevents innovation as other pressures may play an equally important role. Last but not least, there are good examples of cases where the development of new technologies plays a role in facilitating innovation. This is particularly clear in the South African health literacy project and the Danish Cycling without Age but is also significant in the British Open University and the Brazilian electricity-for-waste collection.

In all cases, two or more actors were involved in the innovation process. Many of the cases involved more than a dozen actors dispersed over a large geographical territory. Moreover, except for the case of the electricity for waste collection in Brazil, which merely involves private actors in the design and execution phase, all innovations are based on a close collaboration between public and private actors. In the case of the British Open University, it should be mentioned that collaboration with private partners (mainly potential employers of OU graduates) started well after the establishment of the OU. This seems to substantiate the thesis that innovations – both in the private and public sectors – are rarely created by single persons or producer organizations but more often by a more or less coherent network of public and private actors possessing a broad range of innovation assets (Baldwin and von Hippel 2010; Sørensen and Torfing 2011). What is interesting, however, is that multi-actor collaboration is often combined with elements of market competition. As such, there is a mix of governance mechanisms spurring public sector innovation rather that a singular mechanism.

Public authorities have played a fundamental role in all seven projects. However, their managerial role in the projects varies substantially. Regulatory instruments only played a major role in the three cases involving the attempts to curb criminal activity. In all the cases, except the Brazilian electricity for waste collection, public authorities provided various subsidies or incentives that encouraged multi-actor collaboration. Moreover, in most of the affluent countries (Denmark, the Netherlands and Australia) administrative support from local authorities was provided to the innovation projects. Apart from substantial variation in governing instruments, the management of the processes of collaborative innovation varied in terms of how leadership was distributed. Four innovation projects were led by a lead agency, one project had a Network Administrative Organization and three projects were governed by participants. Moreover, it is interesting to see that, while one lead agent is public, the others are private. Hence, we cannot assume a priori that public innovation projects are led by public actors due to their formal authority and convening power. In sum, the case analysis indicates that processes of collaboration and innovation not only require some form of steering, management and leadership but also that there is a uniform way for steering, managing and leader innovation in the public sector.

Finally, while all projects produced positive short-term results, they did not all seem to have the political support or financial viability necessary to sustain long-term impact. As mentioned above, only one project was based on a principle of complete economic self-reliance, i.e. without public support. At the other end of the spectrum, the housing and employment project in Australia seemed to have dwindling support due to party-political disputes over the role of public intervention in this area. The viability of the rest of the projects is dependent on political and fiscal support from public authorities that is contingent on the continued production of positive results as well as the shifting political preferences of government.

4.11 Conclusion

This chapter has examined seven cases of public innovation from around the world. We analysed them in terms of the social problem addressed, their solution, the initiation process, the collaborating actors, the form of management and the results produced. Since the analysis is descriptive and the sample is neither sufficiently large nor randomly selected, we cannot make any firm analytical conclusions. However, four important observations appear to stand out. First, examples of innovation that create and sustain public value can be found all over the world. Second, public innovation seems to be a team sport involving a host of public and private actors in the development and realization of new and innovative ideas. Third, private actors may initiate and drive public innovation, but in most cases some kind of public support and intervention is needed, although there is no single managerial formula for how this support is provided. Finally, to produce long-term sustainable impact, public innovation relies on political and financial support that is predicated on the continued production of positive results.

While this chapter may have succeeded in adding some flesh and blood to the concept of public innovation and demonstrated its global relevance, further research into the causal mechanisms that create and sustain public innovation is needed. The analysis offered above may help to stimulate our curiosity and formulate testable hypotheses, some of which will be further explored in the subsequent chapters.

References

Australia Bureau of Statistics 2012. *Census of Population and Housing: Estimating Homelessness, 2011*. Canberra: ABS.

Baldwin, C. Y. and von Hippel, E. A. 2010. 'Modeling a paradigm shift: From producer innovation to user and open collaborative innovation', Harvard Business School Finance Working Paper No. 10–38.

Bell, R. and Tight, M. 1993. *Open Universities: A British Tradition?* Milton Keynes: Open University Press.

Borland, J., Tseng, Y. and Wilkins, R. 2013. 'Does coordination of welfare services' delivery make a difference for extremely disadvantaged jobseekers? evidence from the "YP4" Trial', *Melbourne Institute Working Paper Series*, WP No. 12/13.

Castelnuovo, B., Newell, K., Manabe1, Y. C., and Robertson, G. 2014. 'Multimedia educational tool increases knowledge of clinical trials in Uganda', *Journal of Clinical Research and Bioethics* 5: 165. doi:10.4172/2155-9627.1000165.

Cevaal, A., Smits, F., Nootebos, W., Lucassen, J. and Slettenhaar, G. 2010. *Evaluatieonderzoek Doelbewust*. 's-Hertogenbosch: W.J.H. Mulier. URL: htt p://beheer.nisb.nl/cogito/modules/uploads/docs/64291294825128.pdf.

Cipolla, C., Melo, P. and Manzini, E. 2013. 'Collaborative services in informal settlements: A social innovation case in a pacified favela in Rio de Janeiro'. URL: www.scribd.com/doc/191799087/Collaborative-services-in-infor mal-settlements-A-social-innovation-case-in-a-paci%EF%;AC%81ed-fave la-in-Rio-de-Janeiro.

Considine, M. and Hart, A. 2008. 'Integrating homeless young people into housing and employment', in M. Considine and S. Giguére (eds.), *The Theory and Practice of Local Governance and Economic Development*. Basingstoke: Palgrave Macmillan, pp. 161–84.

Dhai, A., Etheredge, H. and Cleaton-Jones, P. 2010. 'A pilot study evaluating an intervention designed to raise awareness of clinical trials among potential participants in the developing world', *Journal of Medical Ethics* 36: 238–42

Engida, E. and Simireta, T. 2013. *Rapid Qualitative Assessment of Maternal and Newborn Health Care (MNHC) Speaking Book in Two Districts in the Amhara Region, Ethiopia*. New York: UNICEF.

European Crime Prevention Network 2011. *European Crime Prevention Award,* 2011. Brussels: EUCPN. URL: eucpn.org/eucp-award/entries.asp? year=2011.

Goldberg, D. 2011. 'A novel intervention for HIV & AIDS: Books of Hope "give voice" to new HIV & AIDS prevention initiatives', *Consultancy Africa Intelligence. Discussion Papers* 18 April, 2011, www.consultancyafrica.com.

Gottfredson, D. C, Najaka, S. S. and Kearley, B. 2006. 'Effectiveness of drug treatment courts: Evidence from a randomized trial', *Criminology & Public Policy* 2(2): 171–96.

Grace, M. and Gill, P. R. 2014. 'Improving outcomes for unemployed and home-less young people: Findings of the YP[4] clinical controlled trial of joined up case management', *Australian Social Work* 67(3): 419–37, DOI: 10.1080/ 0312407X.2014.911926.

Hale, K. 2011. *How Information Matters. Networks and Public Policy Innovation.* Washington, DC: Georgetown University Press.

Head, B. W. and Alford, J. 2015. 'Wicked problems: Implications for public policy and management', *Administration & Society* 47(6): 711–39.

King, R. S. and Pasquarella, J. 2009. *Drug Courts: A Review of the Evidence.* Washington, DC: Sentencing Project.

Kingdon, J. W. 1995. *Agendas, Alternatives, and Public Policies.* 2nd edn. New York: Harper Collins.

Koppenjan, J. and Klijn, E. H. 2004. *Managing Uncertainties in Networks.* London: Routledge.

Light 2014. *Light Recicla.* URL: www.light.com.br/grupo-light/Sustentabilidade/ desenvolvimento-da-area-de-concessao_light-recicla.aspx.

Municipality of 's-Hertogenbosch 2011. *Goalkeepers: One Team, One Result!* Brussels: EUCPN. URL: .eucpn.org/eucp-award/entries.asp?year=2011.

Nolan, J. L. Jr. 2001. *Reinventing Justice: The American Drug Court Movement.* Princeton University Press.

Open University 2014a. *The OU Story.* URL: www.open.ac.uk/about/main/strat egy/ou-story.

    2014b. *International Developments in the 1990s.* URL: www.open.ac.uk/research projects/historyofou/story/international-developments-the-1990s.

    2014c. *Partnerships.* URL: www.open.ac.uk/about/main/strategy/partnerships.

    2014d. *Facts and Figures.* URL: www.open.ac.uk/about/main/strategy/facts-an d-figures.

Provan, K. G. and Kenis, P. 2008. 'Modes of network governance: Structure, management, and effectiveness', *Journal of Public Administration, Research and Theory* 18(2): 229–52.

SADAG 2014a. *SpeakingBooks.* 'About', Sandton, Johannesburg. URL: www.speak ingbooks.com/about.

    2014b. *SpeakingBooks.* 'Partners', Sandton, Johannesburg. URL: www.sp eakingbooks.com/partners.

Spohn, C., Piper, R. K., Martin, T. and Frenzel, E. D. 2001. 'Drug courts and recidivism: The results of an evaluation using two comparison groups and multiple indicators of recidivism', *Journal of Drug Issues* 31(1): 149–76.

Sørensen, E. and Torfing, J. 2011. 'Enhancing collaborative innovation in the public sector', *Administration & Society* 43(8): 842–68.

Van de Ven, A., Polley, D., Garud, R. and Venkataraman, S. 2008. *The Innovation Journey*. New York: Oxford University Press.

Vroom, M. 2006. *Communities on the Move: A Community Approach that Focuses on Promoting an Active Lifestyle among Specific Groups*. Bennekom: Nederlands Instituut voor Sport en Bewegen (NISB).

5   Organizational and Governance Aspects of Diffusing Public Innovation

Jean Hartley

5.1   Introduction

This chapter examines diffusion of innovation from two perspectives: the organization and the governance regime. It explores what it meant by diffusion and how it can be understood as an organizational and inter-organizational phenomenon (the sharing and spread of innovations between organizations). The distinction between 'hard' and 'soft' elements of innovation helps to explain why so much adaptation of innovation often occurs in diffusion – with implications for how governments might conceptualize and stimulate the spread of 'promising practices'. The chapter then turns to consider how the governance context may stimulate or inhibit organizational functioning in relation to diffusion. Throughout the chapter, the focus is on innovation at the product, service or organizational level. It does not concern itself with the diffusion of public policy, which is a field in its own right because the focus is on what happens on the ground, in organizational settings.

The diffusion of innovation has been called the public sector's secret weapon (Hartley 2014) because it has high value to society but interest in and understanding of the diffusion of innovation has been relatively under-theorized and under-researched. There are outstanding systematic reviews, conceptual frameworks and empirical studies of diffusion (e.g. Greenhalgh et al. 2004; Rogers 2003; Berry and Berry 2007) but overall, in studies of innovation, greater attention has been paid to the processes of creativity and invention in innovation than to the processes of diffusion of existing innovations. Additionally, relatively little attention has been paid to how national governance regimes inhibit or foster the diffusion of innovation (Hartley 2005; Windrum 2008).

Yet, the diffusion of innovative technologies and practices is critical to organizations and groups that are concerned with creating public value. Many public and third sector organizations have a social and even moral imperative to share their innovations because society benefits from

95

effective innovations being spread beyond the initial innovator to other organizations and groups. For example, Cycling without Age is a Danish innovation, started in 2012, based on getting elderly people out of their nursing homes on trips by rickshaws ridden by volunteers. The 'right to wind in your hair' has spread to 50 municipalities in Denmark and Norway, and the purchase and use of rickshaws is now diffusing to a number of countries across the world. To give a different example, an effective new hospital treatment increases its value and effectiveness as an innovation where it diffuses to other hospitals because there is limited value created if the innovation is only found in a single hospital. This is not to suggest that diffusion is attempted by all public and third sector organizations, or that such attempts where they happen are successful. However, the public value outcomes of fostering diffusion contrast with the typical private sector organization, which aims to prevent or slow the diffusion of new innovations, through tools such as patents, copyright and design rights so that private value can accrue to the innovating firm (Hartley 2013).

Furthermore, for public service organizations, diffusion can be an effective way of undertaking innovation. By adopting an innovation from elsewhere, the organization reduces or bypasses the practical costs of invention because the adopter may be able to avoid some development costs and some mistakes in invention and prototyping. Diffusion can also reduce the operational and political risks of the innovation because it has been tried and tested in another context, and so politicians and managers can reassure stakeholders on this basis. The argument that risk is a problem for public service innovation is thus mitigated to some extent by drawing on others' experience (Osborne and Brown 2013).

However, just as innovation is not the same as improvement (Hartley 2005), so diffusion is not automatically beneficial for society. Ineffective innovations can diffuse, and we should avoid the 'pro-innovation bias', which assumes that innovations are necessarily valuable or effective (Abrahamson 1991). It has been noted that early work on the diffusion of innovation tended to assume the inherent value of the innovation (Schoeb 2014), and therefore that diffusion was to be fostered where possible. Later contributions have questioned this on two grounds. First, that an innovation may not be an improvement (Hartley 2005), and second, that innovations spread for a range of reasons other than rational, evidence-based reasons, including fads and fashions in management (Abrahamson 1991), isomorphic pressures to conform to what is seen as 'best practice' regardless of suitability (Ashworth, Boyne and Delbridge 2009) and public policy directives from central government (Mintrom 1997; Lewis et al. 2015). This chapter examines diffusion without assuming that it creates value, while recognizing that it has the potential to do so.

Equally, just because there is compelling evidence for the value of an innovation, it does not guarantee spread. Rogers (2003) notes that an innovation which eradicated scurvy among sailors was first practised on British ships in 1601 and was based on clear and robust evidence, but it took the British Navy until 1865 to adopt the policy across the fleet. More recently, there are many examples of the non-spread or slow spread of valuable innovations in the health sector from handwashing to the use of stethoscopes (Buchanan and Fitzgerald 2007).

5.2   What is Diffusion of Innovation?

At first glance, this appears to be a deceptively simple question, but closer analysis suggests this is more complex in highly interesting ways. Some academic studies avoid a definition completely, assuming clarity of the phenomenon. Other studies (e.g. Walker, Avellaneda and Berry 2011) quote the seminal work of Rogers (2003: 5) who defined diffusion as 'the process by which an innovation is communicated through certain channels over time among the members of a social system'. Schoeb (2014: 1) takes a more technical approach: 'the word diffusion is commonly used to describe the process by which individuals and firms in a society/economy adopt a new technology, or replace an older technology with a newer'. On the other hand, Wejnert (2002: 297) takes a more sociological approach and defines diffusion as 'the spread of abstract ideas and concepts, technical information and actual practices within a social system, where the spread denotes a flow or movement from a source to an adopter'.

The first two definitions focus on the innovation itself, implicitly assuming that it is an entity. The last definition allows for the spread of abstract ideas as well as practices, encompassing a wider view of diffusion, and also views the process as a flow from one part of the system to another. Of course, where an innovation is simple (rather than complex), observable and has clear boundaries, then the focus on the innovation as an entity may be realistic and enable the mapping of flows across a population or system. Mapping the spread of the use of hybrid corn seeds (Rogers 2003), or the use of surgical checklists in hospital theatres can provide clear examples of the diffusion of innovation.

However, Greenhalgh, Barton-Sweeney and Macfarlane (2013) note that diffusion is harder to track where the innovation is multidimensional and service-based. How is diffusion analysed when some dimensions are adopted but not others? Furthermore, complex innovations are rarely taken on board de novo but are absorbed into current practices and procedures, such that some elements may be new to the organization but other elements adapted from existing practices. Denis et al. (2002) note that complex innovations have a 'hard' element and a 'soft' element. The hard element may remain unchanged but the soft element may be modified according to circumstances. In such circumstances, what counts as adoption given that the boundaries are blurred? Service innovations are particularly hard to track in terms of spread compared with technological innovations (Alänge, Jacobsson and Jarnehammar 1998; Greenhalgh, Barton-Sweeney and Macfarlane 2013) because they require greater tacit knowledge, have less well-defined system borders and are more subjectively assessed. Service innovations typically have high levels of ambiguity and uncertainty since they are affected by the variability of the human elements of both service givers and receivers (Lewis and Hartley 2001) so an adoption may vary from one service encounter to another service encounter.

Adoption is only rarely an on/off phenomenon. Often, it is more useful to conceptualize diffusion as occurring on a continuum from non-adoption to full adoption. How much, how frequently or how fully does an innovation have to be used to count as adoption? Even technologies (such as smartphones or certain types of medical equipment) may be adopted without all the full features of the technology being used. This is recognized in a number of discussions about the diffusion of innovation, which outline phases in adoption, for example initial versus sustained implementation (Zaltman, Duncan and Holbek 1973); or the sequence of knowledge, persuasion, decision, implementation and confirmation (Rogers 2003); or adoption decision, implementation and routinization (Wolfe 1994). However, such conceptual stages are not always evident in practice, where adoption may be more random, opportunistic and emergent (e.g. van de Ven 1986; Greenhalgh, Barton-Sweeney and Macfarlane 2013).

In addition, adoption is merely replication – i.e. an exact replica of an innovation in a different setting (Berman and Nelson 1997; Szulanski and Winter 2002). While governments sometimes demand strict replication, but where innovations are complex, where the boundaries of the innovation are fuzzy, then adaption to local circumstances is often necessary (Rashman, Downe and Hartley 2005). Local policy entrepreneurs may help an innovation to flourish through awareness of local circumstances and local cultures (Mintrom 1997) and systems may learn to allow more variation over time (Hartley and Rashman 2014). In a large study of sharing innovation in UK local government (Rashma, Downe and Hartley 2005; Hartley and Benington 2006), diffusion was widespread but involved adaptation to local context and conditions. Among the adopting organizations that had used ideas from the innovator, 63 per cent reported that they had adapted the idea from the innovator. This showed that adjustment takes place as the innovation flows from one organization to another. Adaptation happened more than adoption. In addition, 29 per cent reported that they accelerated an idea that they already had, using the adopted innovation with greater confidence. Only 8 per cent based their change closely on the innovator. The small percentage involved in exact copy reflects the wider literature that replication occurs only in relatively infrequent and highly defined circumstances (Szulanski and Winter 2002; Behn 2008). Some have suggested that reinvention aids the sustained implementation of the innovation (Rogers 2003).

Beyond adaption is recombinant innovation (Hargadon 2005). Hargadon notes that breakthrough innovation occurs much less rarely through creating entirely new ideas and more often involves technology brokering, whereby old ideas are recombined in new ways. This is a 'backwards first' approach to innovation whereby the adoption of the innovation, in a new setting or in a new way, becomes the forefront of innovation. Hargadon notes: 'Popular discussions of the innovation process often confuse the origins and impacts of a new technology. According to conventional wisdom, both the introduction of a breakthrough innovation and the revolutionary changes that follow require revolutionary origins. Closer studies of the technical details, however, suggest the opposite: that it is the recombinant (rather than inventive) nature of revolutionary innovations that contribute to their dramatic effects' (2005: 32).

There are many examples of recombinant innovation in the private and public sectors. For example, the electrical transistor was initially thought to have a specialist use only in deaf aids until computer scientists turned it into a central component of early – and now all – computers. In the public sector, a celebrated example is Great Ormond Street Hospital's use of ideas and practices from Formula 1 racing. Doctors were concerned about the transfer of sick children from surgery to intensive care, which involves a change of team and potential loss of key information in the transfer. Watching Formula 1 on television one day, some doctors were struck that a pit stop represented an important concept that could be modified and applied in the hospital. The transferable concepts were the following: a team-based approach, clear communication, rehearsal of procedures and a single person in charge of the decision about completion and safety. The hospital team used these basic practices, modifying and adapting them for the different context and task (Hartley 2014). Another practical example comes from Greater Manchester Fire and Rescue Service, which incorporated thermal imaging (used in a number of sectors), high-pressure water-based cutting equipment (from the construction industry) and extractor

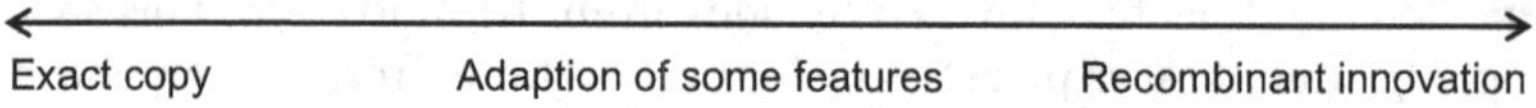

←——→

Exact copy   Adaption of some features   Recombinant innovation

Figure 5.1 A spectrum of variations in degree of diffusion
(Source: Adapted from Buchanan and Fitzgerald 2007)

fans (from fire-fighting in the United States) to innovate in their approach
to high-temperature fires. This required being aware of technological
developments in other fields, sectors and locations and using them creatively in a step-change way in the service.

This consideration of different types or degrees of innovation is captured in a figure adapted from Buchanan and Fitzgerald (2007) which
represents a spectrum from exact copy to recombinant innovation or
'innofusion' (Fleck, Webster and Williams 1990), which involves a
combination of innovation and diffusion. This spectrum recognizes
the variation in how and how far diffusion involves faithful replication
or creative adaptation. This also then suggests some of the processes
which underlie diffusion.

If the focus is on replication, adaptation or recombination, then 'harvesting' innovations which already exist in the world becomes as important as internal organizational creativity (Hartley 2014). Harvesting ideas
rather than (or as well as) inventing them in-house is a radically different
model of innovation. It requires looking outwards, not inwards, because
the innovation may be a novel application of a product or practice in an
entirely different setting. It depends on a positive innovation climate –
energy and curiosity to engage with ideas from the external world beyond
the service or organization.

5.3   Metaphors of Diffusion

The varied approaches to diffusion, along the diffusion spectrum, indicate
why there are so many and so varied metaphors of the diffusion of innovation
(which is a metaphor itself). These provide different assumptions about how
diffusion occurs in organizational settings and can help to explain why both
governments and public services can misunderstand diffusion.

Where exact copy is aimed for, an engineering metaphor of diffusion is
often used or implied – treating the innovator and adopter as though they
are machines which can be tightly controlled, and the innovation clearly
specified, managed and measured. The engineering metaphor can be heard
in language about 'roll-out', or 'replication'. Sometimes the assumption is
that innovation is based on 'copy and paste' or 'plug and play', both of

which are machine-based metaphors (Hartley and Benington 2006). Central governments sometimes have a tendency to seek out exact replication in their policies and programmes, assuming homogeneity of local public services or local contexts. This was characteristic of the early days of the UK's Beacon Scheme in local government, which aimed to share and spread innovation and high performance (Rashman and Hartley 2002), though longer and greater experience with diffusion changed this view from a mechanical metaphor to a learning one (Hartley and Rashman 2014).

However, as noted, 'exact copy' is only rarely a feasible strategy of diffusion and is difficult or impossible where innovations are complex. Adapting some features to the local context or local organization while preserving particular features requires reflection and comparison between the two contexts, working out what is similar and what is different. These are the 'soft' and 'hard' elements of innovation outlined by Denis et al. (2002). Such sharing of promising practices can be facilitated by inter-organizational networks of sharing and comparing (Hartley and Benington 2006), drawing not only on explicit but also on tacit knowledge (Hartley and Rashman 2007). In such circumstances, a horticultural metaphor helps to emphasize the adaption to a different environment – so 'graft and grow' captures the idea of a rootstock onto which other biological live material is bound. As in horticulture, observation and attention to the graft so that it 'takes' and grows is essential. This can partly be based on following instructions, but it also requires understanding of the underlying model, or theory, about what supports and inhibits grafts in particular conditions and why. There is some learning through observation, and perhaps advice from more skilled 'gardeners' about context and culture.

5.4   Organizational and Inter-Organizational Learning Approaches to Diffusion

Where there is diffusion of innovation in many or most features, then a learning approach becomes especially pertinent. The innovation may be based on guiding principles – for example adopting a particular business model or an approach to organizational change, where many of the features need to be worked out through planning and in situ. Or the adoption may take an innovation from another sector in a way which requires not only translation but also interpretation to a new context with most elements of the innovation being adapted not just adopted (often where recombinant innovation takes place).

A learning perspective assumes that learning – by individuals, groups and organizations – is needed each time diffusion occurs because the spread of new knowledge related to the innovation and how to embed it in existing practices requires unlearning old practices and procedures (Behn 2008), working out how the innovation is adapted to fit local circumstances (Hartley and Rashman 2007; Scarbrough et al. 2015), how it is integrated in existing ongoing practices (Denis et al. 2002; Greenhalgh et al. 2004) and how spread can occur beyond professional boundaries (Ferlie et al. 2005). Learning involves both tacit and explicit knowledge (Nonaka 1994; Polanyi 1967) (the former is hard to articulate because it is embodied; the latter can be shared through external means such as websites, PowerPoint slides and books). Innovation and its diffusion generally require tacit as well as explicit knowledge (Kim 1998; Lam 2000). Organizational learning is a key theme in the study of the diffusion of innovation (e.g. Chiva, Ghauri and Allegre 2013; Nonaka 1994; Greenhalgh et al. 2005).

At the organizational level, there is a growing interest in the processes which enable innovations to diffuse or spread between organizations and across populations of organizations (Miner et al. 1999; Hartley and Rashman 2014;), often through knowledge sharing, and inter-organizational learning (e.g. Dixon 2000; Finger and Brand 1999; Downe et al. 2004; Greenhalgh et al. 2004). Both the motivation and the capacity in the organization to 'pull' in innovation are increasingly important (i.e. not just evidence push).

Motivation appears to be less important than capacity, in the view of a number of commentators (e.g. Greenhalgh et al. 2004; Szulanski 2003). Absorptive capacity is the ability to identify, capture, interpret, share, reframe and reuse new knowledge, linked to the existing knowledge base of the organization. Originally conceptualized by Cohen and Levinthal (1990) and since reviewed by writers such as Zahra and George (2002), this provides a way of considering how innovations are selectively taken up and reflect capacity of the organization to understand and utilize new ideas.

Some of the organizational factors and processes which affect the diffusion of innovation through inter-organizational knowledge sharing and learning are shown in Figure 5.2, which is based on research over nine years, with a national initiative in the United Kingdom to foster innovation and improvement in local government (called the Beacon Scheme and outlined in detail by Hartley and Rashman 2007). This model focuses on the characteristics of the innovator, the adopter, the processes of learning between them and the wider policy context.

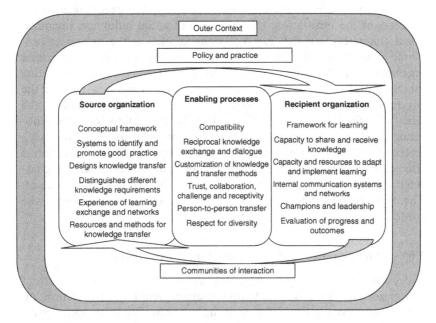

Figure 5.2 Model of inter-organizational learning: factors affecting
diffusion
(Source: Hartley and Rashman 2007)

5.5   Other Factors Affecting Diffusion

From an organizational perspective, the various learning or knowledge-transfer frameworks (of which Figure 5.2 is one example) are particularly dominant, as there has been increasing recognition of the role of learning and knowledge acquisition and use over the last decade or so (see also Scarbrough et al. 2015). However, other factors can act as stimulants or barriers to the diffusion of innovation. The seminal work of Rogers identified a number of features of the innovation, the processes of communication and the characteristics of the adopter of the innovation which shaped extent, degree and vigour of take-up. These have been well rehearsed, though as innovations have become more complex not all elements are supported (e.g. the characterization of individuals as early or late adopters and so on is not supported – Greenhalgh et al. 2004). Other scholars have presented models of diffusion emphasizing both similar and different elements in the processes of diffusion. For example, Greenhalgh, Barton-Sweeney and Macfarlane (2013) describe several components of their model: features of the innovation itself; the potential adopters of the innovation; the processes of social influence; organizational characteristics; the 'external' context such as the prevailing economic and political context along with the behaviour of other organizations in the same sector; and the managerial processes supporting (or not) implementation. The external context suggests a role for the governance arrangements in society. Wejnert (2002) organizes the 'array of variables' affecting diffusion into the characteristics of the innovation itself, the characteristics of the innovators (actors) and the characteristics of the environment. What shines through is that diffusion is affected by wider social, political and economic forces which are characterized as the context or the environment in which diffusion takes place. The next section homes in on this in terms of one specific feature – the governance regimes within the public sector.

5.6   Governance and the Diffusion of Innovation

A decade ago, Hartley (2005) examined the implications of different conceptions of governance and public management for public innovation but did not analyse the diffusion of innovation. The governance paradigms can be seen as competing, in that they exist as layered realities for politicians and managers, with particular circumstances calling forth behaviours and decisions relevant to the diffusion of innovation. In Chapter 1, these widely recognized governance paradigms have been described as 'traditional public administration', 'new public management' and 'collaborative governance'. This is not a normative framework because each paradigm has both strengths and weaknesses for how public innovation develops and is diffused in society.

How might the extent, speed, depth and success of innovation diffusion be affected by the governance arrangements and by particular governance arrangements as exemplified by the three paradigms? First, we know that effective diffusion is influenced by the political and governance arrangements existing in a country (Wejnert 2002; Windrum 2008). This may be due to ideological doctrines (Wejnert 2002) as well as the overall governmental climate which supports innovation or which highlights and aims to minimize risk (Polsby 1984; Bason 2010). Governments can stimulate innovation and its diffusion through economic and technological policies and resource allocation (Crouch and Voelzkow 2009; Mazzucato 2013); they can stimulate the diffusion of innovation through innovation award schemes which not only recognize innovation but also crucially spread promising practices (Hartley and Downe 2007; Borins 2014); elected politicians can champion the diffusion of particular innovations (Polsby 1984;

Berry and Berry 2007; Hartley and Rashman 2010), and they can convene other actors to join them in spreading promising practices (Ansell and Gash 2008; Sørensen and Torfing 2011). Governance arrangements may also affect the institutional pressures which organizations experience in adopting existing innovations: governments can apply coercive pressures to organizations, and the adopters may also experience mimetic and isomorphic pressures to take on board diffused innovations (Di Maggio and Powell 1983; Ashworth, Boyne and Delbridge 2009) in order to enhance their legitimacy and reputation (Westphal, Gulati and Shortell 1997; Downe et al. 2004). Furthermore, networks of organizations, professional associations and communities of practice may also diffuse innovations where there is a permissive climate. However, there is still relatively little theorizing or research about the governance context, and particularly how different governance paradigms may shape the diffusion of innovation.

This chapter therefore extends, in a theoretically informed but empirically speculative way, the approach to considering governance paradigms set out in Hartley (2005). It also draws on more recent analysis in Hartley, Sørensen and Torfing (2013) and in Hartley and Torfing (in press). These show that each governance paradigm (Classical Public Administration, New Public Management and Collaborative Governance) is able to produce innovation, sometimes with large scale and scope across public organizations with impacts on other sectors as well. However, the means to achieve both innovation and its diffusion may be different, and this creates different strengths and weaknesses of each paradigm, as judged by innovation and diffusion goals, impact on stakeholders and contribution to public value (what adds value to the public sphere, Benington and Moore 2011). These elements are shown in Table 5.1. It must be emphasized that these paradigms are 'ideal types' and that in practice, there may be elements of each governance paradigm present at the same time in public organizations. However, ideal types can help to elucidate process and outcomes, in this case in relation to the diffusion of innovation under different governance settings.

The Classical Public Administration approach was particularly evident in the post-war period of the welfare state, though it continues to be highly relevant to certain public services where stable, largely mass-produced services or infrastructure are required in both industrialized and developing countries. There can be a great deal of innovation under this governance paradigm (Mazzucato 2013) although not always discussed in innovation language. The state, particularly elected politicians, drives innovation by creating policies and providing resources for innovations which are ambitious in scale and scope and which are well distributed across the state (Hartley and Torfing, in press). There is little evidence of

Table 5.1 *The role of governance paradigms in the diffusion of innovation*

	Classical Public Administration	New Public Management	New Public Governance
Innovation	Large-scale, and universal innovations, mainly national also local levels of government	Innovations in organizational form more than content	Innovation at both central and local levels and by partners
Role of innovators	Strong role for politicians as policy commanders; managers as implementers	Politicians largely removed from innovation as management comes to the fore. Managers' main responsibility for innovation.	Polycentric governance means that innovation may come from any sector or locality and from various innovation leaders
Role of adopters	Public servants: follow the rules and replicate where possible	Public managers: adopt where clear evidence of performance improvement or where innovator is high status. Adapt to local culture and context if justified	Stakeholders: scan the environment for promising innovations; have confidence to adapt them for local conditions; co-opt potential contributors. Learning orientation
Diffusion of innovation	Top-down through legislation and policy	League tables and performance data encourage imitation. Professional and inter-organizational learning networks are important	Networks across services, sectors, professions and localities aid the spread of innovations
Degree of adaptation	Minimal	Initially adoption but greater adaptation with more experience of using innovation	Large and including recombinant innovation
Strengths	Rapid, wide-scale spread of innovation	Emulation of private sector innovation practices, encouragement (in theory) of entrepreneurial behaviours	Diversity of stakeholders and range of values and experiences involved strengthens adaptation in diffusion and builds ownership. Adapted to local conditions

Table 5.1 (*cont.*)

	Classical Public Administration	New Public Management	New Public Governance
Weaknesses	Little role for citizens Top-down approach reduces 'ownership' of the diffused innovation. Low innovation climate in the organization for future adaptation	Proliferation of performance management approaches increases risk-aversion Little role for stakeholders outside the organization	Cacophony of diffusion opportunities – which stand out? Lack of bureaucracy to ensure longer-term sustainability

local adaptation because the key principle in diffusion is to follow the rules in implementing and spreading the innovation, and this is mainly done by public servants. Replication of initial innovations or the 'rolling out' of inventions across a group of organizations are key terms used which represent 'mechanical' metaphors underlying this approach to diffusion. Innovation and its diffusion can be highly productive under this governance paradigm – as can be witnessed from the innovations in the welfare state period from about 1945 to 1980 in particular, which produced new and effective approaches to health, housing, education and economic development. Diffusion can be widespread and rapid because the approach to diffusion is largely top-down, and the voice of the state is dominant and able to provide large-scale financial, legal and other resources and to give relentless focus through politicians and through policy instruments. However, there is little role for citizens (other than as somewhat passive recipients of state services) or indeed other stakeholders or sectors, and there is little encouragement or incentive for public servants to have a sense of ownership of the diffused innovation or to offer continuing fine-tuning to the innovation (either through learning how it works in practice or as the context or service users change).

When New Public Management and 'reinventing government' first came on the scene (Hood 1991; Osborne and Gaebler 1992), it was widely thought that this approach to governance and management would substantially increase innovation in the public sector, because this was a regime which brought in private sector structures and managerial methods and processes, including market-based competition, which had been thought of as the engine of innovation by many economists (but for a critique of the role of competition in innovation see Hartley, Sørensen and Torfing 2013; Mazzucato 2013). The policy, managerial and even academic discourses of New Public Management (NPM) spoke of innovation and entrepreneurship released from the sclerotic structures of traditional public administration with its rules and procedures. However, in practice, the evidence for innovation and its diffusion was more mixed (Koch and Hauknes 2005; Hartley, Sørensen and Torfing 2013) partly because market competition has more paradoxical influences on competition and partly because the proliferation of and focus on performance data and league tables of comparative performance created a raft of new rules and procedures which encouraged risk aversion and dampened down innovation. In addition, while market competition may in some situations stimulate innovation it conversely makes the diffusion of innovation less attractive (Hartley 2013). However, the existence of comparative performance data across professions, services and types of organization did create some incentives and isomorphic pressures to adopt innovations where the innovator was clearly seen to be rising in performance or in reputation (Ashworth, Boyne and Delbridge 2009). However, for some organizations, this is not solely institutional convergence, as there is evidence of some public organizations shifting, with experience over time, from a focus on exact copy adoption to a greater degree of adaptation (Hartley and Rashman 2014) and with a greater emphasis on inter-organizational learning. Overall, while New Public Management promised innovation and its diffusion, the reality has been less impressive (Windrum 2008; Hartley, Sørensen and Torfing 2013).

New Public Governance, as noted in Chapter 1, is 'the new kid on the block' and is attracting considerable attention as a governance paradigm relevant to innovation. As Sørensen and Torfing (2011) note, innovation in this situation of polycentric governance means that innovation occurs where the stakeholders come together – or are convened, often by public sector actors whether politicians or public managers – to scope a problem or take advantage of an opportunity to innovate. While Classical Public Administration looks upwards (up the hierarchy, including to politicians) for innovation, and New Public Management looks inwards to managers unleashing innovation in the workplace, collaborative innovation looks all around for innovation. It does not take a particular organizational form – it may come from a public organization initially or it may come from a member of the public or a lobby group or a community group. Anyone with an interest in the innovation opportunity and who can mobilize others to pay attention may drive an innovation and mobilize support for it. The public sector, whether politicians, managers or staff, has a particular responsibility to convene actors according to transparent and open rules, without fear or favour, but the initiative really can come from anywhere. So harvesting innovative ideas and practices and sharing and spreading ideas can be important. The diversity of views, values, interests and goals among those convened or assembled to take advantage of an innovation encourages a learning and adaptive approach to diffusion, because following rules and procedures will not appeal (or even seem relevant) to diverse stakeholders. Diffusion may occur with lots of adaptation to local conditions – 'let a thousand flowers bloom'. Collaborative innovation has a number of advantages, particularly where dealing with 'wicked' problems which may necessitate complex innovations (which the literature tells us involve high levels of adaptation in the process of diffusion). What can make collaborative diffusion harder is that there may be a cacophony of innovation, with different innovations, stakeholders, contexts and problems competing for profile, reputation and attention. The variation in approach may make comparative performance analysis difficult (the opposite problem from New Public Management), which may slow diffusion so it may be harder to learn about 'what works' on an evidence base and make collaborative innovation more prone to fads and fashions (Abrahamson 1991). Furthermore, while stakeholders can be convened they can also disband themselves, so there are some questions about the longer-term sustainability of diffusion in networked governance.

Many of these points about the impact on diffusion of different governance regimes are speculative, because there is as yet insufficient evidence. Public innovation is only just coming out of the shadow of the longer-established private sector literature about innovation, where diffusion has been less important. The glamour of the invention phase of innovation has led to less intensity of research on the diffusion stage, despite path-breaking initial work (Rogers 2003). Chapter 1 noted that the literatures on innovation and governance have been largely separate until recently, and so there is much work to be done to build theory and empirical research so that there is a better picture and understanding of the diffusion of innovation. Diffusion is a key part of innovation for any organization concerned with the public sphere, so there is much still to learn about what it is, how it happens and how learning strategies and the overarching governance paradigm help or hinder.

References

Abrahamson, E. 1991. 'Managerial fads and fashions: The diffusion and rejection of innovations', *Academy of Management Review* 16(3): 586–612.

Alänge, S., Jacobsson, S. and Jarnehammar, A. 1998. 'Some aspects of an analytical framework for studying the diffusion of organizational innovations', *Technology Analysis & Strategic Management* 10(1): 3–21.

Ansell, C. and Gash, A. 2008. 'Collaborative governance in theory and practice', *Journal of Public Administration Research and Theory* 18(4): 543–71.

Ashworth, R., Boyne, G. and Delbridge, R. 2009. 'Escape from the iron cage? Organizational change and isomorphic pressures in the public sector', *Journal of Public Administration Research and Theory* 19(1): 165–87.

Bason, C. 2010. *Leading Public Sector Innovation*. Bristol: Policy Press.

Behn, R. 2008. 'The adoption of innovation: The challenge of learning to adapt tacit knowledge', in S. Borins (ed.), *Innovations in Government: Research, Recognition and Replication*. Washington, DC: Brookings Institution Press, pp. 138–58.

Benington, J. and Moore, M. 2011. *Public Value: Theory and Practice*. Basingstoke: Palgrave.

Berman, P. and Nelson, B. 1997. 'Replication: Adapt or fail', in A. Altshuler and R. Behn (eds.), *Innovation in American Government*. Washington, DC: Brookings Institution Press, pp. 319–31.

Berry, F. and Berry, W. 2007. 'Innovation and diffusion models in policy research', in P. Sabatier (ed.), *Theories of the Policy Process*, 2nd edition. Boulder, CO: Westview, pp. 169–200.

Borins, S. 2014. *The Persistence of Innovation*. Washington, DC: Brookings Institution Press.

Buchanan, D. and Fitzgerald, L. 2007. 'The best practices puzzle: Why are new methods contained and not spread?' in D. Buchanan, L. Fitzgerald and D. Ketley (eds.), *The Sustainability and Spread of Organizational Change*. London: Routledge, pp. 41–60.

Chiva, R., Ghauri, P. and Alegre, J. 2013. 'Organizational learning, innovation and internationalization: A complex system model', *British Journal of Management* 25(4): 687–705.

Cohen, W. and Levinthal, D. 1990. 'Absorptive capacity: A new perspective on learning and innovation', *Administrative Science Quarterly* 35(1): 128–52.

Crouch, C. and Voelzkow, H. 2009. *Innovation in Local Economies*. Oxford: Oxford University Press.

Denis, J.-L., Hebert, Y., Langley, A., Lozeau, D. and Trottier, L. 2002. 'Explaining diffusion patterns for complex health care innovations', *Health Care Management Review* 27(3): 60–73.

DiMaggio, P. and Powell, W. 1983. 'The iron cage revisited: Institutional isomorphism and collective rationality in organizational fields', *American Sociological Review* 48(2): 147–60.

Dixon, N. 2000. *Common Knowledge: How Companies Thrive by Sharing What They Know*. Boston: Harvard Business School Press.

Downe, J, Hartley, J. and Rashman, L. (2004) 'Evaluating the extent of inter-organizational learning and change through the Beacon Council Scheme', *Public Management Review* 6: 531–53.

Ferlie, E., Fitzgerald, L., Wood, M. and Hawkins, C. 2005. 'The non-spread of innovations: The mediating role of professionals', *Academy of Management Journal* 48(1): 117–34.

Finger, M. and Brand, S. 1999. 'The concept of the "learning organization" applied to the transformation of the public sector', in M. Easterby-Smith, J. Burgoyne, and L. Araujo (eds.), *Organizational Learning and the Learning Organization. Developments in Theory and Practice*. London: Sage, pp. 130–56.

Fleck, J., Webster, J. and Williams, R. 1990. 'Dynamics of information technology implementation: A reassessment of paradigms and trajectories of development', *Futures* 22(6): 618–40.

Greenhalgh, T., Barton-Sweeney, C. and Macfarlane, F. 2013. 'Exploring the diffusion and sustainability of service innovation in healthcare', in S. Osborne and L. Brown (eds.), *Sage Handbook of Innovation in Public Services*. London: Sage, pp. 540–60.

Greenhalgh, T., Robert, G., Macfarlane, F., Bate, P., Kyriakidou, O. and Peacock, R. 2004. 'Diffusion of innovations in service organisations: Systematic literature review and recommendations for future research', *Milbank Quarterly* 82(4): 581–629.

2005. 'Storylines of research in diffusion of innovation: A meta-narrative approach to systematic review', *Social Science & Medicine* 61(2): 417–30.

Hargadon, A. 2005. 'Technology brokering and innovation: Linking strategy, practice, and people', *Strategy & Leadership* 33(1): 32–6.

Hartley, J. 2005. 'Innovation in governance and public services: Past and present', *Public Money and Management* 25(1): 27–34.

2013. 'Public and private features of innovation', in S. Osborne and L. Brown (eds.), *Sage Handbook of Innovation in Public Services*. London: Sage, pp. 44–59.

2014. 'Eight and a half propositions to stimulate frugal innovation', *Public Money and Management* 34(3): 227–32.

Hartley, J. and Benington, J. 2006. 'Copy and paste, or graft and transplant? Knowledge sharing through inter-organizational networks', *Public Money and Management* 26(2): 101–8.

Hartley, J. and Downe, J. (2007) 'The shining lights? Public service awards as an approach to service improvement', *Public Administration* 85(2): 329–353.

Hartley, J. and Rashman, L. 2007. 'How is knowledge transferred between organizations involved in change?' in M. Wallace, M. Fertig and E. Schneller (eds.), *Managing Change in the Public Services*. Oxford: Blackwell, pp. 173–92.

2010. 'The role of leadership in knowledge creation and transfer for organizational learning and improvement', in K. Walshe, G. Harvey and P. Jas (eds.), *From Knowing to Doing: Connecting Knowledge and Performance in Public Services*. Cambridge University Press, pp. 145–72.

2014. 'Population level learning', Paper presented at the IRSPM Conference, Ottawa, April.

Hartley, J., Sørensen, E. and Torfing, J. 2013. 'Collaborative innovation: A viable alternative to market-competition and organizational entrepreneurship', *Public Administration Review* 73(6): 821–30.

Hartley, J. and Torfing, J. 2016. 'Innovation', in C. Ansell and J. Torfing (eds.), *Handbook on Theories of Governance*. Cheltenham: Edward Elgar, pp. 236–244.

Hood, C. 1991. 'A public management for all seasons', *Public Administration* 69(1): 3–19

Kim, L. 1998. 'Crisis construction and organizational learning: Capability building in catching up at Hyundai motor', *Organization Science* 9(4): 506–21.

Koch, P. and Hauknes, J. 2005. *On Innovation in the Public Sector*. NIFU STEP: Oslo.

Lam, A. 2000. 'Tacit knowledge, organizational learning and societal institutions: An integrated framework', *Organization Studies* 21(3): 487–513.

Lewis, M. and Hartley, J. 2001. 'Evolving forms of quality management in local government: Lessons from the best value pilot programme', *Policy and Politics* 29(4): 477–96.

Lewis, M., Piercy, N., Phillips, W. and Palmer, J. 2015. 'Towards a model of the intervention process', *Policy & Politics* 43(2): 255–71.

Mazzucato, M. 2013. *The Entrepreneurial State*. London: Anthem Press.

Miner, A., Kim, J., Holzinger, I. and Haunschild, P. 1999. 'Fruits of failure: Organizational failure and population-level learning', *Advances in Strategic Management* 16: 187–220.

Mintrom, M. 1997. 'Policy entrepreneurs and the diffusion of innovation', *American Journal of Political Science* 41(3): 738–70.

Nonaka, I. 1994. 'A dynamic theory of organizational knowledge creation', *Organization Science* 5(1): 14–37.

Osborne, D. and Gaebler, T. 1992. *Reinventing Government*. Reading, MA: Addison-Wesley.

Osborne, S. and Brown, L. 2013. 'Risk and innovation: Towards a framework for risk, governance and public services', *Public Management Review* 15(2): 186–208.

Polanyi, M. 1967. *The Tacit Dimension*. New York: Anchor Books.

Polsby, N. 1984. *Political Innovation in America*. New Haven, CT: Yale University Press.

Rashman, L., Downe, J. and Hartley, J. 2005. 'Knowledge creation and transfer in the Beacon Scheme: Improving services through sharing good practice', *Local Government Studies* 31(5): 683–700.

Rashman, L. and Hartley, J. 2002. 'Leading and learning? Knowledge transfer in the Beacon Council Scheme', *Public Administration* 80(3): 523–42.

Rogers, E. 2003. *Diffusion of Innovations*. New York: The Free Press.

Scarbrough, H., Robertson, M. and Swan, J. 2015. 'Diffusion in the face of failure: the evolution of a management innovation', *British Journal of Management* 26(3): 365–87.

Shoeb, A. 2014. 'Diffusion of innovation', *International Journal of Advanced Research in Engineering and Science* 1(1): 1–8.

Sørensen, E. and Torfing, J. 2011. 'Enhancing collaborative innovation in the public sector', *Administration and Society* 43(8): 842–68.

Szulanski, G. 2003. *Sticky Knowledge: Barriers to Knowing in the Firm*. London: Sage.

Szulanski, G. and Winter, S. 2002. 'Getting it right the second time', *Harvard Business Review* 80(1): 62–9.

Van de Ven, A. 1986. 'Central problems in the management of innovation', *Management Science* 32(5): 590–607.

Walker, R., Avellaneda, C. and Berry, F. 2011. 'Exploring the diffusion of innovation among high and low innovative localities', *Public Management Review* 13(1): 95–125.

Wejnert, B. 2002. 'Integrating models of diffusion of innovations: A conceptual framework', *Annual Review of Sociology* 28: 297–326.

Westphal, J., Gulati, R. and Shortell, S. 1997. 'Customization or conformity? An institutional and network perspective on the content and consequences of TQM adoption', *Administrative Science Quarterly* 42(2): 366–94.

Windrum, P. 2008. 'Innovation and entrepreneurship in public services', in P. Windrum and P. Koch (eds.), *Innovation in Public Sector Services*. Cheltenham: Edward Elgar, pp. 3–20.

Wolfe, R. 1994. 'Organizational innovation: Review, critique, and suggested research directions', *Journal of Management Studies* 31(3): 405–31.

Zahra, S. and George, G. 2002. 'Absorptive capacity: A review, reconceptualization and extension', *Academy of Management Review* 27(2): 185–203.

Zaltman, G., Duncan, R. and Holbek, J. 1973. *Innovations and Organizations*. New York: Wiley.

Part II

Changing Roles of Public and Private Actors

6   Collaborative Innovation in the Public Sector

Eva Sørensen and Jacob Torfing

6.1   Introduction

There is a growing effort to spur innovation in the public sector (Borins 2001, 2014). To some people, this may come as a surprise since the competitive pressures on public organizations are still negligible, despite the recent efforts to spur the contracting out of public services. The drivers of public innovation apparently come from somewhere else than competition. Fiscal pressures, political aspirations, professional ambitions and public demands for solutions to the growing number of wicked and unruly problems seem to prompt innovation in the public sector in the face of weak competitive pressures. The efforts to spur public innovation are further encouraged by national policy makers and international organizations that tend to perceive innovation as the silver bullet that can improve the performance and quality of the public sector while cutting the costs (OECD 2014).

If political leaders, public managers and professionally trained public employees agree that public innovation is a favourable alternative to across-the-board cuts because it aims to give us 'more for less' instead of 'less for less', the question becomes how public innovation can be encouraged. A scan of the academic literature reveals a number of competing strategies for spurring public innovation. Some claim that public innovation is driven by scientific breakthroughs and new technologies (Dunleavy et al. 2006). Others have great faith in the entrepreneurship and innovative capacity of political leaders and public managers (Polsby 1984; Osborne and Gaebler 1993) or emphasize the role of service users and local communities as drivers of social innovation (Mulgan et al. 2007). Some scholars regard public procurement as a key driver of public innovation (Edquist and Zabala-Iturriagagotia 2012) and some policy makers call for a growing marketization of the public sector as way of enhancing innovation (European Union 2014). By contrast, other

The corresponding author for this chapter is Eva Sørensen.

researchers claim that competition stifles innovation (Lubienski 2003), and some see the creation of public value and public service motivation as the driver of innovation (Casebourne 2014). Last but not least, some organization theorists insist that stable bureaucratic procedures may help to ensure the exploration and exploitation of new ideas (March and Olsen 1995), whereas others believe that innovation mainly arises as a response to crises, disruptive events and external chocks (Levin and Sanger 1994).

This chapter takes a somewhat different stance as it aims to make the case for collaborative innovation. As such, it is argued that cross-cutting collaboration between public and private actors with different and complementary innovation assets is a potent lever of public innovation (Sørensen and Torfing 2011; Hartley, Sørensen and Torfing 2013). This does not mean that hierarchies and markets do not provide important drivers of public innovation. They most certainly do, as Lotte Bøgh Andersen's chapter in this volume clearly demonstrates. Hierarchical command and control systems enable executive public leaders to put innovation on the public sector agenda, mobilize resources to invest in new solutions, train middle managers in leading innovation, create task forces dedicated to innovation and monitor and reward innovation-enhancing performance of front-line personnel. The creation of quasi-markets in which public and private actors compete for public service contracts and are paid in accordance with the number of customers they attract also tend to force public leaders to create new and better services while reducing the costs by changing their organizational processes and design. However, as we shall see, the problem is that both hierarchically organized public bureaucracies and competing public and private contractors tend to produce innovation in-house and thus fail to tap into the experiences, resources, knowledge and ideas of relevant and affected actors (Hartley, Sørensen and Torfing 2013).

We boldly claim that there is a 'collaborative advantage' in the sense that collaboration is superior to both authority and competition when it comes to producing innovative solutions in the public sector (Sørensen and Torfing 2011), and we want to test our claim in and through a series of empirical case studies in the field of crime prevention. The empirical cases are critical because they belong to a policy area where collaborative innovation is unlikely to appear and succeed.

The chapter is structured in the following way. Section two compares bureaucracy, markets and networks as drivers of public innovation. Section three analyses the conditions for collaborative innovation in the public sector. Section four aims to illustrate and test the theoretical argument through an empirical comparison of Danish and North American cases of innovative crime prevention. Section five reflects on the implications of collaborative innovation for the role perceptions of public and private and the conclusion aims to draw out some of the consequences of collaborative innovation for the future organization and management of the public sector.

6.2   Collaborative Innovation: The Argument

Problems that are publicly recognized as manifest, sizeable, serious and enduring provide important stimuli for public innovation, especially if the problems are framed in ways that make them appear as a threat to core values, common societal goals and the cherished ways of social living. Some problems are simple and can be solved by relatively simple solutions. For example, traffic congestion in big cities can largely be solved by a combination of congestion charges, affordable public transport and bicycle lanes. Other problems are more complex but can still be solved by relatively simple means. For example, the shortage of higher education facilities in sparsely populated rural areas can be solved by creating online study programmes such as those offered by the British Open University, which provides online degree schemes. However, there seem to be a growing number of public problems that are wicked in the sense that they are complex, ill-defined and hard to solve (Koppenjan and Klijn 2004). Such problems can only be solved by thinking out of the box and crafting innovative solutions.

According to Rittel and Webber (1973), wicked problems are unique, multidimensional and tangled and, therefore, difficult to define and put a handle on. We can see that something is not working, or has a negative impact, but it is difficult to say exactly what the problem is because there is no way to tell what distinguishes an observed condition from a desired condition. Indeed, the problem is not fully understood until after the formulation of a solution. Even if we agree on a particular definition of the problem, it is often impossible to locate the root of the problem in the complex web of causalities that characterize open societal systems. Moreover, since there are no clear, objective and undisputed goals in public policy making, but merely a number of ambiguous, contradictory and changing objectives, there are no 'true' or 'optimal' solutions to wicked problems. Solutions can at best be judged as being satisfactory or acceptable. When searching for an acceptable solution, public authorities find it difficult to rely on processes of trial and error since the consequences of an error might do irreversible damage to users, citizens or private firms. There is neither an immediate nor an ultimate test of a solution to a wicked problem because undesirable future repercussions might outweigh the advantages achieved until now.

In addition to these cognitive aspects, there might also be some political aspects of wicked problems that make them unruly in the sense of being conflict-ridden and difficult to tackle through joint action. Political antagonisms between multiple stakeholders, a heavily discounted future, the misalignment of problem and political authority and the belief that solutions are unavailable, objectionable or too expensive might contribute to the creation of what is described as 'super wicked problems' (Lazarus 2009).

Hence, when we are facing wicked and unruly problems such as inner-city decay, negative social heritage, global warming or the lack of employment opportunities in the rural periphery, we need to find new ways of framing the problems and creative ways of solving them that can win political support. None of the known solutions will do, and increased public spending might be wasteful as long as there is no good, promising and acceptable solution in sight.

If wicked problems call for the crafting of innovative solutions, what is then the best strategy for enhancing innovation? Roberts (2000) has made a comparative assessment of authoritative, competitive and collaborative innovation strategies, which concludes that multi-actor collaboration is superior to both authority and competition. Authoritative strategies authorize a particular group of people on the basis of their formal position in the hierarchy, or access to scientific knowledge, to define the problem and produce a matching solution, but formal authorities and scientific experts are often mistaken about which solutions will work in practice and solve the problem. One reason for these frequent mistakes is that authoritative strategies fail to mobilize and exploit the cognitive resources of relevant and affected actors and build a joint ownership of the solution that they are proposing.

Competitive strategies solve this problem by engaging relevant stakeholders in a zero-sum game in which the winner takes all and eventually gets to define the problem and solution by resorting to an authoritative strategy. The advantage of this strategy is that the open competition between different groups and actors prompts the search for new and innovative solutions that challenges the traditional and dogmatic belief of the dominant power elite. However, the problem is that a lot of resources are wasted on conflicts and rivalry and the exchange of ideas among the competitors is obstructed or at least considered as irrational and counterproductive. This means that innovative solutions are often sub-optimal and the winner has over-invested in the race to be the first to cross the finishing line and, therefore, lacks resources to ensure the implementation of the innovative solution (see Teece 1992).

In contrast to both of these strategies, multi-actor collaboration permits the exchange of resources, knowledge and ideas between a broad range of public and private actors and thus facilitates mutual learning that helps improve the understanding of the problem and expand the range of feasible options (Roberts 2000; Weber and Khademian 2008). Collaboration also facilitates deliberation based on reason giving and a willingness to listen to each other and revise one's position in the course of interaction. Deliberation is important because it enables – but does not guarantee – the formation of political compromises that are based on mutual learning processes and challenge common wisdom and established practices.

Having established the basic argument in favour of a collaborative approach to public innovation, the next step is to get a full understanding of the collaborative advantage in different parts of the innovation process. Innovation is a complex, chaotic and non-linear process with frequent leaps, iterations and feedback loops (Van de Ven et al. 1999). Nevertheless, it is possible to identify some constitutive phases that all innovation processes must pass through at some point in order to develop, realize and diffuse new and creative solutions to merging or deep-seated problems. As such, innovation processes all seem to include phases of problem definition, idea generation, idea selection, implementation and diffusion.

Drawing on recent theories of collaboration, learning and creative problem-solving, we find that multi-actor collaboration strengthens and improves all the different phases in the innovation process. First, the definition and framing of problems and challenges is enhanced when public and private actors with different experiences, understandings and forms of knowledge engage in collective processes of reflection, sense-making and agenda setting (Koppenjan and Klijn 2004). Second, the generation of new and creative ideas is spurred when different ideas and suggestions are circulated, challenged, reformulated and integrated through processes of mutual, expansive and transformative learning (Engeström 1987; Mezirow 2000; Swan, Scarbrough and Robertson 2002; Gray and Ren 2014). Third, the selection and testing of the most promising ideas is improved when actors with different vantage points jointly assess the risks and benefits associated with different solutions, decide which risks they are willing to take in order to achieve particular benefits and adjust the preferred solution in and through iterative rounds of design, testing and redesign (Bason 2010; Brown and Osborne 2013). Fourth, the implementation of the new and bold solutions is enhanced by collaboration that facilitates the coordination of actions between actors in order to avoid overlaps and create synergies, the sharing of risks and benefits among the participants and the creation of a common ownership over new solutions in order to reduce implementation resistance

(Eggers and O'Leary 2009). Finally, the diffusion of innovative ideas and practices is propelled by the participation of a plethora of actors who can help to disseminate knowledge and information of the innovative solution through their social and professional networks (Rogers 1995). In sum, collaboration provides a potent method for developing, realizing and diffusing innovative solutions to wicked and unruly problems. It has been argued (Bommert 2010) that multi-actor collaboration is the only method in which it is not the presence of professional, organizational and institutional boundaries that decides who are involved in the production of innovation but rather the possession of relevant innovation assets such as knowledge, experience, ideas, creativity, formal authority, implementation capacity and a wide-ranging network.

The positive impact of collaboration on innovation is found not only in private firms (Powell and Grodal 2004) but also in public organizations and public governance (Roberts and Bradley 1991; Dente, Bobbio and Spada 2005; Steelman 2010; Ansell and Torfing 2014). Indeed, collaborative innovation seems to be on the rise. A recent study of American Government Innovation Awards applicants compares 2010 applicants to semi-finalists from 1990 to 1994 and finds that the proportion of innovation projects with inter-organizational collaboration has increased from 28 per cent to 65 per cent and the proportion of innovation projects with collaboration within government has increased from 21 per cent to 58 per cent (Borins 2014). A recent Danish study confirms the prevalence of collaborative innovation. A survey of 1,255 public organizations shows that eight out of ten innovations are a result of collaboration with other public organizations, civil society organizations, private firms, citizens and users (COI 2015).

6.3   The Conditions for Collaborative Innovation

Until now the notion of collaboration has been left largely undefined. We cannot venture into a lengthy discussion of competing theories of collaboration, but we would like to stress that collaboration does not necessarily involve tiresome and time-consuming attempts to secure unanimous consent to a particular solution. In fact, a total and all-encompassing consensus that eliminates dissent is often predicated on the actors' safe embrace of the least common denominator. Such a consensus will in most cases not be able to solve wicked and unruly problems and fail to bring about truly innovative solutions (Scharpf 1994).

In sharp contrast to the understanding of collaboration as the formation of unanimous consent (Straus 2002), collaboration will here be defined as a process through which multiple actors aim to find a common

ground for solving multi-party problems through a constructive management of difference (Gray 1989). We tend to collaborate with other actors
because they have resources, knowledge, views and ideas that differ from
our own but might help us to find an appropriate solution to the problem
or challenge at hand. Collaboration does not entail eliminating these
differences. It rather involves attempts to harness differences through
processes of cross-fertilizing and mutual learning that are based on deliberation, rivalry and agonistic respect. As such, we should not try to
eradicate or supress conflicts since, if properly managed, they can help
us to problematize conventional thinking and habitual practices and to
revise and sharpen new understandings and ideas. Hence, it is important
that conflicts are framed and regulated in ways that promote constructive
contestations rather than antagonistic clashes. When we are successful in
doing that, conflicts can help us to foster innovative solutions.

Constructive conflicts between interdependent actors are an inherent
part of multi-actor collaboration that provides a key driver of public innovation. However, in real life there is no guarantee that social and political
actors will want to collaborate when facing a problem or challenge in need
of an innovative solution. Strong and resourceful actors will sometimes be
tempted to adopt a 'go-it-alone strategy' that seeks to develop their own
innovative solution and impose it on other actors. This option will not only
tend to create a narrow-minded and partial solution to the problem but will
also generate externalities and conflicts that may be very costly and impede
its implementation and diffusion (Gray 1989). On the other hand, actors
with few resources, low self-esteem and a lack of trust in the responsiveness
of public authorities, or corporate actors, will view participation in collaborative governance as a waste of time and energy.

Spurring collaborative innovation requires more knowledge about why
and when social and political actors choose to collaborate in the search for
innovative solutions to wicked and unruly problems. Five factors affect
the adoption of a collaborative strategy to creative problem-solving. The
first factor concerns the structural conditions for collaboration (Gray
1989; Torfing et al. 2012). Collaboration provides the antidote to
increased political and socio-economic turbulence that tends to encourage people to enhance their collective capacity for responding to structural changes and mitigating their negative effects.

The second factor is the tradition for and experience with collaboration
that varies from country to country, between policy areas and over time
(Ansell and Gash 2008). Strong traditions and positive experiences will
stimulate collaboration and create a virtuous circle of collaboration, trust
building and the crafting of innovative solutions that are appreciated by
the collaborators if they help to solve the problem at hand.

The third factor is the existence of social capital in the sense of the contacts and connections that the actors have with other actors that they trust to be able to provide access to relevant resources (Putnam 2000). The more contacts and the more trust, the more likely it is that people will collaborate.

The fourth factor is the calculation of the individual actors as to whether they want to spend time and energy on collaboration with other actors. This calculation involves a series of judgements about whether the alternative to collaboration is acceptable, whether the other actors will want to collaborate and whether it is likely that the collaborative process will lead to a fair and positive solution (Gray 1989).

The last factor concerns the extent to which the potential collaborators are united by a particular discursive storyline that offers a captivating description of the joint mission or quest (Hajer 2009). A storyline offers a metaphorical description of the problem and the kind of solution that the actors should be looking for. The semantic ambiguity and multi-interpretability of such metaphors is vital for the ability to recruit a broad coalition of actors and to stimulate collaborative interaction.

Just as there is no guarantee that social and political actors will collaborate when they face problems and challenges calling for innovative solutions, collaboration does not always lead to innovation. Hence, collaboration may fail to foster innovation due to the presence of tunnel vision among participants who frequently work together and gradually develop a common world view that prevents them from seeing new and alternative solutions (Skilton and Dooley 2010). The actors may also fail to bridge their differences in norms, values and professional backgrounds and thus prevent mutual learning (Rogers 1995). A high degree of risk aversion among the actors (Koppenjan and Klijn 2004) and an unclear division of tasks and responsibilities in collaborative networks (O'Toole 1997) may hamper the implementation of new and bold solutions. Hence, translating collaboration into innovation requires careful efforts to disturb the actors and get them out of the complacency trap (Eggers and O'Leary 2009), define boundary objects (Engeström 1987, 2008), recruit boundary spanners (Williams 2012), facilitate cross-frame reflection (Koppenjan and Klijn 2004), facilitate the negotiation of risks and gains against each other (Brown and Osborne 2013) and connect creative designers with experienced implementers and integrate the design and implementation phase through an ongoing testing of prototypes (Roberts and King 1996).

In sum, contingent factors may impede collaboration and may prevent collaboration from producing innovative outcomes. However, the actors' recognition of their mutual dependence on the exchange of ideas and resources in order to solve complex but urgent problems provides a stronger driver for collaboration, and deliberate efforts of public leaders and managers to simulate creative problem-solving helps to drive collaborative innovation to a successful conclusion (Sørensen and Torfing 2011).

6.4   Empirical Evidence from Crime Prevention in Copenhagen and Oakland

Public security in general and crime prevention in particular provides an interesting testing ground for collaborative innovation in the public sector. In many large cities around the world, there has been an increasing focus on gang-related crime and violence, which is a wicked problem rooted in poverty, inner-city decay, lack of opportunities, failing ethnic integration, drugs sales, etc. The attempt to prevent gang-related crime calls for innovative measures, but the prospect for a collaborative approach to innovation appears to be limited. First, the 'securization' of public policy, which is at the heart of crime prevention, tends to foster secrecy and the concentration of power in the hand of executive agencies (Wæver 1995) and, second, the police – which is a pivotal actor in crime prevention – is characterized by bureaucratic command structures, red tape rules and silo thinking, and it has strong esprit de corps and a tendency to close ranks in the face of external pressures (Torfing and Krogh 2013). These two factors combine to restrict external collaboration with relevant public and private actors. As such, the attempt to prevent gang-related crime seems to provide a 'least likely' case of collaborative innovation, although the governance discourse is rapidly changing with the new emphasis on community policing (Borch 2005). Hence, if collaborative innovation is possible and plays a significant role in the attempt to enhance public security by reducing gang-related crime, there are good chances that it will work in other policy areas as well.

In order to test the relevance of collaborative innovation as a method for spurring the development of innovative solutions to wicked problems and explore the conditions for its success, we have recently (2010–12) conducted a comparative study of the local attempts to curb gang-related crime in the city of Oakland in California and the Danish capital Copenhagen. The cases are drawn from two liberal democracies that differ in terms of their public welfare systems, but both have relatively strong local governments, who are struggling with gang-related crime. Oakland has suffered from years of gang-related crime in the wake of deindustrialization, urban transformation, racism, rising poverty, and drug sales (Self 2003). The violence involved has cost hundreds of lives. When the funeral of a notorious gang member in the late 1990s gathered large crowds of citizens, the local government in Oakland decided that something had to be done. In 2004, it launched a new strategy named Measure Y that secured a considerable amount of special-purpose funding to boost community policing and initiate new preventive initiatives (see www.measurey.org and www.oaklandnet.com). In 1995–97, Copenhagen was the scene of a large-scale drug-related gang war. After a ceasefire in 1997 things calmed down, but in 2007, the gang war started again, this time involving new gangs consisting of either adults or youth and a growing number of immigrants from ghetto-like neighbourhoods. After a failed attempt to shoot gang members in a popular café in the centre of Copenhagen, the efforts to curb gang-related violence were enhanced and new preventive measures were launched (see www.kk.dk/da/om-kommunen/indsatsomraader-og-politikker/tryghed/sikker-by and www.dkr.dk/bandekriminalitet).

In our studies of crime prevention in Oakland and Copenhagen, we asked local stakeholders to identify new initiatives to reduce gang-related crime and ended up studying six new initiatives in Oakland and 14 in Copenhagen.[1] The initiatives were all more or less innovative, some of them resulting from creative inventions and others from the imitation of innovation projects from elsewhere. Apart from a few exceptions in Copenhagen, the innovative measures were results of multi-actor collaboration either between different public agencies in cross-cutting teams or among public and private actors in partnerships and networks.

Surprised by this empirical finding that clearly demonstrates the prospect of collaborative problem-solving in the area of crime prevention, we focused our attention on the conditions for collaborative innovation to emerge and have a positive impact in terms of contributing to the production of public value. In order to be able to meaningfully compare cases from Oakland and Copenhagen, we looked for matching cases and found two cases of innovative attempts to prevent recruitment to youth gangs by offering different kinds of leisure activities (Youth Uprising and the Resource Centre) and two cases of attempts to facilitate the exit of gang members from the criminal environment in which they are enmeshed (Call Ins and the Exit Strategy).

The efforts to prevent youth from joining gangs and getting gang members to exit their gang are hard to accomplish since criminal gangs tend to provide a lot of things that poor teenagers and adults in a deprived and dangerous neighbourhood find attractive: extra income through criminal activities, access to material goods such as cars, drugs and liquor,

[1] The cases are cases of crime prevention in the sense that they supplement the efforts of the police to put pressure on gang members through surveillance, arrest and imprisonment.

protection from other gangs, thrill and excitement, social identity and a sense of belonging and solidarity. When people first become part of a criminal gang, exiting is difficult because of the simultaneous loss of all these attractions and the fear of being punished by the gang (Jankowski 1991, 2008). The crime prevention projects have been analysed on the basis of a combination of qualitative interviews, document studies and participant observation that allows triangulation. The main findings from our studies are summarized in Table 6.1.

Youth Uprising in Oakland provides leisure activities for at-risk youth in a deprived neighbourhood to keep them off the streets and makes an innovative effort to recruit and train local youth to become future community leaders who can help to reduce gang-related crime by rebuilding

Table 6.1 *Stylized description of the four cases of crime prevention*

	Oakland	Copenhagen
Prevent entry to gangs	Case 1: Youth Uprising (2005–)	Case 2: Resource Centre (2009–)
	Purpose:	**Purpose:**
	Provide resources and competence-building to young people between 14 and 24 years in order to rebuild and transform a deprived neighbourhood with many at-risk youth	Provide attractive and educative leisure activities in an underserved, immigrant neighbourhood in order to keep kids and at-risk youth off the streets and out of gangs
	Innovative design:	**Innovative design:**
	The task is solved by addressing at-risk youth neither as passive recipients of services nor as problems to be solved but as assets for the transformation of the community. A local Youth Centre provides counselling, enhances skills and competences, offers jobs in social enterprises and develops youth leadership through special training programmes	The task is solved by creating a local Resource Centre run by a small staff that recruits and mobilizes local citizens and civil society organizations to organize leisure activities for the local at-risk youth. This creates a meeting not between the local youth and the public system, but between different generations of local citizens
	Participating actors:	**Participating actors:**
	The County, the Department of Health, the Department of Human Services, the director, a hand-picked youth team ('Rise up'), the Juvenile Justice Hall Wrap Around Project, non-profit and for-profit customers to the social enterprises, external board members and local youth in plenary meetings	The Mayor, the municipality of Copenhagen, Danish Red Cross, staff from the non-profit organization running the project, local citizens and civil society organizations, local shops and craftsmen, and local youth in the project's Youth Council

Table 6.1 (*cont.*)

	Oakland	Copenhagen
Facilitate exit from gangs	**Case 3: Call Ins (2006–)** **Purpose:** Provide incentives for local gang members to exit their criminal activities and stop the gang- and drug-related shootings that kill a lot of local citizens **Innovative design:** The task is solved by calling in a carefully targeted group of 15–20 young adults with a history of shooting to a meeting in which they are facing victims of shooting, hearing about the corrective measures of the police, and offered help to stop their criminal behaviour and get an education or a job and join different communal activities **Participating actors:** Mayor's Office, Oakland Police Department, Department of Human Services, Local Outreach Teams, Parole and Probation Department, drug addiction services, housing services, educational and employment services and local community organizations	**Case 4: Exit Strategy (2009–)** **Purpose:** Provide a fast, holistic and hand-held help to gang members who contact the municipality because they want to exit their gang and their criminal activities **Innovative design:** The task is solved by providing a tailor-made package of education, job, housing and perhaps even relocation that none of the traditional public agencies in the field have been able to provide. The project serves a group of criminal young adults over 18 years that has never before been targeted by preventive measures **Participating actors:** The Police, the Social Department, The Children and Youth Department, the Leisure and Culture Department, the Integration and Employment Department, the leader of the interdepartmental unit (SSP) and local politicians

the sense of community and solidarity. The director initially picked a handful of local youngsters to help design the Youth Centre, which works closely together with a variety of public departments in the city of Oakland, funding agencies at the County level, the Juvenile Hall Wrap Around project, which helps young people coming out of detention to integrate, and a variety of stakeholders represented in the board. The programme activates and trains at-risk youth and gives them their first job experience by employing them in a recently created social enterprise that solves a variety of tasks for local for-profit and non-profit customers. The youth are involved in decision making through regular meetings.

The *Resource Centre* in Copenhagen provides attractive and educative leisure activities to at-risk youth in an underserved part of the city. The

Mayor took the initiative to the project after a trip to Oslo where he and a group of local politicians and public managers saw a similar project run by the Norwegian Red Cross. Danish Red Cross helped to design the project, but a local non-profit organization got the contract to run the project and engaged a large number of local volunteers and civil society organizations in the project. This innovative design not only helps to ensure cost efficiency but also helps to provide a rich supply of activities for at-risk youth, empower local citizens and facilitate intergenerational communication. Local shops and craftsmen offer part-time jobs to some of the young people who want to earn some pocket money, and the youth coming to the Resource Centre elect representatives to a Youth Council, which has a small budget to organize trips and events.

Call Ins in Oakland is anchored in the Mayor's Office, the Oakland Police Department and the Department of Human Services. It aims to encourage local gang-members to exit their criminal activities and stop the gang- and drug-related shootings in their local neighbourhood. This is done by getting local outreach teams to carefully select a group of 15–20 gang members with a history of shooting and call them in for a joint meeting, if necessary, with the help of parole and probation officers. At the meeting, the gang members are confronted with horrifying stories from the victims of their shootings. The police tell them about how their activities are monitored and what punishment awaits them if they are caught in criminal activities. Finally, a variety of public agencies offer to help them out of addiction and into education and jobs, and local community organizations invite them to participate in communal activities. In sum, sticks and carrots are used to facilitate exit from gangs and criminal activities.

The *Exit Strategy* in Copenhagen is anchored in the secretariat of an interdepartmental crime prevention unit called SSP that brings together the police and four relevant municipal departments. The SSP unit normally works with youth under 18 years, and the activities include information and crime prevention campaigns and fast and holistic efforts to help at-risk youth who are in danger of becoming criminals or have already had an encounter with the police. However, the target group was recently enlarged to include young adults. Thus, when the police was approached by young gang members who wanted help to leave their gang, the SSP unit formed a small interdepartmental task force that together with local politicians developed the innovative Exit Strategy, which provides a new kind of hand-held service that offers education, jobs and, if necessary, physical relocation to gang members who want to quit their gang. Never before has such a hand-held service been provided to young criminal adults over 18 years.

Since the four cases of crime prevention provide good examples of collaborative innovation, we looked for the case-specific drivers of and

barriers to collaboration and innovation. The *drivers* of multi-actor collaboration were, first and foremost, the shared ambition to help at-risk
youth and improve urban safety and the mutual recognition that no social
or political actors could solve these tasks alone (cases 1, 2, 3 and 4). A
successful effort was also made to facilitate sharing of statistical and
personal data about offenders without the normal restrictions that helped
the projects on their way (cases 1, 3 and 4). In one of the cases, there was
already a well-established collaborative arena that enhanced trust and
facilitated joint action (case 4), while in the other cases sustained interaction helped to build trust and facilitate mutual appreciation of other
actors' ideas about and approaches to crime prevention (cases 1, 2 and 3).
Collaboration at the lower levels was in some cases encouraged by the fact
that that top managers in different public departments and organizations
clearly signalled their commitment to interdepartmental collaboration
(cases 3 and 4). Last but not least, some interviewees reported that a
new generation of externally recruited leaders and managers in the police
department seem to be more open to collaborative problem solving than
previous generations (cases 2 and 4).

A key driver of innovation was that potential users in terms of at-risk
youth and young adults in some cases clearly identified their needs and
also proposed new types of service (cases 3 and 4). Availability of grants
and other types of special-purpose funding that top up existing public
service budgets also helped to lower the transaction costs of collaborating
and made it possible to invest in new and innovative initiatives and
services (cases 1, 2 and 3). We also learned that the police and other
public agencies have started to take a more problem-driven approach in
their attempt to improve performance and also use elements of design
thinking in their work (cases 1 and 4). Reports from visits to innovative
projects in other locations provided inspiration and seem to have propelled the adoption and adaption of new and innovative ideas (cases 2
and 3). Last but not least, local citizens and community organizations
appear to be willing to contribute to the development and implementation of innovative solutions when called upon (cases 2 and 3).

The case studies also revealed a number of *barriers* to both collaboration
and innovation. Hence, in two of the four cases collaboration is limited by
the fact that the targeted gang members were not involved in the design of
the innovative solution because they were regarded as criminals and, therefore, could not be a part of the collaborative governance process (cases 3
and 4). There are also frequent reports that public departments and
organizations are dominated by professionally trained public employees
whose different views, methods, ideas and priorities make it difficult to
collaborate (cases 1, 3 and 4). In one case, collaboration was impeded by

the lack in trust in the police due to some recent incidents of violent law enforcement (case 3). Finally, there are complaints that civil society organizations just want to continue to to do 'their thing' and thus are not always keen to collaborate and innovate (cases 2, 3 and 4).

The barriers to innovation mainly relate to funding and the inability to 'think outside the box'. Hence, at various points slippage in special-purpose funding streams threatened to close down the innovative projects (cases 1, 2 and 3). While the special-purpose funding became subject to political controversy in Oakland, it was the persistent pressure to free money for the funding of new innovations that threatened the survival of a successful innovation in Copenhagen (case 2). However, the local actors in both Oakland and Copenhagen believe that, generally, there is plenty of money for crime prevention and a huge number of public and private actors. However, some actors are more innovative than others. Thus, in one case, the organized stakeholders that constituted the 'usual suspects' are accused of suffering from tunnel vision as they fail to come up with new ideas in brainstorm meetings (case 1). Instead the project leader recruited and trained a team of local youth that helped to design the innovative solution.

In sum, there were both important drivers of collaborative innovation in the four cases and a number of barriers that threatened to jeopardize the process but, for the most part, were mitigated or overcome by the involved actors.

6.5   Improving the Conditions for Collaborative Innovation

The empirical case analysis gives us a more precise idea of what collaborative innovation looks like in practice. It also reveals the importance of the specific conditions for bringing different actors together, triggering collaboration and translating collaboration into new and innovative solutions. One of the key conditions for engaging relevant and affected actors in collaborative processes is their recognition of their mutual dependency. In all four cases, the participating actors realized that they could not solve the problem alone but needed to collaborate in order to exchange resources, competences and knowledge and learn from each other's experiences, views and ideas. However, the way that social and political actors perceive their role and identity may sometimes prevent them from engaging in collaborative processes, despite their recognition of mutual dependence. As such, the future expansion of collaborative innovation hinges on a recasting of the roles and identity of the actors in order to make the actors more inclined to collaborate with other actors. The relevant actors differ from case to case, but let us briefly consider the rearticulation of the roles of the actors who typically are involved in collaborative efforts to spur public innovation.

Politicians tend to see themselves as sovereign decision makers who have all the power and all the responsibility, but in order to engage in collaborative policy innovation they need to perceive themselves as organic political leaders who involve public as well as private stakeholders in defining political problems and developing new solutions (Sørensen and Torfing 2016).

Public managers have in many decades been trained and encouraged to focus their attention on the resource consumption and performance of their agency or department and to take responsibility for the strategic development of their own organization, programmes and services. In order to promote collaboration they need to see themselves both as distributive leaders who facilitate the involvement of middle managers and staff in self-regulating teams (Pearce and Conger 2003; Parry and Bryman 2006) and as collaborative and integrative leaders who appreciate and play an active role in orchestrating inter-organizational and cross-sectorial interaction (Ansell and Gash 2008; Archer and Cameron 2008; Crosby and Bryson 2010).

Public employees with a professional education as doctors, nurses or school teachers tend to perceive themselves as experts with a privileged knowledge of what good service quality is, and they will have to transform their self-perception and view themselves as facilitators, translators and mediators between, on the one hand, politicians and public managers and, on the other hand, the users of public services (Williams 2012).

Interest organizations that primarily define themselves as pressure groups and lobbyists pursuing their own narrow interest will have to perceive themselves as co-creators of innovative solutions to common problems that neither private organizations nor public agencies can solve alone and therefore require some kind of collective entrepreneurship (Roberts and King 1996).

Private firms that have been cast in the role of suppliers and contractors in newly created quasi-markets, characterized by fierce rivalry, need to develop a new identity as partners engaged in processes of knowledge sharing and mutual learning, for example, in and through public–private innovation partnerships (Bloomfield, Westerling and Carey 1998).

Last but not least, *citizens* who have been on a long journey from 'clients' to 'customers' need to adopt a new role and identity as active citizens who have the right and obligation to participate in the production and delivery of services to themselves and to other citizens as volunteers (Gaventa 2002). The recent customization of citizens and users means that they become more demanding and complaining and that they tend to think they have a right to receive top-quality solutions without themselves having to contribute anything.

The development of new collaborative roles and identities will take some time, but it is a part of a 'cultural revolution' that aims to blur the organizational boundaries between public agencies and departments as well as the institutional boundaries between state and society in order to mobilize and merge the capacities, resources and ideas of relevant and affected actors. The agencification of the public sector and the reduction of public and private agencies to competing providers of services, which are distributed to citizens through the newly created welfare markets, tend to keep apart those actors who can help the public sector to benefit from collaborative innovation. Fortunately, new forms of collaborative governance are developing that bring together public and private actors in collaborative processes that can enhance innovation.

Fostering collaboration and translating it into public innovation pose a considerable challenge for public leaders and managers (Hartley, Sørensen and Torfing 2013). This is confirmed by our empirical study of the four cases of crime prevention that all show that collaborative innovation is predicated on the presence of sponsors, conveners and facilitators. The sponsors provide opportunities, resources and encouragement, and they help to remove red tape and secure political support to the collaborative endeavour. The conveners recruit, motivate and empower public and private actors, who may contribute to creative problem-solving. They provide information about the purpose and process of collaboration, and they cover the initial costs of collaborating in terms of providing a venue for meeting and an infrastructure for communication. Lastly, the facilitators spur collaboration by aligning interests, creating a common frame of reference and mediating conflicts. They also play a key role in coordinating action in the implementation phase.

Assembling all the relevant actors and getting them to collaborate only bring us halfway to collaborative innovation. To go all the way, public leaders and managers are faced with the task of catalysing innovation by constructing a sense of urgency, bringing the actors out of their comfort zone, encouraging them to experiment and take risks and securing implementation, consolidation and upscaling of innovative designs that seem to work and produce desirable effects.

Leading and managing innovation requires the ability to govern processes that trigger the future emergence of new and path-breaking solutions. The task of governing the future emergence of new and bold solutions breaks with the backward-looking focus of leaders and managers in the New Public Management era where focus was on minimizing inputs in terms of public expenditure and maximizing outputs in terms of performance. In order to stimulate public innovation, public leaders and managers must shift the focus from input and output to process and outcomes (Osborne 2006, 2010). Hence, the challenge is not merely to cut slack, but to use slack to create collaborative processes that enhance innovation through a collective entrepreneurship. As shown in Chapter 1 and further discussed in Chapter 3, the chance that this challenge will be met is likely to increase if the public sector shifts the balance from New Public Management to New Public Governance.

6.6   Conclusion

This chapter aimed to deepen our understanding of interactive forms of governance by showing that collaborative interaction in networks and partnerships can spur public innovation. As we have seen, collaborative innovation provides a potent tool for solving wicked and unruly problems by stimulating the development and realization of innovative solutions. Collaboration can strengthen all the constitutive phases of the innovation process by bringing new and relevant experiences, competences, ideas and assessments to the table. The chapter has shown the obstacles that must be mitigated or overcome and drivers that must be fully exploited in order to facilitate collaborative innovation and secure desirable outcomes. The theoretical arguments in support of collaborative innovation have been illustrated and tested in an empirical analysis of cases of crime prevention in Oakland and Copenhagen. The analysis demonstrates the viability of processes of collaborative innovation in an area that initially was expected to be hostile to such processes. This increases the likelihood that collaborative innovation has a general applicability in the public sector. If it works in the area of public security, it can work in many other policy sectors too. The fact that the cases are drawn from countries with different welfare systems gives reason to believe that collaborative innovation is a strategy that will work in other liberal democracies as well.

However, more than anything the empirical study reveals contingent conditions that may drive or hamper collaborative innovation. Identifying the necessary and sufficient conditions for collaborative innovation, calls for the collection of a repository of case studies from different countries and policy areas and engagement that lays the ground for systematic comparisons of cases of collaborative innovation. Such comparison will improve our understanding of the conditions of possibility for collaborative innovation and the role that public leaders and managers may play in shaping these conditions.

We have focused exclusively on collaborative innovation in this chapter, but we should not forget that there are many roads to public innovation.

Not only hierarchy and markets but also chance discoveries, organizational learning and social entrepreneurship can enhance innovations (Roberts and King 1996). Nevertheless, as we have aimed to demonstrate, there are strong reasons to expect collaboration to be a superior, yet under-explored and underexploited method for enhancing public innovation.

References

Ansell, C. and Gash, A. 2008. 'Collaborative governance in theory and practice', *Journal of Public Administration Research and Theory* 18(4): 543–71.

Ansell, C. and Torfing, J. (eds.) 2014. *Public Innovation through Collaboration and Design*. Abingdon: Routledge.

Archer, D. and Cameron, A. 2008. *Collaborative Leadership: How to Succeed in an Interconnected World*. Oxford: Elsevier.

Bason, C. 2010. *Leading Public Sector Innovation*. Bristol: The Policy Press.

Bloomfield, P., Westerling, D. and Carey, R. 1998. 'Innovation and risk in a public-private partnership', *Public Productivity and Management Review* 21(4): 460–71.

Bommert, B. 2010. 'Collaborative innovation in the public sector', *International Public Management Review* 11(1): 15–33.

Borch, C. 2005. *Kriminalitet og magt*. Copenhagen: Politisk Revy.

Borins, S. 2001. 'Encouraging innovation in the public sector', *Journal of Intellectual Capital* 2(3): 310–9.

  2014. *The Persistence of Innovation in Government: A Guide for Public Servants*. Washington, DC: IBM Center for the Business of Government.

Brown, L. and Osborne, S. 2013. 'Risk and innovation: Towards a framework for risk governance in public services', *Public Management Review* 15(2): 186–208.

Casebourne, J. 2014. *Why Motivation Matters in Public Sector Innovation*. London: NESTA.

COI. 2015. *Innovationsbarometer*. Copenhagen: COI Publications.

Crosby, B. and Bryson, J. 2010. 'Integrative leadership and the creation and maintenance of cross-sector collaboration', *Leadership Quarterly* 21(2): 211–30.

Dente, B., Bobbio, L. and Spada, A. 2005. 'Government or governance of urban innovation?' *DIPS* 162: 1–22.

Dunleavy, P., Margetts, H., Bastow, S. and Tinkler, J. 2006. 'New public management is dead – long live digital-era governance', *Journal of Public Administration Research and Theory* 16(3): 467–94.

Edquist, C. and Zabala-Iturriagagotia, J. M. 2012. 'Public procurement for innovation as mission-oriented innovation policy', *Research Policy* 41(10): 1757–69.

Eggers, W. D. and O'Leary, J. 2009. *If We Can Put a Man on the Moon: Getting Big Things Done in Government*. Boston: Harvard Business Press.

Engeström, Y. 1987. *Learning by Expanding: An Activity-Theoretical Approach to Developmental Research.* Helsinki: Orienta-Konsultit.

2008. *From Teams to Knots: Activity-Theoretical Studies of Collaboration and Learning at Work.* New York, NY: Cambridge University Press.

European Union. 2014. *Public Procurement as a Driver of Innovation in SMEs and Public Services.* Brussels: The European Union.

Gaventa, J. 2002. 'Introduction: Exploring citizenship, participation and accountability', *IDS Bulletin* 33(2): 1–11.

Gray, B. 1989. *Collaborating: Finding Common Ground for Multiparty Problems.* San Francisco: Jossey-Bass.

Gray, B. and Ren, H. 2014. 'The importance of joint schemes and brokers in promoting collaboration for innovation', in C. Ansell and J. Torfing (eds.), *Public Innovation through Collaboration and Design*, Abingdon: Routledge, pp. 125–147.

Hajer, M. 2009. *Authoritative Governance.* Oxford: Oxford University Press.

Hartley, J., Sørensen, E. and Torfing, J. 2013. 'Collaborative innovation: A viable alternative to market competition and organizational entrepreneurship', *Public Administration Review* 73(6): 821–30.

Jankowski, M. S. 1991. *Islands in the Street: Gangs and American Urban Society.* Berkeley: University of California Press.

2008. *Cracks in the Pavement.* Berkeley: University of California Press.

Koppenjan, J. F. M. and Klijn, E. H. 2004. *Managing Uncertainties in Networks.* Abingdon: Routledge.

Kraemer, K. L. and Perry, J. L. 1989. 'Innovation and computing in the public sector: A review of research', *Knowledge in Society* 2(1): 72–87.

Lazarus, R. J. 2009. 'Super wicked problems and climate change: Restraining the present to liberate the future', *Cornell Law Review* 94(5): 1153–233.

Levin, M. A. and Sanger, M. B. 1994. *Making Government Work: How Entrepreneurial Executives Turn Bright Ideas into Real Results.* San Francisco, CA: Jossey-Bass.

Lubienski, C. 2003. 'Innovation in education markets: Theory and evidence on the impact of competition and choice in charter schools', *American Educational Research Journal* 40(2): 395–443.

March, J. G. and Olsen, J. P. 1995. *Democratic Governance.* New York: Free Press.

Mezirow, J. 2000. *Learning as Transformation: Critical Perspectives on a Theory in Progress.* San Francisco, CA: Jossey Bass.

Mulgan G., Tucker S., Rushanara A. and Sanders B. 2007. 'Social innovation: What it is, why it matters and how it can be accelerated', Working Paper, Skoll Center for Social Entrepreneurship, Oxford Business School.

OECD. 2014. *Innovating the Public Sector: From Ideas to Impact.* Paris: OECD Publications.

Osborne, D. and Gaebler, T. 1993. *Reinventing Government: How the Entrepreneurial Spirit is Transforming the Public Sector.* Reading, MA: Addison-Wesley.

Osborne, S. 2006. 'The New Public Governance?' *Public Management Review* 8(3): 377–88.

Osborne, S. (ed.) 2010. *The New Public Governance?* London: Routledge.

O'Toole, L. J. 1997. 'Implementing public innovations in network settings', *Administration and Society* 29(2): 115–38.

Parry, K. W. and Bryman, A. 2006. 'Leadership in organizations', in S. Clegg, C. Hardy, T. Lawrence and W. Nord (eds.), *The Sage Handbook of Organization Studies*. London: Sage Publications, pp. 447–68.

Pearce, C. L. and Conger, J. A. 2003. *Shared Leadership: Reframing the Hows and Whys of Leadership*. London: Sage.

Polsby, N. W. 1984. *Political Innovation in America: The Politics of Policy Initiation*. New Haven, CT: Yale University Press.

Powell, W. W. and Grodal, S. 2004. 'Networks of innovators', in J. Fagerberg, D. C. Mowery and R. R. Nelson (eds.), *The Oxford Handbook of Innovation*. Oxford University Press, pp. 56–85.

Putnam, R. D. 2000. *Bowling Alone: The Collapse and Revival of American Community*. New York: Simon and Schuster.

Rittel, H. W. J. and Webber, M. M. 1973. 'Dilemmas in a general theory of planning', *Policy Sciences* 4(2): 155–69.

Roberts, N. C. 2000. 'Wicked problems and network approaches to resolution', *International Public Management Review* 1(1): 1–19.

Roberts, N. C. and Bradley, R. T. 1991. 'Stakeholder collaboration and innovation', *Journal of Applied Behavioural Science* 27(2): 209–27.

Roberts, N. C. and King, P. J. 1996. *Transforming Public Policy: Dynamics of Policy Entrepreneurship and Innovation*. San Francisco, CA: Jossey-Bass.

Rogers, E. M. 1995. *Diffusion of Innovations*. New York: The Free Press.

Scharpf, F. W. 1994. 'Games real actors could play: Positive and negative coordination in embedded negotiations', *Journal of Theoretical Politics* 6(1): 27–53.

Self, R. O. 2003. *American Babylon*. Princeton: Princeton University Press.

Skilton, P. F. and Dooley, K. 2010. 'The effects of repeat collaboration on creative abrasion', *The Academy of Management Review* 35(1): 118–34.

Steelman, T. A. 2010. *Implementing Innovation*. Washington, DC: Georgetown University Press.

Straus, D. 2002. *How to Make Collaboration Work*. San Francisco, CA: Berrett-Koehler Publishers.

Swan, J., Scarbrough, H. and Robertson, M. 2002. 'The construction of communities of practice in the management of innovations', *Management and Learning* 33(4): 477–96.

Sørensen, E. and Torfing, J. 2011. 'Enhancing collaborative innovation in the public sector', *Administration and Society* 43(8): 842–68.
  2016. 'Political leadership in the age of interactive governance: Reflections on the political aspects of metagovernance', in J. Edelenbos and Meerkerk, I. (eds.), *Critical Reflections on Interactive Governance*. Cheltenham: Edgar Elgar, forthcoming.

Teece, D. J. 1992. 'Competition, cooperation and innovation', *Journal of Economic Behavior and Organization* 18(1): 1–25.

Torfing, J. and Krogh, A. H. 2013. *Samarbejdsdrevet innovation i bandeindsatsen*. Copenhagen: DJOEF Publishers.

Torfing, J., Peters, B. G., Pierre, J. and Sørensen, E. 2012. *Interactive Governance: Advancing the Paradigm*. Oxford: Oxford University Press.

Van de Ven, A., Polley, D., Garud, R., and Venkataraman, S. 1999. *The Innovation Journey*. Oxford: Oxford University Press.

Weber, E. P. and Khademian, A. M. 2008. 'Wicked problems, knowledge challenges, and collaborative capacity builders in network settings', *Public Administration Review* 68(2): 334–49.

Williams, P. 2012. *Collaboration in Public Policy and Practice: Perspectives on Boundary Spanners*. Bristol: Policy Press.

Wæver, O. 1995. 'Securitization and desecuritization', in R. Lipschutz (ed.), *On Security*. New York: Columbia University Press, pp. 46–86.

7   Public Managers and Professionals in Collaborative Innovation

Victor Bekkers and Mirko Noordegraaf

7.1   Introduction

Innovation is a recurring 'magic concept' in the public sector (Bekkers, Edelenbos and Steijn 2011). A magic concept inspires not only policy makers and politicians but also the general public. Such a concept creates a perspective on change – a perspective which is rather open so that it allows to encompass a variety of manifestations that all embrace the promise that 'transformation' or 'radical change' will happen (Pollitt and Hupe 2011). Very often, the innovations that organizations pursue are perceived as a possible 'game changer', fundamentally altering the role and position of and relation between relevant stakeholders.

During the last five years, innovation in the public sector has been linked to several developments. First, innovation is considered to be vital in order to strengthen the responsiveness and effectiveness of public sector organizations. This can be achieved by really addressing the needs of end-users, given all kinds of societal challenges like the ageing of the population, rising youth unemployment or climate change. End-users might be citizens, but they might also be street-level bureaucrats and public professionals who are confronted with all kinds of pressing and dynamic needs. Second, innovation is considered as a reform strategy that is necessary to legitimize the retreat of government, especially in relation to the emergence of new welfare state arrangements and public health provisions and services that try to fill the gaps that are the result of this retreat. A retreat that opens the door to the development of new governance arrangements that make use of self-organizing capacities of citizens and all kinds of 'grass-roots organizations'. Third, we see that new social practices emerge, also acting as potential 'game changers', in the

The corresponding author for this chapter is Victor Bekkers.
Dr Victor Bekkers is Full Professor of Public Administration at Erasmus University Rotterdam, the Netherlands. Dr Mirko Noordegraaf is Full Professor of Public Management at the Utrecht School of Governance, Utrecht University, the Netherlands.

slipstream of the development of new technologies, such as social media and mobile internet technologies. Fourth, these innovations touch upon the positions, views, interests and domains of many actors as stakeholders of innovation processes.

As a result, innovation – in both public and private sectors – can be seen as the outcome of a process of a exploration and exploitation that is based on collaboration in which ideas, views, experience, knowledge and other resources are shared in order to meet specific challenges. In collaborative innovation, each of these stakeholders is affected, *and* their relations change. The promises of innovation can only be met when multiple actors are connected in new ways, when they collaborate more than they used to do and when their (inter)actions are related to external pressures, needs and demands.

In this chapter, we pay attention to the ways in which two distinctive stakeholders are affected by the rise of innovation: public *managers* and public *professionals*; we analyse their roles and the interplay between them in innovation processes. Public professionals and public managers play a vital role in the innovation of the content, course and outcome of public services. Their interplay very often influences the specific outcomes of public service innovation, also in relation to efficiency, effectiveness and legitimacy (e.g. Noordegraaf 2015a).

We first sketch two models of innovation that can be witnessed in the public sector. These models are 'ideal types', although rooted in empirical findings. In the first model, public innovation is seen as a matter of intended innovation that occurs by initiating top-down actions, backed by strategic agendas. We call this *enforced* innovation. In the second model, public innovation is an emergent activity that occurs by starting from bottom-up actions and organically embedding innovation in work routines, procedures and process, backed by service and client interests. We call this *free* innovation. Next, we analyse the implications of these modes of innovation for both managers and professionals, and their relations. We show how both managers and professionals have become part of collaborative networks in which management and professional logics interact. We argue that the two ideal-types fall short in capturing these dynamics. Instead of emphasizing either 'enforced' or 'free' innovation, we focus on two alternative forms of public innovation, in which managerial and professional logics are interwoven: *guided* and *focused* innovation. Instead of assuming that managerial and professional logics are either 'tightly' or 'loosely' coupled (e.g. Weick 1976; Orton and Weick 1990), as is the case in enforced versus free innovation, we sketch the possibility of 'selective' and 'strong couplings' in which both managers and professionals are important for the success of 'magic' innovation ambitions. Finally, we draw conclusions and we sketch ways forward. We especially discuss how guided and focused innovation can be strengthened *and* how both managers and professionals can be equipped to stimulate viable collaborative innovation.

7.2   Two Models of Innovation

If we explore the ways in which the public sector organizes and manages innovation, two well-known models can be distinguished. In the first model, innovation is viewed as an intended management activity that is backed by strategic agendas. In the second model, innovation is an emergent activity that is rooted in daily work processes, tied to service and client interests. Before we describe these models in the following subsections, one remark on the nature of public services and professionals should be made. Beneath, we treat this in a rather generic way: we speak about services and professionals in rather general ways. When the models are applied to more specific situations, we have to be careful, as services and professionals differ in terms of strength and nature. First and foremost, services depend in terms of their 'publicness' (e.g. Bozeman 1987; Noordegraaf 2015a). They might be part of the state, such as police services, or organized outside the state, such as hospitals or schools. This has strong effects on innovation processes as institutional conditions affect how steering, financing and accounting for innovation might take place. Furthermore, there might be various types of professionals working in and around these services. There are classic or 'pure' professionals (cf. Noordegraaf 2007) like medical doctors, who have lots of institutional autonomy. They are part of strong professions that regulate entrance, education and occupational practices. There are also semi-level, street-level and welfare state professionals (cf. Noordegraaf 2015a; also see e.g. Lipsky 1980) who have less autonomy and are more bound to organizational and welfare state contexts, such as nurses, policemen, teachers and social workers. When they work in state-based organizations, such as welfare organizations, they are more street-level or welfare bureaucrats than 'professionals'. Although we do not really pay attention to these differences, we return to it later, as it affects the applicability of the models we identify. When professionals are 'pure' it will be more difficult to tie them into innovation networks and link them to innovation agendas. When they are less pure, it will be easier to either 'control' them *or* to seek more subtle ways to combine organizational and 'professional' actions. To turn it into a more generic point again, because professionalism throughout public domains becomes less pure and more 'hybrid' (cf. Noordegraaf 2007, 2015b), the latter possibility is more relevant than ever.

7.2.1   Enforced Innovation (Intended, Top-Down)

Innovation is a topic that has systematically been given attention in many policy sectors. Let us begin with three (Dutch) examples. In the Netherlands, the attention of innovation has been organized through special programmes and special projects. In the educational sector, a special law has been implemented which tries to facilitate experiments with new educational practices, thereby bypassing specific educational norms that normally have to be fulfilled.[1] These experiments are focused to assess if specific innovations really work. Questions that have to be answered relate to the following issues: Do they really matter? Do they really make a difference? What are positive and negative effects and side effects? Furthermore, if schools want to implement specific innovations they can hire specific support and advice. Moreover, innovation processes are also supported by a number of portals that are set up. These portals help to access relevant knowledge about what is going on and what are the relevant effects of specific innovations and experiments, as well as to help connect people to other relevant people and organizations.

Another example is the Health Care Innovation Forum (in Dutch: 'Zorg Innovatie Forum'[2]). This forum is a network organization which wants to improve innovation and reform in the health-care sector through the development of a shared vision. It also wants to set up collaboration arrangements in order to tackle the fragmentation of all kinds of innovation efforts in the health sector. The forum wants to set up innovative projects which are worked out in business cases. It tries to scan possible chances, invites experts and market parties to participate and tries to coordinate and monitor the activities that are taking place.

Last but not least the Dutch police have paid attention to the role of innovation in their newly established national police organization. With the creation of a national police force in 2013, a process of centralization and standardization ended, in which fairly autonomous regional police forces were integrated in one national organization.[3] When looking at the role of innovation into the organization plan of the national police, we see that innovation is primarily perceived as change that comes from outside

---

[1] For an overview, see www.rijksoverheid.nl/onderwerpen/innovatie-in-het-onderwijs/stimuleren-innovatie.
[2] For an overview, see www.zorginnovatieforum.nl.
[3] See draft Design plan ['Concept Inrichtingsplan Nationale politie'], 25 June 2012, pp. 64–65.

the organization and that is based on the adoption of new technologies and new knowledge. These new technologies are seen as possible sources of uncertainty and risk that have to be managed. Not every innovation leads to an improvement in the quality of the working processes. Innovation is seen as the outcome of specific strategic, policy and technologically funded considerations that are formulated to establish the ambitions of the national police. The police argue that innovation management is a challenge for the police that can only be managed in a 'top-down manner', while quality improvements in working processes are seen as the outcome of bottom-up process. Furthermore, the Dutch national police also see innovation as the result of a vision of specific societal developments as well as of how the police should develop itself. The board of the national police tries to manage (technological) innovation in such a way that it really leads to innovation in the working processes of the police as well as to an improvement in the goal efficacy of police activities. This is being achieved through planning, prioritizing and budgeting of the innovation efforts. Such a systematic approach helps to reduce all kinds of potential risks. It also helps to improve the goal efficacy of the national police. In order to be aware of what relevant innovations might be available, it is important that the technological environment of the police is scanned systematically so that the possible added value of innovative concepts and technological applications can be explored.

These three examples show that innovation is something that can be 'created'. It is something that systematically can be organized into an organization or into a policy sector. As such innovation is an organized activity, as an intended activity that is consciously formed and implemented. In doing so, resources can be spent to develop and diffuse innovations. More specifically, three forms of enforced innovation can be distinguished:

a. Innovation in terms of facilitating local initiatives and experiments and sharing the knowledge that is gained in these experiments. The innovation programme in the educational sector illustrates this.

b. Innovation in terms of creating collaborative innovation networks in which a shared vision is developed in order to develop projects that are in the common interests of relevant partners. The Health Care Innovation Forum illustrates this. Innovation management is primarily seen as connecting people, organizations, ideas and practices but also funds. The forum is not only a meeting place, it is also a broker.

c. Innovation as a top-down management activity. Innovation is something that can be planned and can be steered from a central position in the organization. Innovation is a question of selection and choice. In order to do so it is necessary that the top of the organization has a vision on the organization, knows what is happening outside the organization in terms of possible new knowledge and technologies that can be adopted and knows what the possible risks of the innovation are. These two considerations in combination with the willingness to allocate budgets for innovation, help to systematically manage the introduction of innovation. This view comes forward in the Dutch police example.

Looking at the three examples of public innovation management, we see that in all the three forms of innovation management a rather rational perspective on innovation prevails, although the emphasis differs. In the first one, the idea is to steer innovation by making use of a number of incentives which help to seduce possible innovators or adopters of an innovation to start, e.g. by helping them to acquire specific funds or to overcome specific legal barriers, or by making knowledge accessible. These incentives are focused on changing the cost–benefit ratio. In the second one, we see that innovation is organized on the basis of a market-model of collaboration in which demand and supply are linked to each other. The forum in the health sector is a place that brings together innovation producers or owners of solutions on the one hand and possible users and problem-owners on the other hand. If these parties find each other, innovations can occur. In the third model, innovation is seen from a rational command and control perspective in which boards, executives and managers are able to steer innovation.

It is also interesting to focus on the sources of innovation. In each of the cases, innovation is closely linked to new knowledge-based concepts and technologies. As a result innovation management is primarily seen as being able to link to the needs of schools, hospitals or the police to these resources in order to exploit them. This is visible not only in the police example but also in the education example. These needs seem to be formulated at the organizational level: what does a school, a hospital or the police need?

Besides, it can be argued – clearly expressed in the police example – that the needs of the organization are closely linked to the goals of the organization. Innovation is very often seen as a way of achieving these goals in a more effective, efficient or more coherent way. As such it can be argued, following March and Olsen (1989), that the logic and values behind the enforced innovation model represent a 'logic of consequence'.

Last but not least, we see that systematic attention is important for achieving intended public innovation. Special programmes, special laws, special organizations are set up in relation to specific goals that have to be accomplished. Innovation is defined as a specific task that can be linked to specific competences and responsibilities, as well as to financial and human resources (money and staff). In that way, innovation is formalized.

In sum, innovation management as far as enforced innovation is concerned can be characterized by

a. a process in which innovation is seen as a systematic organizational activity;

b. rather rational features, although emphases may differ;

c. a focus on making use of new knowledge concepts and new technologies coming from the outside;

d. achieving systematic attention, by institutionalizing innovation in formal positions, programme and units; and

e. links with central goals of organizations and the desire to improve goal efficiency and goal effectiveness in a consequentialist way.

7.2.2   Free Innovation (Emergent, Bottom-Up)

Innovation management can also take place in a different way. It can be seen as an emergent activity that occurs at the shop-floor levels of public service delivery, initiated and carried out by workers including street-level workers and professionals. Individual professionals or groups of professionals with 'entrepreneurial' spirit – perhaps backed by clear interests – try to change ways of working, routines and procedures in order to book better results. This can be caused by contested ambitions, such as financial interests or the strengthening of positions or reputations in professional arenas, but it can (also) come from more 'sincere' ambitions like quality and safety improvements, improving client satisfaction or enhancing learning and improving knowledge. Again, we give several (Dutch) examples.

One example is the so-called Parkinson-net,[4] a Dutch health-care initiative that was started by a few medical professionals, most specifically neurologists, from Radboud academic medical centre, in order to improve treatment of Parkinson's disease. It started as a small-scale project, aimed at establishing collaborative relations between medical specialists (neurologists) and nurses inside the hospital and therapists and nurses outside the hospital, in order to create more integrated care for patients with Parkinson's disease. It specialized the work of nurses, by introducing so-called Parkinson's nurses, and at the same it established more generalist orientations by strengthening links between specialized treatment and therapeutic care. Within a rather short period of time, this initiative grew bigger. At the moment it covers the whole country, which is divided into multiple Parkinson-net regions.

---

[4] See www.parkinsonnet.nl.

Another example is the Dutch organization 'Buurtzorg' ('Neighbourhood care')[5] which was established a couple of years ago in order to renew home care. Instead of working inside 'bureaucratic systems', which negatively affected the quality of care, the innovators coming from the professional rank-and-file tried to break out of the system by a rather radical innovation. They created 'cells' of self-organizing teams of home nurses who would render care on the basis of autonomous professional judgement. Instead of sticking to rigid planning and financing schemes, often linked to time-based performance systems, and instead of making excessive work divisions, these self-organizing teams would provide more integrated care by autonomously making plans, by dividing tasks on the basis of local needs, by forming professional judgement and by creating time for 'high-quality' care. The nationwide organization, Buurtzorg, is a holding company that offers facilities, including ICT facilities, forms strategy and stimulates learning and innovation.

What we can learn from these examples is that innovation 'management' – although 'management' is a misleading term – tries to make use of the experiences of the professionals that play a vital role in all kinds of public service delivery projects, especially when they have to apply specific programmes, standards, formats, routines and procedures as well as when they encounter citizens. The source of innovation is the experiences of these professionals vis-à-vis the needs of the citizens, which are seen as an incentive to look for new routines, formats and procedures. As such, innovations emerge from these experiences and confrontations that take place at the boundaries of the organization. As such, it seems that these innovations primarily focus on changing the relationship and interactions between professionals and citizens and not so much on applying new knowledge concepts and new technologies.

Furthermore, it is important that these professionals are able to redesign the routines, procedures and formats with which they work. This implies a number of things. First, they have to be aware that they are themselves an important source of innovation and that these procedures, routines, working processes and formats can be changed. They should not see themselves as the cogwheels in an implementation machine. They are able to re-design 'the machine'. This implies that innovation and service improvement should be a part of their mindsets, which also have to be addressed in the training and socialization of these professionals. Moreover, it also presupposes that the management in the organization is willing to discuss these innovations and improvements, willing to explore

[5] See www.buurtzorgnederland.com/.

the effects of these innovations, for instance by setting up experiments as well as to support the adoption of these innovations.

Another consequence of this approach is that innovation is embedded in the daily routines of workers and professionals. As such no specific formal arrangements have to be set up to make innovation possible. The most important arrangement is that there is a culture supportive of innovation – a culture in which workers and professionals are willing to explore new ways of working which are applauded by the managers'.

The embeddedness in daily routines and daily contacts may also imply that the legitimacy of the innovation is also rooted in these routines and other daily practices. In doing so, innovations try to improve the fit between the work processes that take place and the specific needs of citizens. The link with the overall goals of the organization, in terms of goal efficiency and effectiveness, is rather *loose*. Relations between professionals and managers are loosely coupled (cf. Weick 1969) and professionals have much leeway to deviate from organizational agendas. In terms of March and Olson's (1989) distinction between the logic of consequence and the logic of appropriateness, it may be argued that this type of innovation predominantly refers to the logic of appropriateness. Innovations should be able to deal with the contingent and thus specific circumstances of public service delivery processes, as they can be derived from the day-to-day interactions between professionals and citizens. Innovations should have added value in terms of feasibility and support, not primarily in terms of the achievement of the overall goals of a specific organization.

Another interesting aspect of this type of innovation management is the rather incremental character of it. Innovation can be considered as a process of continuous improvement which consists of rather small changes. However, given a specific period of time and adding up all these small change, a fundamental change may have occurred. As such an innovation can be seen as the outcome of a process of *layering*, in which different layers of improvement build on each other.

In sum, innovation management as far as free innovation is concerned is characterized by

a. an emergence from daily contacts of professionals and street-level bureaucrats with citizens as clients, as well as from the application of specific routines, procedures, working processes and formats;
b. a more organic interweaving of work and innovation, with a strong social bias, rooted in social relationships and interactions;
c. the layering of continuous improvements, thereby focusing on the introduction of new routines and re-design of existing routines;
d. an emphasis on specific situations in which these professionals have to operate.

7.3   Alternative Innovation Models

Both models can be juxtaposed: the enforced model can be set against the free model; top-down innovations can be set against bottom-up innovations. This can be linked to common approaches in public administration and organizational sciences, in which organizational and professional logics are seen as distinct and treated in oppositional ways (e.g. Exworthy and Halford 1999; Farrell and Morris 2003; for oversight, Noordegraaf 2011). In fact, organizational and professional logics are generally seen as opposite paradigms, which generate contested images of organizational processes – including innovation processes – and conflict-ridden images of daily actions and interactions. In the enforced model, as indicated, executives and managers try to establish *tight couplings* between strategies, goals and implementation between plans and practices. The free model prefers *loose couplings* between managerial and professional spheres (e.g., Weick 1969; Orton and Wcick 1990), so that their individual values, rationales and methods remain rather separate.

In order to analyse organizational and especially innovation processes amidst contemporary circumstances, this black-and-white juxtaposition is problematic. Although both models put a different emphasis either on leading roles of managers or on professionals, it is important to analyse the *interplay* between these domains and to re-conceptualize organizational/professional connections. In the literature, this is known under the heading of *hybridization* (e.g. Kurunmäki 2004; Noordegraaf 2007, 2011, 2015b, 2015c; Kurunmäki and Miller 2006; Dent, Kirkpatrick and Neogy 2012; Kirkpatrick and Noordegraaf 2015). Professional and organizational logics are reconfigured (cf. Noordegraaf 2015b, 2015c) and professional/ organizational principles and values are interwoven (Kirkpatrick and Noordegraaf 2014). This happens because professional and managerial action occurs in changing contexts – various forces change the landscape for managerial/professional action. First, the cases that are treated and the problems that are tackled get increasingly wicked. This means that boundaries between managerial and professional fields are weakened and that these fields are linked to stakeholders. This might happen regionally or locally, but also transnationally. Hospitals or home care organizations might feel the need to organize collaborations with other professional services in order to tackle so-called 'multi-problems', but they might also become part of transnational professional service firms (e.g. Brock, Powell, and Hinings 1999) that render well-organized professional services. Second, there is an increasing need for 'public value' (e.g. Moore 1995), both because end-users become more prominent, as indicated before, and because of growing self-organizing capacities in society. Professional fields can no longer hide behind the proverbial 'walls' of their professions, as many stakeholders demand accountable and trustworthy services. Third, new expert networks and communities arise, facilitated by new technologies that make it easy to communicate, to experiment and to use (big) data and (big) databases. The classic image of the professional as solo-practitioner who treats individual patients on the basis of professional judgement is radically reconfigured. This also affects the professional-driven innovations that were discussed above. Examples like Buurtzorg are interesting for highlighting contemporary innovations, but they also re-install a classic and perhaps nostalgic image of the well-rounded and well-equipped individual professional who solves problems. In case of home care this might be appropriate, but in many other fields this faces obstacles.

In these shifting contexts, innovation requires less instrumental action, less division between fields and more openness and interaction. Conceptually, it calls for more *distributed* images of organizational/professional action. Professionalism is no longer realized by individual professionals but by concerted action of various professionals, support staff, managers and stakeholders. Instead of juxtaposing managerial and professional innovation – or what we call *enforced* and *free* innovation – these two traditional models can be juxtaposed against two other forms of innovation that represent managerial/professional connections. Instead of seeing innovation either as intended and top-down or as emergent and bottom-up, we open up these models and distinguish between their constitutive elements. Instead of lumping top-down and intended as well as bottom-up and emergent together, we differentiate between top-down and bottom-up on the one hand, and between intended or planned and emergent on the other. These other very different dimensions can be combined in multiple ways. Professionals can, for instance, be involved in intended innovation, linked to organizational agendas, and management-driven innovation (top-down) can leave space for open and emergent innovation processes. The matrix that is depicted in Figure 7.1 visualizes these different types of public innovation and the multiple roles managers and professionals can perform. The two alternative models we identify on the grounds of this typology are called *focused* and *guided* innovation.

The two models of top-down, enforced versus bottom-up, free and emergent innovation, which were described before, represent tight and loose couplings between management and professional domains respectively. In the *enforced* model, the work of the professionals is tightly linked with the innovation goals that the management of the organization have formulated. In the *free* model, there is a loose coupling, because the

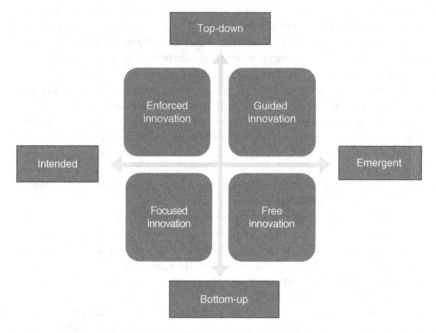

Figure 7.1 Four types of innovation

innovation efforts that take place in the professional world lead to some extent a life of their own. One could even argue that these efforts are linked with the goals of the management when a specific 'policy window', a rather opportunistic opportunity, emerges and which can be used. Chance plays an important role in the adoption of possible innovations by the management. What we call *focused* and *guided* innovation offer two alternative models, encompassing different – 'selective' and 'strong' – couplings between organizational and professional principles. We will briefly describe these two alternative models beneath.

7.3.1   Focused Innovation (Organizational Ambitions, Professionals in the Lead)

In focused innovation, professionals are in the lead, i.e. their work practices are the source of innovation. But they have a clear intention to contribute to innovating working processes in which they participate, and this is accompanied by a clear managerial focus on result. This is not only a matter of individual intentions, as professional groups and segments (cf. Bucher and Strauss 1961) might intend to strengthen public services by aiming for innovative methods, techniques, routines and work systems. Academically, this is discussed under the heading of *organizing professionalism* (cf. Noordegraaf 2011, 2014). Consciously organizing innovation processes increasingly becomes a part of professional acts and repertoires. What we see here is that both professionals and managers share the same goal; they share the idea that working in a resilient organization implies that professionals are permanently engaged in a reflective process, in which they are critical regarding the assumptions that lay behind their work in order to experiment with new ideas, working methods and techniques. The role of the management is, on the one hand, to create an environment in which innovation, as an embedded activity in the work that professionals do, is embraced. In doing so it is important that the management of the organization underline the importance that one of the central values of the organization is innovation. On the other hand, it is important that an innovation *infrastructure* is established which facilitates these embedded innovation processes. This infrastructure refers not only to the creation and maintenance of an innovation culture in which especially 'double loop learning' (Argyris and Schön 1978) is embraced but also to the creation of an organizational climate in which it is possible to experiment and thus to take risks, although there is a clear focus on results as well.

The development of all kinds of supporting services, resources and means that are necessary to help professionals to innovate their work is also an aspect of this infrastructure that should be mentioned. For instance, to have a small budget that helps professionals to spend extra time, or to hire external advice and support. Furthermore, in order to ensure that professionals embrace innovation as an inherent part of their professional work, it is important that they internalize the value of (professional) innovation. Moreover, it is also important that they have acquired or are able to acquire the competences, knowledge and skills that are necessary to be reflective and innovative. This is where training and education come in. Reasoning from this model, it is important that in the professional education curriculum innovation as a subject is being taught. One example can be derived from the Dutch educational field. In the curriculum of their teacher-training colleges, some Dutch universities of higher education pay explicit attention to the question: How can teachers ask themselves the right question to improve their teaching formats, routines and working methods? If innovation is embraced as an embedded activity in the work of professionals, we see that public services are subjected to a rather ongoing process of focused innovation. To some extent, it could be argued that the innovation that takes place has a rather incremental nature, thereby looking for continuous service improvements – step by step – however, looking from a long-term perspective and on a higher, aggregated level, the sum of the small improvements may add up to major improvements and innovations.

We will give a few examples, beginning with innovations in training and education; in one of the Dutch academic medical centres the so-called 'Wonder and Improve' project has been established, aimed at teaching young doctors how to incorporate organizational responsibilities in their professional repertoires. Instead of teaching about management and leadership through courses, lectures and books, the educational leaders link organizational responsibilities to the everyday work of young doctors. They organize special Wonder and Improve sessions which focus on signalling and detecting organizational problems, analysing where they come from and finding solutions. Teams of young doctors are made responsible for implementing these solutions. These sessions and actions are clearly related to a broader organizational agenda, namely a quality and safety agenda, but tackling organizational issues and developing organizational responsibilities occurs quite invisibly. Young doctors are socialized into an organizational world that used to be alien and anonymous, but that become 'manageable' after improving organizational awareness.

Furthermore, the same academic centre also links other innovation mechanisms to the same quality and safety agenda, such as tracing techniques for optimizing patient safety and health-care quality. Tracers are used to analyse how actual care processes occur and whether medical professionals stick to the various guidelines and protocols they are expected to comply with. There are people who can formally act as certified tracers, and the organization consciously stimulates medical professionals, including medical doctors and nurses, to become certified tracers. This means they monitor the delivery of care in other departments and throughout the hospital, which means they are enabled to tell colleagues elsewhere about how they treat patients. Moreover, they are enabled to 'see' problems and vulnerabilities in their own medical practices.

In sum, focused innovation is characterized by

a. an awareness in professional service organizations, also on the side of professionals and professional groups, that innovation is part of professional work;
b. cooperation between professionals/professional groups, as well as between professionals and other internal and external stakeholders;
c. conscious and focused methods for improving and diffusing innovations;
d. management roles aimed at creating an innovation infrastructure in which embedded forms of innovation can flourish; and
e. subtle mechanisms in professional education to embed innovative competencies in training, education and socialization.

7.3.2   Guided Innovation (Situated, Managerial Grip)

In guided innovation, managers play an important role, but instead of intentionally steering and controlling innovation, they 'let things happen'. In doing so a culture is systematically created in which 'a thousand flowers flourish'. To some extent, it can be argued that professionals and experiences on the shop floor, or at the front line of public service delivery processes, are seen as an endless stream of innovative problem definitions as well as new approaches, which only have to be orchestrated in a specific direction. To some extent, the organization is seen as a *'garbage can'*, which can be used as a source of innovation, given the emerging challenges with which the organization is confronted (Cohen, March and Olsen 1972).

Given the variety of possible alternative problem definitions as well aspossible emerging innovative solutions, the main task of the management is, on the one hand, to stimulate the development and maintenance of an organizational context in which variety is embraced as being a condition for innovation. One the other hand, management tries to facilitate and support the process of selection and retention of the innovation to be adopted (Weick 1969). For instance, by looking at new problem definitions and innovative solutions being discussed or even being used in daily practice, specific patterns can be discerned in what they have in common. This view of innovation also resembles Mintzberg's focus on strategy as *pattern*, as opposed to plans (Mintzberg 1978). According to Mintzberg, strategy is a pattern in a stream of decisions (p. 934). Likewise, innovation can be seen as new and changing patterns in streams of actions. This also resembles 'strategy as practice' approaches (e.g. Johnson et al. 2007), which show how strategies are formed in daily practice. As a result, managers try to systematically seek opportunities, respond to events and make use of incidents in order to strengthen innovative potential. To some extent, chance plays an important role in the selection of possible innovations, but the main difference with the bottom-up approach to innovation is that the chance to be able to develop new innovative approaches is systematically organized into the organization.

An interesting example can be found in the use of an 'early warning' system used by the Dutch Rijkswaterstaat, which is the federal agency responsible for the development and maintenance of different traffic infrastructures (Van der Steen et al. 2013). The early warning system retrieves signals from a great number of internal and external respondents. Signals are often retrieved by conducting interviews, which are carried out by an early warning team. This leads to a long list of weak signals, which is then narrowed down by a selection committee to a short list. Before the list of weak signals is presented to the board, further research is done to understand the nature and possible impacts of the selected weak signals. As such these weak signals are embedded in the strategic cycle of the board and are a recurring topic on its agenda. The board then decides which signals should be explored further and deeper (Van der Steen et al. 2013: 23). An example a weak signal that has led to an innovation was focused on the question: How do we deal with phosphate and transform it from a waste product into a valuable good? Phosphate is waste product that one the hand leads to eutrophication problems, like water pollution (water quality for which Rijkswaterstaat is being responsible), while other hand it also an indispensable food substance. The early warning system noted that the global phosphate supply was running out, while the supply production was in hands of rather politically unstable counties. As such this waste product would represent great value for the future. It was also shown that private companies were developing methods for reclaiming it. As a result of this early warning signal, the Rijkswaterstaat was given the opportunity to take on a facilitating role, as a policy entrepreneur, by bringing relevant parties together to develop reclaiming technologies out of the water system managed by the Rijkswaterstaat (Van der Steen et al. 2013: 25).

There are two interesting developments that foster this type of innovation, and both are technology-driven. First, it can be argued that social media can provide an interesting internal and external communication environment that can bring internal and external professionals as well as other relevant actors together to make an inventory of possible weak signals, by discussing them, exploring them and also linking them to other developments. As such it is possible to create virtual policy communities that act as communities of practice (Wenger 1998) which can emerge and can be stimulated and facilitated by managers (Bekkers 2004). However, it is important that the content and results of these discussions are linked to the managerial realm and that communication and feedback channels are created. The second development is that increasingly the large amount of data produced in the daily performance of all kinds of tasks (especially if these tasks are data-driven and ICT-supported) can be made technically available, so that it can not only retrieved but also used, by linking it to other data or data sets. In doing so, weak signals can be retrieved which can be a stimulus for product and service innovation. This development is called 'big data', and it is considered an important source of policy and service innovation (Bekkers and Moody 2014).

In sum, guided innovation is characterized by

a. an awareness that innovation cannot really be controlled by (top-down) plans and techniques;

b. an emphasis on weak signals and strategic details that can be used to discover new patterns and set new innovation streams in motion;

c. an emphasis on organizational practices, to be used as a source of innovation;

d. efforts to mobilize innovative potential by strengthening (inter)orga-nizational interactions, also by making use of new technologies;

e. innovation as a systematically organized process of letting 'a thousand flowers bloom'; and

f. a facilitating and supportive role of management to organize the exploration of weak signals and the linking of signals to the organiza-tion's policies.

7.4   Discussion (Connectivity Matters)

In this chapter, we focused on managers and professionals and identified four specific types of public innovation, which represent different combina-tions of emergent/intended innovation and top-down/bottom-up action. These various types of innovation enable managers and professionals to enrich their innovation repertoires and to establish *connectivity* in everyday practices. That is what the chapter stressed; innovations call for questioning traditional images and roles of managers and professionals and going beyond either professional or managerial domains. Both managerial and profes-sional actions become more dispersed and dependent. Relations between managers and professionals in collaborative innovation force us to renew our own organizational rhetoric. This fits the hybridization of organizational/ professional practices. As professionalism becomes less pure throughout the public sector (cf. Noordegraaf 2007), there will be more possibility to work towards focused and guided innovation.

In order to replace the 'magic concept' of innovation with workable innovation processes, we need to (1) contextualize innovation, (2) identify relevant stakeholders, (3) explore different innovation processes that enable us to understand the interplay between stakeholders, and (4) organize con-nectivity between professionals and managers organically but also system-atically. The various public innovation models that we sketched can be helpful, not only to weaken unproductive analytical distinctions (such as 'managers versus professionals'), but also to seek additional innovative potential which is generated by bringing professionals and managers together, although the emphasis of each model may differ. It is important to acknowledge that professionals and managers, and other stakeholders, are part of collaborative networks in which relations instead of individual actions determine success. These relations might be a matter of 'pragmatic collaboration' (cf. Reay and Hinings 2009). But they might also embody both 'selective' and 'strong couplings' of both managerial and professional logics (for insights on how multiple logics might be combined, see e.g. Skelcher and Smith 2015; Noordegraaf 2015a). Instead of seeking or highlighting conflicts and clashes, managerial and professional fields might seek common ground, either by jointly working on certain projects or activities (selective) or by interweaving work outlooks and values (strong).

In addition, perspectives on innovations count: when managers and professionals act from counterintuitive points of view and 'work against' their own logic, they can generate new opportunities for making innovation happen. When managers relax control ambitions and when professionals act more intentionally and systematically, they might profit from unused innovative potential. Furthermore, the two alternative models on innovation – focused and guided innovation – show that innovation can be organized in a systematic way, thereby trying to exploit the innovation potential that professionals possess. Both managers and professionals can contribute to innovations in ways that are counterintuitive in the light of traditional images of managerial and professional logics. But when these logics are seen as flexible and less oppositional, new prospects for innovation arise. Professional acts can be linked to organizational agendas, by using organizational programmes – such as quality programmes – and by seeing professional action more as distributed action than actions by individual professionals. Managerial acts can be linked to professional values and principles by weakening the emphasis on goals and objectives and by strengthening the focus on signals and surprises.

7.5   Conclusion

The emphasis on focused and guided innovation, in addition to more classic enforced and free innovation, is not meant to get rid of classic models and privilege contemporary models. All of these models – as ideal types – have value, depending on context. In certain organizational and work settings, enforced and free innovation can still occur, and vice versa, and focused and guided innovation does not necessarily lead to better results. It also depends upon the nature and type of professionalism involved. Although the term 'professional' is widely used, there are great differences between different types of professional practices, largely linked to the number and nature of regulatory mechanisms involved. 'Pure' professionalism is scarce, especially in public domains, and is increasingly difficult to maintain. This means not only that the necessity to uphold free innovation is losing ground, but also that the necessity to guard enforced innovation is less strong as well. When professionalism is either reconfigured, to include innovation agendas and acts, or embedded within organizational contexts in meaningful ways, there might be all the more reason to focus on focused and/or guided innovation. In that sense, these alternative models *are* of more value than ever.

Apart from their conceptual value, the rise of alternative models for innovation has various practical implications. First of all, both managers and professionals need to enrich their *repertoires*, in order to act on the basis of these various new models. They need to be aware of the fact that there are multiple ways to establish innovative services and that their traditional roles become one aspect of collaborative action. They more specifically need more connective abilities. Second, they need to be sensitive to *contingencies*, in order to select 'the right type' of innovation. In some cases they can emphasize their traditional role, while in other cases they need to be linked to organizational agendas and programmes. When they do so, they might still feel the tensions that come with hybrid roles, but they are aware of the fact that collaborative innovations call for innovative acts. The third consequence is that innovation, based on the connecting professionals and managers, can be more *naturally* organized in more *systematic* ways. If professional commitment is consciously established in rather organic ways, something which is possible when the alternative innovation models are used, innovation can be linked to the daily processes of both managers and professionals. This paradoxically turns the much-desired and magic concept innovation into a 'natural' instead of exceptional activity in public sector organizations.

References

Argyris, C. and Schön, D. 1978. *Organizational Learning: A Theory of Action Perspective*. Boston: McGraw Hill.

Bekkers, V. 2004. 'Virtual policy communities and responsive governance: Redesigning on-line debates', *Information Polity* 9(3/4): 193–204.

Bekkers, V. and Moody, R. 2014. *Visual Culture and Public Policy. Towards a Visual Polity?* London: Routledge.

Bekkers, V., Edelenbos, J. and Steijn, B. (eds.) 2011. *Innovation in the Public Sector. Linking Capacity and Leadership*. London: Palgrave McMillan.

Bozeman, B. 1987. *All Organizations are Public: Bridging Public and Private Organizational Theories*. San Francisco: Jossey-Bass.

Brock, D., Powell, M. J. and Hinings, C. R. (eds.). 1999. *Restructuring the Professional Organization: Accounting, Health Care and Law*. London: Routledge.

158   *Victor Bekkers and Mirko Noordegraaf*

Bucher, R. and Strauss, A. L. 1961. 'Professions in process', *American Journal of Sociology* 66: 325–34.

Cohen, M. D., March, J. G. and Olsen, J. 1972. 'A garbage can model of organizational choice', *Administrative Science Quarterly* 17(1): 1–25.

Dent, M., Kirkpatrick, I. and Neogy, I. 2012. 'Medical leadership and management reforms in hospitals', in C. Teelken, E. Ferlie and M. Dent (eds.), *Leadership in the Public Sector: Promises and Pitfalls*. London: Routledge, pp. 105–25.

Exworthy, M. and Halford, S. (eds.). 1999. *Professionals and the New Managerialism in the Public Sector*. Buckingham: Open University Press.

Farrell, C. and Morris, J. 2003. 'The neo-bureaucratic state: Professionals, managers and professional managers in schools, general practices and social work', *Organization* 10(1): 129–56.

Johnson, G., Langley, A., Melin, L. and Whittington, R. (eds.). 2007. *Strategy as Practice: Research Directions and Resources*. New York: Cambridge University Press.

Kirkpatrick, I. and Noordegraaf, M. 2014. 'Organizations and occupations: Towards hybrid professionalism in professional service firms?', in L. Empson, L., J. Broschak and D. Muzio (eds.), *The Oxford Handbook of Professional Service Firms*. Oxford: Oxford University Press, pp. 92–112.

Kurunmäki, L. 2004. 'A hybrid profession – The acquisition of management accounting expertise by medical professionals', *Accounting, Organizations and Society* 29(3): 327–47.

Kurunmäki, L. and Miller, P. 2006. 'Modernising government: The calculating self, hybridisation and performance measurement', *Financial Accountability & Management* 22(1): 87–106.

Lipsky, M. 1980. *Street-Level Bureaucracy*. New York: Russell Sage.

March, J. G. and Olsen, J. P. 1989. *Rediscovering Institutions*. New York: The Free Press.

Mintzberg, H. 1978. 'Patterns in strategy formation', *Management Science* 24(9): 934–48.

Moore, M. 1995. *Creating Public Value – Strategic Management in Government*. Cambridge: Harvard University Press.

Noordegraaf, M. 2007. 'From pure to hybrid professionalism: Present-day professionalism in ambiguous public domains', *Administration & Society* 39(6):761–85.

  2011. 'Risky business: How professionals and professionals fields (must) deal with organizational issues', *Organization Studies* 32(10): 1349–71.

  2015a. *Public Management, Performance, Professionalism and Politics*. Basingstoke: Palgrave.

  2015b. 'Hybridity and beyond: (New) forms of professionalism in changing organizational and societal contexts', *Journal of Professions and Organizations* 2(2): 187–206.

  2015c. 'Reconfiguring professional work: Changing forms of professionalism in public services', *Administration & Society* Forthcoming (Available online since November 2013).

Orton, J. D. and Weick, K. E. 1990. 'Loosely coupled systems: A reconceptualization', *Academy of Management Review* 15(2): 203–23.

Pollitt, C. and Hupe, P. 2011. 'Talking about government: The role of magic concepts', *Public Management Review* 13(5): 1–18.

Reay, T. and Hinings, C. R. 2009. 'Managing the rivalry of competing institutional logics', *Organization Studies* 30(6): 629–52.

Skelcher, C. and Smith, S. R. 2015. 'Theorizing hybridity: Institutional logics, complex organizations, and actor identities: The case of nonprofits', *Public Administration* 93(2): 433–48.

Steen, M. van der et al. 2013. *Early Signals Timely Strategy. The Early Warning System at the Dutch Rijkswaterstaat.* The Hague: NSOB.

Weick, K. E. 1969. *The Social Psychology of Organizing.* Reading, MA: Addison-Wesley.

1976. 'Educational organizations as loosely coupled systems', *Administrative Science Quarterly* 21(1): 1–19.

Wenger, E. 1998. *Communities of Practice: Learning, Meaning and Identity.* New York: Cambridge University Press.

8   Bringing the Resources of Citizens into Public Governance
Innovation through Co-production to Improve Public Services and Outcomes

Tony Bovaird and Elke Loeffler

8.1   Introduction

This chapter focuses on the roles of citizens in collaborative innovation, approaching this issue through the lens of user and community co-production with public service providers (from whatever sector) and exploring how citizens' experiences, ideas, energies and resources can be brought into the social innovation process.

Let us state our case clearly from the outset. We believe that the contribution of citizens to public service innovation is already high, but it could be much greater. In a recent summary of the international empirical evidence on co-production (Bovaird et al. 2015b), we have illustrated how the main relevant surveys carried out in recent years (Loeffler et al. 2008; Alford and Yates 2015; Bovaird et al. 2015a; Loeffler et al. 2015; Bovaird et al. 2016) show consistently that the level of co-production activities in all countries tends to be high, and many citizens are willing to do more than they currently do (although social desirability bias may mean that in their responses they have rather exaggerated this willingness). However, there was a widespread tendency for managers and professionals in public services to underestimate how much co-production was actually occurring. This suggests that although co-production is important, it is a social innovation which is more often hidden than publicized. This may be because much co-production practice tends to emerge from the front line, rather than top-down from organization leaders (in spite of the increasing claims by top managers that this is now their espoused strategy).

Another striking finding from these surveys is that demographic variables do not appear to have a strong influence on the level of current co-production or the willingness to undertake more – although gender and

The corresponding author for this chapter is Tony Bovaird.

age sometimes show up as significant, the effects are always weak and other demographic variables (education level, ethnicity, urban/rural location) are rarely important. This characteristic of co-production marks it out from public participation and citizen engagement. As user and community co-production often emerges from the intense interaction of front-line professionals with citizens, it is likely to engage especially those who are keen to make a contribution themselves (the 'willing to do'), rather than simply those who are keen to tell others what to do (the 'willing to talk'), whereas many public participation and citizen engagement initiatives may attract more of the latter. This finding suggests that governments should not prejudge who is likely to (or not likely to) get involved in co-production, to avoid ignoring potential co-producers. This is exciting – it suggests that social innovation in public services can tap into a much larger pool of resources than has traditionally been realized.

After setting out our approach to social innovation, we explore the characteristics of user and community co-production as a social innovation and illustrate these characteristics through four international co-production case studies. We use these case studies to illustrate key elements in our framework for understanding the barriers to co-production and, finally, suggest the need for a new public infrastructure, if user and community co-production is to grow as a social innovation.

8.2   What Is Social Innovation in the Public Sector?

What is social innovation in the public sector? This apparently innocuous question can be opened out to reveal a battlefield of contending definitions. We do not seek to enter this dangerous territory, so we use a concept of social innovation which incorporates but goes beyond service design methodologies, embedding social innovation within the context of public governance.

In this chapter, we wish to focus on social innovation to improve public governance. Consequently, for the purposes of this chapter, we define *social innovation* as *a collaborative process of improving public services and publicly desired outcomes*. This involves at least two actors in collaboration, at least one of which is in the public sector – and consequently the collaborative actions undertaken are subject to democratic accountability.

This wide definition of social innovation allows us to include as actors elected politicians as well as public sector officials and other stakeholders from civil society, such as individual citizen and service users, communities and third sector organizations. It differentiates, however, between *doing* the new activity together and simply talking about it – the latter falls outside the definition. We leave it to the actors themselves to decide for how long the activity must continue before it is no longer 'new'.

Key to the definition is some degree of collaborative action to achieve changes which are jointly regarded as improvements – if the actions undertaken are not agreed, then, under this definition, they are not regarded as 'social'. Non-agreed activities could be regarded as imposed changes, which may be innovations but, if they are imposed, do not seem very 'social'.

Our definition specifies intent to improve public services or publicly desired outcomes. By including outcomes, not just services, we widen the scope for innovative practice, and particularly for co-production activities. Innovations generally cannot flag up clear pathways to improved outcomes, as the complexity of matching multiple intervention pathways to a portfolio of publicly desired outcomes is quite daunting (Bovaird 2012). Some links in the input–output–outcome chains for each outcome pathway are usually missing – by definition, the evidence for innovations tends to be rather thin. Consequently, innovations aimed at improving outcomes are intrinsically less prone to 'capture' by 'professionals' or 'experts' – they have to be creatively fashioned in the light of experience, and the experience of citizens, indeed *all* stakeholders, is relevant.

In exploring the democratic implications of social innovation, we distinguish macro-level from micro-level decisions on resources: the former involve policy choices on resource allocation made *between* services and between stakeholder groups (i.e. which outcomes and which citizens should be prioritized), while the latter involve resourcing choices made *within* services and within the service mix agreed for a specific service user (i.e. *how* outcomes for specific citizens will be achieved). This distinction is important, as rather different stakeholders are involved in social innovation at macro and micro levels.

At the macro level in a democratic society, politicians and their top officials have to make risky choices in formulating policies within a coherent strategy, which joins up complementary outcomes, focuses on the pathways most likely to succeed and decommissions services of low political priority (sometimes thereby overriding 'technically efficient' solutions favoured by officers or 'populist' solutions favoured by local stakeholders). This is usually a dynamic process, demonstrating significant 'churn'. Politicians are usually helped in making these choices by their dense networks of influence, among which are likely to be citizens, although often as members of groups (e.g. service users' associations) rather than as individuals. Political decisions are not simply made in the light of 'expert' advice – innovation can be a reflection of destructive 'initiativitis', where innovations are valued for their novelty rather than because of evidence of their effectiveness. Again, because politicians and top officials operate at macro level, well away from the operational realities of their policies, sub-optimal outcomes can go unremarked for a considerable period. Consequently, when policy failures are eventually noticed, there is often political over-reaction ('throwing the baby out with the bathwater'). Involvement of service users and other citizens can provide a counterweight to both these tendencies at macro level.

At a micro level, social innovations involve front-line professionals, middle managers, service users and their communities in collaboration to change ways of achieving outcomes, either in response to top-down innovations or through emergent bottom-up innovations. Here there is both a representative and a direct democratic input into the change process. The former essentially derives from the overarching framework set by elected politicians for the micro-level process (supplemented by their continuing scrutiny role). However, bottom-up social innovation involving citizens also entails direct involvement of citizens in action and in discourse over public decisions. It therefore promotes what Helmut Anheier (2015) calls 'a more inclusive concept of democracy, and the notion that popular involvement should not be restricted to voting alone'. In this chapter, we therefore consider social innovation as both a product of top-down decision making at the macro level and influences from actors at the micro level.

In line with our definition, the criteria we will therefore use to determine whether specific innovations are 'social innovations' will revolve around whether they involve change, whether this change is collaborative, whether it is democratically endorsed (through the representative democracy route) or supportive of direct democracy in areas of political concern and whether they lead to improvement of public services or publicly desired outcomes.

8.3   Co-production as a Set of Approaches for Collaborative Innovation by Public Service Providers with Service Users and Their Communities

The particular social innovation on which we concentrate in this chapter is user and community co-production of public services and publicly desired outcomes. This we define as follows: *Co-production is about professionals and citizens making better use of each other's assets, resources and contributions to achieve better outcomes or improved efficiency* (www.govint.org).

We distinguish between four key co-production approaches as a 'motor' for initiating and implementing social innovations and sustaining improved public outcomes (Bovaird and Loeffler 2012):

(1) co-commissioning of public services, which puts the focus on planning, procurement and contracting in the public sector;
(2) co-design of public service process or pathways to outcomes;
(3) co-delivery of public services or outcomes; and
(4) co-assessment of the governance of the innovation process and
results achieved.

The contributions made by different stakeholders differ greatly
between these four co-production modes. The co-commissioning mode
often involves mainly a discursive role. This can also apply to some degree
to the co-design and co-assessment modes, but these benefit from the
involved stakeholders having also participated in co-delivery, so that they
have a deeper knowledge of what the services or the outcomes involve.
Co-delivery is primarily action-oriented rather than discussion-oriented,
and here citizens give time, effort and expertise to get things done.

It is this orientation to action and the emphasis on joint contributions
by both citizens and public service organizations which most clearly
differentiate co-production from 'consultation' and 'public participation'
initiatives, both of which tend to be mainly discussion-oriented and to
focus on how many take part in the initiatives rather than the value of the
contribution which is made by the co-producers.

So what are the resources on which these joint contributions from
citizens and public service actors are based? We distinguish three different
types of resources (adapted from Grant 2002):

Tangibles: physical, financial, contracts
Collective intangibles: technology, supplier relationships,
customer relationships, partnership relationships, culture,
reputation
Person-based intangibles: specialized skills or knowledge,
interactive ability, communicative ability, motivation

Clearly, some of these resources are especially likely to be provided by
public service professionals (e.g. specialized skills and knowledge), managers (e.g. technology, supplier relationships) and politicians (e.g. interactive ability, communicative ability). However, other resources are likely
to derive from the strengths of citizens (e.g. customer relationships, motivation). It is the diversity of these resources, and the likelihood that some at
least are likely to be the province of citizens, that generates the potential for
user and community co-production. Interestingly, not all of these resources
are well studied in the literature – in particular, the personal intangible
resources of interactive ability, communicative ability and motivation have
tended to be neglected, especially by economists. It is therefore not surprising that co-production has been underestimated by public sector actors, as
highlighted in the empirical research discussed above.

To what extent does co-production constitute innovation? We argue in this chapter that this has to be carefully evaluated. Our empirical research on co-production in different services in a range of different countries (as summarized at the beginning of this chapter) suggests that there is, in practice, much more co-production than is identified by most public service agencies. Where such longstanding practice is identified for the first time, by practitioners or by researchers, it is often wrongly labelled as 'innovation'. However, the main argument in this chapter is that there is indeed scope for a great deal more user and community co-production of public services and outcomes, and that this will require significant innovation from all the stakeholders involved.

8.4   Co-commissioning of Public Services: Involving Service Users, Citizens and TSOs in the Prioritization and Planning of Public Services

In the following four sections, we use case studies to illustrate the scope for innovative co-production initiatives across the four modes of co-production – co-commissioning, co-design, co-delivery and co-assessment – looking both at the macro (where co-production is embedded in policy) and the micro levels (where co-production emerges from the practice of citizens and professionals, usually at 'the front line'). In each case study, we will show how it fits to our definition of social innovation, and we will explore the lessons for social innovation that emerge. Of course, the international empirical evidence mentioned earlier demonstrates that these case studies are only the tip of the iceberg in terms of the current volume and future potential of co-production activity. However, the value of a case study approach is that it allows a deeper understanding of the drivers for co-production, the barriers which hinder it and the changes required to facilitate more co-production in the future.

8.4.1   Case Study 1 (Macro Level): Co-deciding Improvement Priorities in Berlin-Lichtenberg with Citizens

The Borough of Berlin-Lichtenberg is one of 12 boroughs in the city-state of Berlin, with a very diverse population of 265,000 inhabitants. Its participatory budgeting (PB) process was formally started by an all-party decision in 2004, with the strong support of the directly elected mayor. The Berlin-Lichtenberg approach is now the longest-standing 'participatory budgeting' approach in Germany.

In the first running of PB, citizens were invited to submit and then discuss proposals related to those public services within the responsibility of the Borough that could be altered in the short term (covering about €30 million of the overall €500 million budget), in a five-stage process:

- a launch event for all Borough residents (September 2005);
- five citizen meetings in decentralized Borough neighbourhoods, where residents could submit and vote on proposals;
- a one-day meeting of so-called citizen journalists to edit and aggregate the 20 most popular proposals from each of the five neighbourhood meetings;
- a general citizen assembly in January 2006, an internet vote and a written vote to select the overall 20 best proposals from the set submitted by the 'citizen journalists'; and
- a citizen survey to check the reactions to the prioritized proposals by citizens who had not previously participated.

At the end of this process, the Borough Council debated the proposals at several public meetings and took final decisions on the proposals. Although known as the Berlin-Lichtenberg 'participatory budget', the citizens do not, strictly speaking, set the budget, but rather the service and outcome priorities in the annual budgetary process. Since 2006, the process has taken place every two years and has now been developed further. In particular, the Borough drew up 13 smaller neighbourhoods so that they seemed more relevant to citizens – an important lesson for other countries (like the United Kingdom) where 'neighbourhoods' are often very large. The process now involves nearly 10,000 people in each running and is also used to recruit more activists for local activities.

Again, since not everybody is up for strategic deliberation – some people just want to *do* things for and with other people around them – in 2010 the Borough introduced 'neighbourhood budgets' (Kiezfonds), currently of about €7,000 in each neighbourhood, managed by neighbourhood 'juries', whose members are representative of the demographic make-up of their area (about one member per 1,000 residents) and are frequently changed to bring in people not previously engaged. These neighbourhood budgets provide active citizens with seed-funding to organize events, tackle local environmental problems or take other actions which improve key outcomes at neighbourhood level. The 'juries' meet monthly and fund over 100 projects in some years, although some of these are very small.

This case study highlights how the specific 'social innovation' of PB, involving a dramatic change to the council budgeting process, was collaborative with citizens and indeed involved an element of direct democracy but has simultaneously been endorsed by democratically elected representatives over its ten-year lifespan. This co-production of priorities in the Berlin-Lichtenberg budget not only required a significant innovation impulse at the very beginning from the mayor but has relied upon continuous innovation thereafter by a range of players (service users and other citizens, community organizations, public sector organizations, third sector organizations) in order to refresh it. The key inputs from citizens are their knowledge of the relative impacts of different services on their own welfare and the on the welfare of those for whom they care. The key inputs from the public sector side are information about the budget and its impacts on different groups in the city, plus the organization of the cascaded series of meetings at all levels within the district, through which the citizens' proposals are filtered up to the final decision stages. This organization of the whole process constitutes a new public infrastructure, providing a platform from which citizens can exercise influence on some budget decisions, although of course there is still a considerable way to go before this platform opens up the full budget to direct citizen input.

8.5   Co-designing Public Services: Involving Service Users in Imaginative Service Redesign Processes to Improve Outcomes and Reduce Costs

8.5.1   Case Study 2 (Micro Level): Clean City Linköping – Co-designing Innovative Solutions with Young People

The city centre of Linköping (150,000 inhabitants) in Sweden was experiencing outbreaks of litter and graffiti, particularly during evenings and weekends. Several previous campaigns and projects to convince people to keep the city centre clean had failed. Research suggested that the groups mainly responsible were young people aged 16–22. The Clean City Linköping initiative was therefore specifically targeted at this age group, aimed at changing their behaviour by co-designing campaigns and improvements with them (Timm-Arnold 2014).

The initial project team consisted of a youth liaison officer and an external consultant, together with a young person in the 16–22 age group, the target group for the programme. It proposed the innovative idea of offering young people a very well-paid job during one summer month to drive behaviour change among them. They not only cleaned the city centre streets but also, about half of the time, wrote a daily blog with photos and film clips, showing what the city centre looks like and what young people could do to improve the quality of public spaces.

The Clean City project was launched with a press advert, announcing four jobs for young people. Applicants had to provide a CV and attend an interview with the project team and other council representatives, showing that they had read the project-briefing material. Moreover, they were encouraged to present their own ideas on how to do their job. After this pre-selection process, information on the shortlisted candidates was published on the City of Linköping website for a week, so the local community could have a vote on who they thought were the most qualified candidates. This innovative appointments approach meant that the Clean City project had already achieved a wide public profile even before the young people started work – indeed, the Clean City website www.renstad.nu attracted more than 35,000 single visitors within the first two months of the project, and there were 2,341 applications for the city cleaning jobs.

The project was coordinated by a youth liaison officer, who also kept the website up to date, uploading the fast-growing archive of material from the young co-workers in the form of blogs, experiences and other information. The project had a clear effect, with much less graffiti in the city centre of Linköping and much less litter in the central park. The annual citizen survey in Linköping shows that most citizens now see it as a cleaner city. Moreover, since the start of Clean City Linköping the cost of removing graffiti has fallen by about 3 million Swedish Krona (about £257,000) compared to that in 2009.

After the success in its first year, Clean City continued to be marketed through word of mouth and the website www.renstad.nu, in turn leading to innovative ideas such as the creation of 'talking' bins which started asking (in different languages) people who approached them to throw their rubbish into the bin. Linköping city has moved on to work with schools and pre-school children. For example, a local secondary school produced a commercial which was shown on cinema screens in Linköping.

This social innovation in co-design was triggered by one young project team member working with city council professionals but quickly grew to become a much more extensive co-production exercise with local young people, some of whom became temporary employees of the council. Their input, essentially an understanding of how to get an environmental message across to their peer group, was critical to influencing the behaviours of the young people causing the problems and in designing incentives for young people who want the city-centre-cleaning jobs. The project had no policy (macro) implications for democratic decision makers in the city but may have changed the perception of some young people about the importance of the council, at least in terms of keeping up public places. In this case, the most visible part of the public infrastructure for initiating and rolling out the innovation was relatively traditional, namely the employment of peer-group members by the city council in order to increase the impact of their contribution. However, this was ultimately less important than the contribution to a new public infrastructure by the young people themselves, not only through their word-of-mouth influence on each other but also through a variety of social media-based ways of communicating with each other in a continuous process of influencing behaviour change.

8.6   Co-delivering Public Services and Outcomes: Involving Citizens and People Who Use Services in the Service Delivery Process and in Taking Preventative Action to Improve Outcomes

8.6.1   Case Study 3 (Macro Level): Peer Education of Learner Drivers by (Traffic Law) Offenders in Austria

Young drivers tend to engage in risky behaviour and do not fully understand the risks of driving, so they are particularly vulnerable to accidents. Even after sound training in their driving schools and major accident-prevention publicity campaigns, many young people remain insufficiently aware of the risks they run, particularly as learner drivers, thinking 'It won't happen to me.'

Close To is an ambitious national project in Austria, following up a previous European Union project and financed by the Austrian Department for Traffic, Innovation and Technology, taking a co-production approach to reducing the high number of accidents among young drivers (Lang 2011). Young offenders between 17 and 28 years old complement the theoretical training given in driving schools by telling their peers in a very direct and authentic way how they caused an accident (in most cases under the influence of alcohol) and use their own cases to highlight the implications of risky driving. Since both groups are approximately the same age and meet face to face, driving school pupils are directly confronted with the experiences of young offenders with strong emotional immediacy. This breaks down the normal distance between trainer and trainee and holds up a mirror to the young drivers, in which they can see reflected their own behaviour and its likely consequences.

Some peer trainers, who are often still serving their prison sentence, are recruited through the courts, while others volunteer when they learn about the project through the media. Typically, they get preparatory training, where they themselves learn how to deal with their accident and its consequences and are helped to prepare their presentation, working with a peer coach. Peer trainers are now also being recruited to work in vocational schools, training centres and companies, and, since 2010, even the Austrian army has integrated peer trainers into its driving lessons for young recruits.

The project also aims at behaviour change on the part of the peer trainers. The repeated confrontation in public with their own accident-causing behaviours, and their reflection on their behaviours during the preparatory training, done with mentors, support re-socialization of these offenders and help to change their behaviour. Offenders often say that they are happy about being able to prevent others from making the same mistake that they did. Consequently, many Austrian court judges have recognized participation in Close To as an alternative or complementary punishment to a fine or prison or one reason for grant-ing early parole.

More than 10,000 learner drivers participated in Close To in the three years from 2008, in more than 370 training sessions in driving schools, military facilities, companies, training centres and schools. An evaluation of the project by *Forschungsgesellschaft Mobilität* showed that the project had a significant impact on the behaviour of learner drivers. More than 89 per cent of learner drivers in the programme suggested they will drive more carefully in future (much more than for learner drivers in the control group), and 80 per cent of learner drivers could remember significant details of the story they had heard from their peer trainer, suggesting a sustainable emotional impact.

This social innovation provides the voluntary opportunity for offenders to collaborate in co-production of improved road-safety outcomes, influ-encing their peer group by contributing their own personal experiences in a situation where it has high communicative power. As a national public policy, it demonstrates government commitment to preventative as well as punitive measures to deal with dangerous driving. Here the innovative public infrastructure which is used is an unusually close partnership between the legal system, the offender rehabilitation system and the educational system. While this public infrastructure requires significant resources to organize, the approach has the advantages of fitting well into existing training programmes for learner drivers and providing a low-cost rehabilitation mechanism for previous offenders. However, this is not simply a mechanistic case of strategic 'fit' – an important success factor in the approach is how ex-offenders can engage their audiences emotion-ally, taking them out of their comfort zone and using unusually vivid 'shock and surprise' tactics to confront them with the potentially life-threatening consequences that they too might face, if they do not change their behaviour.

8.7   Co-assessing Public Services and Outcomes: Involving Citizens and People Who Use Services to Evaluate Service Quality and Quality of Life

8.7.1   Case Study 4 (Micro Level): Children Triggering Action as 'District Detectives' in the Borough of Marzahn-Hellersdorf, Berlin, Germany

> We seek and we find, with our magnifying glasses and cameras, the best, coolest and most exciting squares, places and corners around where we live. Road hogs, litter bugs and bellyaching adults – we track them down and take them into custody! Everything we find out is published and lands on the table of our local councillors – so that they know what's actually going on here! We want this place to be child-friendly!
>
> (Translated from www.kijubue.de/kiezdetektive)

This is how the website of the *Kinder- und Jugendbüro* (Children and Young People's Service) in Marzahn-Hellersdorf, one of Berlin's 30 district councils, describes one of its most innovative initiatives. Since 1998 it has encouraged 8–14-year-olds to sign up as 'district detectives' to research what's going on in the district during the school holidays. Positive results are highlighted in the 'Treasure Box', while negatives land in the 'Rubbish Bin'. These findings are then sorted out by the young people themselves, in terms of what they think is most important, and presented to the mayor and relevant council officers at a meeting of the Young People's Council – and the council later outlines what action it intends to take (and this is tracked and reported in following meetings). Proposals at the 2015 Young People's Council included new pedestrian bridges over busy roads, redesign of the some of the city's public spaces and the opening up of school playgrounds. In 2012 and 2014, a variation of this approach was undertaken – the 'climate detectives', where young people were encouraged to seek out and publicize examples of energy wastage in their schools, other public buildings, public transport, etc.

This simple co-assessment case study shows how the energy and imagination of children and young people, an often underestimated and underused resource, can be tapped to identify what isn't working for them in the local area and even to work with district council officials to co-produce positive solutions. By involving schools in the 'game', the range of children and young people involved is greatly widened. As the councillors retain the right to the final decision, this widens direct democratic action without undermining representative democracy – but the minutes of the Young People's Council, the main public infrastructure involved in the initiative, indicate strong pressure from the young people themselves in holding the district council to account for following up their proposals.

8.8   How Can the Barriers to Co-production as Social Innovation Be Tackled?

For all the interest since the early 1980s in user and community co-production, there are still few examples of co-production being mainstreamed in public services. As with most innovation, a key barrier may simply be the very novelty of the approach and the lack of a widely available toolkit – this barrier should reduce over time. However, other barriers may need to be more actively overcome.

We can use the case studies above to illustrate some of the key barriers to co-production which we have explored elsewhere (Bovaird and Loeffler 2012) and how they might be tackled:

- *Funding and commissioning barriers*, where only some of the wide range of outcomes from co-production align with the top priorities of commissioners, e.g. in the priority-setting approach in Berlin-Lichtenberg. Here, there is a strong argument for seeking multiple funders or commissioners, although this is not often done. Berlin-Lichtenberg, for example, relies rather on close negotiation and involvement of citizens with the commissioners throughout the initiative, in order to align purposes.

- *Difficulties in developing a 'business case' to convince stakeholders*, since co-produced services often have effects that are long term and complex, and the benefits often occur in services other than those incurring the co-production costs. Obviously, this is easier where public agencies commission or fund the initiative from the start, as in the two 'macro-level' cases above, but the micro-level case studies also show how the case for public sector support can be developed from experiences on the service front line.

- *Lack of professional and managerial skills* to embed co-production in public services – even where some staff 'get' it, many others can't see or harness the assets that people have, don't know how to encourage people to develop themselves or don't try to use imaginative methods for working with people rather than simply 'processing' them. This needs changes in the way professionals are trained, recruited, developed and performance managed – as exemplified in the Austrian case.

- *Risk aversion* – co-production is still seen as highly risky by many politicians, managers and professionals, although this may simply be because it is less understood than existing service approaches, which may actually be inherently more risky. Again, exposure to both the new approach and to the deficiencies of the old approaches may be the most effective antidote here – as was cleverly achieved by involving decision makers at every stage of the co-production process in Berlin-Lichtenberg. Again, by turning the 'solution-hunting' exercise into a game, as in the 'district detectives' of Marzahn-Hellersdorf, some of the risks are avoided, as participants are likely to find the game is a 'reward' in itself, and the acceptance of the recommended solutions is thereby lower profile, taking some pressure off the politicians.

- *Political and professional reluctance to lose status and 'control'* by sharing it with service users and other citizens (an attitude which Ansell, in Chapter 2 of this book, explores in some detail) – this reluctance, where it occurs, sometimes tempts proponents of co-production (particularly those from the community development tradition) to adopt an antagonistic approach to the public sector and to seek to make co-production a 'social movement' rather than simply a way of working. This can at least partly be alleviated by keeping clear role distinctions, in which the distinctive contributions of politicians and public officials remain clear – as exemplified in the Berlin-Lichtenberg, Linköping and Austrian case studies. And, of course, it is unlikely to be a factor where the alternative expertise is essentially being supplied by children and young people, or other unorganized groups – as, for example, in the Marzahn-Hellersdorf case.

However, we believe that it is important to accept that a social innovation such as co-production is in large part emergent and cannot be conceptualized in simple linear terms (Bovaird and Kenny 2015). Where innovation is occurring in a complex adaptive system, we have to accept that there will be insufficient information on which to rank the cost effectiveness of most pathways to outcomes, including the co-production pathway. In practice, the outcomes are the result of a large number of closely connected variables, only some of which are within the control (or even influence) of local public sector agencies. Consequently, the best way forward is to engage in a meta-strategy of experimentation, prototyping and piloting, as the Berlin-Lichtenberg and Marzahn-Hellersdorf case studies have done.

However, the key lesson from the foregoing case studies is the importance of a new public infrastructure for co-production and partnership working in order to identify, test and evaluate new solutions to 'wicked' social issues. This new public infrastructure may sometimes entail tangibles, such as buildings, transport or communication equipment (most especially, social media platforms, as in the case of Linköping). However, much more often it consists of structures and processes in the public sector and in public services which enable and incentivize citizens to work with public officials and elected politicians in a way which harnesses the resources, assets and capabilities of both parties and allows them to be used for joint benefit. This new public infrastructure can be formally developed by the public sector in order to spur public innovation, as Bekkers and Nordegraaf recommend in Chapter 7 of this book, e.g. through special programmes, special laws and special organizations, which define innovation as a specific task, linked to specific competences and responsibilities as well as to financial and human resources. However, these case studies also emphasize the importance of a more informal infrastructure, where innovation can be incubated, experimented with and learnt from, so that its positive lessons can be more easily embedded within current policies and practices. This corresponds to the emergent innovation identified by Bekkers and Nordegraaf, which emerges from daily contacts of professionals or street-level bureaucrats with citizens as clients, involving a 'more organic interweaving of work and innovation, with a strong social bias, rooted in social relationships and interactions'.

How can this more informal public infrastructure of co-production be built? We would distinguish here between three conceptually different approaches – the science, craft and art of performance improvement (Bovaird and Loeffler 2015). The science of performance improvement, enshrined in the academic literature, focuses on rigorously proven links between organizational or social actions and their results. For the moment, we believe that the literature on how to reduce barriers to co-production as a form of social innovation is still quite weak – the fact that such innovation is often emergent means that cause-and-effect relations between innovation triggers and innovation consequences are far from clear and hard to prove rigorously. The craft of performance improvement is more promising, focusing on the long-standing build-up of experience on how social change can be generated and sustained, through both organizational action and community action. Although, here too, the emergent nature of innovation means that many ways of overcoming barriers will only work in some contexts, understanding the role of context is the essence of the craft of innovation. Finally, the art of performance improvement requires immersion by key actors in the needs and opportunities of the moment, improvising relevant solutions in the light of their specific context, but simultaneously transcending these contexts through creativity. This is in line with the recommendation by Bekkers and Noordegraaf that organizations need to strengthen their focus on signals and 'surprises', e.g. through 'wonder and improve' sessions with front-line practitioners. In our case studies, the capacity to improvise an emotional engagement was most evident in Case Study 3 (where people who had caused traffic accidents used the 'shock and surprise' of their own experiences to confront learner drivers with the potential consequences of their behaviour), but the value of emergent practice, with its concomitant of improvised 'surprise' tactics, was present in all four case studies. We suggest that the barriers to co-production are most likely to be overcome by exploring in more depth lessons emerging from the craft of co-production in specific contexts and from encouraging stakeholders, whether they be citizens, professionals, managers or politicians, to have confidence in their ability to improvise creative solutions together in the 'art' of co-production.

Such creative improvisation presupposes that each stakeholder has confidence in the potential value of the contributions to be made by the others. This is closely related to the concept of 'self-efficacy' (the belief that 'people can make a difference') which, we noted earlier, emerges from our surveys of co-production as critical in encouraging co-production. How can this confidence in the 'power of the people' be developed and grown? Again, the literature provides few rigorously proven recommendations here, but it suggests that trust in others partly derives from emotional sources, so rational approaches (policies, strategies, promises) mean less than experience. This suggests that co-production is more likely to be understood and accepted through the experience of doing it than through rational business cases as to why it should be done. Consequently, the new public infrastructure needed for co-production must contain spaces and opportunities for experimentation, for risking failure, for admitting to uncertainty and for expressing humility about how much we already know and optimism about what others can contribute through collective efforts.

8.9   Conclusion

Co-production is sometimes regarded by the public sector as simply a low-cost way of delivering public services by replacing paid staff by unpaid volunteers. However, this is misguided. Not only does such an interpretation fall outside our definition of co-production – where both citizens and professionals make a contribution – but it also ignores that co-production often delivers to citizens a range of outcomes not available from traditional service approaches, and a range of extrinsic and intrinsic rewards.

We have therefore argued that user and community co-production of public services and publicly desired outcomes is a collaborative social innovation with the potential not only to improve services but also to achieve social change, in line with the democratic policies and decisions which lie behind those public services. Sometimes this co-production is democratically initiated or endorsed (through the representative democracy route), while in other cases it consists of some elements of direct democracy in relation to issues of political concern. In all cases, the joint activities of citizens and public services open up the potential to make democratically governed social action both more effective and more democratic.

As such, co-production is an integral element of collaborative governance. When done well, it can support the legitimacy of government and of public governance, help to transform public services, radically improve outcomes and/or bring about significant efficiency gains. When done badly, of course, it may convince citizens of the bad faith or incompetence of government and can convince government that only professionalized services can be effective and efficient.

So what will determine whether this social innovation is likely to be done well or badly? A key lesson from the case studies in this chapter is the need to invest in a new public infrastructure – co-production is not 'free', it requires both sides to make inputs in order to release the potential synergies in collaboration with each other. And such investment is generally not simply a 'rational' calculation; it is a social action, which links innovative practice to social purpose. This highlights the precarious nature of the current political interest in co-production – if it is based simply on a fanciful belief that governments in financial crisis can cut their budgets by passing the buck to citizens, it is doomed to failure. Co-production, by definition, requires joint commitment from citizens and governments. Without citizen-powered innovation, public services are likely to repeat the deficiencies of the past; however, without investment from the public sector, even imaginative innovation is likely to be ineffective and wasteful.

References

Alford, J. and Yates, S. 2015. 'Co-production of public services in Australia: The roles of government organisations and co-producers', *Australian Journal of Public Administration*, first published online, DOI: 10.1111/1467-8500.12157.

Anheier, H. 2015. 'Democracy requires the critical engagement of practitioners and experts alike if it is to thrive in these challenging times', Democratic Audit UK, www.democraticaudit.com/?p=15068.

Bovaird, T. 2012. 'Attributing outcomes to social policy interventions – "Gold standard" or "fool's gold" in public policy and management?', *Social Policy and Administration* 48(1): 1–23.

Bovaird, T. and Kenny, R. 2015. 'Managing complex adaptive systems to produce public outcomes in Birmingham, UK', in P. Cairney and R. Geyer (eds.), *Handbook of Complexity and Public Policy*. Cheltenham: Edward Elgar, pp. 261–83.

Bovaird, T. and Loeffler, E. 2012. 'From engagement to co-production: The contribution of users and communities to outcomes and public value', *Voluntas* 23(4): 1119–38.

2015. 'Public management and governance: the future?' in T. Bovaird and E. Loeffler (eds.), *Public Management and Governance*. London: Routledge.

Bovaird, T., van Ryzin, G., Loeffler, E. and Parrado, S. 2015a. 'Activating citizens to participate in collective co-production of public services', *Journal of Social Policy* 44(1): 1–23.

Bovaird, T., Loeffler, E., van Ryzin, G., Alford, J. and Yates, S. 2015b. 'International comparisons of user and community co-production of public services and outcomes: Survey evidence from six countries', Paper presented to PMRA Conference, Minneapolis, MN.

Bovaird, T., Stoker, G., Loeffler, E., Jones, T. and Pinilla Roncancio, M. 2016. 'Activating collective coproduction for public services: Influencing citizens to participate in complex governance mechanisms', *International Review of Administrative Science* 82, first published online, DOI: 10.1177/0020852314566009.

Grant, R. M. 2002. *Contemporary Strategy Analysis*. London: Wiley.

Lang, R. 2011. 'Peer training of learner drivers by offenders in Austria', *Governance International*, www.govint.org/good-practice/case-studies/close-to-peer-train ing-of-learner-drivers-by-offenders-in-austria/.

Loeffler, E. Bovaird, T., Parrado, S. and van Ryzin, G. 2008. '"If you want to go fast, walk alone. If you want to go far, walk together": Citizens and the co-production of public services', Report to the EU Presidency. Ministry of Finance, Budget and Public Services.

Loeffler, E., van Ryzin, G., Bovaird, T. and Timm-Arnold, P. 2015. 'Improving the quality of life of younger and older generations in Germany through co-production: A quantitative and qualitative study of the levels, drivers and barriers', Paper presented at IRSPM Conference, University of Birmingham, Birmingham.

Timm-Arnold, P. 2014. 'Clean City Linköping: Co-designing innovative solutions with young people', *Governance International*, www.govint.org/good-practice/case-studies/clean-city-linkoeping-co-designing-innovative-solutions-with-young-people/.

9   The Role of Elected Politicians in Collaborative Policy Innovation

Eva Sørensen

9.1   Introduction

As described in Chapter 1, public innovation is moving to the top of the political agenda in Western liberal democracies as well as among public sector researchers (Agger et al. 2015). While much thought has been given to the question of how to innovate public service provision (Mulgan and Albury 2003; US Government 2009; OECD 2010; Osborne 2010) few considerations have been made about policy innovation in terms of new political visions, goals and strategies. A comprehensive analysis of public innovation should include analyses of the public sector's policy innovation capacity, e.g. to what extent public authorities, and not least elected politicians, have the capacity to develop, implement and diffuse new political visions, goal and strategies (Sørensen and Waldorff 2014). In particular, more knowledge is needed about the impact of existing forms of governance on the development of new innovative public policies and what can be done to reform Western liberal democracies in ways that enhance their policy innovation capacity.

The limited focus on policy innovation is striking in light of the growing distrust of politicians and general disenchantment with representative democracy (Stoker 2006; Femia, Korosenyi and Slomp 2009; Norris 2011). Moreover, the growing number of wicked and unruly problems that governments have placed at the top of the policy agenda, but are unable to solve, warrants intensive efforts to improve politicians' capacity for policy innovation (Rittel and Webber 1973; Levin et al. 2012). Among these problems are global warming, poverty, crime, drug abuse, lifestyle-related illnesses, terrorism, negative social heritage, and refugees and migration. In their dealings with these complex and sensitive policy issues, governments face mounting policy execution problems in the form of ill-designed policies that do not result in the intended outcomes (Macmillan and Cain 2010) and political stalemate and deadlock between political actors with fixed and opposed political positions and

178

interests (Goodin 1996). One way for governments and other political actors to overcome this predicament is to improve their ability to develop new innovative policies that reduce policy failures and pave the way for compromise and agreements that make collective political action possible.

This chapter explores the institutional conditions for policy innovation in representative democracies and considers how institutional changes can contribute to enhancing the policy innovation capacity of elected politicians. Drawing on recent developments in innovation theory, it is argued that mainstream models of representative democracies do not fully exploit all available drivers of policy innovation, but that this short-coming can be remedied though relatively moderate institutional changes in the formal and informal set-up of policy-making procedures that accommodate collaboration between elected politicians and relevant and affected stakeholders. The chapter starts out by identifying three potential drivers of policy innovation. Then follows a discussion of how mainstream models of representative democracy exploit these drivers. I identify a new role for politicians as metagovernors of collaborative policy innovation and conclude by pointing to some of the ways in which the policy innovation capacity of elected politicians can be enhanced.

9.2   Three Drivers of Policy Innovation

Classical innovation theories are mainly developed with the private sector in mind. They assign entrepreneurial business leaders and competitive market pressures as the key drivers of innovation (Schumpeter 1976). Entrepreneurial leaders generate new ideas, commission missions and establish teams consisting of actors with relevant innovation assets such as experience, knowledge, creativeness, competence, courage, resources and authority. Competitive pressures motivate actors to try something new despite considerable risk of failure and the large costs involved in moving into unknown territory. In the 1980s, the New Public Management (NPM) programme brought this line of thinking into the public sector (Osborne and Gaebler 1993) by recasting public managers as entrepreneurial leaders of public innovation and competition between public service providers as a means to motivate street-level bureaucrats to innovate in an attempt to enhance the efficiency and effectiveness of public governance. While NPM mainly considered leadership and com-petition from a managerial perspective, classical theories of liberal democracy from James Mill to Robert A. Dahl (Dahl 1961; Held 1989; Mill 1992; Helms 2015) saw political leadership and competition as important drivers of policy innovation. Hence, they more or less explicitly

relate the success or failure of political leaders to their ability to launch
new political programmes and ideas (Kingdon 1984; Polsby 1984).
Likewise, analyses of inter- and intra-party policy making view competition as an important driver of policy innovation (Bara and Weale 2006;
Bouchey 2010; Bullinger et al. 2010; Buchler 2011). In other words, it is
generally agreed that political leadership and competition are key drivers
of policy innovation. As we shall see below, however, recent developments in innovation theory suggest that although these drivers are important they are insufficient and should be supplemented by collaboration.

In recent years, innovation theorists have expressed an increasing
interest in the role of collaboration in driving innovation. Students of
private sector innovation increasingly view business clusters, triple helix
arrangements and lead and end-user involvement as essential for promoting innovations in products, production methods and business models
(Von Hippel 1986; Rosenfeld 1997; Novell, Schmitz and Spencer 2006;
Ranga, Miedema and Jorna 2008; Bishop and Riopelle 2011). An upcom-
ing field of social innovation theory highlights partnership formations in
civil society as an invaluable means to develop new ways of meeting
unfulfilled social needs (Mulgan and Albury 2003; Paulus and Nijstad
2003; Moulaert et al. 2013). Finally, public innovation researchers show
a growing interest in the innovative potentials of networks and other
interactive forms of public governance (Borins 2001; Eggers and Singh
2009; Bommert 2010; Sørensen and Torfing 2011a; Ansell and Torfing
2014).

What unites these new theoretical developments in innovation theory is
the idea that collaboration, defined as the constructive exploitation of
differences in a group of actors, accommodates innovation through a
creative destruction of existing ideas, beliefs, perspectives and practices
and an explorative search for something new to replace what has been
destroyed (Gray 1989). It is exactly because of the fact that collaboration
involves conflicts and contestations between actors with different interests, perspectives, values, experiences and knowledge that transformative
learning and innovation can take place (Torfing 2016). The theories also
agree that whether or not collaboration in clusters, partnerships or networks results in innovation depends on the presence of interdependencies
between the participating actors that motivates them to overcome the
difficulties they encounter. The level of innovation also depends on the
costs related to the exchange of ideas and viewpoints and the engagement
in heated debates that might and might not lead to new innovative positions, recognitions and patterns of action.

It should be noted that collaboration is mostly seen as a supplement
rather than as an alternative to the two classic drivers of innovation:

leadership and competition. Following this line of thinking, I shall argue that each of the three drivers of innovation – political leadership, competition and collaboration – has an important role to play in promoting policy innovation. *Political leadership* is important for bringing policy innovation onto the political agenda, commissioning innovative missions, allocating sufficient resources and authorizing relevant actors to innovate. In representative democracies, the task consists in building institutions that place elected politicians in the position as leaders of policy innovation processes. *Political competition* is important for different reasons. Its particular strength is that it motivates political actors to develop their political ideas and policy programmes. Therefore, the policy innovation capacity of representative democracies is related to the level of competition it provides, which again depends on the number of actors that are given the capacity, opportunity and access to battle for political power and influence. Finally, *political collaboration* between actors with relevant innovation assets can produce new understandings of a policy problem and inspire the formulation of new innovative political visions, strategies and goals (Roberts and Bradley 1991; Roberts and King 1996; Sherranden, Slosar and Sherraden 2000). Representative democracies can exploit this last innovation driver through the institutionalization of policy innovation arenas that accommodate collaboration between actors with relevant innovation assets including politicians from different parties, policy experts, organizations and associations, and lead and end-users.

In agreement with the general recognition of the importance of all three innovation drivers, I propose that a political system's capacity for policy innovation, defined as its ability to formulate, implement and diffuse new political visions, goals and strategies (Agger and Sørensen 2014), depends on the extent to which its political institutional set-up accommodates both political leadership, political competition, and political collaboration (Hartley, Sørensen and Torfing 2013; Helms 2015). Moreover, the political institutions must seek to reduce the potential tensions between the three innovation drivers to ensure a happy marriage between them. Although they are supplementary, they can also easily undermine each other if the formal and/or informal institutional design allows one to dominate the others. Political leadership can hamper competition and collaboration; competition can weaken the exercise of political leadership and the willingness to collaborate, and collaboration can reduce competition and weaken political leadership. This means that whether or not a policy process leads to policy innovation depends on the mix between them. The concrete mix we find in different representative democracies is an expression of historical choices in institution building as well as of the ongoing task of reformers, described in Chapter 1, to establish a productive balance and tension between and mix of the forms of governance advocated by the Classical Public Administration (CPA) paradigm, NPM and New Public Governance (NPG).

9.3   Limits to Policy Innovation in Representative Democracy

To what extent then do mainstream models of representative democracy exploit the three drivers of policy innovation described above? This is a complex question to answer due to the considerable variation in the way they are formally and informally institutionalized at different levels of governance as well as in various countries (Stoker and Batley 1991; Lijphart 1999). Compared to national governments, local governments are often formally designed to accommodate consensus and overcome conflicts more than to spur competition, and the political culture tends to accommodate collaboration not only between political leaders and ordinary politicians, and politicians from different parties, but also between politicians and local citizens and stakeholders. There are also huge differences in the conditions for policy innovation in majoritarian two-party systems such as the United States and United Kingdom and in multi-party systems such as those found in the Scandinavian countries, and differences in the political cultures in the countries further deepen these differences (Almond and Verba 1961; Lijphart 1999; Dalton and Welzel 2014). Despite these systematic institutional differences in the way representative democracy is formally and informally institutionalized, some similarities can be detected in the way they exploit the three innovation drivers.

At a general level of analysis, the formal institutional set-up of representative democracies is primarily designed to promote political leadership and political competition as well as a fruitful co-existence between these two innovation drivers. A key goal is to ensure that political leadership is possible in a context characterized by political pluralism and that the institutions accommodate political competition between politicians who seek election as well as between those who have obtained it (Helms 2015). Less is done, however, to accommodate collaboration. Although some institutional mechanisms, e.g. veto powers and multi-party election systems, do put pressure on politicians to seek political compromise and engage in bargaining, these incentives for intra- and inter-party collaboration are relatively weak and enjoy limited institutional support. Moreover, the formal rules and procedures are rarely designed to promote collaboration between politicians and stakeholders with relevant innovation assets (Lees-Marshment 2015). The politicians are by and large left with the full burden of developing new innovative policies among themselves and must do so in policy arenas, which are heavily dominated by political leadership and competition such as meetings in the individual political parties, in representative assemblies and in standing political committees. These arenas can undoubtedly produce new political ideas and perspectives, but they limit the policy innovation capacity of representative democracy because they provide very few formalized procedures for collaborative policy making. The collaborative arenas that do exist are for the most part heavily exposed to the centrifugal forces of political hierarchy and competition. Moreover, they rarely bring politicians into dialogue with relevant and affected stakeholders.

Studies of informal practices in representative democracies show, however, that elected politicians do have some opportunity to develop new policies in cross-party collaboration as well as in dialogue with public administrators in arenas that escape the public limelight and thus the centrifugal forces of hierarchical leadership and competition. Analyses of coalition building show that informal inter-party and intra-governmental negotiations and agreements among party leaders play a key role in developing new policies (Dupont 1996; Strøm, Müller and Bergman 2008), but ordinary politicians tend not to be allowed to participate in these negotiations, which leaves them with few opportunities to engage in collaborative policy innovation. Other studies show that politicians often involve executive public managers in policy development but again it is mostly executive politicians who benefit from these collaborations (Svara 1998, 2001; Peters 2002). Politicians also seek informal dialogue with external actors. They meet delegations of interest groups, participate in thematic conferences and visit public institutions, businesses, organizations and local communities. However, these events rarely take the form of collaboration. Instead politicians are put under pressure to give clear and affirmative answers and show responsiveness to demands from stakeholders who advocate for and dictate policies that serve their particular interests, and in doing so they sometimes hamper rather than enhance the policy innovation capacity of elected politicians (Echstein 1969; Smith 1990; Jones and Baumgartner 2005; Bijlsma et al. 2011). Politicians also gain valuable inspiration from think tanks and expert committees, but politicians often end up as passive receivers of policy advice rather than as co-producers of new innovative policies (Stone 1996).

In light of the limited access to collaborative policy arenas, and the huge institutional pressures on elected politicians to come up with new innovative policies, many politicians develop a personal political network (Fenno, 1978). These networks mainly consist of hand-picked actors that the politicians trust, and who possess relevant knowledge, ideas and insights that can assist the politicians in developing new political visions, goals and strategies as well as in considering how to respond to policies proposed by others (Sørensen 2006). Such networks can serve as important arenas for collaborative policy innovation to the extent that they give the politicians an opportunity to discuss, develop and diffuse their political position in dialogue with a set of selected public and/or private actors who are willing to move beyond a narrow interest perspective or expert truisms. Moreover, the politicians get a chance to test and develop their political ideas at a safe distance from intra-party hierarchies, inter-party competition and merciless media scrutiny. As evidenced in a number of studies, access to an informal personal political network is highly valued by elected politicians (Mintrom and Vergari 1998; Devere 2011) as well as by other actors (Chun 2009) that are involved in policy innovation processes. As it stands, however, the degree to which a network serves this purpose depends on the ability of individual politicians to engage actors with relevant innovation assets in an open-ended search for new policies.

In conclusion, the formal set-up of representativeness provides few and relatively weak arenas and procedures for promoting collaboration between politicians and internal and external actors with relevant innovation assets, and although informal collaboration does take place, it is up to the individual politician to find ways to engage in collaborations that promote their policy innovation capacity. An institutionalization of formal arenas and procedures for collaboration between politicians and relevant actors is therefore a promising strategy for enhancing the policy innovation capacity of representative democracy (Lees-Marshment 2015).

9.4   Politicians as Metagovernors of Collaborative Policy Innovation

Before advocating for a closer collaboration between elected politicians and relevant and affected stakeholders, there is good reason to consider the possible dangers involved and, in particular, how the collaboration will affect the two other drivers of policy innovation. Will enhanced collaboration weaken the exercise of political leadership and the level of political competition? I shall argue that whether it is possible to avoid trade-offs between the three innovation drivers depends on the extent to which it is ensured that the politicians who engage in collaborative policy innovation are empowered rather than taken hostage by those involved in the collaboration process (Klijn and Koppenjan 2000; Torfing et al. 2012; Helms 2015). In other words, we need to consider under what conditions collaboration will assist elected politicians in their endeavours to develop new policies that qualify their political leadership and provide a strong platform for participating in competitive battles for political power and influence.

Recent developments in theories of public leadership, management and governance are helpful in clarifying how public authorities can collaborate with relevant and affected stakeholders and at the same time maintain their political autonomy and authority (Klijn and Koppenjan 2000; Agranoff and McGuire 2003; Burns 2003; Kooiman 2003). James MacGregor Burns (2003) re-conceptualizes leadership as the act of transforming followers into creative co-governors, and public management research investigates how public authorities seek to govern through the mobilization and empowerment of employees and citizens (Agranoff and McGuire 2003). Finally, governance theories have introduced the term metagovernance to specify a number of techniques that make it possible for public leaders to address and sometimes actually solve complex societal problems through the governance of self-governing actors (Kooiman 1993; Jessop 1998; Sørensen and Torfing 2007). The significance of these theories is that they view collaboration as a governance tool rather than as a barrier to governance. The mobilization of, and engagement with, relevant and affected actors can enhance public governance and do so without undermining the leadership position of public authorities.

The proposed list of tools by which public authorities can metagovern participating stakeholders includes political, financial and legal framing of governance objectives, the composition of collaborative policy arenas, incentives steering, and facilitation of and participation in co-governance (Sørensen and Torfing 2007, 2009). Different forms of framing allow public authorities to determine what is up for discussion and what is not. Being in charge of the composition of participants allows public authorities to monitor the collaborative governance process in ways that are in line with the intended purpose of involving external actors. Incentives steering can help to accommodate collaboration between selected actors through the creation of strategic interdependencies, and process facilitation and direct participation in the collaboration, and accommodate knowledge exchange and the development of shared meaning, purpose and ownership to governance initiatives. While some of these metagovernance tools are exercised hands-off and at a distance from the collaboration process others involve hands-on engagement in the collaboration process. Through a balanced combination of hands-off and hands-on tool kits, public authorities can prosper from the insights and resources that grow out of the collaboration while still maintaining a relatively high level of independence. While hands-off metagovernance involves institutional reform of governance procedures, hands-on metagovernance mainly involves changes in the day-to-day practices of political actors (Klijn and Koppenjan 2004; Meuleman 2008).

Metagovernance theories and research into how public authorities can promote public governance through the mobilization of relevant and affected actors have for the most part taken departure in a managerial approach to public governance. The focus of attention has been on how public managers can metagovern collaborative processes in ways that enhance the efficiency, effectiveness and innovativeness of public service provision. Less has been said about how politicians can exercise political leadership through the metagovernance of collaborative policy innovation. A few studies have focused on how public authorities can metagovern to ensure the democratic quality of collaborative forms of governance (Klijn and Koppenjan 2000; Sørensen and Torfing 2005, 2009; Koppenjan, Kars and Van der Voort 2011), but these studies fail to explicate the strictly political aspects of metagovernance and how politicians can metagovern collaboration in the pursuit of new innovative policies. In other words, we need to know more about how politicians can metagovern collaborative policy innovation processes in ways that strengthen their capacity to launch new innovative policies that give them an advantage in competitive battles for political leadership and re-election within the individual parties as well as between parties.

As a first step in trying to specify the strictly political aspects of metagovernance, and clarify further how politicians can metagovern collaborative policy innovation, it is necessary to draw a distinction between politics and administration. As evidenced in numerous studies, the division of labour between politicians and administrators in the real world of political life tends to be messy rather than clear cut and concise (Lindblom 1959; Svara 2001; Overeem 2012). So, rather than making claims regarding what politicians and administrators do, respectively, I will make an analytical distinction between politics and administration as two distinct aspects of public governance (Peters and Pierre 2003). Politics, on the one side, involves contestations between actors with different perceptions of what constitutes a good society and of what counts as morally acceptable strategies and methods for getting there. Administration, on the other, is concerned with designing and implementing policies efficiently, effectively and innovatively in accordance with existing laws, prevailing professional norms, standards and management techniques.

What are the implications of this analytical distinction between politics and administration when it comes to defining a distinctly political approach to metagoverning collaborative policy innovation? While managerial metagovernance of collaborative policy innovation aims to bring together actors who can engage in a creative cognitive endeavour to develop the content, procedures and working methods used in the provision of public services, political metagovernance aims to stage and direct political debates that contribute to the development of new political visions of, and goals and strategies for realizing good society. Political metagovernors set the political agenda, enrol and commit selected actors to contribute with new ideas and propositions while excluding others, design the process in ways that ensure that the output and outcome of the collaboration levels with the overall political perspectives and aspirations of the metagovernor, stage debates that produce convincing political arguments for and against new policy ideas, and initiate conflicts that illuminate the political realism of bringing policy innovations into the political process in representative democracy. As such, political metagovernance can be seen as a laboratory for metagovernors, and in this case politicians, to develop new innovative political programmes, test the political viability of these programmes in a safe environment and refine their political position and argumentation before they venture into hardnosed intra-party and inter-party battles for political power (Sørensen 2015).

However, politicians who engage in the exercise of political metagovernance face a huge dilemma. Collaboration is valuable for politicians because it allows open-ended political debates that can potentially produce new policies. At the same time the political relevance of the new policies depends on how they fit into the larger political perspectives, strategies and contestations at play on the political scene at a given time. It is a constant temptation for politicians to regulate the collaborative policy process too tightly in order to control the agenda and the outcomes, although this over-regulation will most likely reduce the innovativeness of the collaboration process. As such, an enforcement of the policy innovation capacity of representative democracy calls not only for institutional reform but also for an enhancement of the capacity of elected politicians to find a productive balance between over-regulation and under-regulation in their exercise of political metagovernance of collaborative policy innovation.

9.5 Improving the Policy Innovation Capacity of Elected Politicians

As noted earlier, the institutions of representative democracy provide few formal and informal opportunities for elected politicians to engage in collaborative policy innovation. The situations where they can step into the role as political metagovernors of collaborative policy innovation are also rare. Rather than calling for major institutional reform, however, I claim that this limitation to policy innovation in representative democracies can be remedied through a step-by-step promotion of occasions where individual politicians, parties, representative assemblies and governments can step into the role as metagovernors of collaborative policy innovation.

Let us first consider ways of improving the conditions for individual politicians to seek dialogue with relevant and affected stakeholders in ways that assist them in developing new innovative political ideas and policy programmes. Although personal networks might to some extent serve this purpose, these networks do not necessarily include the relevant stakeholders, and in the cases where they are formed over a long time period and function as a closed circle, they tend to preserve rather than innovate and bring new ideas and perspectives to the table. As suggested by the results of a Danish case study of collaborative policy innovation, the policy innovation capacity of individual politicians could be more systematically enhanced by granting them the opportunity to step into the role of political metagovernors of policy innovation workshops on selected policy topic and composed of selected stakeholders with relevant competences, experience and know-how. The study points out how a series of policy innovation workshops debating the use of force in psychiatric care triggered a radical change among the participating members of parliament (MPs) in their perception of the policy problem as well as of possible policy solutions (Sørensen and Waldorff 2014). This did not lead them to agree on what needed to be done. Rather it changed their individual political positions on the matter, and, in consequence, the content of the political debates, contestations and alliances between them. Although the collaboration reinvigorated the political debate between the individual politicians, however, the new policy positions did not get an easy path into the larger political debate due to the dominance of hierarchy and competition within the individual parties.

Accordingly, the next question we need to consider is how collaborative policy innovation involving relevant and affected actors can promote the policy innovation capacity of political parties. The need for collaborative spaces for policy innovation arenas depends, among other things, on the number and variety of party members, and the general decline in party membership enhances the need for political parties to engage in open-ended political debate with the population. The required collaborative policy innovation also depends on the political culture in the individual parties. The need to stage collaborative policy innovation is particularly large in centralized political parties and in homogenous political parties where members have similar backgrounds and life experiences. Hence, political parties easily develop political tunnel vision, which can seriously hamper their policy innovation capacity and reduce their ability to capture the hearts and minds of the electorate (Kitschelt 2000). The danger of political stagnation is particularly pertinent in situations where a political party has stable or even growing voter support, while the incentives to develop new policies tend to be stronger when parties face a decline in public support (Hersey 2014). Recent changes in the way political parties develop new policies indicate that there is a growing recognition of the important role collaborative policy innovation between the members of a political party and non-party members can play for enhancing the party's capacity to formulate, implement and diffuse new innovative policies (Dalton 2008). The new social media, e.g. different kinds of crowdsourcing, could enhance the policy innovation capacity of political parties, but the development of new party structures that more systematically involve non-party members in face-to-face political debates is another promising avenue for enhancing the policy innovation capacity of political parties. This strategy faces some resistance, however, because the involvement of non-party members in political debate can destabilize the internal power balance between different fractions in the party as well as well-consolidated and relatively clear differences and divisions between the political parties that are the foundation for inter-party competition for support on election day.

Small changes in the way representative assemblies work can also promote the policy innovation capacity of elected politicians. Although much policy innovation takes place within the political parties, dialogue between politicians from different parties can also spur policy innovation. A reinvigoration of the inter-party policy debates in the standing political committees is a good place to start. Many standing political committees tend to focus on day-to-day law or rule making more than on policy innovation, and often they function as arenas for party competition rather than as arenas for collaborative policy innovation (Pilkington 1997; Bradley and McCubbins 2002). Recent experiments with political committees in Danish municipalities suggest, however, that advisory ad hoc committees composed of politicians and selected stakeholders can function as spaces for collaborative policy innovation (Sørensen and Torfing 2011b; Agger and Sørensen 2014). What triggers policy innovation seems to be that stakeholders participate in the debate, that the committees do not hold decision-making powers and that the activities and debates take place in seclusion and escape public scrutiny (Fung, Graham and Weil 2007; Torfing et al. 2012). Inter- and intra-party battles for political power take place elsewhere, and it is possible for politicians as well as for stakeholders to test and elaborate on preliminary policy ideas in a safe environment under the radar of day-to-day politics and media attention. The studies also show, however, that there is a tendency in these new committees to avoid discussions of heavily contested political issues to the effect that the committees do not fully exploit their potential to contribute to the development of new innovative solutions.

Finally, it should be pointed out that governments can prosper from collaborative policy innovation, too. When politicians first get into office after a period in opposition, they tend to be loaded with new political ideas and innovative policy programmes that have been developed in the years in opposition. As time moves on, however, governments often run dry and opportunities for developing new ideas are few and far between. Therefore, governments often end up relying more or less exclusively on inputs from the administration and expert commissions and lobbyists. A systematic political metagovernance of collaborative policy innovation process can enhance the capacity of governments to stay on top of the political process through the continuous proactive launching of new policy programmes rather than gradually ending up in a reactive position as commentators on policies developed by others (Burley 2003). The Open Government initiative launched by President Obama could be seen as an attempt to engage citizens directly in the development of new policies, although further research is needed in order to clarify the impact of Open Government for the policy innovation capacity of his administration (Ginsberg 2011). The highly competitive and antagonistic climate in American federal policy making raises some doubts, however, regarding the extent to which the government is ready to be more open to citizen inputs.

In sum, many small steps can be taken to enhance elected politicians' capacity for policy innovation. An institutionalization of more spaces for collaboration can foster policy innovation without undermining the political leadership and competition that also play a key role in driving policy innovation in representative democracies. Individual politicians as well as political parties, representative assemblies and governments can prosper from small reforms in the policy-making processes that with regular intervals and when need exists place them as political metagovernors of collaborative policy innovation. Experiments of the kind described above are taking place but further research is needed in order to clarify how widespread these experiments are, and to what extent they contribute to enhancing the policy innovation capacity of elected politicians. Such studies could, among other things, produce valuable knowledge about the problems and potential related to the intersection between and co-existence of collaboration, competition and hierarchy in democratic decision-making. Under what conditions do the three drivers enforce each other and when do they deactivate each other in ways that weaken the policy innovation capacity of elected politicians?

9.6 Conclusion

Public innovation has risen to the top of the political agenda among governments all over the Western world, and research into public innovation is mushrooming. The focus of interest has mainly been on the innovation of public service delivery while little attention has been given to policy innovation. The limited attention given to assessing and enhancing the policy innovation capacity of representative democracies is striking in light of the mounting policy problems that governments seem unable to solve and the growing distrust in elected politicians. There is ample reason to include policy innovation in analyses of the current level of innovation in the public sector as well as in debates about how to promote public innovation. In light of the overall purpose of this edited volume, the purpose of this chapter has been to analyse to what extent and how contemporary models of representative democracy fully exploit three key innovation drivers: political leadership, competition and collaboration. What I am arguing here is that it is time for elected politicians to ripen the potential fruits of the collaborative forms of governance proposed by the NPG paradigm while continuing to draw on the innovation drivers offered by the CPA and NPM paradigms. While political leadership is essential for placing policy innovation on the political agenda, and political competition motivates political actors to innovate, collaboration between actors with relevant ideas, creativity, courage, experiences and ideas provide the creative destruction that paves the way for the formulation, implementation and diffusion of new innovative policies. I conclude that although the formal and informal set-up of representative democracy does promote policy innovation, there is room for improvement by enhancing the space for collaboration between elected politicians and relevant and affected stakeholders. As suggested in recent studies, small-scale institutional reforms that place national as well as local politicians in the role of metagovernors of collaborative policy innovation appear to be a promising way of enhancing the policy innovation capacity of representative democracy, although it is going to be far from easy to strike a productive combination of political leadership, competition and collaboration in the promotion of new innovative policies.

References

Agger, A. and Sørensen, E. 2014. 'Designing collaborative policy innovation: Lessons from a Danish municipality', in C. Ansell and J. Torfing (eds.), *Public Innovation through Collaboration and Design*. New York: Routledge, pp. 188–208.

Agger, A., Damgaard, B., Krogh, A. H. and Sørensen, E. 2015. *Public Innovation in Northern Europe*. London: Bentham Press.

Agranoff, R. and McGuire, M. 2003. *Collaborative Public Management: New Strategies for Local Government*. Washington, DC: Georgetown University Press.

Almond, G. and Verba, S. 1961. *The Civic Culture: Political Attitudes and Democracy in Five Nations*. Washington, DC: Georgetown University Press.

Ansell, C. and Torfing, J. (eds.) 2014. *Public Innovation through Collaboration and Design*. New York: Routledge.

Bara, J. and Weale, A. (eds.) 2006. *Democratic Politics and Party Competition*. New York: Routledge.

Bijlsma, R. M., Bots, P. W. G., Wolters, H. A. and Hoekstra, A. Y. 2011. 'An empirical analysis of stakeholders' influence on policy development: The role of uncertainty handling', *Ecology and Society* 16(1): 51. online URL: www.ecologyandsociety.org/vol16/iss1/art51/.

Bishop, A. and Riopelle, K. 2011. 'Identifying potential collaborative innovation networks to support emerging chemical legislation and global design', *Social and Behavioral Sciences* 26(3): 38–45.

Bommert, B. 2010. 'Collaborative innovation in the public sector', *International Public Management Review* 11(2): 15–33.

Borins, S. 2001. 'Encouraging innovation in the public sector', *Journal of Intellectual Capital* 2(3): 310–19.

Bouchey, G. 2010. *Policy Diffusion Dynamics in America*. New York: Cambridge University Press.

Bradley, D. W. and McCubbins, M. D. (eds.) 2002. *Party, Process and Political Change*. Washington, DC: CQ Press.

Buchler, J. 2011. *Hiring and Firing Public Officials*. Oxford University Press.

Bullinger, A. C., Neyer, A.-K., Rass, M. and Moeslein, K. M. 2010. 'Community-based innovation contests: Where competition meets cooperation', *Creativity and Innovation Management* 19(3): 290–303.

Burby, R. J. 2003. 'Making plans that matter: Citizen involvement and government action', *Journal of the American Planning Association* 69(1): 33–49.

Burns, J. M. 2003. *Transforming Leadership*. New York: Grove Press.

Chun, L. 2009. *The Governance Structure of Chinese Firms: Innovation, Competitiveness, and Growth in Dual Economy*. Dordrecht: Springer.

Dahl, R. A. 1961. *Who Governs? Democracy and Power in an American City*. New Haven: Yale University Press.

Dalton, R. J. 2008. *Citizen Politics: Public Opinion and Political Parties in Advanced Industrial Democracies*. Washington, DC: CQ Press.

Dalton, R. J. and Welzel, C. (eds.) 2014. *The Civic Culture Transformed*. Cambridge: Cambridge University Press.

Devere, H. 2011. 'The resurrection of political friendship', in B. Descharmes, C. S. Hauser, C. Kruger and T. Loy (eds.), *Varieties of Friendship. Interdisciplinary Perspective on Social Relationships*. Göttingen: V&R Unipress, pp. 17–42.

Dupont, C. 1996. 'Negotiation as coalition building', *International Negotiations* 1(1): 47–61.

Echstein, H. 1969. 'Pressure group politics', *Journal of Medical Education* 35(11): 1069–82.

Eggers, B. and Singh, S. 2009. *The Public Innovators Playbook*. Washington, DC: Harvard Kennedy School of Government.

Femia, J. V., Korosenyi, A. and Slomp, G. (eds.) 2009. *Political Leadership in Liberal and Democratic Theory*. Exeter: Imprint Academic.

Fenno, R. F. Jr. 1978. *Home Style. House Members in Their Districts*. Boston: Little Brown and Company.

Fung, A., Graham, M. and Weil, D. 2007. *Full Disclosure: The Perils and Potentials of Transparency*. Cambridge: Cambridge University Press.

Ginsberg, W. 2011. *Obama Administration's Open Government Initiative: Issues for Congress*. Washington, DC: Congressional Research Service.

Goodin, R. E. 1996. 'Institutionalizing the public interest: The defense of deadlock and beyond', *American Political Science Review* 90(3): 331–43.

Gray, B. 1989. *Collaborating: Finding Common Ground for Multiparty Problems*. San Francisco: Jossey-Bass.

Hartley, J., Sørensen, E. and Torfing, J. 2013. 'Collaborative innovation: A viable alternative to market competition and organizational entrepreneurship', *Public Administration Review* 73(6): 821–30.

Held, D. 1989. *Models of Democracy*. Cambridge: Cambridge University Press.

Helms, L. 2015. 'Democracy and innovation: From institutions to agency and leadership', *Democratization*, ahead of print, DOI: 10.1080/13510347.2014.981667.

Hersey, M. (ed.) 2014. *Guide to U.S. Political Parties*. Thousand Oaks: CQ Press.

Jessop, B. 1998. *The Rise of Governance and the Risk of Failure: The Case of Economic Development*. UNESCO no. 155. Oxford: Blackwell Publishers.

Jones, B. D. and Baumgartner, F. R. 2005. *The Politics of Attention*. Oxford: Oxford University Press.

Kingdon, J. W. 1984. *Agendas, Alternatives, and Public Policies*. Boston: Little Brown.

Kitschelt, H. 2000. 'Linkages between citizens and politicians in democratic politics', *Comparative Political Studies* 33(6/7): 845–79.

Klijn, E. H. and Koppenjan, J. 2000. 'Interactive decision making and representative democracy: Institutional collisions and solutions', in O. van Heffen, W. J. M. Kickert and J. A. Thomassen (eds.), *Governance in Modern Society: Effects, Change and Formation of Government Institutions*. Dordrecht: Kluwer Academic Publishers, pp. 114–24.

Kooiman, J. 1993. *Modern Governance: New Government Society Interactions*. London: Sage.

2003. *Governance as Governing*. London: Sage.

Koppenjan, J. and Klijn, E. H. 2004. *Managing Uncertainties in Networks*. New York: Routledge.

Koppenjan, J., Kars, M. and van der Vaart, H. 2011. 'Politicians as metagovernors – Can metagovernance reconcile representative democracy and network reality?' in J. Torfing and P. Triantafillou (eds.), *Interactive Policy Making, Metagovernance and Democracy*. Colchester: ECPR Press, pp. 129–48.

Lees-Marshment, J. 2015. *The Ministry of Public Input*. Houndsmill: Palgrave-Macmillan.

Levin, K., Cashore, B., Bernstein, S. and Auld, G. 2012. 'Overcoming the tragedy of super wicked problems: Constraining our future selves to ameliorate global climate change', *Policy Sciences* 45(2): 124–52.

Lijphart, A. 1999. *Patterns of Democracy: Government Forms and Performance in Thirty-Six Countries*. New Haven: Yale University Press.

Lindblom, C. 1959. 'The science of "Muddling Through" ', *Public Administration Review* 19(2): 79–88.

Macmillan, P. and Cain, T. 2010. *Closing the Gap: Eliminating the Disconnect between Policy Design and Execution*. Vancouver: Deloitte.

Mill, J. 1992. *Political Writings*, edited by Terence Ball. Cambridge: Cambridge University Press.

Mintrom, M. and Vergari, S. 1998. 'Policy networks and innovation diffusion: The case of state education reforms', *The Journal of Politics* 60(1): 126–48.

Meuleman, L. 2008. *Public Management and the Metagovernance of Hierarchies, Networks and Markets*. Heidelberg: Springer Press.

Moulaert, F., MacCallum, D., Mehmood, A. and Hamdouch, A. (eds.) 2013. *The International Handbook on Social Innovation*. Cheltenham: Edward Elgar.

Mulgan, G. and Albury, D. 2003. *Innovation in the Public Sector*. Strategy Unit, UK: Cabinet Office, October 2003.

Norris, P. 2011. *Democratic Deficit: Critical Citizens Revisited*. New York: Cambridge University Press.

Novelli, M., Schmitz, B. and Spencer, T. 2006. 'Networks, clusters and innovation in tourism: A UK experience', *Tourism Management* 25(6): 1141–52.

OECD 2010. *The OECD Innovation Strategy: Getting a Head Start on Tomorrow*. Paris: OECD.

Osborne, D. and Gaebler, T. 1993. *Reinventing Government: How the Entrepreneurial Spirit is Transforming the Public Sector*. Reading, MA: Addison-Wesley.

Osborne, S. 2010. *The New Public Governance?* New York: Routledge.

Overeem, P. 2012. *The Politics-Administration Dichotomy. Towards a Constitutional Perspective*. Boca Raton: CRC Press.

Paulus, P. B. and Nijstad, B.A. (eds.) 2003. *Group Creativity: Innovation through Collaboration*. New York: Oxford University Press.

Peters, B. G. 2002. 'Politicians and bureaucrats in the politics of policy-making', in S. Osborne (ed.), *Public Management: Critical Perspectives on Business and Management*. London. Routledge, pp. 156–82.

Peters, B. G. and Pierre, J. 2003. 'Introduction: The role of Public Administration in governing', in B. G. Peters and J. Pierre (eds.), *Handbook of Public Administration*. London: Sage, pp. 1–11.

Pilkington, C. 1997. *Representative Democracy in Britain Today*. Manchester: Manchester University Press.

Polsby, N. W. 1984. *Political Innovation in America: The Politics of Policy Initiation*. New Haven: Yale University Press.

Ranga, L. M., Miedema, J. and Jorna, R. 2008. 'Enhancing the innovative capacity of small firms through triple helix: Challenges and potentials', *Technology Analysis and Strategic Management* 20(6): 697–716.

Rittel, H. W. J. and Webber, M. M. 1973. 'Dilemmas in a general theory of planning', *Policy Sciences* 4(2): 155–69.

Roberts, N. C. and Bradley, R. T. 1991. 'Stakeholder collaboration and innovation: A study of public policy initiation at the state level', *The Journal of Applied Behavioural Science* 27(1): 209–27.

Roberts, N. C. and King, P. J. 1996. *Transforming Public Policy*. San Francisco: Jossey-Bass.

Rosenfeld, S. A. 1997. 'Bringing business clusters into the mainstream of economic development', *European Planning Studies* 5(1): 3–23.

Schumpeter, J. A. 1976 [1942]. *Capitalism, Socialism and Democracy*. Abingdon: Routledge.

Sherranden, M. G., Slosar, B. and Sherraden, M. 2000. 'Innovation in social policy: collaborative policy advocacy', *Social Sciences* 47(3): 209–21.

Smith, M. J. 1990. 'Pluralism, reformed pluralism and neo-pluralism: The role of pressure groups in policy-making', *Political Studies* 38(2): 302–22.

Sørensen, E. 2006. 'Metagovernance: The changing role of politicians in processes of democratic governance', *American Review of Public Administration* 36(1): 98–114.

2015. 'Enhancing policy innovation by redesigning representative democracy', *Policy & Politics*, available online. www.ingentaconnect.com/content/tpp/pap/pre-prints/content-PP_072;jsessionid=5pkfj3nffginl.alice.

Sørensen, E. and Torfing, J. 2005. 'The democratic anchorage of governance networks', *Scandinavian Political Studies* 28(3): 195–218.

2007. *Theories of Democratic Network Governance*, Basingstoke: Palgrave Macmillan.

2009. 'Enhancing effective and democratic network governance through metagovernance', *Public Administration* 87(2): 234–58.

2011a. 'Enhancing collaborative innovation in the public sector', *Administration and Society* 43(8): 842–68.

2011b. 'Kommunalpolitikere som ledere af politikinnovation', *Økonomi og Politik* 86(4): 33–47.

Sørensen, E. and Waldorff, S. B. 2014. 'Collaborative policy innovation', *The Innovation Journal* 19(3): 1–17.

Stoker, G. 2006. *Why Politics Matters: Making Democracy Work*. Basingstoke: Palgrave Macmillan.

Stoker, G. and Batley, R. 1991. *Local Government in Europe: Trends and Developments*. Basingstoke: Macmillan Education.

Stone, D. 1996. *Capturing the Political Imagination: Think Tanks and the Policy Process*. London: Frank Cass.

Strøm, K., Müller, W. C. and Bergman, T. (eds.) 2008. *The Democratic Life Circle in Western Europe*. Oxford: Oxford University Press.

Svara, J. H. 1998. 'The politics-administration dichotomy model as aberration', *Public Administration Review* 58 (1): 51–8.

2001. 'The myth of the dichotomy: Complementarity of politics and administration in the past and future', *Public Administration Review* 61(2): 176–83.

Torfing, J. 2016. *Collaborative Innovation in the Public Sector*. Washington DC: Georgetown University Press.

Torfing, J., Peters, B. G., Pierre, J. and Sørensen, E. 2012. *Interactive Governance: Advancing the Paradigm*. Oxford University Press.

US Government 2009. 'Open Government Initiative', *The White House*, www.white house.gov/open/documents/open-government-directive.

Von Hippel, E. 1986. 'Lead users: A source of novel product concepts', *Management Science* 32(7): 791–806.

10 The Role of Private Actors in Public Sector Innovation

Ole Helby Petersen, Veiko Lember, Walter Scherrer and Robert Ågren

10.1 Introduction

The changing forms of governance stemming from the rise of New Public Management (NPM) and New Public Governance (NPG) have brought about significant changes in the relationship between the public and private sectors (Christensen and Lægreid 2007; Torfing and Triantafillou 2013). Not only have we witnessed a gradual increase in the involvement of private actors in the provision of public services, but we have also seen an upsurge of new forms of public–private interaction based on quasi-markets, partnerships and networks.

This development, which has unfolded over the past four decades, entails two parallel but distinct trends. First, the gradual replacement of public with private solutions across a broad range of services, such as health, eldercare, employment services and childcare, many of which are services that have traditionally been seen as the family silver of the modern welfare state. While this trend has developed incrementally, it has nonetheless resulted in significant transfers of activities from the public to the private domain (Petersen and Hjelmar 2013). Second, we have witnessed the emergence of a growing number of innovation-oriented forms of public–private interaction under catchy titles such as 'public–private partnerships' (PPPs) (Hodge and Greve 2005), 'public procurement of innovation' (Lember, Kattel and Kalvet 2014), 'innovative contracting out' (Lindholst and Bogetoft 2011) and 'public–private innovation partnerships' (Brogaard and Petersen 2014). Today, perhaps more than ever before, there is a search for new forms of public–private collaboration that have the potential for delivering efficient public services, enhancing innovation and safeguarding public value in its widest sense (Moore 1995).

This chapter examines how governments can enhance public sector innovation by utilizing new as well as old forms of public–private interaction

The corresponding author for this chapter is Ole Helby Petersen.

that mobilizes the knowledge, competencies and resources of the private sector. We focus on three major yet distinct forms of public and private interplay: contracting out, public procurement and public–private partnerships (PPPs). The aim is to examine how these widely used interaction forms fit into the emerging NPG paradigm and how they can contribute to enhanced innovation, learning and collaboration under the evolving NPG framework.

As outlined by the editors in Chapter 1 of the book, innovation and learning are embedded into collective action and institutions governing the public–private collaboration. At the same time, as we are witnessing both a critique of the shortcomings of NPM-based solutions, as well as a return of NPM interventions through austerity policies, there is a need to reassess the market-based forms of public–private interaction as well. On the one hand, debates on marketization under the NPM paradigm have been mainly focused on competition and cost effectiveness and less on innovation and learning. Hence, relationships between the public and private sectors were expected to be of a static and discrete nature. Though most scholars would agree that even transactional market relationships have relational elements (Macneil 1980), the market-based coordination mechanisms characteristic of the NPM era were nonetheless often characterized by a rather narrow focus on contractual rather than relational aspects (Lindholst and Bogetoft 2011). On the other hand, under the NPG paradigm, it is the role of collaborative relations engaged in the co-creation of public value that captures the focal attention (Torfing and Triantafillou 2013). Thus, in the context of wicked problems and societal grand challenges, mutual learning through dynamic or relational user–producer relationships becomes gradually more central in the attempt to facilitate public–private interaction that is conducive to public sector innovation.

The remainder of the chapter is structured as follows. We first examine the conceptual background for discussing the role of private actors in public sector innovation. Next, we examine how the interplay between public and private actors has evolved in the context of public sector innovation with a focus on innovative aspects of contracting out, public procurement and PPPs. In the penultimate section, we move on to discuss how the current governance framework can be improved to enhance the contribution of private actors in public innovation. Finally, we provide a conclusion and discuss themes for future research.

10.2   Private Actors in Public Sector Innovation

Private actors have always played a key role in bringing forth transformative change in public service delivery in modern territorial states. The private sector has enabled governments to introduce new public services, e.g. rescue services (Hodge and Greve 2005), and innovate and transform the existing ones, such as tax collection in medieval times (Wettenhall 2003) or various e-services today. Yet, governments have not only been passive consumers of private sector innovation, but they have in fact been important market makers where no ready-made solutions to tackle societal problems were available. By formulating new demand, creating lead markets and offering valuable feedback, governments have spurred private actors to engage with research, development and innovation activities (Edquist, Hommen and Tsipouri 2000; Mazzucato 2013). The history of technology development from air jets to semi-conductors illustrates that best: when public procurement was part of larger and more systemic public policies (e.g. defence, health, energy, etc.) it has facilitated radical innovation and learning in and between public and private sectors (Lember, Kattel and Kalvet 2014).

When addressing the nexus between public–private interaction and innovation, an important distinction should be made between innovation *in* the public sector and *through* the public sector (Kattel et al. 2014). Innovation in the public sector can be broadly understood as significant changes in public service delivery leading to alteration of the core tasks in the public sector, which broadly aligns with the definition given in Chapter 1 of this book. The link between public sector innovation and public–private interactions has at least three important dimensions (Kattel et al. 2014).

First, public–private interaction may significantly influence and alter the organizational routines of public organizations, as decisions to engage in public–private interaction may lead to developments of new public sector capabilities and learning patterns. Second, public–private interaction may give access to private competencies, resources and know-how, and thereby lead to the introduction of new or significantly improved public services. Governments are key players in tackling complex problems, such as ageing, national security or environmental change, but may lack knowledge or capacity to address these issues in an effective and innovative way. Third, public–private interaction can bring about important change in governance by altering strategic capacities of various social and market agents (Jayasuriya 2005). Either for legitimacy or efficiency reasons (or a combination of the two), changing forms of public–private interaction therefore have potential for altering not only the relationship between government and market but also the fundamental accountability and legitimacy structures between government and citizens (see Chapter 15 by Christensen and Lægreid in this volume).

From an economic perspective, government intervention in technology and innovation policy can be justified if the difference between private and social returns of research and development (R&D) is largely due to market failure (Stiglitz and Wallsten 1999). Such intervention in the private market can be further motivated by the presence of systemic failures; public–private interaction acts as a variety-creation mechanism by linking agents from different sectors in the innovation process and thereby creating new opportunities for user–provider interactions and mutual learning (Lundvall 1992/2010). In this way, public–private interaction contributes to the performance of both governments and markets by strengthening the feedback linkages in the economy as a whole. Also, there may be reasons for governments to contribute to the 'making' of new markets if there is a social need for new solutions in areas that the private sector regards as too risky for immediate investments (Mazzucato 2013). Public–private interaction can therefore be seen as a means of fostering the generation and exploitation of innovation activities by providing the organizational frame for 'producing' innovations and bringing new products, processes, modes of organization and other innovations to the market.

While innovation *in* the public sector manifests itself through changes in public sector capabilities, innovation *through* the public sector is essentially about using the public sector to create (positive) change in private sector capabilities. More specifically, this can take place in three principal ways (Edquist, Hommen and Tsipouri 2000; Edquist, Vonortas and Zabala-Iturriagagoitia 2015).

First, the public sector can procure or contract for so-called off-the-shelf solutions, i.e. standard solutions that neither require nor lead to any innovation. Governments simply continue to purchase private sector services on the basis of 'business as usual'. This type of interaction is characteristic of routine tasks that are contracted out mostly through price-dominated competition and which usually lead to no change in public sector services, solutions or organizational routines. This form of contracting may, however, increase public sector productivity through better exploitation of economies of scale and/or lower salaries paid in private organizations (Hodge 2000; Vrangbæk, Petersen and Hjelmar 2015). Being the least risky strategy, this is often the standard operating procedure in public procurement of goods and services, which often leads to little or no significant upgrading of private sector capabilities (Lember, Kattel and Kalvet 2014).

Second, governments can facilitate more radical innovation where private actors develop new-to-the-world products or solutions. Here the government explicitly sources for non-existing and/or unknown solutions, thus motivating and creating incentives for the private sector to engage in exploratory innovation processes. In order for this type of innovation to succeed, governments often need to nurture specific private sector know-how, resources and/or competencies to call forth and mediate as well as exploit radical innovations. In addition to creating innovation in services, processes, etc., the private sector capability to develop radical innovation may also change the relationship, accountability and legitimacy structures between government, market and citizens (think only about the potential effects of emerging data-driven services on these relationships). At the same time, this kind of contracting has the largest potential to spur private sector capabilities and development of new markets, as well as support innovation infrastructure and effective innovation policy making. Here the quality of demand or the ways government articulates the user needs for private partners is a key factor affecting market behaviour. Surely, this is also the riskiest option for governments, both organizationally as well as politically.

Third, governments can spur incremental innovation, meaning that the contracted services or solutions are new only to the particular service area or user organization but not to the broader society as such. Here the innovation is adaptive or exploitive in its nature. This type of contracting combines both the positive as well as problematic aspects of the previous two types.

All three types of public–private interaction involve collaboration and inter-organizational learning to a greater or lesser extent (Edquist, Vonortas and Zabala-Iturriagagoitia 2015). Systemic innovation theory emphasises interaction and feedback loops among agents involved in the innovation process as a key success factor (Lundvall 1992/2010). Interaction, in turn, hinges on proximity between agents not only in spatial distance terms, but also in social, organizational, institutional and cognitive terms (cf. Boschma 2005). For public–private interaction, such proximities are likely to affect both collaboration processes and innovation outcomes. Moreover, knowledge bases and expertise often differ significantly across sectors, and so do modes of organization and the institutional frameworks governing the public sector and private business, respectively (see also Rolfstam 2013).

In some cases, fostering innovation does not require intensive interaction between public and private agents and merely market-based relations (e.g. traditional public procurement and contracting out) will turn out as the preferred solution, both for the public sector and for private business. In such a setting, government policy clearly has its main focus on the demand side: it either deliberately aims at procuring innovative products or services without much collaboration with the private supplier, or innovation may occur more or less by coincidence as a side-effect of existing procurement activities. Yet in other cases, governments may need to first invest in public and/or private sector's absorptive capacity (i.e. the organizational ability to obtain, understand and use new knowledge) before opting for more genuine forms of collaborative interaction.

10.3   Evaluating Different Forms of Public–Private Interaction

The use of various forms of public–private interaction for the delivery of public services has long antecedents, as exemplified by the use of private tax collectors, construction of private railways, privately contracted vessels and the provision of schools and hospital services by the Church for many centuries (Wettenhall 2003; Hodge and Greve 2005). In the following, we scrutinize recent experiences with public–private interaction with a focus on contracting out, public procurement and PPPs. They constitute three noticeable and distinct forms of interplay between governments and markets, each of which produces specific conditions for achievement of public sector innovation.

10.3.1 Contracting Out

At the time when the high level of economic growth following World War II came to an end in the early 1970s, the following waves of liberalization, deregulation and contracting out broadened the role of private markets in the delivery of public services. Contracting out is here defined as the process whereby the production responsibility for a publicly financed service is transferred temporarily to a private sector actor in return for a financial compensation, whereby the public sector takes the role of buyer but retains the financing and supervision responsibility (Petersen and Hjelmar 2013).

While the ideological roots of liberalization, privatization and contracting out were neoconservative, the theoretical foundations for this shift were provided by neoclassical economics. In particular, public choice theory provided theoretical inspiration by claiming that the public sector is inherently inefficient compared to the private sector, because it lacks the profit motive to reduce cost, raise productivity and improve the quality of goods and services (Niskanen 1971). Moreover, public sector agents work under a different incentive structure, because they neither risk their own money nor that of shareholders, which can exert controls. Their individual reward for raising efficiency and effectiveness of public activities is thus usually small. Therefore, according to neoliberal and public choice theorists, bringing these services to the competitive market provides a mechanism for bringing the disciplining power of the private sector into public service delivery (Niskanen 1971).

The roll-out of contracting out across more functions and policy fields gained momentum with the Thatcher and Reagan governments from the late 1970s onwards. This development reflected, first, a shift in the general ascription of the relative efficiency of public and private sector activities in favour of the latter. Second, increasing private sector involvement in the process of public sector innovation was expected to help spur public innovation because private sector technological capabilities and management techniques would also be superior with regard to producing innovative public services.

Increasing private agents' involvement in public innovation thus enables the public sector to tap into the discipline, incentives, skills and expertise that private sector firms have developed in the course of their everyday business (HM Treasury 2000). It also allows greater asset utilization, exploiting economies of scale and scope, spreading risks to those agents that are most experienced in managing them, and 'cradle-to-grave' or whole-life asset management (McQuaid and Scherrer 2010). Most of all, as the prevailing systemic perspective on innovation, which was developed in the late 1980s and 1990s, points out: innovation is an interactive process among a variety of agents. Therefore, setting up and fostering relations between the public and private sectors is by itself considered conducive to innovation in the public sector.

Yet, placing innovation in the context of contracting out is tricky, because the competition focus in public choice and property rights theory place little, if any, explicit emphasis on innovation. The comparative advantage of nations to produce more, better and cheaper goods and services is essential, and competition will pressure companies to incessantly innovate and outcompete the competitors and to push costs downwards, thus increasing efficiency (Kattel and Lember 2010). In many countries, there has been a long tradition of public–private interaction, mostly in sectors of strategic military importance (arms industry, space industry), in traditional infrastructure development (Edquist, Hommen and Tsipouri 2000) and in technical services such as cleaning, refuse collection and street maintenance (Hodge 2000; Petersen and Hjelmar 2013). Both the neoclassical and the public-choice traditions argue that trade and competition are the main drivers of innovations and growth. Therefore, it is no surprise that the role of competition and private agents has gained prominence in public innovation, too.

At the same time, contracting out as way to increase competition was mainly seen as a means of efficiency improvement, and innovation was only implicitly assumed to be more prevalent in the private domain.

Indeed, most studies of the time pay little if any notice to the topic of innovation. If innovation was part of the (assumed) gains of transferring public activities to the market domain, this was mainly an implicit form of innovation related to arguments about incremental efficiency gains stemming from the competitive pressure on private organizations. Moreover, many have observed that the neoclassical and neoliberal winds actually radically reduced governments' willingness to explicitly engage with procuring innovation (Edquist, Hommen and Tsipouri 2000). Therefore, in the privatization and contracting-out era, public innovation was mainly present as an implicit and incremental activity related to the use of private actors as a means to increase competition and thereby public sector efficiency.

10.3.2 *Public Procurement*

The focus on using market discipline and public–private interaction as drivers of public sector efficiency, and implicitly innovation, has led to further policy developments focusing on increased market efficiency. Traditional procurement typically entails procurement of off-the-shelf services or goods, but also some variants of public procurement of innovation may be included, such as pre-commercial procurement (Lember, Kattel and Kalvet 2014). The public agent may procure each service separately with the benefit of promoting a maximum level of competition when seeking private suppliers, thus providing as much leverage for private innovation as possible (Asker and Cantillon 2010). But, as a consequence, this compartmentalizing approach also leads to an increase of disconnected contracts, where risk is distributed through enforceable contractual rules. By promoting discrete relationships and maximum competition among private suppliers, traditional public procurement was thus well embedded in the NPM paradigm.

Important developments in public procurement took place with the launch of the Private Finance Initiative (PFI) in the United Kingdom and elsewhere from the early 1990s onwards (Broadbent and Laughlin 1999; English and Guthrie 2003). Policy initiatives were essentially targeting procurement of infrastructure services. However, due to the complexities involved in this type of project, it needed to reduce the distance between agents and reinvent public/private risk-sharing mechanisms (Hart 2003; Hoppe, Kusterer and Schmitz 2013).

While PFI predominantly was impelled by a perceived need for alternative ways of financing infrastructure delivery, it did represent development of a more collaborative approach to public–private interaction as well (Terry 1996). The vision was that the private sector could provide knowledge on how to deliver services efficiently while the public sector still remained the principal for defining the scope of public service delivery. This perception, though, gradually has shifted to a view of the private sector as an equal partner, who would be able to also design public goods and services. Perceiving the private sector as a knowledgeable partner thus shifted focus from seeing innovation as occurring in a competitive market to a view where innovation could be achieved by means of strategic engagement with an external private actor.

However, in order to achieve innovation, the collaborative dimension of public–private interaction would need to be explicitly supported. This clashed with the policy agenda earlier laid down, which had an arm's-length distance, a discrete view of public–private interaction. While the clash did not explicitly hamper the ability to spur innovation through public–private interaction (Rolfstam 2013), the discrete nature of the relationship did seem to inhibit continuous collaborations based on trust, experience and shared goals (Ågren and Rolfstam 2014). The lack of collaborative elements affected the delivery of services more significantly than delivery of goods.

As a result of the tension between the market efficiency policy, driven predominately on an EU level, and the national collaborative policy driven in the UK, a national practice of side-stepping the regulatory efforts from the EU level developed. This approach was characterized by what can be described as a very liberal interpretation of EU-level regulations (Martin, Hartley and Cox 1997), and thus allowing for a more flexible, relational model of public–private interaction, showing the perceived deficiencies of entrusting public innovation on market efficiencies. Eventually, from the late 1990s onward, this need for collaborative relationships was acknowledged also on an EU level. With the introduction of the 2004 legislative package on public procurement, new procedures for starting public–private interactions were introduced, such as the competitive dialogue procedure (Petersen 2010). Furthermore, the EU started to promote the benefits of extended collaborative public–private interaction.

This policy trend is also visible in the 2014 legislative package on public procurement, where new procedures, such as innovation partnerships, have been added together with an increased access to the competitive negotiated procedure. Thus, since the mid-2000s, the view of public procurement as a means of stimulating public innovation has been gradually changing. Instead of seeing innovation as something implicit, taking place mainly in the private sector, innovation is increasingly regarded as something that could (and should) be explicitly procured by the public sector. The prevailing view was still that innovation was exogenous from the public sector, but by addressing it more explicitly in public procurement policies, it was possible to deliberately promote public innovation policy. Consequently, by bringing these collaborate forms of public–private interaction more deliberately into public procurement, the innovativeness of the private market could be utilised to improve public service delivery as well.

10.3.3 Public–Private Partnerships

Since the mid-2000s significant changes in public–private interaction practice and rhetoric have been witnessed. Instead of focusing purely on market discipline (as under the PFI initiative) more genuine attempts to combine the application of competitive pressure with creating more collaborative linkages and explicit attempts to foster innovation have emerged (see Cropper et al. 2008 for an overview). For instance, governments increasingly attempt to create new state, policy and administrative capacities, and in many of these approaches, innovation plays a prominent role, e.g. public procurement of innovation and demand-side innovation policy (Edler and Georghiou 2007) or citizen-driven innovation (see chapter by Bovaird and Loeffler in this volume). These new approaches have led to a demand for a re-conceptualization of risk in public affairs. More collaborative forms of public–private interaction imply a need for risk sharing between public and private agents instead of full delegation of risk, which often dominates transactional views of public–private interaction.

This new notion denotes the public sector as a risk taker, because it is seen as better placed to encounter long-term risks. Thus, risk sharing is necessary in order to enable transformative change in society (Mazzucato 2013). This signifies an increase of public agent risk tolerance where risk management is made more explicit in order to trade-off risk-avoiding practices vis-à-vis promotion of innovation. The risk perspective is accompanied by other managerial and legal principles, such as a preference for open output specifications instead of detailed input specifications and a greater emphasis on the use of functional requirements in public procurement. These tendencies require by definition more interaction and engagement with market stakeholders, since the public sector's knowledge and capacity to translate needs into functional requirements is limited (Edquist, Vonortas and Zabala-Iturriagagoitia 2015). As previously mentioned, recent EU legislative changes support increased interaction during the early stages of public–private interaction, by extending the availability of negotiated procedures, competitive dialogue and by the introduction of innovation partnerships (Caranta 2015).

Technological change, emerging global and specialized business models and ongoing economic stagnation all importantly shape the conditions for public sector innovation through private actors. Rapid technological changes are altering the nature of the existing public–private interaction patterns. Not only is the exponential growth in computing power fundamentally changing the existing models of public service delivery (e.g. from 3D printing to autonomous vehicles to smart cities) as we speak, but the same is happening also in health, energy, environment and other sectors from advances in bio-, nano- and other technologies. Grassroots innovators, such as civic hackers, put citizens at the centre of public sector innovation (Hui and Hayllar 2010). These and other examples provide governments with unprecedented opportunities but also present governments with a huge challenge – not only how to cope and adjust but also how to shape and guide the markets and society.

At the same time, many public sector markets are increasingly consolidating (solid waste collection provides a classic example). Global conglomerates today are able to provide public services, ranging from office cleaning to welfare services to nuclear weapons maintenance, pointing towards the tendency that variety and size rather than innovation capabilities is what determines who wins public service contracts (Crouch 2011). Moreover, economic stagnation in the Western hemisphere, together with the concerns over the effects of public debt on economic development, have in many countries reinforced rather than diminished the desire to introduce market discipline into public service delivery (Alonso, Clifton and Diaz-Fuentes 2015 provide recent statistics). Consequently, innovation and collaboration are oftentimes used not as genuine policy goals but rather as new branding tools to legitimize change.

While public–private collaboration and innovation have clearly gained prominence in rhetoric, there remain a number of pertinent issues that call for rethinking of the interaction. The developments outlined above are still merely examples of what could perhaps be new times of involving the private sector in public sector innovation. A key question at this stage is how governance frameworks can be improved to further support the development of more innovative forms of public–private interaction in policy practice. This question leads to the next section, where we discuss ways in which the governance framework can be changed to enhance public sector innovation.

10.4   Changing Governance to Enhance the Contribution of Private Actors in Public Innovation

The efforts of governments to bring together public and private actors in achieving innovative solutions to the current societal challenges have been increased over the past years but are still impeded by both formal and informal barriers, while recent empirical evidence of innovative outcomes of collaboration, as examined above, still remain rather scarce. So what are the main hurdles and potential solutions for greater private sector contribution to public sector innovation?

One of the most persistent legacies of the NPM era is how government's role in the public–private knowledge creation process was expected to evolve. Understood primarily as a passive user of existing private sector knowledge, the government's role in creating new knowledge and innovation was reduced to competition organizer rather than active player in shaping and creating new market capacities to deliver public services. Yet, in public–private interaction, the problem of little or no cognitive proximity might exist frequently as one side – probably the public side in many cases – might not sufficiently reach the same level of expertise as the other side. In such cases, the public side more or less buys goods off the shelf; consequently, innovation occurs by coincidence, and thus it is the role of the public side, which ought to be enhanced in order to induce innovation. Re-designing civil service recruitment and career systems to attract and maintain people with different knowledge sets (e.g. engineers and other professions as policy makers) may be a useful step to consider here.

Conversely, in cases where there is a long-term and very close connection between actors, and the knowledge base has developed in close collaboration between private suppliers and public sector users (e.g. in some military technologies), strengthening cognitive proximity is not likely to have much effect on innovation. Instead, to spur knowledge creation and innovation, the capacity to coordinate the exchange of complementary pieces of knowledge owned by a variety of actors within and between organizations needs to be increased (Boschma 2005: 64). But achieving sufficient organizational proximity between public and private actors may turn out to be difficult, because public organizations must abide by a number of laws, regulations and accountability requirements that private actors need not, which may impede collaboration across sectors. Forming joint entities comprising public and private agents (e.g. in institutional PPPs) might be a possibility to overcome low organizational proximity (see e.g. Weiss 2014 on the recent experiences of the US security sector).

Institutional proximity between public and private agents reflected by the 'sets of common habits, routines, established practices, rules, or laws that regulate the relations and interactions between individuals and groups' (Edquist and Johnson 1997: 46) clearly vary across countries and sectors. Basically, some of these institutions – possibly the formal institutions more easily than the informal ones – can be influenced by the public sector, which thus could enhance the role of private agents in public innovation. However, for a relationship to be successful in inducing innovation, both formal and informal institutions need to be coordinated within the relationship between the agents (Ågren and Rolfstam 2014), i.e. they need not be aligned but rather positioned so as to provide mutual benefits for both sides. Routine industry engagement through developing common technological platforms and implementing technological foresight exercises are examples among many others that can serve this purpose (Georghiou 2008).

In addition to changing their role in innovation, governments of today engage in public–private interactions that intend not only to support innovation of policy implementation but also policy formulation processes. In this respect, there could be possibilities for creating more innovation-enabling forms of public–private interaction under the NPG paradigm than were the case under NPM. These new types of collaboration and innovation-oriented partnerships are still in their infancy, and as discussed in the previous section, actual empirical examples remain rather limited.

In spite of much recent focus on innovation-oriented forms of partnerships and procurement, the vast majority of public–private interaction still takes place in the marketplace and is still largely governed by traditional lowest-cost-driven (non-collaborative) contracts (Uyarra et al. 2014) that leave little room for interaction, innovation and dynamic feedback loops.

Interestingly, while NPM represented an attempt to copy private sector practices, large tracts of the private sector have – due to technological change – for the past decades mostly used a mix of collaborative and competition-based contracting strategies in order to cope with uncertainties when pursuing innovative but risky cross-organizational cooperation (Gilson, Sabel and Scott 2009). The need to design better frameworks for enabling dynamic feedback and continuous interaction calls not only for new forms of governance under the NPG paradigm but also for a redesign of existing forms of governance under the classic NPM paradigm. Formalized and rather rigid procurement and contract regimes can constitute a barrier to innovation under the market-based forms of public–private interaction associated with the NPM, whereas innovation under the NPG is still hampered by lack of experience, risk averseness and few empirical examples of innovations that were successful for both the public and private sectors (Brogaard and Petersen 2014).

Therefore, if public–private collaboration is part of the answer to the current challenges that Western governments face, a dual approach, which recognizes the importance of stimulating innovation under NPM forms of public–private interaction while supporting the development of collaborative and partnership-oriented forms of interaction under the NPG, is warranted. What is needed, in other words, is an approach that addresses innovation from a market-centred perspective and utilizes the private sector's capacity to innovate under the pressure of competition. This approach should ideally support innovation in market-based forms of public–private interaction, such as contracting out and traditional (transactional) public procurement by redesign of well-known market models to facilitate and enhance innovation. This requires the development of procurement and contracting-out regimes that change the game by shifting the focus from purchasing standardized (off-the-shelf) services and products to open-ended output and outcome specifications that let the private sector come up with innovative solutions. For that to happen, public servants need to be entrusted with more explicit room for experimentation and legitimization of risk-taking with regard to wicked problems, such as ageing, environmental sustainability or security (for various specific strategies see Lember, Kattel and Kalvet 2015).

What is moreover needed is an approach to innovation in the public sector that builds on collaborative forms of interaction and utilises the trust and joint decision making provided by mutually binding forms of collaboration and partnerships – an approach that can be associated with the emerging NPG paradigm. In order to support public innovation in relevant ways, this paradigm needs to provide clearer answers as to how – by what designs and instruments – different types of interaction can bring about innovation in public services and policies. Again, that endeavour might require increased room for experimentation and risk-taking in the public domain and among civil servants. While both concepts are at the core of private market-centred innovation, they need to be developed in public organizations that are governed by more formal and rigid command-and-control procedures.

Besides bureaucratic capacities (from contracting to risk-management skills) it is clear that politicians have an important role to play in creating the space for experimentation and innovation in the public domain. Increased public innovation therefore requires not only new (and less rigid) procedures at the administrative level but also changes in the governance framework at the political level. At the same time, collaboration and increased risk-taking in public organizations opens up and intensifies accountability issues that need to be addressed as well (see chapter by Christensen and Lægreid in this volume).

10.5   Conclusions

The roles of the public and private sectors in the context of public sector innovation have historically been closely intertwined. Under the traditional contracting-out and public procurement approaches, innovation was mainly seen as an implicit result of competition among private providers in the marketplace. Private providers were chosen on the basis of cost efficiency, and while this in some instances led to reduced spending, especially in low-transaction-cost services, there was little if any explicit focus on extracting ideas, know-how and innovation capacity from the private sector. Innovation was thus most of all a supply-side phenomenon. Subsequently, from the late 1980s and into the 1990s, new forms of public procurement that focused more explicitly on innovating public goods and services were introduced. Thereby, innovation increasingly became a demand-side tool that provided governments with the possibility of using its market-dominating purchasing power to buy off-the-shelf services and products.

Finally, recent years have seen the most radical change – at least in rhetoric – in the role of governments in public sector innovation. Rather than taking the role as passive purchasers (as in the first phase) and active buyers (as in the second phase) governments seem increasingly to engage deliberately and actively in public innovation through collaboration and partnerships, i.e. innovation through something that is akin to NPG. The view on public innovation has thus evolved from one regarding it as external to public service delivery (efficiency gains) to one regarding these interactions as internal to public service delivery. Thus, the active engagement of the public sector can essentially spur innovation if there is a collaborative effort on dimensions other than mere efficiency gains.

Today, innovation is not something that takes place only in the marketplace but in collaboration between the public and private sectors. In this context, several possibilities for changing the governance framework and thereby supporting innovation, both with regard to policy implementation and formulation, are present. Amidst NPG promises of more joined-up, collaborative and trust-based forms of public–private interaction, we should not disregard the sustained importance of traditional and competition-based models, such as contracting out and public procurement. These models still constitute the majority of interactions between the public and private sectors, whether measured in number or economic value of interactions, and still deserve attention as vehicles for enhancing the (incremental) innovative outcomes of public–private sector interaction.

What is needed to enhance the contribution of private actors to public sector innovation, therefore, is a reformed version of NPM that embeds innovation more firmly within public procurement and contracting out *and* a refined and more concrete version of NPG that provides more clear answers to how networks and partnerships can spur public innovation, both with regard to innovation in service delivery and innovation in policy formulation and governance.

References

Ågren, R. and Rolfstam, M. 2014. 'A conjecture on institutional rationalities and property rights in public procurement of innovation', in F. Decarolis, G. Piga and M. Frey (eds.), *Public Procurement's Place in the World: The Charge Towards Sustainability and Innovation*. New York: Palgrave Macmillan, pp. 131–54.

Alonso, J. M., Clifton, J. and Díaz-Fuentes, D. 2015. 'Did New Public Management matter? An empirical analysis of the outsourcing and decentralization effects on public sector size', *Public Management Review* 17(5): 643–60.

Asker, J. and Cantillon, E. 2010. 'Procurement when price and quality matter', *RAND Journal of Economics* 41(1): 1–34.

Boschma, R. 2005. 'Proximity and innovation: A critical assessment', *Regional Studies* 39(1): 61–74.

Broadbent, J. and Laughlin, R. 1999. 'The private finance initiative: Clarification of a future research agenda', *Financial Accountability & Management* 15(2): 95–114.

Brogaard, L. and Petersen, O. H. 2014. *Offentlige-Private Innovationspartnerskaber (OPI): Evaluering af Erfaringer med OPI på Velfærdsområdet*. Copenhagen: KORA.

Caranta, R. 2015. 'The changes to the public contract directives and the story they tell about how EU law works', *Common Market Law Review* 52(2): 391–459.

Christensen, T. and Lægreid, P. (eds.) 2007. *Transcending New Public Management: The Transformations of Public Sector Reforms*. Aldershot, UK: Ashgate.

Cropper, S., Ebers, M., Huxam, C. and Smith Ring, P. (eds.) 2008. *The Oxford Handbook of Inter-Organizational Relations*. Oxford: Oxford University Press.

Crouch, C. 2011. *The Strange Non-Death of Neo-Liberalism*. Cambridge: Polity Press.

Edler, J. and Georghiou, L. 2007. 'Public procurement and innovation: Resurrecting the demand side', *Research Policy* 36(7): 949–63.

Edquist, C., Hommen, L. and Tsipouri, L. (eds.) 2000. *Public Technology Procurement and Innovation*. Boston/Dordrecht/London: Kluwer Academic Publishers.

Edquist, C. and Johnson, B. 1997. 'Institutions and organizations in systems of innovation', in C. Edquist (ed.), *Systems of Innovation: Technologies, Institutions and Organizations*. London: Pinter, pp. 41–60.

Edquist, C., Vonortas, N. S. and Zabala-Iturriagagoitia, J. M. 2015. 'Introduction', in C. Edquist, N. S. Vonortas, J. M. Zabala-Iturriagagoitia and J. Edler (eds.), *Public Procurement for Innovation*. Cheltenham: Edward Elgar, pp. 1–34.

English, L. and Guthrie, J. 2003. 'Driving privately financed projects in Australia: What makes them tick?' *Accounting, Auditing & Accountability Journal* 16(3): 493–511.

Georghiou, L. (ed.) 2008. *The Handbook of Technology Foresight: Concepts and Practice*. Cheltenham: Edward Elgar.

Gilson, R. J., Sabel, C. F. and Scott, R. E. 2009. 'Contracting for innovation: Vertical disintegration and interfirm collaboration', *Columbia Law Review* 109(3): 431–502.

Hart, O. 2003. 'Incomplete contracts and public ownership: Remarks, and an application to public–private partnerships', *The Economic Journal* 113(486): C69–76.

HM Treasury 2000. *Public Private Partnerships: The Government's Approach*. London: GSO.

Hodge, G. A. 2000. *Privatization: An international Review of Performance*. Boulder, CO: Westview Press.

Hodge, G. A. and Greve, C. (eds.) 2005. *The Challenge of Public–Private Partnerships: Learning from International Experience*. Cheltenham: Edward Elgar.

Hoppe, E. I., Kusterer, D. J. and Schmitz, P. W. 2013. 'Public–private partnerships versus traditional procurement: An experimental investigation', *Journal of Economic Behavior & Organization* 89: 145–66.

Hui, G. and Hayllar, M. R. 2010. 'Creating public value in E-Government: A public–private-citizen collaboration framework in Web 2.0', *Australian Journal of Public Administration* 69(1): 120–31.

Jayasuriya, K. 2005. 'Capacity beyond the boundary: New regulatory state, fragmentation and relational capacity', in M. Painter and J. Pierre (eds.), *Challenges to State Policy Capacity: Global Trends and Comparative Perspectives*. Houndmills, Basingstoke: Palgrave Macmillan, pp. 19–37.

Kattel, R., Cepilovs, A., Drechsler, W., Kalvet, T., Lember, V. and Tõnurist, P. 2014. 'Can we measure public sector innovation? A literature review', *LIPSE Working Papers* 2: 1–45.

Kattel, R. and Lember, V. 2010. 'Public procurement as an industrial policy tool: An option for developing countries', *Journal of Public Procurement* 10(3): 368–404.

Lember, V., Kattel, R. and Kalvet, T. (eds.) 2014. *Public Procurement, Innovation and Policy: International Perspectives*. Heidelberg: Springer.

Lember, V., Kattel, R. and Kalvet, T. 2015. 'Quo vadis public procurement of innovation?' *Innovation: The European Journal of Social Science Research* 28(3): 403–21.

Lindholst, A. C. and Bogetoft, P. 2011. 'Managerial challenges in public service contracting: Lessons in green-space management', *Public Administration* 89(3): 1036–62.

Lundvall, B.-Å. (ed.) 1992/2010. *National Systems of Innovation: Toward a Theory of Innovation and Interactive Learning*. London: Anthem.

Macneil, I. R. 1980. *The New Social Contract: An Inquiry into Modern Contractual Relations*. New Haven: Yale University Press.

Martin, S., Hartley, K. and Cox, A. 1997. 'Public purchasing in the European Union: Some evidence from contract awards', *International Journal of Public Sector Management* 10(4): 279–93.

Mazzucato, M. 2013. *The Entrepreneurial State: Debunking the Public vs. Private Myth in Risk and Innovation*. London: Anthem Press.

McQuaid, R. W. and Scherrer, W. 2010. 'Changing reasons for public private partnerships', *Public Money and Management* 30(1): 27–39.

Moore, M. H. 1995. *Creating Public Value: Strategic Management in Government*. Harvard University Press.

Niskanen, W. 1971. *Bureaucracy and Representative Government*. Chicago: Aldine-Atherton.

Petersen, O. H. 2010. 'Emerging meta-governance as a regulation framework for public–private partnerships: An examination of the European Union's approach', *International Public Management Review* 11(3): 1–21.

Petersen, O. H. and Hjelmar, U. 2013. 'Marketization of welfare services in Scandinavia: A review of Swedish and Danish experiences', *Scandinavian Journal of Public Administration* 17(4): 3–20.

Rolfstam, M. 2013. *Public Procurement and Innovation: The Role of Institutions*. Cheltenham: Edward Elgar.

Stiglitz, J. E. and Wallsten, S. J. 1999. 'Public–private technology partnerships promises and pitfalls', *American Behavioral Scientist* 43(1): 52–73.

Terry, F. 1996. 'The private finance initiative – Overdue reform or policy breakthrough?' *Public Money and Management* 16(1): 9–16.

Torfing, J. and Triantafillou, P. 2013. 'What's in a name? Grasping New Public Governance as a political-administrative system', *International Review of Public Administration* 18(2): 9–25.

Uyarra, E., Edler, J., Garcia-Estevez, J., Georghiou, L. and Yeow, J. 2014. 'Barriers to innovation through public procurement: A supplier perspective', *Technovation* 34(10): 631–45.

Vrangbæk, K., Petersen, O. H. and Hjelmar, U. 2015. 'Is contracting out good or bad for employees? A review of international experience', *Review of Public Personnel Administration* 35(1): 3–23.

Weiss, L. 2014. *America Inc.? Innovation and Enterprise in the National Security State*. Ithaca: Cornell University Press.

Wettenhall, R. 2003. 'The rhetoric and reality of public–private partnerships', *Public Organization Review* 3(1): 77–107.

Part III

Transforming Governance to Enhance
Innovation

11 Public Innovation and Organizational Structure
Searching (in Vain) for the Optimal Design

Mads Leth Felsager Jakobsen and Claus Thrane

11.1 Introduction

The relationship between innovation and organizational structure is an important issue for scholars seeking to explain public sector development and policy actors seeking to improve the performance of public sector organizations. Competing governance paradigms prescribe different structural solutions for the design of public organizations. It is the dominant view that bureaucratic organizational structures prescribed by the Classical Public Administration (CPA) paradigm are likely to diminish innovation, although research has increasingly become focused on the ways bureaucracy can enhance innovation (Torfing and Triantafillou, Chapter 1). In particular, organizational structures such as formalization, division of labour, specialization, hierarchy, centralization and high ratios of administrative employees have been blamed for the alleged problems with innovation in the public sector (Osborne 1993; Eggers and Singh 2009; Bason 2010; Torfing 2011).

On the basis of this critique, the New Public Management (NPM) paradigm has prescribed decentralization, incentives and performance management, and the New Public Governance (NPG) paradigm has prescribed inter-organizational networks and co-production as alternative ways to enhance innovation (Hartley, Sørensen and Torfing 2013; Torfing and Triantafillou, Chapter 1). This chapter analyses and discusses the relationship between organizational structures and innovation within a public sector where the prescriptions of the NPM paradigm and in particular the NPG paradigm have been added to the traditional CPA structures.

We address three specific questions. First, what is the evidence from the existing body of literature on the impact of organizational structures on innovation? We find that there is a somewhat ambiguous impact of

The corresponding author for this chapter is Mads Leth Felsager Jakobsen.

these structures, which runs counter to very negative accounts of the impact of bureaucracy on innovation. Furthermore, the NPM prescription of decentralization and prescriptions for internal and external communication, which can be derived from the NPG paradigm, also seem to have a positive impact on innovation.

Second, is there an optimal organizational structure for innovation? We find it difficult to develop strong prescriptions for an optimal structure from the theoretical arguments and the empirical evidence. Still, centralization in general seems like something to avoid while the division of labour and specialization as well as high levels of communication should be promoted in order to further innovation.

Third, are we searching in vain for an optimal structural design for public sector innovation? To the extent that we assume the existence of a single optimal structural design fit for all contexts, we argue that it is a potentially misleading endeavour because it overlooks the inherently contingent and subjective nature of entrepreneurship as a key element of innovation. Entrepreneurship arises from a nexus between entrepreneurial opportunities and enterprising individuals, which cannot be reduced to organizational structures (Shane and Venkataraman 2000). Organizational structures can and do play a role in such a process, but this role is always contingent upon the individual and his or her nexus. From this micro-level perspective, which is profoundly different from the deductive macro-level approach of the first part of the chapter, we argue that a promising research question is how public actors can be enabled to act entrepreneurially in terms of coping with uncertainty and acting collaboratively in a specific context. The prescriptions of the NPM paradigm are then likely to be more suitable as a governing context in cases of low uncertainty, whereas the NPG prescriptions would in general provide a better context for innovation in situations with high uncertainty and where entrepreneurial opportunities need to be developed through creative, experimental and collaborative efforts.

11.2   How Do Organizational Structures Affect Innovation?

Following Sørensen and Torfing (2011: 849), we define innovation as 'an intentional, yet inherently contingent, process that involves the development and realization of new and creative ideas that challenge conventional wisdoms and break with established practices in a particular context'. This innovation process can be divided into an adoption phase with development of and decision to adopt solutions, and an implementation phase where the solution is put into practice (Rogers 2003).

There are many types of innovation. This chapter focuses on administrative innovations that deal with administrative structures and systems as
well as technical innovations that relate to the product or service delivered
by an organization and therefore are directly related to the basic activities
of the organization (Damanpour 1991; Jaskyte 2011: 78). Furthermore,
policy innovation, which is a key type of innovation in a public sector
context, can be seen as a subtype of both administrative and technological
innovation on a highly aggregated level as policies relate to how the public
sector should be organized and what goods it should deliver. This leaves
out broader and different kinds of innovation, e.g. democratic and discursive (see Torfing and Triantafillou, Chapter 1), to which we should be
wary of generalizing the findings of this chapter.

11.3   Conceptualizing Structure

Organizational structures are 'recurrent set(s) of relationships between
organizational members' (Donaldson 1999: 51), such as reporting,
authority and communication relationships.

Much debate on the design of public organizations in relation to innovation has centred on the calamity caused by bureaucratic structures prescribed by the CPA. The Weberian bureaucracy is the cornerstone of the
CPA paradigm. It is an ideal-type model of organization consisting of
several dimensions: (a) hierarchy in the form of the number of organizational levels; (b) centralization as the degree to which decision making
resides at higher hierarchical levels; (c) formalization, which is governance
through formal rules; (d) division of labour, which is the structuring of the
organization into functional units; and (e) specialization as the development of highly specialized competences for specific tasks (Albrow 1970;
Weber 1971). These bureaucratic structures are not always strongly correlated (Hall 1963: 19; Walton 2005), and organizations can be bureau-
cratized in many different ways. Another organizational structure often
linked to the concept of bureaucracy is the administrative intensity of
organizations, which is the ratio of administrative employees to other
employees – oftentimes more positively referred to as administrative capacity (Fernandez and Wise 2010; Walker 2014: 26).

We also look into a key prescription of the NPM paradigm, namely
decentralization (Hood 1991). Decentralization is the extent to which
decision-making competences are located at lower hierarchical levels
within an organization. It is the opposite of centralization, but the two
phenomena are measured on the same scale. In addition, we look at two
organizational structures that are implicitly prescribed by the NPG paradigm as they make collaborative processes – the key mechanism of the

paradigm – across boundaries possible (Torfing and Triantafillou, Chapter 1). Internal communication describes the level of communication within an organization, vertically between levels and horizontally between actors in functionally differentiated units. External communication is the level of communication between actors inside and outside the organization.

11.4   Theoretical Arguments on the Impact of Structure

Hierarchy, formalization and centralization are often the prime targets of innovation bashing in the public sector. Key arguments are that such structures reduce employee motivation and room for innovation by decreasing commitment, involvement and flexibility (Delbecq and Pierce 1978; Thompson 1965) and hamper employees' opportunities to seek new knowledge and ideas outside the organization (Zaltman, Duncan and Holbek 1973: 138–43). Furthermore, hierarchical layers are often assumed to constrain the vertical flow of new ideas within the organization (Hull and Hage 1982; Torfing 2011: 120).

Still, the picture need not be so grim. In contrast to the adoption of ideas, hierarchy, centralization and formalization can be less detrimental or even beneficial when it comes to the implementation of adopted ideas (Delbecq and Pierce 1978; Rogers 2003: 441). They can create clarity, reduce conflict and uncertainty and secure coordination within organizations and within extra-organizational networks involved in the innovation process (Zaltman, Duncan and Holbek 1973: 138–46; O'Toole 1997). The latter is particularly important in the light of the NPG prescriptions for more network-based innovation, as the productive running of such networks requires participants with a certain stability and integrity, which can be provided by clear competences and explicit rules. The same could be argued for administrative intensity in relation to the NPM prescriptions of outsourcing and procurement, which requires administrative capacities to manage intricate contractual relations and to absorb the transaction costs of the exchanges with private actors in general.

Furthermore, the idea that organizational structures such as hierarchy, formalization and centralization have a definite impact on innovation is basically problematic. Studies have shown that formalization and hierarchy are ambiguous as they can be both enabling and coercive (Adler and Borys 1996) and formalization can cause both inefficient red tape rules (Bozeman and Feeney 2011) and efficient green tape rules (DeHart-Davis 2009). This demonstrates the importance of considering not only more or less hierarchy, centralization and formalization but also how these structures are designed (Hammond 1993; Dixit 2002), the leadership process through which they are created and communicated (van der Voet 2015), and how organizational members acting within the structures perceive the rules (Mikkelsen, Jacobsen and Andersen 2015).

In contrast to centralization, hierarchy and formalization, the mainstream view of the impact of the division of labour and specialization on organizational innovation is more positive. Diversity follows from functional differentiation, and highly specialized competences create different perspectives, knowledge bases and competences within the organization, which further creativity and innovation (Thompson 1965; Kimberly and Evanisko 1981; Hage 1999; Bason 2010: 15). The more complex the division of labour, the higher the organization's learning capacity as different professions provide channels with the environment where profession-based knowledge and ideas can flow (Hage 1999: 604–5). A more negative view has also been proposed as the division of labour as well as specialization could limit the flow of ideas within and between organizations, which could restrict creativity and in particular hamper the collaboration necessary for the implementation of adopted ideas (Torfing 2011: 120). A positive impact of specialization and division of labour is particularly important in the context of the NPG paradigm as it explicitly requires collaboration between a multitude of organizational actors (Hartley, Sørensen and Torfing 2013). Collaboration within an organization should, however, be easier to promote in a hierarchical structure, which reduces problems of collective action, than via inter-organizational collaboration, which to a higher degree has to rely on trust (Scharpf 1994).

Another facet of the bureaucracy is the number of bureaucrats (the administrative staff) relative to the number of employees in the organization. This can be conceptualized as administrative capacity (Ingraham, Joyce and Donahue 2003), which is argued to increase, at least up to a certain point, an organization's ability to control and adapt to its environment through innovation (Andrews and Boyne 2011). A more negative interpretation is to see higher levels of administrative intensity as waste piling up, which arises from various interests that are not directed at promoting innovation, but rather at securing more narrow interests in the form of positions, tasks and job security (Parkinson 1960; Niskanen 1974; Dunleavy 1989).

The level of internal and external communication is generally expected to be positively associated with innovation (Damanpour 1991). When people communicate within an organization, ideas spread and learning takes place (Aiken and Hage 1971). External communication has the same effect, as interaction with, e.g., professional associations makes outside ideas flow into the organization. Both forms of communication could also improve the implementation of adopted innovations by transferring knowledge and expectations between implementation actors. Still, the impact of communication relationships must, like other structures, depend on its substance and direction as top-down directives with little learning are unlikely to further innovation.

In sum, none of the structural factors characterizing the classic bureaucracy constitute a slam dunk case on the theoretical level. The overall picture is an expected positive impact of specialization and the division of labour and an unclear impact of the other bureaucratic structures including administrative intensity. This is also the case for centralization and decentralization as prescribed by the NPM paradigm. With internal and external communication as prescribed by the NPG paradigm, the main expectation is a positive impact, depending on the purpose and content of this communication. Hence, the theoretical arguments are ambiguous and indicate that most structures are somewhat open ended in terms of their innovation impact.

11.5   The Empirical Evidence

What do we know empirically about the impact of organizational structures on public sector innovation? There are few broad, systematic studies of public sector organizations (Walker 2008: 591; Nauta and Kausbergen 2009) and a recent comprehensive meta-review of the public sector innovation literature concludes that it is mostly conceptual and normative rather than empirical (De Vries, Bekkers and Tummers 2016: 2).

The studies examined in this chapter measure innovation in terms of adoption and implementation of new ideas by an organization. Thus, we do not directly measure innovative activity by individuals (Scott and Bruce 1994) or broader phenomena such as an innovative culture (Wynen et al. 2014). Due to the limited number of empirical studies, we draw on two meta-reviews from the wider organizational literature, including both public and private organizations (Damanpour 1991, 1996; Zornoza, Boronat Navarro and Cipres 2007), identified through a literature search in 2012.[1] Damanpour (1991, 1996) covers studies

---

[1] The literature search was conducted in 2012 on CSA (Cambridge Scientific Abstracts) with relevant search terms (see Jakobsen 2013). 57 of 541 articles were selected for further inspection based on their abstract. Of the 57 articles, only two (Walker 2008; Jaskyte 2011) were selected after reading because they were (a) quantitative studies with (b) innovation as the dependent variable and (c) included organizational structures as an independent variable. Neither Jaskyte (2011) nor Walker (2008) is included in Walker (2014). Based on the references in the 57 articles, two meta-analyses were identified that fulfilled the above selection criteria. Walker (2014) was identified through a general literature research of innovation studies in key public management journals (*JPART, Public Administration, Public Administration Review* and *Public Management Review*) in August 2015.

from 1960 to 1988 with both profit and non-profit organizations, and Zornoza, Boronat Navarro and Cipres (2007) cover profit organizations from 1970 to 2001. These meta-studies only use individual studies that measure innovation as the adoption rate of multiple innovations, which is highly preferable to only studying single innovations as it increases consistency (Hage 1999: 600). We also draw on a recent meta-study by Walker (2014), which examines the determinants of process innovations in public sector organizations and does include studies of single innovations. The search identified two recent single studies that examine the impact of organizational structures in public and non-profit organizations: Walker's (2008) broad study of innovation in UK local government and Jaskyte's (2011) study of US non-profit organizations. This allows us to contrast the patterns of the general but older meta-analyses with recent public administration studies of the same subjects. Given their much broader information bases, the meta-analyses are given the highest weight in the analysis.

The relevant results from these studies are presented in Table 11.1, where the studies are included on the vertical dimension, and type of study, design and structures on the horizontal dimension.

Hierarchy, which is only reported in Damanpour (1991, 1996), is on average not related to organizational innovation, and nor is formalization in the meta-analyses (Damanpour 1991, 1996; Zornoza, Boronat Navarro and Cipres 2007) or in Jaskyte's recent study of US non-profit organizations. Only Walker's (2008) study of UK local governments finds a negative impact but only for service innovation, which is a form of technical product innovation. There is thus little evidence that hierarchy and formalization in general should be detrimental to innovation.

Only in the case of centralization is the negative view of the impact of the CPA structures supported. Centralization is, however, the opposite of decentralization, which is a prescription of the NPM paradigm. The negative relationship between centralization and organizational innovation in two meta-analyses (Damanpour 1991, 1996; Zornoza, Boronat Navarro and Cipres 2007) hence supports the prescriptions of the NPM paradigm. The results are a bit more mixed in relation to Jaskyte's (2011) and Walker's (2008) individual studies, but overall the evidence supports the claim that decentralization is positively associated with organizational innovation.

The relationship between division of labour and specialization on the one hand and organizational innovation on the other is mainly positive. Meta-studies (Damanpour 1991, 1996; Zornoza, Boronat Navarro and Cipres 2007) find a positive relationship, while the two individual studies of non-profit (Jaskyte 2011) and public sector organizations (Walker 2008)

Table 11.1 *The empirical relationship between organizational structures and innovation*

	Type of study	Units of study	Hierarchy	Formalization	Division of labour	Specialization	Administrative intensity	Centralization/decentralization	Internal communication	External communication
Damanpour (1991) supplemented by Damanpour (1996)	Meta-analysis (administrative and technical + process and product innovations)	For profit and non-profit	None	None	Positive	Positive	Positive	Negative	Positive	Positive
Zornoza et al. (2007)	Meta-analysis (administrative and technical)	For profit	NA	None	Positive	Positive	NA	Negative	NA	NA
Walker (2014)	Meta-analysis (process innovations)	Public	NA	NA	NA	NA	Positive	NA	NA	NA
Jaskyte (2011)	Cross-sectional (Administrative and technical innovations)	Non-profit	NA	None	–	None	NA	Mixed (none for technical and positive for administrative)	NA	NA
Walker (2008)	Panel analysis (administrative and technical – but with other terms)	Public	NA	Mixed (varies with type of innovation)	None	None	NA	Mainly negative (none for some types of innovation)	NA	Mainly none (but positive for service innovation)

find no relationship. This overall positive relationship is in accordance with the argument that division of labour and specialization allow for the development of stronger competences as well as more diversity of actors within an organization, which furthers the development and implementation of new ideas. Furthermore, neither specialization nor division of labour seem on average to create coordination problems leading to an overall negative relationship with innovation.

Such a positive pattern is also evident in relation to bureaucratic capacity measured as administrative intensity, which is reported in Walker's (2014) meta-analysis of public organizations. Administrative intensity is found to be positively related to organizational innovation. This is somewhat surprising as a rising number of administrative relative to non-administrative front-line workers are often argued to be a dead weight on the public sector as it is driven by other factors than genuine needs to improve public service provision (Parkinson 1960; Niskanen 1974). Yet, it is consistent with the argument that administrative intensity can further innovation as it provides the analytical tools, the necessary knowledge and the ability to coordinate how the organization adapts to its environment, as well as how new ideas are nurtured, chosen and implemented.

There is a similar positive pattern between internal and external communication and innovation in the meta-analysis (Damanpour 1991). However, Walker (2008) only identifies a positive impact of these structures on one out of four types of innovation. Still, there is general support for a positive impact of the two organizational structures that can be derived as prescriptions from the NPG paradigm. The result was expected based on the theory that communication furthers the spread of ideas.

11.6   What is the Optimal Organizational Structure?

Given the relations between different organizational structures pertaining to different governance paradigms and innovation, what is the optimal organizational structure? Unfortunately there is no straightforward answer. The theoretical arguments as well as the empirical patterns are somewhat ambiguous, but they do point to some general arguments about the relationship between organizational structures and innovation. On this basis, we can approach the question of an optimal organizational structure.

First, the fact that there is no strong and consistent relationship between organizational bureaucratic structures and public sector innovation is an important finding. The optimal organizational design for innovation is not public sector organizations without bureaucracy. This is important as bureaucratic structures also embody widely shared values for the public sector, such as accountability, equity, consistency and equality (Albrow 1970; Weber 1971; Caiden 1991; Goodsell 2004; Du Gay 2007). Indeed, promoting innovation by completely removing bureaucratic structures would, most likely, hinder any innovation, as key values legitimizing public sector organizations would be undermined. This is also consistent with the historical development of layering first NPM and then NPG on top of the Classical Public Administration thereby modifying, but not eradicating, earlier forms of governance (Christensen, Lie and Laegreid 2008; Jakobsen and Mortensen 2016). As pointed out by Torfing and Triantafillou (Chapter 1), the case for the NPG paradigm is also based on a continued presence of key structures prescribed by both the CPA and the NPM paradigms.

Second, we can stretch the empirical evidence a bit further. When designing organizational structures for innovation, we should be particularly sceptical of centralizing decision making at the top of the organization. We should be less worried about the level of formalization and hierarchy and instead focus on the design, communication and exercise of rules and decision-making power. Furthermore, administrative capacity, specialization, division of labour and internal and external communication are likely to further innovation. As far as administrative capacity, we should keep in mind that its positive impact is likely to become negative at some point as administrative staff become ever more dominant within the organization (Andrews and Boyne 2011). Relating to governance paradigms, CPA, NPM and NPG all prescribe structures that are positively related to innovation, while other structures prescribed by CPA, except centralization, have no relationship. The lack of a 'winner' paradigm is consistent with the continued layering of paradigm prescriptions as many of them seem to work in the same direction.

Third, it is difficult to move beyond such relatively simple generalizations for individual dimensions of organizational structure. One starting point would be the observation that the impact of organizational structure varies between different types of innovations and contexts (Downs and Mohr 1976; Hage 1999; De Vries, Bekkers and Tummers 2016). This implies that a structural configuration that is optimal in one setting is not optimal in another, which is in line with the contingency theory of organizations (Mintzberg 1980; Donaldson 1999; Walker 2014). Unfortunately, there is little empirical evidence on public organization or meta-studies of innovation in general that examine the interactive impact of different organizational structures in different settings. If we were to make optimal designs, it would, for instance, be beneficial to know whether the impact of specialization varies with different levels of formalization and hierarchy and how this is conditioned by the environment and the type of innovation.

Fourth, theoretical models of structural designs that combine many types of structures do exist and can be assessed based on the evidence. One classic design argued to further innovation is the organic model of organizations, which prescribes structures with little formalization, hierarchy, division of labour and specialization combined with fluid leadership and horizontal channels of communication (Burns and Stalker 1979). Such a model closely resembles what has been coined adhocracy (Mintzberg 1980: 336–8) due to its claimed ability to respond immediately (ad hoc) to new challenges and ideas and to generate innovation. In a contingency perspective, such structures should be optimal in very specific situations, such as highly fluid and changing environments that require a very high level of innovation (Mintzberg 1980). The relevance of such models in other environments – which is relevant to consider given the agenda to promote innovation broadly in the public sector – is nevertheless more questionable. The evidence presented above is consistent with the organic model in a few dimensions as centralization has a negative impact and communication has a positive impact on innovation. Still, the positive impact of specialization and division of labour and the lack of negative impact from hierarchy and formalizations do not fit the model.

Hybrid forms of organization that are characterized by several design principles (Mintzberg 1979: 474) can contain bureaucratic as well as more ad hoc-based structures. They have a better fit with the empirical evidence as they allow the pros of the different structures to supplement each other. This is reflected in the prescription for safe innovation havens that are close to, but still separated from, the day-to-day operations of the organization (Eggers and Singh 2009: 134; Bason 2010: 113). Government innovation units such as MindLab and NESTA are examples of such units. Their impact can also be understood based on the positive impact of the division of labour as such units increase the complexity of the division of labour within the organization (Hage 1999: 604–5). Hybrid organizations also deliver a possible interpretation of why some bureaucratic structures have little relationship with innovation. If organizations have some areas that are structured in a way that is conducive to innovation like division of labour, decentralization and lots of communication, they can maintain more classic bureaucratic features in other areas of the organization were other goals than innovation are pursued.

Yet, even with these modest conclusions, several caveats are at play. Very little of the empirical evidence presented above is based on longitudinal and experimental designs, which makes it difficult to rule out two-way causality. For example, innovative organizations could become more decentralized as they work innovatively. Furthermore, there is evidence that the impact of structural features, such as formalization, depend not only on how they are designed but also on how these rules are developed, communicated and perceived. This clearly indicates that it is difficult to design optimal structures without taking leadership, culture and motivation into account. This makes us consider whether asking about optimal structural design is really the right or the most important question to ask if we want to understand how to enhance public innovation.

11.7   Are We Searching in Vain for the Optimal Design?

We now change from a hypothetical-deductive approach to a more explorative and theoretical approach where we, based on assumptions about individual entrepreneurship, seek to develop an alternative to the question about optimal design.

If we assume that entrepreneurship is a key element in innovation, the whole issue of furthering innovation through organizational structures becomes highly complicated. Indeed, plenty of research seeks to explain entrepreneurship with macro-level organizational structures (Eckhardt and Shane 2003). However, while this research has generated considerable insights, it does not adequately explain entrepreneurship because it does not consider micro-level factors in terms of human agency (Shane 2003; Korsgaard et al. 2015). Indeed, defining innovation as 'an intentional, yet inherently contingent, process' (Sørensen and Torfing 2011: 849) maintains that contingencies and thereby complexity do not only pertain to macro-level factors. Even though theory on macro-level organizational structures is typically without such complexity, it may be a useful approximation to direct and govern micro-level entrepreneurial processes (Stinchcombe 1991). However, making inferences from macro-level organizational structures to govern and support profoundly different and more complicated processes at a micro-level, such as creativity, social interactions and subjectivity, is intrinsically problematic (Baker and Nelson 2005).

In a seminal paper, Shane and Venkataraman (2000) proposed a conceptual framework for entrepreneurship revolving around the structural factors shaping entrepreneurial opportunities as well as entrepreneurial individuals (Venkataraman et al. 2012; Eckhardt and Shane 2013; Fiet, Norton and Clouse 2013). According to Shane and Venkataraman (2000: 218), 'entrepreneurship involves the nexus of two phenomena: the presence of lucrative opportunities and the presence of enterprising individuals'. Moreover, the conceptual framework revolves around the process of discovery, evaluation and exploitation of lucrative entrepreneurial opportunities, while maintaining that the entrepreneurial process unfolds within an individual–opportunity nexus. However, this nexus cannot be directly governed through macro-level organizational structures as these are alien to micro-level elements such as creativity and subjectivity.

The innovative component is comprised in the term 'entrepreneurial opportunities'. This encompasses the introduction of new goods, services, markets, policies and/or organizational methods through the formation of a new means-end framework that is not restricted to any particular organizational form (Shane and Venkataraman 2000). Adding the term 'lucrative' to opportunities makes explicit the connotation that opportunities are perceived as favourable by the individual – even opportunities that turn out to be non-lucrative later on. Rather than being independent of specific actors and readily available to everybody, opportunities thus represent a perception and assessment of circumstances as a function of the individual (Davidsson 2015). Basically, opportunities for everyone are opportunities for nobody since opportunities require a certain element of idiosyncrasy.

This view on entrepreneurship introduces subjectivism as a core contingency emphasizing the non-deterministic nature of innovation and entrepreneurial activities. Thus, from this point of view, innovation is not reducible to individual or organizational structures but is co-created in an entrepreneurial process. Also, each individual's starting point in the nexus, in terms of entrepreneurial identity and personal opportunities, is different. Therefore, it is conducive to innovation when employees are assigned to work on entrepreneurial activities that are linked to their knowledge, interests and everyday practice. Indeed, Spinosa, Flores and Dreyfus (1997) refer to entrepreneurship as history making through the perception and sensitivity towards disharmonies and anomalies in our own everyday practice. Within this line of thinking, entrepreneurial opportunities to innovate arise from sensitivity towards disharmonies in employees' everyday practice.

In this perspective, which is profoundly different from the deductive macro-level approach presented earlier, the search for an optimal structural design for public innovation is potentially a misleading endeavour. The relationship between macro-level organizational structures and genuine entrepreneurship driving innovation is too distant and too complex to pursue the ambition of identifying an optimal design. Instead, a more promising and explorative question relates to how public actors can be enabled to act entrepreneurially from a nexus perspective in terms of coping with uncertainty and acting collaboratively in a specific context. Accordingly, the key question is: How do we support and govern a process of discovery, evaluation and exploitation of entrepreneurial opportunities that unfolds within an individual–opportunity nexus? On the one hand, organizational structures are likely to play a minor role in the answer to this question. On the other hand, organizational structures such as division of labour and decentralization may be able to provide contingencies and stepping stones within which public sector innovation can unfold as a co-creation process between the individual and his or her opportunities.

Using the concept of discovery, Shane and Venkataraman (2000) argue that opportunities are objective and predate the entrepreneurial process. They are literally just waiting to be discovered. This perspective is grounded in a fairly traditional discovery model, in which an alert entrepreneur discovers an entrepreneurial opportunity, evaluates its potential gains and exploits it for economic or political reasons (Kirzner 1973). Except for the instantaneous act of discovering the entrepreneurial opportunity, this process resembles a simple process of optimization with only limited uncertainty (McMullen and Shepherd 2006; Korsgaard et al. 2015). An example is a public physician who discovers an entrepreneurial opportunity to make an efficiency improvement in a production process at the hospital that is easily evaluated and implemented, even though it may contain elements of calculated risk. Such processes can be referred to as a risky decision based on the Knightian distinction between risk and uncertainty (Alvarez and Barney 2007). Hence, the act of entrepreneurship, which introduces the contingency at the individual level, is the act of alertness carried out with the lure of, e.g., economic or political gains. The contingency hence stems from individuals' idiosyncratic prior knowledge and/or access to specific information and networks, i.e. the doctor knows management consultants through private networks who have alerted him to the inefficiency at the hospital (Shane 2000). With low uncertainty and processes resembling optimization, the discovery view of entrepreneurial opportunities offers a useful interpretation of the entrepreneurial process (Alvarez and Barney 2007; Korsgaard et al. 2015). In such situations, structures to advance public innovation need to address extrinsic performance incentives to enhance efficiency through continuous efforts to optimize existing practices, which is basically at the core prescription of the NPM paradigm.

The discovery model has been questioned and moderated in many ways by scholars representing a creation view of discovery (Sarasvathy 2001; Alvarez and Barney 2007; Korsgaard 2013). In this view, opportunities do not exist prior to the entrepreneurial process, but are created through a genuinely uncertain entrepreneurial process (Alvarez and Barney 2007; Korsgaard 2013; Alvarez, Young and Woolley 2015). For example, Sarasvathy shows how opportunities are created in the face of uncertainty through iterative social processes with potential stakeholders using the resources and interests of the entrepreneur as the starting point (Sarasvathy 2001, 2008; Venkataraman et al. 2012). In these cases, employees engage in entrepreneurial activities in highly unstable environments where neither employees nor employer possess knowledge that allows them to foresee the effects of their actions. Hence, in entrepreneurial processes characterized by uncertainty, which is the case with wicked problems (see Torfing and Triantafillou, Chapter 1), opportunities must be developed through creative, experimental and collaborative efforts (Garud and Karnøe 2003; Baker and Nelson 2005; Korsgaard et al. 2015). The physician would thus not just discover the inefficiency at the public hospital, but based on his subjective and personal background and everyday practice develop a sense of disharmony between ideals and practices and co-create this to an entrepreneurial opportunity through an entrepreneurial process. A governance regime to advance public innovation needs to address the aspects of output uncertainty and collaborative elements in the entrepreneurial process by focusing structures and incentives on the process, while uncertainty makes prediction and outcome-based incentives unattainable. This resembles the core prescription of the NPG paradigm that allows employees to work and create opportunities across borders without a strict performance-based governance regime.

NPM may hence be suitable for the governance of public innovation in cases of low uncertainty that resemble optimization processes, whereas NPG should be preferred in cases with high uncertainty. In such cases, entrepreneurial opportunities need to be developed through creative, experimental and collaborative efforts. However, accepting that entrepreneurship and innovation revolve around an individual–opportunity nexus to some extent contradicts the entire concept of 'governance'. This is particularly the case for the assumption that specific forms of governance contribute directly to the realization of a political goal such as public sector innovation. Viewing entrepreneurship as a nexus implies that entrepreneurship and innovation are and must be what the employees and other involved actors make it.

11.8   Conclusion

The purpose of the chapter was to examine the relationship between organizational structures and public sector innovation. In relation to this purpose, the chapter has delivered three key points.

First, the classic Weberian bureaucracy is not the enemy of public sector innovation as it is often proclaimed to be. From a theoretical perspective, there are both pros and cons of the impact on innovation from most of the dimensions of bureaucracy, and there are in particular strong arguments that the impact of most structures like formal rule systems is open-ended and contingent. Furthermore, empirically the impact of the various structures is not strong and uniform. Only centralization seems to be at odds with innovation, while the division of labour, specialization and administrative capacity are positively related to innovation. Consistent with the NPG prescription, internal and external communication are also positively related to innovation.

Second, it is not possible to develop an optimal organizational design based on the empirical evidence. The possible recommendations for designers of organizational structures would be (a) that they should not be too wary of bureaucracy in general, (b) that they should try to avoid high degrees of centralization, and (c) that they could increase the potential for innovation by promoting division of labour, specialization and high levels of communication and secure a solid administrative capacity within the organization. These results are only partly consistent with organic forms of organizations and could be interpreted to support some form of hybrid organization that combines ad hoc features with bureaucratic structures. By not abandoning bureaucracy altogether, the organization also upholds public values which are promoted by bureaucratic structures and legitimize public organizations.

Third and finally, the inability to develop an optimal structural design implies that the search for a single best organizational design for innovation could be misplaced. By focusing on the entrepreneurial component of innovation that emphasizes how entrepreneurship arises in specific nexuses between the individual and their specific opportunities, elements such as creativity, subjectivity and collaboration take centre stage. These elements are difficult to reach with organizational structures. An alternative to asking about optimal structural design is to ask how public sector actors can be enabled to act entrepreneurially in terms of coping with uncertainty and acting collaboratively. While other factors than organizational structures are likely to be more important answers to the question, organizational structures could play a contingent and enabling role. In particular, we suggest that the organizational structures prescribed by the NPG paradigm could support entrepreneurial public sector behaviour in cases of high uncertainty, which is for instance the case for the many wicked problems confronted by the public sector.

References

Adler, P. S. and Borys, B. 1996. 'Two types of bureaucracy: Enabling and coercive', *Administrative Science Quarterly* 41: 61–89.

Aiken, M. and Hage, J. 1971. 'The organic organization and innovation', *Sociology* 5: 63–82.

Albrow, M. 1970. *Bureaucracy*. London: Macmillan.

Alvarez, S. A. and Barney, J. B. 2007. 'Discovery and creation: Alternative theories of entrepreneurial action', *Strategic Entrepreneurship Journal* 1: 11–26.

Alvarez, S. A., Young, S. L. and Woolley, J. L. 2015. 'Opportunities and institutions: A co-creation story of the king crab industry', *Journal of Business Venturing* 30: 95–112.

Andrews, R. and Boyne, G. 2011. 'Corporate capacity and public service performance', *Public Administration* 89: 894–908.

Baker, T. and Nelson, R. E. 2005. 'Creating something from nothing: Resource construction through entrepreneurial bricolage', *Administrative Science Quarterly* 50: 329–66.

Bason, C. 2010. *Leading Public Sector Innovation: Co-Creating for a Better Society*. Bristol, UK: Policy Press.

Bozeman, B. and Feeney, M. K. 2011. *Rules and Red Tape: A Prism for Public Administration Theory and Research*. Armonk, NY: M.E. Sharpe.

Burns, T. and Stalker, G. M. 1979 *The Management of Innovation*, 2nd edition. London: Tavistock Publications.

Caiden, G. E. 1991. 'What really is public maladministration?' *Public Administration Review* 51: 486–93.

Christensen, T., Lie, A. and Laegreid, P. 2008. 'Beyond New Public Management: Agencification and regulatory reform in Norway', *Financial Accountability & Management* 24: 15–30.

Damanpour, F. 1991. 'Organizational innovation: A meta-analysis of effects of determinants and moderators', *The Academy of Management Journal* 34: 555–90.

1996. 'Bureaucracy and innovation revisited: Effects of contingency factors, industrial sectors, and innovation characteristics', *The Journal of High Technology Management Research* 7: 149–73.

Davidsson, P. 2015. 'Entrepreneurial opportunities and the entrepreneurship nexus: A re-conceptualization', *Journal of Business Venturing* 30: 674–95.

De Vries, H., Bekkers, V. and Tummers, L. 2016. 'Innovation in the public sector: a systematic review and future research agenda', *Public Administration* 94(1, March): 146–66,

DeHart-Davis, L. 2009. 'Green tape: A theory of effective organizational rules', *Journal of Public Administration Research and Theory* 19: 361–84.

Delbecq, A. L. and Pierce, J. L. 1978. 'Innovation in professional organizations', *Administration in Social Work* 2: 411–24.

Dixit, A., 2002. 'Incentives and organizations in the public sector: An interpretative review', *The Journal of Human Resources* 37: 696–727.

Donaldson, L. 1999. *The Normal Science of Structural Contingency Theory. Studying Organizations: Theory and Method*. Thousand Oaks, CA: Sage

Downs, G. W. and Mohr, L. B. 1976. 'Conceptual issues in the study of innovation', *Administrative Science Quarterly* 21: 700–14.

Du Gay, P. 2007. *Hyldest til bureaukratiet: Weber, organisation, etik.* Copenhagen, DK: Hans Reitzel Publishers.

Dunleavy, P. 1989. 'The architecture of the British central state, part I: Framework for analysis', *Public Administration* 67: 249–75.

Eckhardt, J. T. and Shane, S. A. 2003. 'Opportunities and entrepreneurship', *Journal of Management* 29: 333–49.

2013. 'Response to the commentaries: The individual-opportunity (IO) nexus integrates objective and subjective aspects of entrepreneurship', *Academy of Management Review* 38: 160–3.

Eggers, W. D. and Singh, S. K. 2009. *The Public Innovator's Playbook: Nurturing Bold Ideas in Government.* Deloitte.

Fernandez, S. and Wise, L. R. 2010. 'An exploration of why public organizations "ingest" innovations', *Public Administration* 88: 979–98.

Fiet, J. O., Norton, W. I. and Clouse, V. G. H. 2013. 'Search and discovery by repeatedly successful entrepreneurs', *International Small Business Journal* 31: 890–913.

Garud, R. and Karnøe, P. 2003. 'Bricolage versus breakthrough: Distributed and embedded agency in technology entrepreneurship', *Research Policy* 32: 277–300.

Goodsell, C. T. 2004. *The Case for Bureaucracy: A Public Administration Polemic,* 4th edition. Washington DC: CQ Press

Hage, J. T. 1999.'Organizational innovation and organizational change', *Annual Review of Sociology* 25: 597–622.

Hall, R. H. 1963. 'The concept of bureaucracy: An empirical assessment', *American Journal of Sociology* 69(1): 32–40.

Hammond, T. H. 1993. 'Toward a general theory of hierarchy: Books, bureaucrats, basketball tournaments, and the administrative structure of the nation-state', *Journal of Public Administration Research and Theory* 3: 120–45.

Hartley, J., Sørensen, E. and Torfing, J. 2013.'Collaborative innovation: A viable alternative to market competition and organizational entrepreneurship', *Public Administration Review* 73: 821–30.

Hood, C. 1991. 'A public management for all seasons?' *Public Administration* 69: 3–19.

Hull, F. and Hage, J. 1982. 'Organizing for innovation: Beyond burns and stalker's organic type', *Sociology* 16: 564–77.

Ingraham, P. W., Joyce, P. G. and Donahue, A. K. 2003. *Government Performance: Why Management Matters.* Baltimore: Johns Hopkins University Press.

Jakobsen, M. L. F. 2013. 'Bureaukrati: ven eller fjende af (offentlig sektor) innovation?' *Politica* 45: 250–66.

Jakobsen, M. L. F. and Mortensen, P. B. 2016. 'Rules and the doctrine of performance management', *Public Administration Review* 76: 302–312.

Jaskyte, K. 2011. 'Predictors of administrative and technological innovations in nonprofit organizations', *Public Administration Review* 71: 77–86.

Kimberly, J. R. and Evanisko, M. J. 1981. 'Organizational innovation: The influence of individual, organizational, and contextual factors on hospital adoption of technological and administrative innovations', *Academy of Management Journal*, 24: 689–713.

Kirzner, I. M. 1973. *Competition and Entrepreneurship.* Chicago, IL: The University of Chicago Press.

Korsgaard, S. 2013. 'It's really out there: A review of the critique of the discovery view of opportunities', *International Journal of Entrepreneurial Behaviour & Research* 19: 130–48.

Korsgaard, S., Berglund, H., Thrane, C. and Blenker, P. 2015. 'A tale of two Kirzners: Time, uncertainty and the "nature" of opportunities', *Entrepreneurship: Theory & Practice.* Epub ahead of print 12 February. DOI: 10.1111/ etap.12151.

McMullen, J. S. and Shepherd, D. A. 2006.'Entrepreneurial action and the role of uncertainty in the theory of the entrepreneur', *Academy of Management Review* 31: 132–52.

Mikkelsen, M. F., Jacobsen, C. B. and Andersen, L. B. 2015. 'Managing employee motivation: Exploring the connections between managers' enforcement of command systems, employee perceptions, and employee intrinsic motivation', *International Public Management Journal* 1 early view (accepted author version).

Mintzberg, H. 1979. *The Structuring of Organizations.* Englewood Cliffs, N.J.: Prentice-Hall.

　1980. 'Structure in 5's: A synthesis of the research on organization design', *Management Science* 26: 322–41.

Nauta, F. and Kausbergen, P. 2009. 'OECD literature review. Public sector innovation', *Lectoraat Innovatie Rapport*, https://hbo-kennisbank.nl/en/record/oai:repository.samenmaken.nl:smpid:15206.

Niskanen, W. A. 1974. *Bureaucracy and Representative Government.* New Brunswick, NJ: Aldine Transaction Publishers.

O'Toole, L. J. 1997. 'Implementing public innovations in network settings', *Administration & Society* 29: 115–38.

Osborne, D. 1993. 'Reinventing government', *Public Productivity & Management Review*, 16 ('Fiscal Pressures and Productive Solutions: Proceedings of the Fifth National Public Sector Productivity Conference'): 349–56.

Parkinson, C. N. 1960. *Parkinsons lov eller stræben efter fremgang,* 8th edition. Copenhagen, DK: Fremad.

Rogers, E. M. 2003. *Diffusion of Innovations,* 5th edition. New York: Free Press.

Sarasvathy, S. D. 2001. 'Causation and effectuation: Toward a theoretical shift from economic inevitability to entrepreneurial contingency', *Academy of Management Review* 26: 243–64.

　2008. *Effectuation: Elements of Entrepreneurial Expertise.* Cheltenham: Edward Elgar.

Scharpf, F. W. 1994. 'Games real actors could play positive and negative coordination in embedded negotiations', *Journal of Theoretical Politics* 6: 27–53.

Scott, S. G. and Bruce, R. A. 1994. 'Determinants of innovative behavior: A path model of individual innovation in the workplace', *Academy of Management Journal* 37: 580–607.

Shane, S. 2000. 'Prior knowledge and the discovery of entrepreneurial opportunities', *Organization Science* 11: 448–69.
    2003. *A General Theory of Entrepreneurship: The Individual-Opportunity Nexus.* Cheltenham: Edward Elgar.
Shane, S. and Venkataraman, S. 2000. 'The promise of entrepreneurship as a field of research', *Academy of Management Review* 25: 217–26.
Sørensen, E. and Torfing, J. 2011. 'Enhancing collaborative innovation in the public sector', *Administration & Society* 43: 842–68.
Spinosa, C., Flores, F. and Dreyfus, H. L. 1997. *Disclosing New Worlds: Entrepreneurship, Democratic Action and the Cultivation of Solidarity.* Cambridge, MA: MIT Press.
Stinchcombe, A. L. 1991. 'The conditions of fruitfulness of theorizing about mechanisms in social science', *Philosophy of the Social Sciences* 21: 367–88.
Thompson, V. A. 1965. 'Bureaucracy and Innovation', *Administrative Science Quarterly* 10 (Special Issue on Professionals in Organizations): 1–20.
Torfing, J. 2011. 'Teorier om offentlig administration og styring: Fra stillestående bureaukrati til samarbejdsdrevet innovation', in E. Sørensen and J. Torfing (eds.), *Samarbejdsdrevet innovation i den offentlige sektor* (Vol. 1.). DJØF Publishers, pp. 117–36.
van der Voet, J. 2015.'Change leadership and public sector organizational change: examining the interactions of transformational leadership style and red tape', *The American Review of Public Administration*, OnlineFirst.
Venkataraman, S., Sarasvathy, S. D., Dew, N. and Forster, W. R. 2012. 'Reflections on the 2010 AMR decade award: Whither the promise? Moving forward with entrepreneurship as a science of the artificial', *Academy of Management Review* 37: 21–33.
Walker, R. M. 2008. 'An empirical evaluation of innovation types and organizational and environmental characteristics: Towards a configuration framework', *Journal of Public Administration Research and Theory* 18: 591–615.
    2014. 'Internal and external antecedents of process innovation: A review and extension', *Public Management Review* 16: 21–44.
Walton, E. J. 2005. 'The persistence of bureaucracy: A meta-analysis of Weber's model of bureaucratic control', *Organization Studies* 26: 569–600.
Weber, M. 1971. *Makt og byråkrati: Essays om politikk og klasse, samfunnsforskning og verdier.* Oslo: Gyldendal Norsk Forlag.
Wynen, J., Verhoest, K., Ongaro, E. and Van Thiel, S. 2014. 'Innovation-oriented culture in the public sector: Do managerial autonomy and result control lead to innovation?' *Public Management Review* 16: 45–66.
Zaltman, G., Duncan, R. and Holbek, J. 1973. *Innovations and Organizations.* New York: Wiley.
Zornoza, C. C., Boronat Navarro, M. and Cipres, M. S. 2007. 'A meta-analysis of organizational innovation', in J. Saee (ed.), *Contemporary Corporate Strategy – Global Perspectives.* New York: Routledge, pp. 61–75.

12 Can Command and Incentive Systems Enhance Motivation and Public Innovation?

Lotte Bøgh Andersen

12.1 Introduction

Imagine that you have a candle, a book of matches and a box of thumb-tacks. Your task is to fix and light the candle on a wall (a cork board) in a manner so that the candle wax will not drip onto the table below. What would you do? Some people melt the candlewax and use it to stick the candle to the wall. That does not work. Neither does trying to tack the candle directly to the wall. The innovative solution is to empty the box of thumbtacks, put the candle into the box, use the thumbtacks to nail the box (with the candle in it) to the wall and light the candle with the match. This type of idea generation is an important part of public innovation (as defined in Chapter 1). Due to implicit or explicit rules concerning the function of the box, however, many people cannot re-conceptualize it in a manner allowing them to solve the problem. One of the key questions in this book is how public governance can facilitate this type of innovative behaviour in the public sector, and this chapter focuses on the effects of incentives and command systems.

There is a potential trade-off between incentivizing individuals to do their best and risking a shift towards extrinsic motivation, undermining their pre-existing intrinsic motivation (and thus weakening their creative joy). Letting individuals solve the candle problem with and without a financial incentive to work fast, Glucksberg (1962) found that the result depended on the task. If the task was complex (the original setup), individuals without the financial incentive performed best; conversely, if the task was made simple by delivering the box and thumbtacks separately, the individuals with a financial incentive prevailed. The key message appears to be that complex tasks demand that creativity is set free from incentives and rules. Other studies do, however, contradict this message. Manso (2011), for example, shows how an incentive scheme motivates innovation if it exhibits substantial tolerance (or even reward) for early failure and reward for long-term success, and Scotchmer (2004) argues that rules concerning, for example, copyrights and the protection of intellectual property are important to innovation.

This implies that knowledge about the use of incentives and rules in organizations in which idea-creating types of innovation are important is very relevant. Given that it is impossible to cover all types of rules, this chapter focuses on rules (concerning employee effort or performance) that are monitored and sanctioned by supervisors (also called command systems). Correspondingly, the focus (among the many types of financial incentives) is on performance-related pay. Improving our understanding of the relationship between these important public governance measures and innovation can hopefully enable public managers to make more informed decisions about whether and how they should use command and incentive systems. Do rules and potential bonuses stop people from having good ideas? Or can the careful application of thought-out incentives and command systems actually induce employees to 'think outside the box'?

It is sometimes asserted that the strong adherence to rules and lack of incentives (e.g. bonus payments) stifle public sector innovation (Borins 2001; Sørensen and Torfing 2011), but this is not necessarily true. Motivation crowding theory (Frey 1997) suggests that if incentives and command systems are seen as controlling, they crowd out employee motivation; if, however, they are seen as supportive, they might have the opposite effect. In many public organizations, the only direct incentives to innovate are those of internal career politics and upward mobility within the hierarchy. Potts and Kastelle (2010: 126) argue that these incentives are so weak that the 'question of how to instrumentally improve public sector innovation efficacy notably contrasts with the economist's amazement that it ever happens at all'. In line with this, Borins (2001: 310) argues that the public sector is characterized by asymmetric incentives that punish unsuccessful innovations much more severely than they reward successful ones. According to Damanpour and Schneider (2009: 498–9), this leads many authors to refer to the lack of incentives as a specific barrier to innovation in the public sector. Public managers might, however, be just as able as private managers to influence the motivation of their employees and create a work and social climate that encourages and rewards innovation (Damanpour and Schneider 2009). Bellé (2014), for example, argues that public employees are inherently required to consider the well-being of the greater community, which renders it easier to motivate them to transcend their immediate self-interest. This chapter discusses both motivation and innovation, because they are expected to reinforce each other mutually (Unsworth and Clegg 2010; Rosenblatt 2011) and the same mechanisms might be relevant for their relationships with command and incentive systems.

While we have some knowledge about the relationships between incentives, command systems and motivation, we know too little about how different types of incentives can be used to enhance innovation in the public sector, and the relationship between command systems and innovation has also been neglected. We know a bit more about innovation and red tape, which is the perceived level of burdensome administrative rules and procedures with negative effects on the effectiveness of the organization. Rules are an important part of a command system, and the perceptions of rules have been seen as important in motivation crowding theory as well as in the red tape literature itself. Research on the red tape–innovation relationship is, however, inconclusive, suggesting that this literature could also benefit from more knowledge about different managerial interventions and innovation.

The antecedents of innovation are complex (Damanpour 1991; Walker 2008: 592), and this chapter does not try to cover this complexity. Instead, it focuses on two types of managerial intervention that can potentially both facilitate and hinder innovation, namely financial incentives and command systems or, in more popular terms, organizational carrots and sticks. Can public managers use financial incentives and command systems to foster the motivation and innovativeness of their employees? Existing studies have found that command systems and financial incentives can increase and decrease motivation, depending on how employees perceive such interventions, and this might also be the case for innovation. Both financial incentives and command systems are often accused of stopping people from being creative, but the literature is mixed. Some authors argue that offering extrinsic rewards for creativity will enhance creative performance (Eisenberger and Armeli 1997), while others argue that the use of contingent, extrinsic rewards will diminish creativity by undermining individuals' intrinsic motivation (e.g. Amabile, Hennessey and Grossman 1986). Given that several studies find positive effects (Baer, Oldham and Cummings 2003; Rosenblatt 2011; Bysted and Jespersen 2014), it is highly relevant to investigate whether extrinsic intervention such as command and incentive systems always relate negatively to innovation or whether they (used in a supportive manner) can enhance both employee motivation and innovation. Existing studies have found a negative association between a controlling perception of extrinsic intervention and both public service motivation and intrinsic motivation (e.g. Jacobsen, Hvitved and Andersen 2014), and this is relevant for innovation, because both types of motivation may enhance innovation. The basic argument is that employees with these types of motivation experience a higher sense of choice in terms of initiating their own actions and that this makes them integrate a given demand (e.g. to create and implement innovation) into their own sense of self, resulting in greater persistence and better performance (Ryan and Deci 2000).

After a theoretical discussion of different reasons for expecting associations between financial incentives, command systems, motivation and innovation, four sections examine the empirical relationships between financial incentives and motivation, command systems and motivation, financial incentives and innovation, and command systems and innovation. The chapter concludes with a discussion of how public managers can best enhance motivation and innovation using financial incentives and command systems.

12.2   Theoretical Relationships between Command and Incentive Systems, Motivation and Innovation

The first step towards disentangling the relationships between financial incentives, command systems, motivation and innovation is to clarify the concepts. As mentioned in Chapter 1, innovation can be seen as the intentional introduction and application of ideas, processes, products or procedures that are new to the relevant unit of adoption. This chapter focuses exclusively on idea generation (rather than idea adoption), because idea generation normally demands the highest level of creativity, making it especially vulnerable to the potentially harmful effects of incentive and command systems. In other words, the chapter focuses on novelty in general (e.g. doing something in a totally new manner) rather than novelty in a given organization (e.g. adopting a different way of doing things that is new to the organization).

Being motivated means to be moved to do something; accordingly, Ryan and Deci (2000: 54) consider individuals motivated if they are 'energized or activated toward an end'. Motivation can be either intrinsic or extrinsic. Extrinsic motivation is derived from benefits that are not part of the work, whereas intrinsic motivation is 'interest in or enjoyment of the work for its own sake' (Le Grand 2003: 53). For example, employees might be motivated to participate in innovation involving technology because they enjoy learning about and mastering new technology. This may make them want to contribute to the success of a specific new technological innovation. In the public sector, public service motivation can also be very relevant. Doing good for others and shaping the well-being of society are motivating (Perry and Hondeghem 2008). It can be seen as a specific type of integrated, extrinsic motivation. If employees feel that they participate in innovation because they want to contribute to society of their own free will, this higher sense of choice can make them integrate the demand to be innovative into their own sense of self, which can in turn result in greater persistence and better performance (Ryan and Deci 2000).

Managers can enhance their employees' motivation and willingness to innovate in different ways. Several studies have shown how transformational leadership in particular can enhance employees' public service motivation (Bellé 2014; Krogsgaard, Thomsen and Andersen 2014), and this leadership strategy is also positively related to innovation (e.g. Gumusluoglu and Ilsev 2009). It can be defined as attempts at motivating employees to transcend their immediate self-interest for the sake of the team, the organization or the larger polity (Bellé 2014: 110) and involves developing, sharing and sustaining a vision for the organization. While the creation of meaning is key to this type of leadership and for public service motivation, intrinsic motivation depends more on task autonomy (e.g. Cadwallader et al. 2010: 225). This concerns the job design – ensuring that tasks are seen as interesting and giving the employees room to feel the above-mentioned sense of choice. This can clash with external interventions (incentives and command systems) if they are seen as controlling. While positive interventions (e.g. pay and recognition) increase the net benefits of doing something, negative interventions increase the net costs of not doing it (e.g. through a potential firing or criticism). Compared to negative interventions (command systems), it is easier to implement positive interventions (incentives) in a manner that is seen as supportive rather than controlling (Frey 1997), but both types of intervention can be perceived very differently, depending on the signal they send (either as a 'pat on the back' or a control device). Both positive and negative interventions come in material as well as non-material forms, but this chapter focuses on material interventions. Following the terminology in motivation crowding theory, financial incentives are seen as rules that link pecuniary rewards to certain levels of effort or performance, whereas command systems are rules demanding a specific behaviour and/or performance, which are monitored and (in the case of non-compliance) sanctioned.

While there is little doubt that intrinsic motivation is positively related to innovation (e.g. Rosenblatt 2011), the use of extrinsic interventions, such as financial incentives and command, is often accused of inhibiting creativity. If we look at the effect on extrinsic motivation alone, financial incentives increase the payoff of hard work (functioning as carrots), while command systems render it less attractive to shirk because of the sanctions (functioning as sticks). Motivation crowding theory does, however, argue that external interventions also affect intrinsic motivation, especially for interesting tasks (Weibel, Rost and Osterloh 2010). The argument is that they can potentially crowd out intrinsic motivation, thereby decreasing productivity and hindering innovation, because they reduce individual self-determination and signal a low acknowledgement of individuals' autonomous motivation (Frey and Jegen 2001: 594–5). Self-determination is, in other words, expected to mediate the effect of command and incentive systems on intrinsic motivation and innovation (Alexy and Leitner 2011). Therefore, in addition to a positive direct effect of 'sticks and carrots', they might crowd out other forms of motivation driving innovation in the public sector; that is, have a negative indirect effect. This can also be the case for both public service motivation and intrinsic motivation, and motivation crowding theory suggests that extrinsic interventions will be positively associated with motivation and innovation if the employees perceive them to be supportive, whereas the association is expected to be negative if the employees see the interventions as controlling.

In addition to the potential motivation crowding effects of command systems and financial incentives, there are other reasons why these interventions can be important for innovation in the public sector. Especially if the task involves horizontal collaboration, it is very important that the incentives and command systems do not have a tournament structure where the compensation (punishment) is solely a function of rank. The best (worst) employees receive a prize (punishment), meaning that it can be just as useful to sabotage others as to apply oneself. Innovation often demands knowledge sharing and the exchange of ideas, which is hardly going to happen if only the best are rewarded (or the worst punished).

Bysted and Jespersen (2014) also argue that, in many public organizations, lacking goal clarity means that financial incentives may positively influence the level of innovation among public employees because they increase the goal clarity concerning organizational objectives. By rewarding a given type of innovation, the reward system makes the goals more distinct, incentivizing the employees to innovate. Potts and Kastelle (2010: 128) argue that the currency of successful innovation in public organizations is reputation with pay-off in career advancement within the public sector organizations. While innovation often leads to higher job security in private organizations due to a stronger organizational position on the market, this is seldom the case in public organizations. These organizations are rarely able to use innovation to expand their areas of operations, and the politicians who are the ultimate principals in the public sector have many types of considerations, leading to a multitude of different goals for most public organizations. Especially in the context of financial austerity, the rhetoric of innovation is often used in the same sentences as downsizing the public sector (Bysted and Jespersen 2014).

The employees in public organizations therefore often regard innovation as leading to a reduced number of jobs. If public managers can use financial incentives to send the signal to the employees that innovation is important and safe, possibly even improving their job security, they might be able to improve the inner climate for innovation.

Similar arguments can be made for command systems, although there are also reasons to expect command systems to be negatively associated with innovation (and motivation) in the public sector. Command systems can give rise to cumbersome administrative procedures and therefore higher transaction costs associated with innovation. The perceived level of burdensome administrative rules and procedures with negative effects on the organization's effectiveness is often conceptualized as 'red tape' (Bozeman 2000). Part of the literature argues theoretically that red tape can be expected to reduce innovation (e.g. DeHart-Davis and Pandey 2005) and motivation (Moynihan and Pandey 2007), but it has also been argued that red tape can motivate organizations to seek alternative solutions, generating a demand within the organizations for better forms of communication and coordination to reduce the high transaction costs, thereby enhancing innovation (Pandey and Bretschneider 1997). Some researchers capture the potential positive effects of rules by calling effective rules 'green tape' (DeHart-Davis 2009); but while it is useful to study when rules are seen as red or green, it is almost built into the definition that the relationship between green tape and motivation (and possibly also innovation) is positive. Whether the positive or negative effect of the *perceived* level of burdensome rules (red tape in the sense defined above) dominates might depend on the context in which the organization is placed. This means that there are reasons to expect both positive and negative associations between incentives and command systems, on the one hand, and motivation and innovation on the other. The next sections discuss the empirical evidence of these associations.

12.3   Empirical Evidence Concerning Financial Incentives, Command Systems and Motivation

The associations between incentives and motivation have been investigated in several recent studies (e.g. Andersen and Pallesen, 2008; Bertelli 2006; Georgellis, Iossa and Tabvuma 2011; Holmaas et al. 2010; Weibel, Rost and Osterloh 2010) that generally support the argument that incentives can have crowding effects on motivation (Jacobsen 2012). The key finding concerning incentives and motivation across the studies is thus simple: Incentives seen by employees as supportive can increase motivation, while incentives perceived as controlling tend to reduce motivation.

Motivation crowding theory has also been tested for command systems, studies which also tend to indicate that the controlling perceptions of command systems are negatively associated with employee motivation (Jacobsen, Hvitved and Andersen 2014) and ultimately with performance (Jacobsen and Andersen 2014b). In line with this, studies of the perception of burdensome rules (red tape) and motivation find negative associations (Scott and Pandey 2005; Moynihan and Pandey 2007). Although these cross-sectional studies cannot determine the causal direction, the negative correlations support the notion that the perception of command systems is important for motivation.

12.4   Empirical Evidence Concerning Financial Incentives and Innovation

Due to the cross-disciplinary character of innovation research, it has been investigated in many ways: historically (e.g. Scotchmer 2004), using survey data with individuals (e.g. Bysted and Jespersen 2014; Walker 2008) and qualitatively (e.g. Torfing and Ansell 2014; Unsworth and Clegg 2010). Historical analyses typically focus on the legal and institutional contexts in which innovation takes place, emphasizing, for example, the economic design of intellectual property, different models of cumulative innovation, patent enforcement and the funding of research and development investments (Schotchmer 2004). This can be relevant as the context for the specific question in this chapter, because the context might determine what constitutes innovation barriers and innovation drivers. For example, the institutions governing universities can affect researchers' incentives to be secretive, and their motive to publish can become an impediment to sharing and therefore to innovation (Scotchmer 2004: 254). Below, I discuss the results separately for qualitative studies, quantitative studies with self-reported data, and ultimately quantitative studies of external measures of innovation. This discussion is more detailed than the discussion earlier, because the results are more complex (and rarely discussed together in the literature).

Qualitative interviews are primarily used to study the association between incentives and innovation within a given context. Sehested et al. (2010), for example, investigate the barriers and drivers of innovation in the public sector. They find that many of their respondents think that an incentive structure supporting collaborative innovation in the public sector will reduce risk aversion and increase the motivation of leaders and employees to work across sectors and groups of actors. For example, they analyse whether their respondents think that there is a lacking focus on incentives and lacking acceptance of market principled in the public sector, and whether this hinders innovation. Their respondents do not agree on this; one-third agree that lacking incentives and market mechanisms hinder innovation, while the rest view the question as being too general and un-nuanced. Some of these respondents do not see the market being able to stimulate innovation. Several of them mention that a visionary leadership style is far more important than financial incentives for stimulating innovation. Generally, the results from this type of research are difficult to generalize, although doing so produces important insights into how individuals see the mechanisms.

Quantitative studies building on self-reported data on innovation normally use surveys. Based on answers from 3,743 public and 4,567 private employees in Denmark, Norway and Sweden, Bysted and Jespersen (2014) find that salary bonuses linked to performance do not influence employee creativity but that such bonuses actually reduce idea realization. Still, they also find that public employees' willingness to implement new ideas is motivated by salary bonuses, and their overall conclusion is that employees in the public sector respond well to clear performance rewards. This is in line with a study based on panel data on more than 6,000 Canadian establishments drawn from the 1999–2003 Canadian Workplace and Employee Survey. Zoghi, Mohr and Meyer (2010) thus find that establishments with incentive pay plans are significantly more likely to innovate than other establishments. The authors do, however, argue that their data indicate that this relationship is not necessarily causal, given that controls for unobserved heterogeneity weaken results and lagged variables give no clear evidence that organizational changes predate innovation. This could also be due to moderation effects, for example from managerial implementation or the type of task performed by the employees. Alexy and Leitner (2011) thus argue that the effect of payment in distributed innovation settings is very complex, and their findings from a scenario experiment with open-source software developers show that payment does not have a positive effect for individuals with strong norms against payment. In line with this, Baer, Oldham and Cummings (2003) find a positive relation between extrinsic rewards and creativity for employees with an adaptive cognitive style and relatively simple jobs, a weak relation between rewards and creativity for employees with an innovative cognitive style and complex jobs, and a negative relationship for employees with the combinations adaptive style/complex job and innovative style/simple job. The general result from survey-based studies of incentives and innovation is, thus, a weak positive association.

In the economic approach to innovation research, patent counts have become one of the standard measures of innovation, because the measure is external to the persons who are innovative (Moser 2013: 23–4).

Analysing patents also enables us to perform panel data studies of innovation, and Potts and Kastelle (2010) argue that studies of knowledge-producing organizations are uniquely fitted to illustrate how public sector innovation in general can be enhanced. They argue that the incentive structures between public sector innovation and science are more similar than those between public and private sector innovation, because the reward structure in science for successful innovation accrues to reputational capital and upward mobility in the scientific community. The use of patent data as a proxy for innovation output was pioneered by Schmookler (1966) and Scherer (1965) and later continued in the Patent Data Project as described by Cockburn, Hall, Powell and Trajtenberg (2005). Using the data from Andersen and Pallesen (2008), Jacobsen and Andersen (2014a) analyse 66 Danish university departments with valid information on patents in 2000 and 2005. The data combines the quantitative coding of local salary agreements with register data on the patent applications. In 2000, none of the departments had direct individual financial incentives linked to research outcome (although most of them had career incentives linked to publications and other types of performance), whereas many of the departments had introduced such financial incentives to a varying degree in 2005. The financial incentives are classified on a scale from no publication incentive to a very strong publication incentive with specific, non-discretionary release of publication bonuses when a given performance is met. The reason for studying publication incentives (instead of bonuses for patents) is that none of the departments had incentives linked to patents. While both patents and publications are outcomes of innovative research, we cannot study the direct incentives to take out a patent on the research. Still, it is relevant to know whether the incentives linked to research output are positively or negatively related to innovativeness in research, operationalized as the number of patents.

Only departments where the number of patents can be reliably measured in both 2000 and 2005 are included in the analysis, and the number of patents per full-time-equivalent researcher is the dependent variable. Both logistic and tobit panel regressions indicate that there is a positive association between the introduction of financial incentives and number of patents. If no incentive was implemented between 2000 and 2005, the number of patents is estimated to be lower in 2005 than in 2000, while this is not the case if an incentive had been introduced. If more than a minimum effort is demanded to receive pay supplements, the effect is estimated to be positive. The difference is statistically significant, also when controlling for the type of department (science and health versus humanities and social science). Other outputs in the research sector also appear to be positively associated with financial incentives: Sauermann and Cohen (2010) use data from more than 1,700 private sector scientists and engineers to investigate the antecedents of innovation, finding that motives regarding intellectual challenge, independence and money have a strong positive relationship with innovative output. Again, taken together, the trend seems to be a weak positive association.

Although the evidence from qualitative, survey and patent-based studies of innovation is complex, the results generally point towards a positive association between the use of performance-related incentives and innovation. This association might very well only be present when incentives are seen as supportive and when employees have at least some public service motivation (making them want to contribute to society with their innovations) or some intrinsic motivation (making them enjoy the process).

12.5   Empirical Evidence Concerning Command Systems and Innovation

As mentioned above, command systems are rules demanding a specific behaviour and/or certain performance, which are monitored and (in the case of non-compliance) sanctioned. One strand of relevant research considers the rule-aspect conceptualized as emphasis on following rules and procedures when conducting organizational activities. According to Damanpour (1991), the associations between innovation and formalization tend to be non-significant. Similarly, in a study of non-profit organizations, Jaskyte (2011) finds that formalization affects neither administrative nor technological innovation in non-profit organizations. Recent studies do indicate, however, that the strength and direction of the association may depend on the type of innovation and whether the organization is private or public (Walker 2008; Jakobsen 2013). Turning to studies of the direct association between rules and public innovation, it is again relevant to differentiate between survey-based studies and studies using patents as a measure of innovation.

Several survey-based studies analyse the red tape–innovation relationship, the general finding being that they are negatively correlated, either because red tape creates an organizational climate that reduces motivation and productivity or because it disrupts the internal processes associated with adopting innovation (Bozeman and Crow 1991; Bozeman and Kingsley 1998; DeHart-Davis and Pandey 2005). Still, some studies find positive red tape–innovation associations (Pandey and Bretschneider 1997; Moon and Bretschneider 2002). Applying a two-stage least squares model on NASP data (survey data with 386 public top managers, 284 private top managers and 207 non-profit top managers) to account for the endogenous red tape–innovativeness relationship, Moon and Bretschneiber (2002) thus find that high levels of perceived red tape may lead organizations to innovative solutions. They also find that IT innovativeness can help organizations reduce red tape levels. Similarly, Panday and Bretschneider (1997) find that top managers perceiving high red tape levels in their organization can lead to organizational pressure for alternative solutions to the red tape problems, which in turn can lead to increased organizational interest in new information technologies. In line with these results, Welch and Pandey (2007) do not find support for their expectation that organizations with higher levels of red tape will be less likely to implement intranet technology. Although survey-based studies produce mixed findings, the general message is that the *perception* of burdensome rules can be detrimental to innovation. This does not mean that rules are always a barrier, however, given that employees might also see them as supportive.

Patent data has also been used to study the command systems–innovation relationship. Jacobsen and Andersen (2014a) thus investigate whether the introduction of different command systems at 12 university departments within the same university affected the number of patent applications in the nine years between 2001 and 2009. In this analysis, the financial incentives are held constant, as all 12 departments had the same incentive system. This study is based on register data on patents and utilizes the fact that the relevant university demanded that the departments introduced command systems in 2001, which they went about very differently. Qualitative interviews and documentary material were collected in both 2007 and 2009 to classify these command systems on a scale from general statements of intent without directives, monitoring or sanctioning (score 1) to diffuse demands, casual monitoring and soft sanctions (score 2) to firm, but unspecific demands not linked to individual performance, occasional monitoring and moderate sanctions (score 3) and, finally, firm, frequently monitored and sanctioned demands linked to individual performance (score 4). The coding of the command systems is similar to Jacobsen and Andersen (2014b). The total number of patents per organization per year is the dependent variable. Analysing the 12 departments (from the same university) over nine years shows a weak, positive, non-significant association between the command system introduced in 2001 (when the university forced them to introduce some sort of command system) and the number of patents. There might be a positive association (statistical power is quite low, so the lacking rejections of the null hypothesis should not be given too much weight), but our interpretation is, still, that there is no noteworthy association between command systems and innovation.

In sum, the empirical evidence concerning the relationship between command systems and innovation does not allow any firm conclusions. Still, the results tentatively suggest that we cannot preclude that command systems can enhance innovation. As documented by Jacobsen and his colleagues (Jacobsen and Andersen 2014b; Jacobsen, Hvitved and Andersen 2014), command systems appear to be able to increase motivation when seen as supportive, and given that other studies have documented an effect of intrinsic motivation on innovation, it seems plausible that command systems that are perceived to be supportive enhance innovation as well as motivation.

12.6   Discussion and Conclusion

Based on existing studies and new analyses, the question in the title 'Can command and incentive systems enhance motivation and public innovation?' can be answered with a tentative 'yes' in terms of idea generation. The discussions and empirical studies in this chapter suggest that much depends on the individual manager and how they implement external interventions. DeHart-Davis (2009), for example, argues that the probability of rule effectiveness depends on whether the stakeholders understand their purpose, and the Mikkelsen, Andersen and Jacobsen (2015) analysis of the relationship between how school principals have implemented the Danish student plan requirement and how teachers have perceived this command system shows that dialogue led the teachers to perceive it to be more supportive. In line with this, Zhang and Bartol (2010: 107) argue that empowering leadership positively affects psychological empowerment, influencing both intrinsic motivation and creative process engagement. These two variables have a positive influence on creativity, and Zhang and Bartol also show that leader encouragement of creativity moderates the connection between psychological empowerment and creative process engagement. Bysted and Jespersen explain: 'the key to successful innovative work behaviour is whether the internal climate that management creates motivates employees to engage in innovation' (Bysted and Jespersen 2014: 2). This internal climate relates to organizational culture and, thus, also to recruiting employees who are able and willing to engage in innovative efforts, but it is also a question of the managerial recognition of the fact that innovation requires the acceptance of failure and a willingness to try new things. This is very much in line with Manso's (2011) finding that the ideal incentive scheme in relation to innovation exhibits substantial tolerance (or even reward) for early failure and reward for long-term success. Bysted and Jespersen (2014) argue further that public employees require a clear signal to supply innovative work behaviour, because innovation is often extra-role behaviour in public organizations. Here, it is important to stress that it cannot be taken for granted that public managers will even try to spur innovation if their incentives do not induce them to do so (see Chapter 7 by Bekkers and Mirko Noordegraaf, in this volume).

If the salary bonuses for innovative behaviour or command systems intended to increase this type of behaviour are used in public organizations, it is very important to be aware of the potential crowding-out effects of commands and incentives (which will occur if this intervention is seen as controlling rather than supportive). Alternatively, public managers can provide motivation and direction by developing, sharing and sustaining a vision intended to encourage employees to transcend their own self-interest and achieve organizational goals – for example, by engaging in innovative behaviour. When the leaders–employees dialogue leads to a more positive perception among the employees, it often relates to sharing a vision, which can involve both convincing employees about the desirability of the vision and allowing them to influence the vision and its implementation.

These different ways of showing how innovation is appreciated might very well supplement each other (van Wart 2013: 558). Bysted and Jespersen argue that the lack of goal clarity in public organizations increases the need for credible signals from managers (Bysted and Jespersen 2014: 18–9), while motivation crowding theory argues that the importance of the perception of managerial interventions is more generic. The importance of how incentives are implemented is further supported by Ederer and Manso (2013), who carry out a laboratory experiment that finds that the combination of tolerance for early failure and reward for long-term success is more effective in motivating innovation than fixed-wage incentive schemes. The participants in this experiment were recruited from the Harvard Business School Computer Laboratory for Economic Research (HBS CLER) subject pool using an online recruitment system, but the results are in line with other studies of real public employees, suggesting that the credibility of the direct manager is crucially important for innovation (Leonard-Barton 1995).

In times of financial austerity, enhancing innovation is especially challenging for public managers, because the need to create bottom-line savings can narrow the focus to innovation that simplifies processes, reducing the required number of employees, and this can be a problem for the motivation to innovate. In this context, Bysted and Jespersen (2014) show that the creative performance of public employees requires managerial recognition and a feeling of employment safety in order to reduce the risk associated with innovation. In sum, it seems as though management can create an innovation-supportive environment by using financial incentives and command systems but that this does not happen automatically when these interventions are used. How can this be done in a context in which the three paradigms discussed in Chapter 1 (Classical Public Administration (CPA), New Public Management (NPM) and New Public Governance (NPG)) are layered on top of one another? The paradigms have different understandings of the employees (as being driven by public duty, extrinsic motivation and different types of intrinsic motivation) and therefore place different emphasis on rules, incentive-based management and trust-based leadership. But the results presented in this chapter suggest that it can be useful to have more than one type of arrow in one's quiver': Innovation in hierarchies may be enhanced by NPG tools such as financial incentives if they are implemented in a meaningful, trust-based manner, respecting the employees' self-determination and acknowledging their autonomous motivation. An important factor is, thus, to ensure that financial incentives and command systems are perceived as supportive rather than controlling, as they may otherwise crowd out the employees' public service motivation and intrinsic motivation.

This can be seen as part of a larger trend in which the attention is on boosting employee motivation directly or indirectly. Transformational leadership has, thus, especially been shown to foster public service motivation (Moynihan, Pandey and Wright 2012), and Le Grand (2003, 2010) has convincingly argued that the models of public service delivery chosen by decision makers depend highly on their assumptions about employee motivation and user capacity. Considering employee motivation is therefore an important part of facilitating innovation in the public sector. Even for an organization in which stability is important and idea generation is of lesser consequence, making sure employees see incentive and command systems as supportive is useful, because a supportive perception is positively related to motivation in general, which again is positively related to performance. Still, it is important to remember that 'one size does not fit all', and this chapter does not suggest that all managers should use commands and incentives to boost motivation and innovation. But the general conclusion is that if they use it, they should be in dialogue with their employees, working to ensure that they see these measures as supportive rather than controlling. This chapter thus contributes to a better understanding of the relationship between public governance, motivation and innovation by showing how neither incentives nor command systems are in themselves harmful for innovation or motivation but that public managers should be aware that if employees see incentives or command systems as controlling, it can be a serious barrier to a productive link between these types of governance and innovation and motivation.

References

Alexy, O. and Leitner, M. 2011. 'A fistful of dollars: Are financial rewards a suitable management practice for distributed models of innovation?' *European Management Review* 8(3): 165–85.

Amabile, T. M., Hennessey, B. A. and Grossman, B. S. 1986. 'Social influences on creativity: The effects of contracted-for reward', *Journal of Personality and Social Psychology* 50(1): 14–23.

Andersen, L. B. and Pallesen, T. 2008. ' "Not Just for the Money?" How financial incentives affect the number of publications at Danish research institutions', *International Public Management Journal* 11(1): 28–47.

Baer, M., Oldham, G. R. and Cummings, A. 2003. 'Rewarding creativity: When does it really matter?' *The Leadership Quarterly* 14(4): 569–86.

Bellé, N. 2014. 'Leading to make a difference: A field experiment on the performance effects of transformational leadership, perceived social impact, and public service motivation', *Journal of Public Administration Research & Theory* 24(1): 109–36.

Bertelli, A. M. 2006. 'Motivation crowding and the federal civil servant: Evidence from the U.S. internal revenue service', *International Public Management Journal* 9(1): 3–23.

Borins, S. 2001. 'Encouraging innovation in the public sector', *Journal of Intellectual Capital* 2(3): 310–19.

Bozeman, B. 2000. *Bureaucracy and Red Tape*. Upper Saddle River, NJ: Prentice-Hall.

Bozeman, B. and Crow, M. 1991. 'Red tape and technology transfer success in government laboratories', *Journal of Technology Transfer* 16(2): 29–37.

Bozeman, B. and Kingsley, G. 1998. 'Risk culture in public and private organizations', *Public Administration Review* 58(2): 109–18.

Bysted, R. and Jespersen, K. R. 2014. 'Exploring managerial mechanisms that influence innovative work behaviour: Comparing private and public employees', *Public Management Review* 16(2): 217–41.

Cadwallader, S., Jarvis, C. B., Bitner, M. J. and Ostrom, A. L. 2010. 'Frontline employee motivation to participate in service innovation implementation', *Journal of the Academy of Marketing Science* 38(2): 219–39.

Cockburn, I., Hall, B. H., Powell, W. and Trajtenberg, M. 2005. *Patent Data Project – NSF Proposal*. http://emlab.berkeley.edu/users/bhhall/papers/CHPT_NSF_%20litreview_updated.pdf, accessed 10 May 2013.

Damanpour, F. 1991. 'Organizational innovation: A meta-analysis of effects of determinants and moderators', *Academy of Management Journal* 34(3): 555–90.

Damanpour, F. and Schneider, M. 2009. 'Characteristics of innovation and innovation adoption in public organizations: Assessing the role of managers', *Journal of Public Administration Research and Theory* 19(3): 495–522.

DeHart-Davis, L. and Pandey, S. 2005. 'Red tape and public employees: Does perceived rule dysfunction alienate managers?' *Journal of Public Administration Research and Theory* 15(1): 133–48.

DeHart-Davis, L. 2009. 'Green Tape: A Theory of Effective Organizational Rules', *Journal of Public Administration Research and Theory* 19(2): 361–84.

Ederer, F. and Manso, G. 2013. 'Is pay-for-performance detrimental to innovation?' *Management Science* 59(7): 1496–513.

Eisenberger, R. and Armeli, S. 1997. 'Can salient reward increase creative performance without reducing intrinsic creative interest?' *Journal of Personality and Social Psychology* 72(3): 652–63.

Frey, B. 1997. *Not Just for the Money: An Economic Theory of Personal Motivation.* Cheltenham & Brookfield: Edward Elgar.

Frey, B. and Jegen, R. 2001. 'Motivation crowding theory', *Journal of Economic Surveys* 15(5): 589–611.

Georgellis, Y., Iossa, E. and Tabvuma, V. 2011. 'Crowding out intrinsic motivation in the public sector', *Journal of Public Administration Research and Theory* 21(3): 473–93.

Glucksberg, S. 1962. 'The influence of strength of drive on functional fixedness and perceptual recognition', *Journal of Experimental Psychology* 63(1): 36–41.

Gumusluoglu, L. and Ilsev, A. 2009. 'Transformational leadership, creativity, and organizational innovation', *Journal of Business Research* 62(4): 461–73.

Holmaas, T.H., Kjerstad, E., Lurås, H. and Straume, O. R. 2010. 'Does monetary punishment crowd out pro-social motivation? A natural experiment on hospital length of stay', *Journal of Economic Behavior & Organization* 75(2): 261–7.

Jacobsen, C. B. 2012. *Management Interventions and Motivation Crowding Effects in Public Service Provision.* Aarhus: Politica.

Jacobsen, C. B. and Andersen, L. B. 2014a. 'Performance management in the public sector: Does it decrease or increase innovation and performance?' *International Journal of Public Administration* 37(14): 1011–23.

2014b. 'Performance management for academic researchers: How publication command systems affect individual behavior', *Review of Public Personnel Administration* 34(2): 84–107.

Jacobsen, C. B., Hvitved, J. and Andersen, L. B. 2014. 'Command and motivation: How the perception of external interventions relates to intrinsic motivation and public service motivation', *Public Administration* 92(4): 790–806.

Jakobsen, M. L. F. 2013. 'Bureaukrati: ven eller fjende af (offentlig sektor) innovation?' *Politica* 45(3): 250–66.

Jaskyte, K. 2011. 'Predictors of administrative and technological innovations in nonprofit organizations', *Public Administration Review* 71(1): 77–86.

Krogsgaard, J. A., Thomsen, P. and Andersen, L. B. 2014. 'Only if we agree? How value conflict moderates the relationship between transformational leadership and public service motivation', *International Journal of Public Administration* 37(12): 895–907.

Le Grand, J. 2003. *Motivation, Agency, and Public Policy.* New York & Oxford: Oxford University Press.

2010. 'Knights and knaves return: Public service motivation and the delivery of public services', *International Public Management Journal* 13(1): 56–71.

Leonard-Barton, D. 1995. *Wellsprings of Knowledge: Building and Sustaining the Sources of Innovation.* Boston: Harvard Business Press.

254   *Lotte Bøgh Andersen*

Manso, G. 2011. 'Motivating innovation', *The Journal of Finance* 66(5): 1823–60.

Mikkelsen, M. F., Andersen, L. B. and Jacobsen, C. B. 2015. 'Managing employee motivation: Exploring the connections between managers' enforcement actions, employee perceptions, and employee intrinsic motivation', *International Public Management Journal*. Accepted author version posted online: 16 July 2015, http://dx.doi.org/10.1080/10967494.2015.1043166.

Moon, M. J. and Bretschneiber, S. 2002. 'Does the perception of red tape constrain IT innovativeness in organizations? Unexpected results from a simultaneous equation model and implications', *Journal of Public Administration Research and Theory* 12(2): 273–92.

Moser, P. 2013. 'Patents and innovation: Evidence from economic history', *Journal of Economic Perspectives* 27(1): 23–44.

Moynihan, D. P. and Pandey, S. K. 2007. 'The role of organizations in fostering public service motivation', *Public Administration Review* 67(1): 40–53.

Moynihan, D. P., Pandey, S. K. and Wright, B. E. 2012. 'Setting the table: How transformational leadership fosters performance information use', *Journal of Public Administration Research and Theory* 22(1): 143–64.

Pandey, S. K. and Bretschneider, S. 1997. 'The impact of red tape's administrative delay on public organizations' interest in new information technology', *Journal of Public Administration Research and Theory* 7(1): 113–30.

Perry, J. L. and Hondeghem, A. 2008. 'Directions for future theory and research', in J. L. Perry and A. Hondeghem (eds.), *Motivation in Public Management: The Call of Public Service*. New York and Oxford: Oxford University Press, pp. 294–310.

Potts, J. and Kastelle, T. 2010. 'Public sector innovation research: What's next?' *Innovation: Management, Policy & Practice* 12(2): 122–37.

Rosenblatt, M. 2011. 'The use of innovation awards in the public sector: Individual and organizational perspectives', *Innovation: Management, Policy & Practice* 13(2): 207–19.

Ryan, R. and Deci, E. 2000. 'Intrinsic and extrinsic motivations: Classic definitions and new directions', *Contemporary Educational Psychology* 25(1): 54–67.

Sauermann, H. and Cohen, W. M. 2010. 'What makes them tick? Employee motives and firm innovation', *Management Science* 56(12): 2134–53.

Scherer, F. M. 1965. 'Firm size, market structure, opportunity, and the output of patented inventions', *American Economic Review* 55(5):1097–125.

Schmookler, J. 1966. *Invention and Economic Growth*. Cambridge: Harvard University Press.

Scotchmer, S. 2004. *Innovation and Incentives*. Cambridge, MA: MIT Press.

Scott, P. G. and Pandey, S. K. 2005. 'Red tape and public service motivation: Findings from a national survey of managers in state health and human services agencies', *Review of Public Personnel Administration* 25(2): 155–80.

Sehested, K., Sørensen, E., Schultz Larsen, T. and Hedensted Lund, D. 2010. 'Barrierer og drivkræfter for samarbejdsdreven innovation: Resultater fra et ekspertpanel (Delphi-studie)', Working Paper. Roskilde: Roskilde University http://rudar.ruc.dk//bitstream/1800/6266/1/Working_paper_no._3_Delphi_rapport_1_.pdf, accessed 4 February 2014.

Sørensen, E. and Torfing, J. 2011. 'Enhancing collaborative innovation in the public sector', *Administration & Society* 43(8): 842–68.

Torfing, J. and Ansell, C. 2014. 'Collaboration and design: New tools for public innovation', in J. Torfing and C. Ansell (eds.), *Public Innovation through Collaboration and Design*. Abingdon: Routledge, pp. 1–18.

Unsworth, K. L. and Clegg, C. W. 2010. 'Why do employees undertake creative action?' *Journal of Occupational and Organizational Psychology* 83(1): 77–99.

Van Wart, M. 2013. 'Lessons from leadership theory and the contemporary challenges of leaders', *Public Administration Review* 73(4): 553–65.

Walker, R. M. 2008. 'An empirical evaluation of innovation types and organizational and environmental characteristics: Towards a configuration framework', *Journal of Public Administration Research and Theory* 18(4): 591–615.

Weibel, A., Rost, K. and Osterloh, M. 2010. 'Pay for performance in the public sector: Benefits and (hidden) costs', *Journal of Public Administration Research and Theory* 20(2): 387–412.

Welch, E. W. and Pandey, S. K. 2007. 'E-government and bureaucracy: Toward a better understanding of intranet implementation and its effect on red tape', *Journal of Public Administration Research and Theory* 17(3): 379–404.

Zhang, X. and Bartol, K. M. 2010. 'Linking empowering leadership and employee creativity: The influence of psychological empowerment, intrinsic motivation, and creative process engagement', *Academy of Management Journal* 53(1): 107–28.

Zoghi, C., Mohr, R. D. and Meyer, P. B. 2010. 'Workplace organization and innovation', *Canadian Journal of Economics* 43(2): 622–39.

13   Administrative Leadership for Innovation

Montgomery Van Wart

There are many sources of and reasons for successful innovation. One significant contributor to innovation is administrative leadership (Senge 1990; Albury 2005; Pollitt and Hupe 2011). Leadership itself is a complex process and frequently quite difficult (Van Wart 2011). When innovation is one of the major aspects of leadership, leadership becomes even more difficult (Kotter 1990; Light 1997; Dean 1999). The aim of this chapter is to examine the conventional wisdom about the pragmatic steps that increase the likelihood of success in implementing innovations and reforms, as well as the effect of different governance styles on the implementation process. This short chapter will provide: a definition of administrative leadership with some caveats about the role it plays with innovation; a definition of innovation in the context of administrative leadership; an overview of some of the major theories of change related to leadership and a series of practical steps and concomitant competencies that practising leaders should strive to achieve. The chapter contributes to the literature by pointing out that strong skills in innovation and transformation are needed by most leaders in today's dynamic governmental environment, and that taking account of the prevailing governance paradigms, often called political savvy, is a particularly important competency in the selection, support and planning steps of the change process.

13.1   Defining Administrative Leadership and the Context of Innovation

Leadership can be defined in many ways – such as in terms of individuals or process or in terms of applied functions or theoretical notions. Here, we use a heuristic approach and thus focus on individuals in the leadership process and what they need to do to be successful in relatively concrete behavioural terms. The definition of administrative leadership is 'a complex process involving the acts of assessing one's environment and one's leadership constraints, developing numerous leadership traits and skills, refining and modifying one's style (behaviours) for different situations, achieving predetermined goals, and continually evaluating one's own performance and developing one's potential' (Van Wart 2012: 26).

Of course, innovation in its various forms is not the only function of leaders; sometimes it is the most important function (Zalznik 1978; Kotter 1990; Van Wart 2011). Examples of cases where innovation is key abound, such as when:

• the organization is out of alignment with environmental needs of clients, taxpayers or users;
• the cost structure or business model has become outmoded or dysfunctional;
• new technology or processes have revolutionized similar organizational processes;
• the structure of the organization needs to be reorganized to provide reinvigorated focus on the mission and vision; and/or
• the workforce has become unengaged or poorly equipped for the current jobs.

However, there are also many cases in which innovation is not the primary function of leaders. Sometimes a series of changes have already been introduced and refined, and it is not yet time for a new change cycle. Sometimes leaders introduce minor changes gradually and successfully, mitigating the need for and likelihood of major changes. Sometimes organizations are simply not following their own dictates, and thus change is no more than reintroducing the discipline of past practice.

Several other truisms regarding change should be kept in mind. First, those seeking to innovate and reform must remember that they need normally start from where the organization is, not from where one would like it to be (Windrum and Koch 2008). If one were building a prison, education or health system from scratch, one might do things in an entirely different way than one can when working with innovating through the current system (Pollitt and Bouckaert 2011).

This leads to the second truism – that the more dramatic the change, the longer it will take to implement, the more capacity it will take to implement, the more it can go wrong and the more likely it will simply fail (Kanter, Stein and Jick 1992; Wheatley 1992; Talbot and Johnson 2007). This is not to dissuade attempts at innovation but rather to encourage caution and pragmatism. The high failure rate of 'grand plans' is an acceptable aspect of the private sector which is built on 'creative' destruction and reward for risk but not particularly well suited to the public sector with its purposefully risk-averse, long-term perspective.

The third truism is that innovation is not just about logic and planning but involves a bit of luck and timing too (Boal and Hoojiberg 2001).

Windows of opportunity are often as important as the need for or sensibility of change itself (Kingdon 1984). Conversely, allowing for an opportune moment is wise, as the adage 'good things come to those who wait' avers. Patience can provide the opportunity to build up one's capacity and resources for the right time to innovate.

13.2   Defining Innovation in the Context of Administrative Leadership

Innovation has been defined in this text as the use of *new* 'ideas, processes, products, or procedures'. The level of change is really on a spectrum from very minor to comprehensive, but for our purposes, we will emphasize significant change – that is, we will focus more on radical change over incremental change, sweeping change over continuous improvement and customized adaptations over simple mechanical adoptions of standard technology or managerial practices.

Innovation can certainly occur at different levels or echelons in administration. It can apply to both the managerial-level competency sometimes labelled 'managing technical innovation and creativity' and executive level competency related to 'managing organizational change' (Van Wart 2011). Both need to be supported by the ability to 'manage personnel change' that always accompanies these efforts, which is generally a critical element of any successful wholesale innovation initiative.

It should also be noted that change in the form of innovation and reform varies in many ways that extend beyond the current discussion. The breadth of the innovation can be quite narrow, affecting only a small part of the organization, or it can affect everyone. The complexity of the change can be quite simple, such as introducing a novel but straightforward computer program, or it can be creating a new database system for the organization's clientele. It can be relatively undemanding on followers who have ample time and training to move to a new method, or it can be one that requires extensive training and entirely new work practices. Innovation and change can be implemented quite quickly if it is a simple replace-and-use protocol, or it may take many years if it involves adjusting multiple, interdependent systems, as often happens in major organizational overhauls in which both custom and culture are being changed.

Finally, it should be noted that the change and innovation can come from many directions (Morison 1966; Borins 2000). Sometimes senior managers take their lead from their political masters, sometimes from the field staff, sometimes from subordinates and only occasionally from themselves (Borins 2002). The drivers of change may be modernization and rationalization, or conventional Classical Public Administration

(CPA) types of reforms. Or the driver may come from opportunities to be more business-like, such as contracting out, in line with New Public Management (NPM) philosophies. Or the driver may be about utilizing collaborative energies more effectively, such as moving to a shared services model with another agency, and much recommended in the New Public Governance (NPG) model. The argument in this article is that good administrative leaders (1) create a conducive environment for change apart from and prior to innovation efforts and (2) pay close attention to the political environment for what is, and is not, possible in selecting and implementing change. Further, (3) the governance paradigm holding sway may emphasize some types of change over others, but organizational needs can and should dictate the final selection of change initiatives over which administrative leaders have discretion (Vigoda-Gadot 2009).

13.3 Theories of Leadership and Change

The transactional school of leadership that dominated leadership theory from the 1950s to the early 1980s emphasized the importance of the basics: getting the ideal match between the needs of the work itself and workers. The transformational school of leadership theory upended the internally oriented approach of the transactional leader by broadly asserting that the primary responsibility of leaders was largely an alignment of the organization to the external environment and that entailed change or transformation (Burns 1978; Tichy and Devanna 1986). Perhaps the most widely adopted model, however, was called the full-range leadership theory, which proposed that transformational leadership is built on transactional leadership in an additive relationship (Bass 1985). In other words, you can only transform and go beyond expectations by using leadership that combines both transactional and transformational aspects. It identifies six factors. Bass's first transactional factor is called management-by-exception; this aspect of leadership occurs when management reacts to various problems or exceptions. The second transactional factor is called contingent reward; this aspect of leadership is based on the exchange and contractual relationship that exists between employers and employees. One of the four transformational factors is individualized consideration, which is supportiveness of employees. A second transformational factor is idealized influence, which is a result of trusting the leader as well as the persuasiveness of the leader. A third factor is inspirational commitment, which results in employees bonding as a group and transcending self-interests. The final factor is intellectual stimulation, or the vision, planning and implementation of change. This critical role of transformational leaders is well articulated in the applied change management literature. The basics of change management (Fernandez and Rainey 2006) include establishing the need for change, providing a plan, building internal support, ensuring top-management support, arranging external support, providing resources and institutionalizing change.

More recent perspectives have provided different points of view without necessarily contradicting the Bass model. Complexity leadership emphasizes the need for adaptive learning and providing enabling structures to harness that learning (Uhl-Bien, Marion and McKelvey 2007). Strategic leadership emphasizes the ability to learn and survive in a competitive environment (Boal and Hoojiberg 2001). Social change leadership focuses on the need for community-based policy change and the role of leaders in being good facilitators and brokers of change by exercising integrity, cultural sensitivity, openness, consensus building and other collaborative skills (Bryson and Crosby 1992; Cayer, Baker and Weschler 2010). See Table 13.1 for a comparison of the competencies emphasized by contemporary schools of thought on leadership and change.

13.4   Practical Steps for Leaders in Achieving Innovation

There is a general order to most change management initiatives. Below are seven 'steps' that are consistent with the leadership of change literature. Each of the steps is accompanied by two to four behavioural competencies.

13.4.1   *The First Step: Create a Supportive Environment for Innovation*

Administrative innovation is much more likely when organizations have cultures favourable to creativity, use appropriate strategies to encourage participation and reduce resistance and take a pragmatic approach to change in general. Managing innovation and creativity requires an environment that fosters learning, flexibility and change. There must be a focus on the benefits of learning itself, as well as learning from surprises and problems. Innovative organizations find ways to challenge assumptions and mental models and encourage lateral thinking, e.g. brainstorming. Such organizations invest in learning despite turbulent times and ensure that they provide the appropriate tools and opportunities. Finally, as transformational leadership theory suggests, innovation and performance beyond expectations depend on good transactional management practices being in place. Leaders need to ensure that dysfunctional practices and poor performance are discouraged and/or eliminated.

The first competency required for this step is the ability to *develop a culture of consideration and goodwill*. This, in turn, requires skills at (or

Table 13.1 *Comparing Bass' full range leadership theory with other leadership theories emphasizing change*

Traditional transformational approach	Traditional transformational: comprehensive approach from an organizational, skill-based emphasis	Alternative perspectives			
		Complexity leadership: theory-based organizational focus on adapting in complex environment	Strategic leadership: theory-based organizational focus in competitive environment	Social change leadership: policy focus in collaborative environment	Change management theory: applied focus
Management by exception		Administrative leadership	Managerial leadership	Political and administrative competence	Provide resources
Contingent reward					
Consideration					
Intellectual stimulation		Adaptive leadership	Adaptive leadership	Comfort with ambiguity and complexity	Ensure the need
					Provide a plan
Idealized influence; trust, communication		Enabling leadership	Absorptive leadership	Personal integrity	Build internal support
Inspirational commitment: teamwork, perseverance				Sense of egalitarianism	Ensure top-management support
				Cultural sensitivity	Ensure external support
				Openness to ideas of others	Institutionalize changes
				Consensus building	Pursue comprehensive change

providing opportunities for) training, coaching, delegation and empowerment. Training ensures that employees are capable of doing their jobs no matter whether they are new hires trying to master the basics or veteran workers being asked to change past practices (Van Wart 1998). Coaching may provide employees with the necessary support in their work environment (Van Wart, Cayer and Cook 1993). Delegation ensures that employees are given authority to match their responsibilities and monitoring is reduced as competence increases (Van Wart 2011). Empowerment, the highest level of employee engagement, means that delegated authority extends to the creative use of resources and planning.

The second required competency is the ability to be able to examine and deal with *structural issues such as pay and life–work balance to the degree possible*. In this area, legislative and organizational rules and realities may provide little flexibility. Nonetheless, leaders must be highly sensitive to the perceptions of employees and be perceived as genuinely interested in the situations of employees (see also Chapter 12 by Andersen). They must be seen as working to improve conditions that are substandard. Otherwise, those same employees will become cynical about the leader and resistant to change in a setting which they feel is indifferent to their interests.

Leaders must also be able to *stabilize the organization if necessary*. Sometimes a new leader takes over an organization that has just experienced a scandal or is simply in managerial chaos. The changes required in these situations may require management replacement or a return to following rules more strictly. Sometimes an organization gets a shock or a scandal erupts during a leader's tenure, requiring work in public relations, reorganizing, redistribution of resources, downsizing, etc.

A final reality is that leaders must also have the competency to be able to effectively *deal with low performers and performance lapses head-on*. Such issues diminish productivity and squander resources. Additionally, it is exceedingly annoying to high-performing employees to watch others who are poor performers or incompetent.

13.4.2   Second Step: Select Problems to Solve Carefully After Thorough and Realistic Assessment

As already noted, there is no single set of contextual demands, and the challenges also vary extensively. So the path is not immediately self-evident, and good and thorough assessment is critical, no matter whether those needs and demand for change arise from within the organization or originate from policy makers acting through legislation.

From the internal perspective, one competency in problem selection is the ability to *examine organizational needs*. There are many standard tools for organizational assessment, and one should use as many as one can but not so many as to overwhelm the system. Tools that can ascertain the structural effectiveness of an organization and its technical performance include reviews of organizational purpose (detailed assessments of mission and vision statements), performance checks of both outputs and outcomes, ethics audits, customer and citizen assessments, comparative performance (benchmarking), strategic performance reviews (e.g. use of regulations versus incentives) and appraisals of internal and external coordination and adaptability (comprehensive quality assessments). Such strategies are well documented elsewhere (Van Wart 1995) and will not be reviewed here for reasons of space. While having accurate and balanced data about organizational functioning is fundamental to good administrative leadership and critical to the selection of problems, leaders must ensure that monitoring systems do not become excessively burdensome and problematic themselves and select auxiliary assessment tools with care because of the resources that they consume.

Another aspect of assessing organizational needs is at the level of employee competence and follower development. What is the level of task skills, role clarity, subordinate effort and cohesiveness and cooperation? The tools used for ascertaining the quality of employee competence can include consultations, observation and monitoring, employee attitude and culture assessments, and employee focus groups. While not all strategies need to be as comprehensive as the award programmes require, they should be balanced enough to give a broad picture of both organizational performance and deficiencies (Kaplan and Norton 1996).

Administrative leaders must also realistically assess the *ability to reform and innovate itself within the political context*. The more substantial the innovation or reform, the more it will entail resource shifts, affect programme recipients (and generate new complaints) and possibly spark internal resistance that will try to align with external political power centres. Thus, administrative leaders must ensure an increasingly wide base of executive and political support as the innovation and reform initiatives are proposed. Without external support, major changes should rarely be enacted administratively, no matter whether that locus is an elected executive or a legislative group such as policy committees overseeing an agency. Not only may support be needed at the executive and legislative levels, but public relations campaigns may also be necessary to counteract the inevitable opposition to change that would otherwise occur. An awareness of the prevailing governance paradigm is needed here in order to select innovations that either fit with it naturally or can be promoted in alignment with it.

A third competency is the ability to deal with *changes that stem from policy makers or which need legislative changes that require policy makers' action.* This is somewhat easier at the local government level where the connection between management executives and policy makers is tighter and less formal, and partisan issues are generally, but not always, less likely. When dealing with the innovations of policy makers (e.g. a new law), leaders need to be able to grasp the intent quickly, foresee likely implementation challenges, forewarn policy makers of implementation delays and work with the organization to implement the changes as discussed in the steps that follow. Sometimes administrative leaders envision how new legislative changes would expedite, support or refine programmes. Even in systems in which administrative executives enjoy unusual power (parliamentary systems) or political trust (some local governments), such changes must be approved by central offices or be formally passed by legislative authorities. Administrative leaders must be highly careful about what they propose and may have to prepare the argument and wait for years for the right time to push for legislative changes (Kingdon 1984).

13.4.3   *The Third Step: Ensure Internal Support Before, During and After Implementing Innovation*

Just as external support is critical before proceeding, it is critical that internal support be maximized before, during and after devising a strategy for planned change.

One widely held recommendation is to be sure to *create a sense of urgency.* Urgency provides the energy and attention that innovation and reform need for the rigours and distractions that change creates. Leaders must ensure that those in the organization understand the managerial and/or political necessity of change. What has happened requiring change, what was the process of change and what must be done? While the understanding that some change must occur helps, it does not ensure the acceptance of a particular plan, necessitating other competencies.

In order to aid in the support of a particular plan, it is important to *create a sense of shared fate* to the degree possible (Brown 2003; Bason 2010). Although creating a sense of urgency is important to arouse people to the need for change, it can also arouse a sense of fear of the unknown, fear of victimization and loss of control. Creating a sense of shared fate works to reduce the negative side effects that the anticipation of change often produces. At the same time, it can increase the effectiveness of planned change. First, it is important to share the data underlying the need for change as broadly as possible. Although few may ultimately access original documents, it is reassuring to followers that they do not have to rely entirely on the interpretations of leaders. Second, it is highly useful to get as much input on the possible ramifications of changes as time and circumstance allows. In the case of legislative change, the amount of input may be limited initially, but as the implementation rolls down the administrative system, input will invariably improve the details of administrative execution. Third, it is critical to calm fears by reducing discussion of unlikely options and ensuring that the less pleasant aspects of change will occur with fairness and consideration.

In order to convey both urgency and shared fate, as well as to maximize effectiveness, leaders must be inclined to *communicate extensively and be able to do so with dynamism*. Ensuring that people are well informed about the progress of change is the rule of thumb for communication during times of change, so the emphasis is nearly always more, rather than less, communication. The only caveat to this recommendation is to ensure that it is consistent and clear, because message confusion causes enormous emotional havoc. In terms of personal dynamism as Bennis and Nanus (1985) noted, personal charisma is not required to have idealized influence, although it is a highly useful asset when present. However, while few leaders are personally charismatic, all can and should be able to convey dynamism of message through emotive language. Good leaders during change not only use the clarity of administrative language to convey technical information but they also ensure that some language and messaging connects with the emotional side of recipients who are more effective when their hearts and souls are engaged. Good leaders will find opportunities to use evocative language via symbols, aspirational statements, sentiments reflecting the ability of employees to succeed, expressions of empathy for the challenges of change and so on. The best administrative leaders are able to foster healthy resilience among those implementing change, as well as courage if the change is particularly debated and criticized as mistakes and weaknesses are highlighted by detractors.

13.4.4 The Fourth Step: Provide a Realistic Strategy for Innovation or Reform

Administrators should be good at planning, but planning for innovation and change requires special competence (Koch and Hauknes 2005).

A first aspect is to *develop a plan with well-articulated enabling structures*. Sometimes change will be managed entirely by the administrative leader, but this is rare. More frequently successful change implementation plans will be some combination of study groups, drafters of the legislative orders into regulatory language (and drafters of administrative manuals), delegation to specific managers for implementation by functions, training personnel and cross-management teams to ensure coordination. The competence here is for highly articulated and detailed strategies, plans and procedures.

Additionally, it is important for administrative leaders to *provide enough time for the changes to work*. Small innovations may result in immediate productivity improvements, but this is extremely rare for major innovation and governmental reform. In fact, it is likely that there will be an immediate loss of productivity as new systems are put in place, employees transition between systems, kinks are worked out in new systems, and the organization builds up administrative speed and competence with new ways of conducting business.

13.4.5   *The Fifth Step: Be a Good Change Manager*

Getting people on board for change cannot be assumed (Damanpour and Schneider 2009). Strategies for people-inclusive change include being a leader that can be trusted, demonstrating flexibility during the change process, being aware of one's own limitations and mitigating them, inspiring resilience in the change process as it unfolds with bumps and challenges and ensuring that the necessary resources are available.

Leaders who *model high levels of integrity* are far more likely to be followed willingly in the first place, and especially if the change process is difficult and long. Administrative leaders are far less likely than their political cousins to experience personal scandals because of their lower visibility and less political lifestyles, but when personal scandals do erupt, it is hard for planned change not to suffer or become entirely derailed. The subtler aspects of trust based on integrity are equally important. A reservoir of integrity-based trust means that plans are more likely to be accepted and requests for shared sacrifice will be believed to be truly communal.

Complex planned change, no matter whether it is the installation of a cross-agency database or the reorganization of multiple agencies into one, cannot be accurately planned in advance because there are too many unknown factors related to programmes, processes, recipients, organizational culture, etc. Thus, administrative leaders must *demonstrate flexibility and adaptability*. While plans need to be well articulated, they also need to be flexible as changes in the plan are inevitably required. Major innovations and reforms predictably require changes in implementation plans as the organization learns from overcoming challenges and mistakes (Naveh, Meilich and Marcus 2006; Pollitt 2011) – for example, when at all possible, learn through pilot projects, beta tests, practice exercises, etc.; announce in advance that it will take adjustments and improvements both to the innovation or the system itself as the implementation proceeds; define adjustments as progress towards goal, not as errors in planning.

Another important competency in being a good change manager is *knowing your own limitations to mitigate them*. As much as optimism and ambitious visions have their place, it is critical for administrative leaders to understand their constraints (Lombardo and McCauley 1988). Planning for more than what one's realistic constraints allow is a common problem that leads to disappointments and failures for ambitious and idealistic administrators. Of course, one can push back constraints (to a degree) over time with planning and determination. Three important types of constraint are the following: (a) within administrative leaders' jobs and organizational strictures, (b) with their resources and (c) with their personal leadership capabilities. This last type of constraint on the development of administrative leadership is of particular interest to this discussion. An excellent assessment tool for the capabilities of leaders is 360° assessment in which one gets feedback potentially from subordinates, colleagues and one's superior. Several areas are of particular importance in this process for the purpose of knowing one's ability to develop and support reform and innovation. One is the analysis of one's assessment skills, which can be much enhanced by education and quality training. Already mentioned in the theories section of this chapter are competencies such as flexibility, cognitive complexity, openness to change, collaboration, integrity and goodwill, cultural sensitivity and long-term perspective. Finally, frequently referenced contemporary skills of leaders in political and dynamic environments are political savvy (so necessary in managing political reform) and e-leadership skills (being able to manage and motivate through virtual means) (US OPM 2006; Avolio et al. 2014).

Finally, it is critical to *provide the necessary resources for change*. Resources may include special staffing, time for change processes, new equipment, funds for preliminary studies or pilot programmes, special or organization-wide training, etc. Change adds work as it is, and without the necessary resources, the likelihood of errors and widespread discouragement become highly likely.

13.4.6   The Sixth Step: Institutionalize Changes

Initial implementation of an innovation or reform is only the technical part of the process. It requires finalizing regulations and/or rules after adjustments have been made, and building out these changes in manuals, websites, training programmes and other published locations. Furthermore, if innovations are not properly institutionalized, there will be backsliding or uneven application of changes. Several competencies are related to this step.

A critical part of institutionalizing changes is *redesigning individual incentive systems*. One type of incentive is acknowledgement, so celebrating early successes is critical, as well as noting how well the organization has done as a whole. Another powerful form of acknowledgement is conducted in annual reviews in which accomplishment of new innovations is featured. Tangible individual incentives are frequently altered in major change initiatives, to acknowledge new priorities or ways of doing things. In many larger change initiatives, personnel practices will be altered, affecting promotions and other perquisites.

Another aspect of institutionalization is *redesigning organizational accountability systems*. Key among the imperative elements of changing accountability is to integrate new performance indicators where the innovation is substantial enough to merit them. Equally important is providing accountability to eliminate or disband old and outdated measures, incentives, programmes, etc. (see also Chapter 15 by Christensen and Lægreid). Not removing outmoded indicators, incentives or programmes can lead to a loss of focus. Finally, it is very important to have regular monitoring of the new system until it has been fully operational for some time and it is ensured that the new measures will provide an early warning of systemic problems. Generally, such reviews are done by both quantitative and qualitative means as in productivity reports and error reports on one hand and employee interviews and complaint analysis on the other.

13.4.7   The Final Step: Evaluate

Ultimately, one must evaluate the level of success and decide if further action is necessary. Two competencies are necessary for this step.

First, one must *assess the success of changes and innovations after they have matured*. What is the overall level of success? Are a few of the elements of an innovation or reform in need of further improvement (i.e. refinement)? Is it too early to tell? Does the innovation need more time to come up to capacity (see also Chapter 14 by Dooren and Willems)?

Second, one must *assess the need for altogether new change*. When an innovation is relatively successful, one may then evaluate whether there are the resources and energy to move onto another administrative innovation. Such innovations may build on a prior innovation or may simply mean that there is the organizational capacity to move to a different area needing attention. Good leaders have an agenda of change but are pragmatic about not overwhelming the organization or division with more change than is necessary and plausible at any given time.

Table 13.2 summarizes the various steps and the related competencies.

Table 13.2 *A summary of 20 pragmatic steps leading to effective innovation and reform*

1. Create a supportive environment for innovation
   a. Develop a culture of consideration and goodwill: coaching, delegation, training opportunities, empowerment
   b. Examine structural issues such as pay and life–work balance
   c. Stabilize the organization if necessary
   d. Deal with low performers and performance lapses head-on
2. Select problems carefully to solve after thorough and realistic assessment
   a. Examine organizational needs (issues largely under administrative leader's direct purview)
   b. Ensure external support for internally developed innovation
   c. Examine policy needs (issues in which laws, regulations, rules or past practices need approval before modifying)
3. Ensure internal support before, during and after implementing innovation
   a. Create a sense of urgency
   b. Create a sense of shared fate
   c. Communicate extensively and with dynamism
4. Provide a realistic strategy for innovation or reform
   a. Develop enabling structures
   b. Provide enough time for the changes to work
5. Be a good change manager
   a. Model integrity (exemplary behaviour)
   b. Demonstrate flexibility and adaptability
   c. Know your own limitations and mitigate them
   d. Provide the necessary resources
6. Institutionalize changes
   a. Redesign incentive system
   b. Redesign accountability system
7. Evaluate innovations
   a. Assess the success of changes and innovations after they have matured
   b. Assess the need for further change, refinement and/or celebration

13.5   Conclusion

Leadership is complex, and the implementation of innovation and reform makes it much more difficult (Battilana et al. 2010; Pollitt 2011). Administrative leadership is a complex process involving the acts of assessing one's environment and one's leadership constraints, developing numerous leadership traits and skills, refining and modifying one's style (behaviours) for different situations, achieving predetermined goals and continually evaluating one's own performance and developing one's potential. Thus, while instituting innovation and reform is not the only function of leaders, it is not uncommon for change functions to be among the most important, and sometimes the most important, depending on an organization or unit's point of evolution. The worldwide demand is everywhere for increased levels of change based on rationalization and modernization projects such as information system upgrades (a major preoccupation of CPA), incorporating market forces and the private sector (a concern of NPM) and increased collaboration by governments both internally and externally for both better inclusiveness as well as efficiencies (as promoted by NPG). A number of theories of leadership reviewed here emphasized the importance of change: transformational leadership, complexity and strategic leadership, social change leadership and change management theory. While the recommendations were drawn from all of these schools of thought, this presentation relied on the change management literature most because of its applied focus and more articulated and sequential approach to the requirements for successful administration of change. Seven steps were identified along with 20 related competencies as summarized in Table 13.2. While the presentation uses a linear format, in reality the process tends to be circular, overlapping and often quite messy. Nonetheless, change masters who are adept at the process seem to not only sail through it but also have a good time in the process (Doig and Hargrove 1987). On the other hand, change processes involving innovation and reform, especially large ones, can be difficult for those without most of the competencies identified, and leaders deficient in these competencies may encounter failures and career humiliations (Van Wart 2015).

References

Albury, D. 2005. 'Fostering innovation in public services', *Public Money & Management* 25(1): 51–6.

Avolio, B. J., Sosik, J. J., Kahai, S. S. and Baker, B. 2014. 'E-leadership: Re-examining transformations in leadership source and transmission', *Leadership Quarterly* 25(1): 105–31.

Bason, C. 2010. *Leading Public Sector Innovation: Co-Creating for a Better Society*. Bristol: Policy Press.

Bass, B. M. 1985. *Leadership and Performance Beyond Expectations*. New York: Free Press.

Battilana, J., Gilmartin, M., Sengul, M., Pache, A. and Alexander, J. 2010. 'Leadership competencies for implementing planned organization change', *Leadership Quarterly* 21(3): 422–38.

Bennis, W. and Nanus, B. 1985. *Leaders: Strategies for Taking Charge*. New York: Harper and Row.

Boal, K. B. and Hoojiberg, R. 2001. 'Strategic leadership research: Moving on', *Leadership Quarterly* 11(4): 515–549.

Borins, S. 2000. 'Loose cannons and rule breakers? Some evidence about innovative public managers', *Public Administration Review* 60(6): 498–507.

2002. 'Leadership and innovation in the public sector', *Leadership & Organization Development Journal* 23(8): 467–76.

Brown, M. M. 2003. 'Technology diffusion and knowledge barrier: The dilemma of stakeholder participation', *Public Performance and Management Review* 26(4): 345–59.

Bryson, J. M., and Crosby, B. C. 1992. *Leadership for the Common Good: Tackling Problems in a Shared-Power World.* San Francisco: Jossey-Bass.

Burns, J. M. 1978. *Leadership.* New York: Harper and Row.

Cayer, N. J., Baker, D. and Weschler, L. F. 2010. *Social Change and Adaptive Management.* San Diego: Birkdale Publishers.

Damanpour, F. and Schneider, M. 2009. 'Characteristics of innovation and innovation adoption in public organizations: Assessing the role of managers', *Journal of Public Administration Research and Theory* 19(3): 495–522.

Doig, J. W. and Hargrove, E. C. 1987. *Leadership and Innovation: A Biographical Perspective on Entrepreneurs in Government.* Baltimore, MD: Johns Hopkins University Press.

Dean, M. 1999. *Governmentality: Power and Rule in Modern Society.* London: Sage.

Fernandez, S. and Rainey, H. G. 2006. 'Managing successful organizational change in the public sector', *Public Administration Review* 66(2): 168–176.

Kanter, R. M., Stein, B. A., and Jick, T. D. 1992. *The Challenges of Organizational Change: How Companies Experience It and Leaders Guide It.* New York: Free Press.

Kaplan, R. S. and Norton, D. K. 1996. *The Balanced Scorecard: Translating Strategy into Action.* Boston: Harvard Business School Press.

Kingdon, J. W. 1984. *Agendas, Alternatives, and Public Policies.* Boston: Little, Brown.

Koch, P. and Hauknes, J. 2005. *On Innovation in the Public Sector.* Publin, NIFU Step: Oslo, Norway.

Kotter, J. P. 1990. *A Force for Change: How Leadership Differs from Management.* New York: Free Press.

Light, P. 1997. *The Tides of Reform: Making Government Work, 1945–1995.* New Haven: Yale University Press.

Lombardo, M. M. and McCauley, C. D. 1988. *The Dynamics of Management Derailment.* Greensboro, NC: Center for Creative Leadership.

Morison, E. E. 1966. 'Gunfire at sea: A case study of innovation', in E. E. Morison (ed.), *Men, Machines, and Modern Times.* Cambridge, MA: MIT Press, pp. 17–44.

Naveh, E., Meilich, O. and Marcus, A. 2006. 'The effects of administrative innovation implementation on performance: An organizational learning approach', *Strategic Organization* 4(3): 275–302.

Pollitt, C. 2011. '30 years of public management reforms: Has there been a pattern?' Working Paper, Washington, DC: World Bank, siteresources.world bank.org/EXTGOVANTICORR/Resources/Politt.doc.

Pollitt, C. and Bouckaert, G. 2011. *Public Management Reform: A Comparative Analysis: NPM, Governance and the Neo-Weberian State*, 3rd ed. Oxford University Press.

Pollitt, C. and Hupe, P. 2011. 'Talking about governance: The role of magic concepts', *Public Management Review* 13(5): 1–18

Senge, P. 1990. *The Fifth Discipline: The Art and Practice of the Learning Organization*. New York: Doubleday Currency.

Talbot, C. and Johnson, C. 2007. 'Seasonal cycles in public management: Disaggregation and re-aggregation', *Public Money and Management* 27(1): 53–60.

Tichy, N. M. and Devanna, M. A. 1986. *The Transformational Leader*. New York: Wiley.

Wheatley, M. J. 1992. *Leadership and the New Science: Learning About Organizations from an Orderly Universe*. San Francisco: Berrett-Koehler.

Windrum, P. and Koch, P. M. (eds.) 2008. *Innovation in Public Sector Services: Entrepreneurship, Creativity, and Management*. Cheltenham: Edgar Elgar.

Uhl-Bien, M., Marion, R. and McKelvey, B. 2007. 'Complexity leadership theory: Shifting leadership from the industrial age to the knowledge era', *Leadership Quarterly* 18: 298–318.

U.S. Office of Personnel Management (OPM). 2006. 'Guide to senior executive service qualifications', www.opm.gov/ses/references/sesqualsguide2006.pdf.

Van Wart, M. 1995. 'The first step in the reinvention process: Assessment', *Public Administration Review* 55(5): 429–38.

1998. *Changing Public Sector Values*. New York: Garland Publishing.

2011. *Dynamics of Leadership: Theory and Practice*. Armonk, NY: M. E. Sharpe.

2012. *Leadership in Public Organizations*, 2nd edition. Armonk, NY: M. E. Sharpe.

2015. 'Evaluating transformational leadership: The challenging case of Eric Shinseki and the VA', *Public Administration Review* 75(5): 760–769.

Van Wart, M., Cayer, J. and Cook. S. 1993. *Handbook of Training and Development for the Public Sector: A Comprehensive Resource*. San Francisco: Jossey-Bass Publishers.

Vigoda-Gadot, E. 2009. *Building Governability and Public Management*. Farnham, UK: Ashgate Publishing.

14   Thinking Allowed
Reforming Indicator-Based Accountability to Enhance Innovation

Wouter Van Dooren and Tom Willems

Indicator-based accountability was a key tenet of New Public Management (NPM). Public organizations and the people working within those organizations were held to answer for their results rather than for following rules and processes. Unfettered from processual regulation and controls, a blend of creativity and pragmatism was expected to cause better performance and make room for innovation. It turned out differently. NPM-flavoured accountability regimes in many instances stifle innovation rather than foster it. Today, New Public Governance (NPG) creates new challenges for indicator-based accountability systems. NPG raises questions on how to reform indicator-based accountability to make it work in complex multi-actor settings. What is the use of performance indicators when dealing with unruly problems? How to stimulate innovation without calling accountability in itself into question? This chapter proposes some prospective directions based on a critical analysis of indicator-based accountability. We argue that performance indicators should be used for learning and innovation rather than for indicator-based accountability. Accountability can only enhance innovation when it allows for staff and stakeholders to critically think about the results. They have to engage in a performance dialogue on the meaning of indicators that also accounts for complexity. Indicator-based accountability, however, typically does not allow for such thinking. The target is the truth. In our view, reforming accountability therefore implies that results-based accountability needs to be saved from its indicators.

Accountability is foundational to all variants of governance: the Classical Public Administration (CPA), NPM and NPG. In each governance paradigm, however, accountability takes on a particular interpretation. While CPA accountability is based on rule-following in a hierarchy, NPM accountability focuses on results in a (quasi-)market. In NPM,

The corresponding author for this chapter is Wouter Van Dooren.

results-based accountability is typically narrowed down to indicator-based accountability. One of the catchphrases of NPM is that only what is measured matters. NPM hence assumes that we cannot talk about results in a qualitative, judgemental way. In this chapter, we look at indicator-based accountability as a subset of results-based accountability. The accountability model in NPG is more diffuse than the CPA and NPM approaches (Willems and Van Dooren 2011). There is some rule-following of general principles rather than detailed regulations. There is a result orientation but at a cross-cutting, more general level. NPG accountability also puts a stronger emphasis on accountability mechanisms within professional groups. In what follows, we will first critically address NPM's indicator-based accountability. We then will argue that indicator-based accountability is entangled in a diffuse web of multiple accountabilities, which bars the prospect for innovation. Finally, we discuss how indicators can foster innovation. We propose not to use indicators for accountability but to enrich professional learning and dialogue. Performance measurement should build on intrinsic motivation rather than be an external control. This view is more consistent with the NPG paradigm.

14.1   The Promise and Practice of Indicator-Based Accountability

The NPM diagnosis of the established bureaucracies under the CPA model was straightforward. The excessive density of rules and regulations obstructed all creativity and pragmatism at the front line of public services. Read the examples of Osborne and Gaebler's (1993) acclaimed text on NPM. The parks department in Visalia, California, could provide a deposit of $60,000 overnight to buy a $400,000 castoff swimming pool because budget rules allowed for managerial freedom. A defaulting community school in East Harlem became the best in class after the district did away with assignment by zone. Free school choice created a quasi-market and led to competitive pressures to improve. In the US Department of Defense, a deputy assistant secretary for installations cut the rules for military base construction from 400 to 4 pages and those for housing from 800 to 40. Base commanders could make the decisions autonomously now. As an experiment, one military base was even completely relieved from regulation. The gains could be reinvested in the base. As a result, thousands of regulations have been put into question, costs have been cut and performance increased 3 per cent. Efficiency gains were believed to be 10 per cent or $3 billion. The driver in all cases was front-line innovation.

The remedies of the NPM advocates promised the best of both worlds: fewer rules, more innovation, matched with better accountability. More flexibility would lead to creativity, innovation and better performance. Account holders would retreat for months, years or any other time-to-target. Relieved of continuous account giving on processes and the use of resources, public managers would be more prepared to take the risks needed for innovation. Yet, this did not imply that politics had to clear the way. On the contrary, politicians would be able to focus on what 'really matters', and what really matters are results, not rules.

In reality, the bifurcation between NPM and CPA was clearly not as sharp as presented. Well before NPM, the implementation literature had amply demonstrated the importance of front-line discretion (Hill and Hupe 2002). Similarly, indicator-based steering was not an invention of the managerial movement of the 1990s. The application of indicator-based management, however, has never been as intensive, i.e. integrated in the incentive structures of daily management, and extensive, i.e. applied in virtually all corners of the public sector (Van Dooren 2008).

The practice of indicator-based accountability proved to be challenging. Radin (2000) succinctly summarized her critique of NPM arguing that it is fitting square pegs in round holes. Rather than a failure of implementation, indicator-based accountability is flawed in its design: the main default being its naïve view on information. NPM audaciously assumed the forthright availability of performance information (Bouckaert and Peters 2002). Measurement of performance is a critical feature of results-based accountability schemes. Yet, as Osborne and Radnor argue in Chapter 3, robust measurement is only feasible in production environments with tangible routine tasks (Noordegraaf and Abma 2003). Precisely those routine tasks have become increasingly rare in public services for at least three reasons. First, wicked policy issues lead to more complex service-delivery arrangements and less routine. This is most evident in the services dealing with multi-problems. Think of the drug addict who is also homeless, unemployed and poorly educated. Effective service delivery for multi-problems relies on networking and counselling rather than the mere production of methadone programmes, shelter and training courses. Second, services are increasingly embedded in professional disciplines and subject to professional expertise that objects routine work. Few professionals would or could describe their work in production terms (Jos and Tompkins 2004). Third, many (but not all) constituencies have been outsourcing the remainder of routine tasks in government to the private sector, which further reduce the prospect of sensible performance measurement in the public realm (Radin 2006).

Also the assumption that results-based accountability schemes would substitute existing rules and regulations proved to be naïve and partly flawed. Poulsen (2009) for instance describes the co-existence of competing public administration traditions, with often contradictory interpretations of accountability, as different 'archaeological layers'. Rather than substitution, regulation is a historical sedimentation process in which new mechanisms add onto older ones (see also Laegreid and Verhoest 2010; Schillemans 2010; Van Dooren, Voets and Winters 2015). Indicator-based accountability proved to be just another layer to the sediment of regulation.

The practice of the next decennium proved the critics right. People in public services resorted to gaming the performance metrics (see Pollitt 2013 for an overview). Gaming of indicators in high-stakes accountability schemes is rampant; police officers reclassify crimes, researchers set up citation circles, teachers teach for the test and hospitals reduce waiting lists by operating a waiting list for the waiting list. The options for creative accounting at the front line seem endless (Bohannon 2013; Van Dooren, Bouckaert and Halligan 2015). If the gamer were only a statistics juggler, not too much harm may be done. Yet, this is often not the case. Indicator-based accountability can affect the core processes and outcomes of public services. Several studies show that the impact on front line work is complex, subtle, but definitely real. A study by Soss, Fording and Schram (2011: 225) in a Florida welfare programme falling under an indicator-based accountability scheme found that 'the discretion possessed by case managers is broad, in the sense that they are authorized to make a wide variety of decisions affecting the client, and it is ineradicable, in the sense that they almost always know some way to push a decision in a preferred direction'. But, they argue, the broad discretion does not run very deep. Time pressure of the performance regime prevents front line workers from pursuing the treatments they would have advised otherwise. Brodkin's (2011) study of welfare reform introduces the concept of street-level calculus. Street-level practitioners do more than simply respond to performance incentives; they also adjust to them as they manage the imbalance between the demands of their jobs, the indicators and resource constraints.

14.2   Multiple Accountabilities, Indicators and Innovation

But why is indicator-based accountability leading to gaming and rigidity rather than to service improvement and innovation? In order to answer this question, we first need to refine our understanding of accountability. We argue that accountability takes place in five accountability forums that

Table 14.1 *Forums and processes of accountability*

Accountability forums	Processes of accountability
Political	Elections, parliamentary scrutiny, political debate within political parties, ministerial responsibility, ...
Administrative	Hierarchical command, diverse government auditors, regulatory bodies, ombudsmen, other types of government monitoring agencies, performance contracts, budgets, ...
Judicial	Judicial courts, administrative tribunals, mediation ...
Public	Mass media, social media, civic action, ...
Market	Shareholders' reports, consumer choice, rating agencies, ...

(*Source:* Willems and Van Dooren 2012)

host the main processes of contemporary accountability (Table 14.1). We take the metaphor of a forum quite literally – an approach which is slightly different from the functional approach used in Chapter 15 by Tom Christensen and Per Lægreid (see also Schillemans and Bovens 2011). A forum is a marketplace where actors are held to account by account holders, following the rules of that particular marketplace. Account givers and account holders typically belong to a specific forum: administrative agencies and cabinet ministers for instance to the administrative forum or media players to the public forum. However, willingly or not, account givers are regularly drawn to other forums: for instance when an agency has to answer to court for violating legislation or when the media challenges a minister. Since public–private collaboration is increasingly strong, we include the market as a relevant forum where public account givers have to answer for their actions.

Indicator-based accountability is developed in the administrative forum, where a principal 'lets' and 'makes' managers manage through the use of performance contracts with targets. During the time-to-target, the principal unloads most accountability demands. The period in between contract evaluations allows at least in theory for risk-taking and innovation. Without the permanent immanence of accountability, accountees have the time to correct for experiments and innovations that went wrong. Yet, the impact of indicators transcends the principal-agent setting of the administrative forum. Indicators play out in other forums in a very unpredictable way. Politicians, journalists and investors for instance do not follow the orderly cycles of performance contracting. Rather, they grab the indicators they need, when they need them. The oxygen for risk-taking and innovation that performance contracts are supposed to offer is drained off again, because indicators can be used in other forums than the administrative forum at any moment.

The combined action of multiple accountabilities can be seen as a case-specific field of forces that creates incentives for rule following, improvement, gaming or any other organizational behaviour, including the behaviour that stimulates innovation. These multiple accountabilities define the interests at stake in performance indicators, and in second order also define the freedom of action that is needed for innovation. In many, but not all contexts, the use of performance indicators for multiple accountabilities leads to indicator rigidity rather than an environment supportive to innovation.

Indicator-based accountability is primarily developed within the *administrative forum*. Executive politicians hold public managers to account for results. The whole endeavour rests on performance indicators that are typically found in institutional instruments such as annual reports, management contracts, scorecards and performance budgets. Performance management in the public sector is moreover becoming a specialization in itself, with increasingly more staff devoted to measurement, evaluation and auditing (Van Dooren 2008). Interestingly, there is usually not much political opposition against performance-based management reform. In many countries, NPM reforms have been approved quasi-unanimously in parliament (Pollitt and Bouckaert 2004). The issue is depoliticized, it seems.

Accountability processes within the administrative forum can perfectly explain indicator rigidity that stands in the way of innovation. A rigid focus on indicators occurs when performance targets are consequential for individual careers. Performance pay schemes have been demonstrated to have a strong impact on gaming behaviour (Perry, Engbers and Jun 2009). The detrimental effect of the bonus culture in the financial sector is a case in point for the displacement effect of performance incentives. Rigidity also occurs when performance targets have an impact on budgets of organizations (Hood 2006). When money is tied to the results, the temptation to juggle the indicators is high.

Yet, we cannot suffice by looking only at the administrative forum. In many instances, performance indicator schemes are noncommittal at first sight. Performance scorecards for instance only make information available without targets, punishments or rewards. Nonetheless, rigidity regularly occurs in such apparently low-pressured accountability schemes (Wiggins and Tymms 2002; Hood 2006). Moreover, many seemingly high-pressured performance schemes such as performance pay and budgeting turn out to be relatively low-pressured because sanctions often fail to materialize (Schick 2003). Yet, even when high pressure becomes low pressure, gaming is looming because performance indicators unfold in other forums. When indicators are used in other accountability forums, they also follow the rules of these forums.

Performance indicators play a somewhat dubious role in the political forum. There is ample evidence that Members of Parliament or local councils use performance information rather reservedly, if at all (Johnson and Talbot 2008; Van Dooren, Bouckaert and Halligan 2015). On some occasions, however, there are outbursts of political debate on performance metrics: on punctuality of trains for instance, or educational attainment and the incidence of hospital bacteria. Suddenly, performance indicators are politically significant. Yet, rather than following the orderly march of administrative reporting, performance indicators are frequently used as ammunition in political guerrilla warfare. In the garbage can of policy making, political players can use performance indicators to make problems politically relevant at any time (Cohen, March and Olsen 1972; Kingdon 1984).

Indicators also play out in the public forum. News value generally increases when stories are framed negatively (Galtung and Ruge 1965). The performance literature refers to this phenomenon as negativity bias (James and John 2007). The reputational impact of public exposure hence can be substantial, and public organizations devote considerable efforts to avoid public blame (Hood 2010). Arguably, blame management has shifted gears with the surge of social media that cause public blame to go viral. Media exposure of performance targets has become increasingly unpredictable and the threat of bad press is always in the air. Performance indicators can certainly fuel the blame game (Hood 2010).

In addition to media and politics, there is also accountability in markets or quasi-markets. Quasi-markets that are driven by league tables of school performance are a good example. The performance information is supposed to inform parents on school choice. The policy theory behind these reforms has been typified as the choice revolution (Blomqvist 2004). The provision of an exit option is supposed to put pressure on public services. The choice discourse was strong in Sweden, the United Kingdom and the Netherlands. The European Union used the concept of choice to argue for liberalization of public services (Jilke and Van de Walle 2012). Market pressure can be quite substantial and a good deal of gaming occurs on league table indicators. The teaching-for-the-test tactic is probably one of the best-known instances of gaming (Hood 2006). Gaming should not come as a surprise. Public services are concerned that league tables may lure them in a vicious spiral. Fewer consumers may opt for a particular public service, which in turn may lead to demotivation and scale ineffi-ciencies. For human services such as education, the vicious circle also affects the intake of the public service. A high-ranking school can be selective at the gate. At the same time, the low-ranking schools are left with the deprived pupils.

Accountability processes hosted by the legal forum are seldom a direct cause of performance indicator rigidity. Failures to deliver upon performance targets can rarely be taken to court. But legal obligations have an impact in a different way. They can explain why regularly no use is made of the discretion, if any, that a focus on results would create. The use of discretion to reach targets may also lead to legal liabilities. The use of discretion holds a risk of being held accountable in court for failure. Sticking to the rules and routines is generally the safer option (Bardach and Kagan 1982). Clearly, the risks of risk-taking are found in all governance arrangements that rely on front-line discretion.

The different demands for accountability point organizations towards an inflexible, rigid dealing with performance indicators. Whereas the hope within the administrative forum is that accountability for results creates room for innovation, other forums of accountability lead organizations to treat indicators as cast in concrete. Whereas the administrative principal-agent logic proposes that managers are free to manage as long as they measure results, the message heard from the other accountability forums is that everything they measure can be used against them, anytime.

Why does indicator-based accountability often stand in the way of innovation? The answer is essentially the same as why old-fashioned bureaucracy can obstruct innovation. Indicator-based accountability discourages risk-taking in several ways. First, the reputational damage that could result from bad media coverage leads public organizations to a more narrow focus on indicators. Second, in quasi-market contexts, pressure further increases. Teachers who mainly teach for a test are a case in point. Bad results may lead to lower enrolment and hence in the long run threaten organizational survival. Third, political blame games may lead to bureaucracy bashing when targets are not met, but also to political recuperation when targets are reached. Fourth, organizations often fall back on indicators of processes when output or outcome measures are not available. In this case, experimentation with processes becomes difficult. Fifth, when innovation leads to higher performance, it may trigger a ratchet effect (Hood 2006). Targets are typically set at a higher level when performance increases. This creates an incentive to ensure not to overshoot the targets because surpassing them would lead to higher targets the next year (Van Thiel and Leeuw 2002). After performance targets are introduced in a scheme of accountability, results tend to cluster around the target. Low performers make efforts to reach the target, but high performers tend to relax their effort. Finally innovation often results in an S-shaped performance improvement curve. Performance peaks immediately after introducing an innovation but declines when the innovation momentum fades away. Due to ratchet effects, innovators fear the immediate dip in performance after innovation since it is penalized in the target regime.

14.3   Accountability beyond NPM: A Pro-Innovation Agenda

Performance information will only lead to learning and innovation when the pressure emanating from indicator-based accountability is driven under the gaming threshold. As we argued above, we have reasons to believe that this threshold is rather low. The discussion of accountability forums suggests that performance indicators can be taken to the political and public forum any time. It has also been suggested that political and public accountability follow a garbage can model that makes accountability for performance unpredictable. Real, biting challenges of accountability rarely coincide with formal cycles of management reporting. The unpredictability creates uncertainty and risk-avoidance, which in turn discourages experimentation.

So how to reform indicator-based accountability to enhance innovation? The first and foremost reform of accountability mechanisms to enhance innovation would be to take performance *indicators* out of the formal processes of accountability, such as budgeting, contracting and performance appraisal. Indicator-based accountability should move away from formal schemes that usually lead to compliance at best. What are needed are performance indicators that trigger learning. Performance information can trigger the disruptive questions that lead to innovation. The high scores for Finland on the OECD education rankings, for instance, should challenge educational policies. They should not lead to naïvely copying the Finnish education system or to a political blame game in low-performing countries (Meyer and Benavot 2013). The education indicators should trigger policy learning. This requires a deeper understanding of what is going on. Is it really the structure of the education system? Or is the schooling of the teachers better in Finland? Are class sizes maybe smaller or is the student population less diverse? Policy learning should also critically question the value of the indicators themselves. What do comparative tests actually measure for instance? Is it mainly cognitive test results? And if so, what about values such as creativity or citizenship? The same goes for indicators within organizations. Lotte Bøgh Andersen (Chapter 12) shows that command and incentive systems can work only when transformative leadership enables dialogue on the indicators. Indicator-based accountability schemes, however, often do not make room for asking challenging questions. Explaining the past is more important than preparing for the future (Carter, Klein and Day 1992).

Cutting back on indicator-based accountability offers an exiting prospect for performance management. Contemporary performance management is often reduced to performance *indicator* management. This has led to many adverse effects that fundamentally challenge the utility of performance management. Yet, performance management is more than performance measurement. It implies that managers look at results and outcomes rather than inputs and processes. Performance managers in theory attach great importance to the decentralization of responsibilities; as long as results are obtained managers are free to manage, and staff are free to organize their work. Similarly, results-based accountability is more than indicator-based accountability. Many results, and particularly innovative results, are hard to quantify beforehand but nonetheless very real. Contrarily, many quantified results lack meaning in practice. Genuine performance management should build on meaningful conceptions of performance.

When management no longer prescribes how results need to be obtained, high trust is placed in front-line workers to do their job. A focus on results offers an opportunity to engage with staff to make meaning of performance. Arguably, people are quite willing to account for results, but only when they can do so in a meaningful way. Accountability for results can only work when real, meaningful results and impacts are discussed. This is not the case in many indicator-based accountability schemes, as the literature on gaming extensively demonstrates. Such schemes subvert the trust in front-line workers and professionals that is needed to make performance management work (Soss, Fording and Schram 2011). Indicators can also enable what Noordegraaf (2008) calls discursive craftsmanship. Indicators play a role in crafting policy stories that are considered to be meaningful. The metaphorical power of numbers to build meaningful policy stories has also been documented by Stone (1997). Performance management is mainly about sense making. Many performance indicators, however, are not making sense.

We do not suggest abandoning performance indicators altogether. In order to save performance management from its indicators, new connections need to be made. Performance management systems that tightly couple measurement to evaluative judgements need to be replaced by loosely coupled systems that allow for deliberation, learning and ultimately innovation (Van Dooren 2006; Van Dooren, Bouckaert and Halligan 2015). Performance management scholars have already studied this new approach to performance indicators. Moynihan (2008) proposes to embed performance indicators into a performance dialogue that allows for interpretation and learning. A performance dialogue, according to Moynihan, is a routine event that takes all relevant stakeholders on board. The main purpose is to make meaning from performance indicators by using both quantitative and experiential data. The discussion should be non-confrontational and be based on equality among participants. Performance dialogues should focus on goals, but could also serve as a breeding ground for innovation. The dialogue on performance should make sense of the mostly ambiguous performance information. Kroll (2013) adds to this notion of routine dialogues the idea of non-routine feedback in performance management. Much of the value of performance indicators does not originate from the indicator-based accountability schemes. What is more important are these spontaneous mechanisms of feedback that lead to ad hoc learning.

Cutting down on indicator-based accountability would by no means be the end of results-based accountability either. Indicator-based accountability is a limited approach to results-based accountability. Forums of accountability can perfectly thrive and be results-oriented without catalogues of performance indicators (Bovens 1998; Willems and Dooren 2011). Accountability mechanisms such as legal appeal and media exposure, hierarchy and market exit are still in place. Politicians can still question the performance of the education system when the PISA study comes out. Media can and will still critique the railway company when punctuality of the trains is lacking. Performance audits are still published and interest groups are still issuing standpoints. These external pressures can be beneficial for innovation. Yet, as we argued above, large and high-pressured performance indicator schemes are generally at odds with innovation. When schools are held accountable for test scores, teachers teach the test. Similarly, there are many ways in which railway companies can improve punctuality without improving the quality of service. Public organizations may even use indicators to divert questions of accountability, rather than to answer them. In this way, indicators shield off pressures for innovation rather than take innovation to heart.

NPG aspires to respond to complex societal contexts. Faced with complexity, results-based accountability needs thick descriptions of performance to allow for performance dialogue and meaningful innovation. The main critique on indicator-based accountability has targeted the thin evidence base of performance indicators. As the gaming literature has demonstrated abundantly, performance indicators are often not valid because they only measure performance very partially. They are also not reliable because strategic behaviour skews measured results. Rather than publicizing a laundry list of performance indicators, public services could bring a documented evaluation of performance and goal attainment to the table. The development of thick descriptions comes with a warning, however. Lewis and Triantafillou (2014) argue that thick description is more likely to supplement than to replace existing performance indicator regimes of accountability; that it is likely to demand more not less data; that it requires extensive participation and dialogue; and that it may reinforce the logic of constant organizational change in the name of improvement. They warn that such 'learning systems' may simply increase administrative overload rather than reduce it. The layering of oversight mechanisms may indeed suffocate innovation capacity and should be avoided.

Innovation typically builds on smart information gathering, with a good combination of both thin and thick descriptions. Thin performance indicators may be used to scratch the surface and to trigger debate. They may also direct our attention to issues that are worthwhile of thick description. Thick descriptions are better suited to finding explanations for differences in performance and for designing future strategies. Thick descriptions may also raise critical voices on thin performance indicator schemes. A good performance dialogue should reveal the instances of gaming that may have affected the performance data. In fact, most developed countries have a longstanding tradition of policy evaluation. The evidence base for innovation will be strengthened when evaluation studies and performance indicators are both put to use. Smart combinations of thick and thin evidence on performance should also be useful for scrutiny on different forums of accountability.

A step further would be to hold organizations and programmes accountable for innovation rather than for results. The innovation literature offers some clues on the responsibilities for which organizations could be held accountable: creating an open environment that fosters the intake and circulation of ideas, providing for a safe context for change, attention for diversity in the organization, scanning of the environment, prototyping and piloting (Albury 2005; Hartley 2005). These dimensions describe the capacity for innovation rather than the occurrence of innovation or the impact of innovation on society. More capacity assumes a higher *probability* of relevant innovation. The occurrence of innovation itself is too unpredictable and the impact of innovation is too diffuse to be a basis for accountability (Osborne and Brown 2013). Clearly, it will be hard to quantitatively measure capacity for innovation. We should not fall victim to the same mistakes of traditional indicator-based management. Are we able to quantitatively measure an inherently complex and context-dependent concept such as innovative capacity? Thick descriptions of innovative capacity might be more meaningful. Mazzucato (2013), for instance, critiques the number of patent registrations as an indicator of private sector innovativeness. She demonstrates that while private companies register most patents, the most innovative work comes out of the public sector, with government labs and government-backed universities investing in the research responsible for producing the most radical new drugs. Clearly, a thick description that assesses the quality of the drugs is needed to really understand innovation in the pharmaceutical sector.

Third, chance events seem a particularly relevant subject for both accountability and innovation (see also Chapter 13 by Montgomery Van Wart). Political crises, natural disasters and policy failures put pressure on the resilience of the political and administrative system. Chance events also activate processes of accountability on all forums (Schneider 2005; Rixen 2013). A crisis is a lightning switch for all accountability forums. Recent terrorist attacks in Paris and Copenhagen, for instance, led to public scrutiny of the role of government in politics, media and the courts. After a foiled terrorist attack in Belgium, a discussion ensued on quasi-market 'voting with the feet' by Jewish communities from allegedly inadequate protection by police forces. A key issue is whether accountability pressure leads to innovation (Osborne and Brown 2013). In any case, processes of accountability do have the potential to translate disruptive events into discontinuous change. Although not everyone agrees that it has been an innovation for the better, the 9/11 attacks without any doubt led to such a major overhaul of public governance (Roberts 2011).

Fourth, a politicization of accountability mechanisms may be fruitful. Governance mechanisms in general and performance indicator regimes in particular are only to a limited extent scrutinized in political and public forums. The news values and political salience of policy content are generally higher than the governance arrangements for these policies (Roberts 2011; Willems and Van Dooren 2016). Yet, liberal democracies should be capable of having a political debate on the advantages and disadvantages of accountability arrangements and decide on how much and what kind of accountability is required. Until now, mainly scandals have sparked off a politicized debate on indicator-based accountability. Patient neglect at Stafford Hospital (United Kingdom) for instance has been attributed to indicator rigidity and accountability (Mid Staffordshire NHS Foundation Trust Public Inquiry 2013). In the United States, a public debate on performance incentives unfolded after Veteran Affairs hospitals were scrutinized for disregarding patient follow-up (Moynihan 2014). A more sustained and systematic review of accountability mechanisms may be useful. Such a review should go beyond scandals and investigate the many functions of accountability; including innovation.

14.4   Conclusion

The overall argument of this chapter has been that indicator-based accountability, as proposed by the NPM paradigm, often drives out innovation. The promise of freedom to manage and to innovate does not materialize due to a rigid focus on performance indicators. NPM thus reduces results-based accountability to indicator-based accountability. Moreover, NPM only acknowledges the administrative forum of accountability, where (political) principals set targets for bureaucrats and agencies. In reality, organizations face multiple accountabilities. Performance indicators thus play out in different forums of accountability such as politics, media and markets. Indicators are used in an unpredictable way. Overall, it seems that indicator-based accountability following the NPM logic insufficiently acknowledges the complexity of contemporary governance. The simplicity of the model – set target, measure and sanction – is often a barrier to innovatively solving complex policy issues.

In contrast to NPM, NPG takes complexity as its problem diagnosis. Innovation can only materialize in governance systems that cope with (and thrive in) complex settings. A reform of indicator-based accountability can only enhance innovation if it is able to deal with complexity too. We argue that performance indicators can help to understand complexity when used for a performance dialogue outside of an accountability context. This is a learning perspective that has a better probability of understanding complexity and getting to innovation. Furthermore, indicator-based accountability may benefit from a good combination of thick and thin description. Another suggestion is to demand accountability for innovation rather than results. Since innovation typically is unpredictable, the focus should be on innovation capacity rather than actual innovations. Finally, accountability and innovation should be politicized. Thriving accountability forums in a liberal democracy should not only discuss the contents of policies but also the nature of accountability and the value of innovation.

References

Albury, D. 2005. 'Fostering innovation in public services', *Public Money & Management* 25(1): 51–6. http://doi.org/10.1111/j.1467–9302.2005.00450.x.
Bardach, E. and Kagan, R. A. 1982. *Going by the Book the Problem of Regulatory Unreasonableness*. Philadelphia: Transaction Publishers.

Blomqvist, P. 2004. 'The choice revolution: Privatization of Swedish welfare services in the 1990s', *Social Policy & Administration* 38(2): 139–55. http://doi.org/10.1111/j.1467–9515.2004.00382.x.

Bohannon, J. 2013. 'Who's afraid of peer review?' *Science* 342(6154): 60–5. http://doi.org/10.1126/science.342.6154.60.

Bouckaert, G. and Peters, B. G. 2002. 'Performance measurement and management: The Achilles' heel in administrative modernization', *Public Performance & Management Review* 25(4): 359–62.

Bovens, M. 1998. *The Quest for Responsibility: Accountability and Citizenship in Complex Organisations.* Cambridge, MA: Cambridge University Press.

Brodkin, E. Z. 2011. 'Policy work: Street-level organizations under new managerialism', *Journal of Public Administration Research and Theory* 21(S2): i253–77. http://doi.org/10.1093/jopart/muq093.

Carter, N., Klein, R. and Day, P. 1992. *How Organizations Measure Success. The Use of Performance Indicators in Government.* London: Routledge.

Cohen, M. D., March, J. G. and Olsen, J. P. 1972. 'A garbage can model of organizational choice', *Administrative Science Quarterly* 17 (1):1–25. http://doi.org/10.2307/2392088.

Galtung, J. and Ruge, M. H. 1965. 'The structure of foreign news: The presentation of the Congo, Cuba and Cyprus crises in four Norwegian newspapers', *Journal of Peace Research* 2 (1):64–90. http://doi.org/10.1177/002234336500200104.

Hartley, J. 2005. 'Innovation in governance and public services: Past and present', *Public Money and Management* 25(1): 27–34. http://doi.org/10.1111/j.1467–9302.2005.00447.x.

Hill, M. and Hupe, P. 2002. *Implementing Public Policy: Governance in Theory and in Practice.* London: Sage.

Hood, C. 2006. 'Gaming in targetworld: The targets approach to managing British public services', *Public Administration Review* 66(4): 515–21.

2010. *The Blame Game: Spin, Bureaucracy, and Self-Preservation in Government.* Princeton: Princeton University Press.

James, O. and John, P. 2007. 'Public management at the ballot box: Performance information and electoral support for incumbent English local governments', *Journal of Public Administration Research and Theory* 17(4): 567–80.

Jilke, S. and Van de Walle, S. 2012. 'Two track public services? Citizens' voice behaviour towards liberalized services in the EU15', *Public Management Review* 15(4): 465–76. http://doi.org/10.1080/14719037.2012.664015.

Johnson, C. and Talbot, C. 2008. 'UK parliamentary scrutiny of public services agreements: A challenge too far?', in S. Van de Walle and W. Van Dooren (eds.), *Performance Information in the Public Sector: How it is Used.* Basingstoke: Palgrave McMillan, pp. 140–57.

Jos, P. H. and Tompkins, M. E. 2004. 'The accountability paradox in an age of reinvention: The perennial problem of preserving character and judgment', *Administration & Society* 36(3): 255–81.

Kingdon, J. 1984. *Agenda, Alternatives and Public Policies.* Boston: Little, Brown & Company.

Kroll, A. 2013. 'The other type of performance information: Nonroutine feedback, its relevance and use', *Public Administration Review* 73(2): 265–76. http://doi.org/10.1111/j.1540–6210.2012.02648.x.

Laegreid, P. and Verhoest, K. 2010. 'Reforming public sector organizations', in *Governance of Public Sector Organizations: Proliferation, Autonomy and Performance*. Basingstoke: Palgrave Macmillan, pp. 1p.

Lewis, J.M. and Triantafillou, P. 2014. 'From performance measurement to learning: a new source of government overload?' *International Review of Administrative Sciences* 78 (4): 597–614.

Mazzucato, M. 2013. *The Entrepreneurial State: Debunking Public vs. Private Sector Myths*. New York: Anthem Press.

Meyer, H.-D., and Benavot, A. 2013. *PISA, Power, and Policy: The Emergence of Global Educational Governance*. Oxford: Symposium Books.

Mid Staffordshire NHS Foundation Trust Public Inquiry. 2013. *Report of the Mid Staffordshire NHS Foundation Trust Public Inquiry: Executive Summary*. The Stationery Office.

Moynihan, D. 2014. 'The problem at the VA: "Performance perversity" ', *Los Angeles Times* (June 1). www.latimes.com/opinion/op-ed/la-oe-moynihan-va-scandal-performance-perversity-20140602-story.html.

Moynihan, D. P. 2008. *The Dynamics of Performance Management: Constructing Information and Reform*. Washington, DC: Georgetown University Press.

Noordegraaf, M. 2008. 'Meanings of measurement', *Public Management Review* 10(2): 221–39. http://doi.org/10.1080/14719030801928672.

Noordegraaf, M. and Abma, T. 2003. 'Management by measurement? Public management practices amidst ambiguity', *Public Administration* 81(4): 853–71.

Osborne, D. and Gaebler, T. 1993. *Reinventing Government: How the Entrepreneurial Spirit is Transforming the Public Sector*. New York: Plume Press.

Osborne, S. P. and Brown, K. 2013. *Handbook of Innovation in Public Services*. Cheltenham: Edward Elgar.

Perry, J. L., Engbers, T. A. and Jun, S. Y. 2009. 'Back to the future? performance-related pay, empirical research, and the perils of persistence', *Public Administration Review* 69(1): 39–51. http://doi.org/10.1111/j.1540–6210.2008.01939_2.x.

Pollitt, C. 2013. 'The logics of performance management', *Evaluation* 19(4): 346–63. http://doi.org/10.1177/1356389013505040.

Pollitt, C. and Bouckaert, G. 2004. *Public Management Reform: A Comparative Analysis*. Oxford: Oxford University Press.

Poulsen, B. 2009. 'Competing traditions of governance and dilemmas of administrative accountability: The case of Denmark', *Public Administration* 87(1): 117–31. http://doi.org/10.1111/j.1467–9299.2008.00727.x.

Radin, B. A. 2000. 'The government performance and results act and the tradition of federal management reform: Square pegs in round holes', *Journal of Public Administration Research and Theory* 10(1): 111–35.

   2006. *Challenging the Performance Movement: Accountability, Complexity, and Democratic Values*. Washington, DC: Georgetown University Press.

Rixen, T. 2013. 'Why reregulation after the crisis is feeble: Shadow banking, offshore financial centers, and jurisdictional competition', *Regulation & Governance* 7(4): 435–59. http://doi.org/10.1111/rego.12024.

Roberts, A. 2011. *The Logic of Discipline: Global Capitalism and the Architecture of Government.* Oxford: Oxford University Press.

Schick, A. 2003. 'The performing state: Reflection on an idea whose time has come but whose implementation has not', *OECD Journal on Budgeting* 3(2): 71–103.

Schillemans, T. and Bovens, M. 2011. 'The challenge of multiple accountability: Does redundancy lead to overload?', in M. Dubnick and G. Frederickson (eds.), *Accountable Governance: Problems and Promises.* New York: ME Sharpe, pp. 3–21.

Schneider, S. K. 2005. 'Administrative breakdowns in the governmental response to Hurricane Katrina', *Public Administration Review* 65(5): 515–6.

Soss, J., Fording, R. and Schram, S. F. 2011. 'The organization of discipline: From performance management to perversity and punishment', *Journal of Public Administration Research and Theory* 21(s2): i203–32. http://doi.org/10.1093/jopart/muq095.

Stone, D. 1997. *Policy Paradox: The Art of Political Decision Making.* New York: W. W. Norton and Company.

Van Dooren, W. 2006. *Performance Measurement in the Flemish Public Sector: A Supply and Demand Approach.* Thesis, faculty of social sciences. Leuven, Belgium.

  2008. 'Nothing new under the sun? change and continuity in the twentieth century performance movement', in S. Van de Walle and W. Van Dooren (eds.), *Performance Information in the Public Sector: How It Is Used.* Basingstoke: Palgrave McMillan, pp. 15–45.

Van Dooren, W., Bouckaert, G. and Halligan, J. 2015. *Performance Management in the Public Sector*, 2nd edition. London: Routledge.

Van Dooren, W., Voets, J. and Winters, S. 2015. 'Autonomy and reregulation: Explaining dynamics in the Flemish social housing sector', *Public Administration.*

Van Thiel, S. and Leeuw, F. L. 2002. 'The performance paradox in the public sector', *Public Performance & Management Review* 25(3): 267–81.

Wiggins, A. and Tymms, P. 2002. 'Dysfunctional effects of league tables: A comparison between English and Scottish primary schools', *Public Money and Management* 22(1): 43–8.

Willems, T. and Van Dooren, W. 2011. 'Lost in diffusion? How collaborative arrangements lead to an accountability paradox', *International Review of Administrative Sciences* 77(3):505–30. http://doi.org/10.1177/0020852311408648.

  (2012): 'Coming to terms with accountability', *Public Management Review* 14(7): 1011–36. http://dx.doi.org/10.1080/14719037.2012.662446.

  2016. '(De)Politicization dynamics in public–private partnerships (PPPs): Lessons from a comparison between UK and Flemish PPP policy', *Public Management Review* 18(2): 1–22. http://doi.org/10.1080/14719037.2014.969759.

15 Organizational Innovations and Multiple Forms of Accountability in the Post-New Public Management Era

Tom Christensen and Per Lægreid

15.1 Introduction

Processes of innovation in the public sector will often reveal dilemmas, tensions and conflicts. Conversely, successful innovations in the political-administrative system imply an ability to balance different values, interests and actors. Attention must be paid not only to efficiency and effectiveness but also to trustworthiness and accountability as important values. Thus, key institutions in a democracy, such as the administrative apparatus, require a better knowledge base if they are to be able to innovate successfully and they must also garner support for new organizational arrangements from citizens, users and clients (Olsen 2004). It is especially important to have an innovative public sector capable of tackling the 'wicked' social challenges posed by the welfare state. Innovations in the public sector differ from those in the private sector because their ultimate goal is enhanced legitimacy, and they must also take the specific institutional context into account (Bekkers, Edelenbos and Stejn 2011). Thus, it is not only the logic of consequentiality that matters to innovation and accountability but also the logic of appropriateness (March and Olsen 1989).

The focus of our analysis is on organizational innovations in the welfare state and multiple accountability dynamics. We pose the following research questions:

- What characterizes the organizational innovations in the welfare, hospital and immigration sectors in Norway?
- How are these innovations affecting changes in formal and actual accountability relations?

The main working hypothesis in this chapter is that political accountability will constrain other types of accountability in organizational innovation processes, especially in politicized policy areas.

The corresponding author for this chapter is Tom Christensen.

We will describe and compare three organizational innovations, which we regard as hybrid and complex reorganizations that combined both NPM and post-NPM reform measures. We will then discuss how the three organizational innovations have affected formal and actual accountability relations. We look at the different types of accountability (political, administrative, professional, legal and social accountability) and how different tasks matter. We will also address the different areas for which public officials and politicians are held accountable (finance, procedure and performance). Bovens (2007) and Schillemans (2013) have already examined the challenges of multiple and overlapping accountability systems. We try in particular to add to this literature, in the context of organizational innovation, focusing on the importance of political accountability in accountability dynamics.

This chapter addresses three organizational innovations in reforms of the welfare administration carried out in Norway from 2001 onwards. First, as part of the reform of the employment and welfare administration a new form of local welfare office based on a partnership agreement between local and central government was introduced in 2005 and implemented through 2012. Second, the Hospital Reform introduced regional and local health enterprises from 2002 based on a specific law. Third, in the field of immigration a new 'court-like' central agency with extended autonomy from the ministry was introduced in 2001 to handle complaints from immigrants and asylum seekers.

We will start by introducing central concepts such as innovation, accountability, governance and reform. Second, we will briefly describe the overall reform context in Norway in order to illustrate the hybrid character of the three welfare reforms. Third, we will analyse the hybrid organizational innovations within the three reform areas and their implications for accountability dynamics, with a special focus on political accountability. Finally, we will draw some conclusions.

15.2   Central Concepts: Innovation, Accountability and Reforms

Innovation. Innovation is an ambiguous and multi-dimensional concept. On a general level, it can be defined as an idea, practice or object that is perceived as new by a unit of adoption (Rogers 2003; Fagerberg, Mowrey and Nelson 2005).[1] A standard definition of innovation is the development and realization of new ideas that break with established practices

---

[1] A reform may not necessarily imply an innovation, and an innovation could be the result of other processes than reform processes.

and common wisdom (cf. Chapter 1 this book; Damanpour 1991; Rogers 2003). Because of its broad scope, great flexibility and positive flavour, Pollitt and Hupe (2011) label innovation as a magic concept. Often innovation tends to include both the creation and implementation of new processes, services and methods of delivery and organizations (Damanpour and Evan 1984; Lægreid, Roness and Verhoest 2011). Our focus is on organizational innovation (Stenbæk and Treppendahl 2006; Windrum 2008; Balle Hansen 2010).

The public sector has traditionally been seen as resistant to innovation (Borins 2001), but in recent years this conventional wisdom has been challenged (Frederickson and Johnston 1999; Mulgan and Albury 2003). A series of recent studies claims that public sector innovation is widespread (NAO 2006; Borins 2008; Pollitt 2011; Sørensen 2012). Often motivated by internal problems, civil servants and managers have in practice been responsible for many innovations (Borins 2001), but political executives may also become reform entrepreneurs. In this chapter, we will contribute to this changing view.

A recent UK study confirmed that initiating public sector innovation is predominantly a top-down story involving senior management, middle management and to some extent politicians (NAO 2006). Top-down radical or systemic innovations are led either by politicians in response to crises or by newly appointed agency heads undertaking organizational turnarounds (Borins 2008). We mainly focus on top-down innovations, i.e. the development of new organizational forms.

As for the effects of innovation the general picture is that innovation is a risky business (Pollitt 2011). Many innovations do not work well and they might prove to be dysfunctional or have undesired side effects, which imply that innovations do not necessarily lead to improvements (Moore and Hartley 2008). That said, public sector research has found evidence that innovativeness has an impact on organizational performance as well as on individual job satisfaction and motivation (Damanpour 1991; Vigoda-Gadot et al. 2005). The effects of innovation on accountability relations have been less well studied.

Accountability. Schillemans (2013) emphasizes that a minimum definition of accountability should include answerability and adds that it is a relational concept and a retrospective and layered process. Bovens (2007: 450) defines accountability as '. . . a relationship between an actor and a forum, in which the actor has an obligation to explain and to justify his or her conduct, the forum can pose questions and pass judgments, and the actor may face consequences'. One key question is the problem of many eyes or the '*accountability to whom*' question, which focuses on the type of forum. The rationales for accountability and *why* an actor accounts to a forum will also be addressed (Bovens, Curtin and t'Hart 2010). We take it for granted that accountability relations are multiple and complex, and we examine what the true implications of innovation are for such accountability systems or regimes.

Bovens (2007) elaborates on five types of accountability based on the various types of forums an actor must report to (cf. also Romzek and Dubnick 1987). He sees *political accountability* as built on delegated popular sovereignty to representatives in elected bodies, who further delegate authority to the cabinet and the civil service. Thus, political accountability can include accountability to the minister or the cabinet within the executive branch as well as to the parliament (Mulgan 2003).

Administrative accountability is related to an organization's location within a public hierarchy in which a superior calls a subordinate to account for the performance of delegated duties, with a focus on process and procedures. Managerial accountability, as a version, reflected in modern reforms, is about monitoring output and results and making those with delegated authority answerable for carrying out tasks according to agreed performance criteria (Day and Klein 1987).

> *Legal accountability* reflects the increasing formalization of social relations and may be either external – i.e. to the courts – or internal – i.e. securing individual rights and fair treatment of users or citizens.

> *Professional accountability* deals with the mechanism of professional peers or peer review. In typical professional public organizations the various professions are constrained by professional codes of conduct – a system marked by deference to expertise (Mulgan 2000).

> *Social accountability* arises out of a lack of trust in government and the existence of several potential social stakeholders in the environment. Public organizations feel obliged to account for their activities vis-à-vis the public at large, stakeholders, or (civil) interest groups and users' organizations, via public reporting, public panels, information on the Internet or through the media (Malena, Forster and Singh 2004).

Bovens, Curtin and t'Hart (2010) distinguish between mandatory *vertical accountability* and voluntary *horizontal accountability*. In the first instance, the forum has formal power over the actor, as in political and legal accountability characterized by a hierarchy. In the second instance, there is more room for choice and moral convictions about duty with no direct intervention from leaders, as in social and professional accountability based on informal accountability relations. Accountability *for what* varies with different tasks and distinguishes between procedural accountability, underlining impartiality and fairness; financial accountability, focusing on economy; and accountability for performance or results.

The puzzle we are focusing on is that all organizational innovations studied intended to strengthen administrative accountability, in one way or another, without weakening political accountability, but in practice it turned out to be difficult to fulfil.

Accountability and reform. Two reform waves have been prominent in recent decades: New Public Management and post-New Public Management, both adding to and partly modifying what we can label Weberian or Old Public Administration features (Christensen and Lægreid 2007). NPM implies proliferation and unbundling, contractualization, marketization, a private sector management style, explicit performance standards and output/outcome control (Pollitt and Bouckaert 2011). Post-NPM reforms not only represent centralization meaning vertical reintegration, reflecting elements of Old Public Administration in new settings, but also seek to improve the horizontal coordination of governmental organizations and to enhance coordination between the government and other actors, alluding to New Public Governance (Osborne 2010; Lodge and Gill 2011; Klijn 2011).[2] Under NPM politicians have a strategic, goal-setting role, and civil servants are supposed to be autonomous managers held to account through performance arrangements and incentives (Pollitt and Bouckaert 2011). Under post-NPM politicians are guarantors of compromise deals between multiple stakeholders, while civil servants are network managers and partnership leaders. While NPM has a more internal focus on improving efficiency and promoting competition based on innovative strategies, post-NPM governance-inspired reforms are mainly inter-organizationally oriented and enhance collaboration strategies (Sørensen 2012). While NPM promotes competition-based innovative strategies, post-NPM enhances collaborative strategies. We have seen one main reform wave supplementing another in a complementary process whereby the trade-off between different administrative modes has changed, resulting in increased complexity and hybrid organizational forms.

The effects of innovative reforms on accountability are often inconclusive. Dublick (2011) addresses this by introducing the 'reformist paradox' in which efforts to improve accountability through reforms generate consequences that might alter, complicate or undermine existing forms of

---

[2] Post-NPM with its emphasis on combining structural reintegration and coordination covers better than New Public Governance the organizational innovations we are analysing, since the three cases do not focus on creating networks, which is a central part of NPG.

accountability. One may focus on what kind of accountability is related to different reforms and their dynamics (Romzek 2000). Accountability in a multi-functional public sector means being responsible for the achievement of multiple and often ambiguous objectives.

In a hierarchical model the concept of accountability is primarily related to upward accountability to political sovereigns (Christensen and Lægreid 2002). The network and partnership models are different. Partnerships need some level of independence, but at the same time they should be accountable upwards to politicians, horizontally to other agencies and local government, and downwards to citizens. They thus have to face the challenges of political as well as administrative and bureaucratic, legal and professional accountability (Pollitt 2003). Networks in partnership models supplement rather than replace the traditional welfare state hierarchy (Bouckaert, Peters and Verhoest 2010).

Reform processes normally represent unstable, unsettled and unexpected situations that go beyond the more stable routine situations of business as usual (Olsen 2014). The answers to questions such as who has the right to call to account, to discuss and debate the information given and to face consequences and judgements are more fluid. A further question is then how this is related to the innovative organizational models that reforms involve. What are the dynamics between accountability and innovation? Will even dynamic and unstable situations between innovative organization forms and multiple and overlapping accountability regimes be constrained or dominated by political accountability?

We now turn to the Norwegian case, which illustrates the complex relationship between hybrid organizational innovations and various accountability relations.

15.3   A Short Methodological Note

The three reforms are all related to highly politicized policy areas and directed towards efficiency gains and better treatment of users. They all represent multiple forms of accountability, but in different ways, so they represent different types of changes and potential tensions between accountability types. Another common similarity between the three reforms is that they intended to strengthen administrative accountability without having negative side effects on political accountability. A third common feature is that they all introduced different organizational innovations. The organizational innovation in the welfare reform (the partnership model) enhanced administrative accountability and challenged potentially political accountability especially at local level. The organizational innovation in the hospital reform (the health enterprise model) also enhanced administrative accountability and challenged professional accountability as well. A main concern of this reform was sustaining political accountability. The organizational innovation in the immigration reform (the court-like independent agency model) enhanced administrative accountability but focused more on professional and legal accountability and pointed towards autonomy and potentially challenging for political accountability. High political salience may also make social accountability challenging.

The data in the study consist of around 50 interviews, mostly among top political and administrative leaders in the three areas (Byrkjeflot, Christensen and Lægreid 2014: 177). Diverse public documents like public committee reports, government reports and proposals, Parliamentary debates, etc. are also used. This study is adding to many published studies based on the same type of data in the way that innovation is focused.

15.4   The Overall Reform Context: Hybrid Reforms

The welfare administration reform was initiated in 2001, approved in 2005, and implemented between 2006 and 2011. The reform merged the employment administration, represented by the Directorate of Labour (DOL) and the National Insurance Administration (NIA), into one new labour and welfare agency (Christensen, Fimreite and Lægreid 2007). It established new local, one-stop shops based on a new partnership between the central agency and locally based social services, thus combining central control and formalization with some local flexibility and variety. The whole new organization also received a new performance-management system. The main aim of the reform was to coordinate a fragmented structure better, thus reflecting the post-NPM trend. So the holistic aspect of the reform was central. However, unifying three different professional cultures into a new single culture proved to be a major challenge.

The hospital reform. In 2002, the main responsibility for Norwegian hospitals was transferred from the counties to central government, a typical post-NPM feature. The reform centralized the ownership function to the Ministry of Health, aided in administrative and oversight functions by two subordinate central agencies – The Norwegian Directorate of Health and The Norwegian Board of Health Supervision. Five (later merged to four) regional health enterprises with separate professional boards were established, comprising 33 local health enterprises overseeing 250 health institutions of different types. The NPM elements in this reform are rather evident. The hospitals were transformed into enterprises, which were supposed to have a large amount of managerial autonomy. A performance-management system (NPM-related), whereby central targets were set, resources provided and results reported from regional and local enterprises, was also established. A small part of the hospital reform was reversed when the new Red-Green government came to power in 2005, because it brought politicians back onto the boards of hospitals. The hospital reform introduced a rather complex combination of centralization, decentralization and corporatization.

The immigration reform. In 2001, a major reform of the central immigration administration took place in Norway. In addition to making the Norwegian Directorate of Immigration more autonomous, it also established a new 'court-like' body with a lot of formal autonomy – the Immigration Appeals Board (IAB). The main motives behind the reform were to alleviate capacity problems and the burden on the central political and administrative executive by hiving off immigration control cases, and it also involved a blame-avoidance component (Christensen, Lægreid and Norman 2007). After the reorganization, political executives could no longer interfere in most ordinary individual cases, but later on the political leadership took various steps to try to modify this feature, implementing less successful control measures. Steering was to be done from a distance, via general policy directives, thus furthering professional autonomy. Overall, this case shows a marked NPM-oriented structural devolution reform focusing on agencification while its focus on hierarchy, specialization and rule-based behaviour are post-NPM features.

Not one of the reforms uses a 'pure' set of principles taken from either NPM or post-NPM. They are all hybrid, combining and balancing different and partly opposing principles of organization, and they introduce organizational forms that are new and innovative. In the two cases where post-NPM dominated the aims, the hospital and welfare cases, formal vertical and horizontal reintegration or de-specialization was used, blended with NPM instruments like decentralization/delegation and corporatization. In the immigration case, the main goals involved NPM-type measures, the main reorganizational measure being structural devolution, but there was also a stronger focus on user participation, professional features and rule-based decision making, later blended with attempts to introduce more central control.

15.5   Organizational Innovation and Accountability in Administrative Reforms

Organizational innovation. The reforms in these three welfare state fields each came up with their own organizational innovation to handle the

298   *Tom Christensen and Per Lægreid*

challenges they face. The welfare administration reform brought about the largest merger of agencies ever in Norway, while the real innovation was the *partnership model*. In contrast to the traditional steering doctrines of separate ministerial responsibility and local self-government, this innovation was supposed to solve the tension between them by stronger integration into one local organizational form, which reflected a political compromise. So the main focus was on political accountability and how to live with simultaneous accountability to local politicians and to central government, i.e. combining two hierarchies.

In the hospital reform, the first element was centralized ownership, but the real organizational innovation was the establishment of *health enterprises*, which were supposed to bolster administrative or managerial accountability. In contrast to the traditional Norwegian agency model and the public sector company model, this arrangement was a hybrid, allowing regional/local enterprises a lot of discretion but at the same time giving the ministry the option to interfere in cases of political urgency. The managerial autonomy of the health enterprises is constrained by a number of steering devices from the ministry that illustrate the inbuilt ambiguity of the reform when it comes to balancing autonomy and central control (Christensen, Lægreid and Stigen 2006). The ministry exercises control through the Health Enterprise Act, through the articles of association, through steering documents (contracts), through decisions adopted by the enterprise meeting and through signals (Opedal 2004).

In the immigration reforms, the organizational innovation was the establishment of an Immigration Appeals Board (IAB) – a *court-like central agency with super autonomy* to handle complaints/appeals; it was originally conceived as a result of blame-avoidance related to 'wicked issues' (Christensen, Lægreid and Norman 2007). In contrast to the traditional Norwegian agency model with semi-autonomous agencies under the supervision of their parent ministry, or a court model, used in Sweden, the new hybrid solution granted this agency more formal autonomy from the ministry, giving it the rather ambiguous label of 'court-like'. Politicians could not interfere in single cases but could change the rules and regulations.

Organizational innovation and accountability. Organizational forms tend both to constrain and enable accountability relations, but normally they allow for some variation in actual behaviour, partly because they are ambiguous and have a hybrid character and partly because it is in practice difficult to live up to the formal organizational model (Byrkjeflot, Christensen and Lægreid 2014). Organizational innovations not only tend to solve some accountability issues but also produce new accountability challenges (Table 15.1). It is difficult to solve political conflicts via

Table 15.1 *Dynamics of accountability relationships through organizational innovations in three sectors*

	Accountability to whom?		Accountability for what?
	Formal and actual changes in political accountability.[3]	Major dynamics and tensions with other types of accountability.	
Welfare: Partnership	Both formal and actual changes. New local offices represent two competing hierarchies, but the central one has the upper hand.	Tensions between political accountability at central and local level. Administrative accountability more crucial for political accountability.	Focus on performance and efficient service delivery, but also side effects on procedural and financial aspects.
Health: Health enterprises	Formally a change towards hybrid governance – centralization, decentralization and corporatization at the same time. There has not been the same degree of change in governance practices.	Political accountability is challenged by professional and administrative/ managerial accountability. Social accountability dynamics represent a potential problem for political accountability primarily at the regional/local levels.	Focus on financial accountability, but also has side effects on procedural and performance accountability.
Immigration: Court-like agency	Both formal and actual changes – increased formal delegation and a de facto undermining of political control.	A combination of administrative, professional and legal accountability challenges political accountability, in a dynamic relationship with social accountability.	Focus on procedural accountability, fairness and impartiality but side effects on financial and performance accountability.

[3] Just like the distinction between formal structure and actual behaviour made by Egeberg (2012), the distinction between formal and actual accountability alludes to what is formally the changes in accountability and what is actually happening concerning accountability behaviour after these formal changes (Byrkjeflot, Christensen and Lægreid 2014).

organizational innovations. Rather than bring about de-politicization by strengthening managerial accountability at the expense of political accountability, the organizational innovations tend to encourage arena-shifting (Flinders and Buller 2006). The organizational innovations do not cause political conflicts to disappear, but instead tend to move them from one organizational arena to another.

The three reforms represent different agency strategies concerning innovation and also different vertical political accountability relationships. Delegation is a main organizational tool in all three reforms but with different levels of clarity and distance between delegated bodies and the core of government. Such multi-agency hybrid arrangements represent shared responsibilities and organizational complexity. In the hospital field, the ministry has overall ownership responsibility and may use frame steering, but at the same time it can also interfere in specific cases. Delegation of responsibility from the ministry to the agencies is a core element not only in the immigration reform but also in the hospital reform. The welfare administration represents an agency strategy focusing on partnership structures and trans-organizational elements. The IAB case represents hard-core delegation with a high level of distance and very clear delegation, while the health enterprises represent a more mixed or soft delegation with a less clear-cut and more fuzzy delegation pattern (Hood 2010: 78). The IAB type of delegation is more likely than the welfare case to clarify accountability relations because it makes policy or administrative responsibility clearer (Hood 2011).

The reforms in these three welfare state fields have each come up with their own organizational innovation to handle the accountability challenges they face. The welfare administration reform was supposed to resolve the tension between ministerial accountability and local self-government but in practice cooperation between administrative levels has been problematic (Christensen, Fimreite and Lægreid 2014). It did, however, have side effects on legal, professional and social accountability, and in practice the partnership model has proved difficult to implement because it tends to make accountability relations more ambiguous. Thus, the partnership model is a quasi-solution (Fimreite 2011).

In the hospital reform, the health enterprises were supposed to bolster administrative or managerial accountability and autonomy, implying increased efficiency. In practice it has, however, been difficult to live up to this model. The political executive has taken a more hands-on approach to single cases owing to high political salience, and the strong professional influence of doctors prevails (Lægreid, Opedal and Stigen 2005).

In the immigration reforms, the establishment of a *court-like central agency with super autonomy* to handle complaints/appeals, originally conceived as a result of blame-avoidance related to 'wicked issues', was supposed to increase administrative, legal and professional accountability. But, in practice, the political executive has tended to get the blame anyway. The politicians' reaction was to try to re-institute political control, with limited success, the least so with IAB.

Tasks matter. The three reforms studied deal with different task areas and service provision. If we compare the three organizational innovations, one important conclusion is that *tasks matter*. There are both similarities and variations among the reform areas with respect to political salience, level of professionalization and complexity, and the degree of acceptance of local variations. First, they are all *highly politically salient*, which makes political accountability central. All three reforms aim to strengthen administrative/managerial accountability without having negative side effects on political accountability. In the welfare reform, the existence of two, potentially competing hierarchies makes political accountability internally challenging. In the hospital reform, professional accountability is critical and potentially challenges political accountability. In the immigration reform, professional and legal accountability point towards autonomy and potentially challenge political accountability. High political salience may also make social accountability challenging for political accountability and legitimacy.

The role of political leaders is ambiguous in all three reform cases: elected officials have a role as strategists in defining the long-term goals of the public sector and assessing the results, but at the same time they are expected to give considerable discretion to administrative leaders and operative agencies, entities they should control through administrative/managerial accountability. However, they can interfere in individual cases to a greater or lesser extent. In both the welfare administration reform and the hospital reform accountability has shifted from the political to the administrative/managerial sphere and from input and processes to output and outcomes, without actually undermining political accountability much. But in the partnership arrangement, we see a tension between political accountability at the local municipal level and at the central government level.

Attempts to strengthen other accountability mechanisms have, however, been overshadowed by political accountability, and there seem to be clear limitations on how far one can go in constraining political accountability in such politicized areas. Eventually the reforms have tended to strengthen central government capacity and political accountability even if they initially tried to upgrade other accountability relations. The political dynamics have also tended to produce unstable trade-offs and tensions between accountability mechanisms. The reforms have revealed the true nature of

302   *Tom Christensen and Per Lægreid*

accountability as multidimensional, dynamic and hybrid, but with political accountability having the upper hand, most clearly seen in the hospital reform and somewhat less so in the welfare reform, especially regarding the partnership at local level where administrative accountability tended to get the upper hand (Christensen and Lægreid 2014).

Second, we would expect a degree of *professionalism* in service provision. Day and Klein (1987) argue that services involving a high level of professionalism like hospital care are also likely to be more complex. Even if professionalism does not always correlate with complexity, we would thus expect professional accountability to be associated with complexity in areas where service provision is diverse, such as in hospitals, whereas both pensions and immigration services will be more standardized and less varied and hence less complex and less professionalized. Hospitals resemble professional bureaucracies with a high level of professionalism and complexity in service provision at the same time. The reforms in this sector focused more strongly on balancing the power of professionals by introducing more mechanisms for administrative control. This has been difficult since there is a major tension between both professional and administrative accountability on the one hand and political accountability on the other. But political accountability mechanisms have also been used frequently, in a dynamic relationship with social accountability, especially in crisis cases.

Third, we would expect the *acceptance of local variation* in service provision to make a difference (Bogdanor 2010; Fimreite 2011). If there are strong norms of impartiality and equal services for the same kind of users or clients all over the country, we would expect services to be standardized and legal and administrative accountability to be strong, as in immigration cases. For service provision with more local variation, like employment and benefits cases in the welfare administration, we would expect professional and social accountability to be more prominent. Immigration (especially control and regulation) and welfare services (especially pensions) are more like machine bureaucracies and have a stronger focus on legal accountability than the hospital sector does. While hierarchical accountability might be better applied to routine tasks, professional accountability might be more suitable for non-routine tasks (Romzek 2000).

Summing up, we have shown that the organizational innovations in the three reform areas studied are rather hybrid, meaning that complexity is combined with partly inconsistent or tension-ridden organizational principles. This in turn tends to produce multiple accountability relations, changing the balance between different accountability forms and resulting in trade-offs. Common to all the sectors is the salience of political accountability, with formal and actual accountability relations in the three sectors changing according to complex and varied patterns. As a result, administrative accountability involves more of a focus on control and performance, professional accountability is beset with internal and external tensions, judicial accountability places more emphasis on individual rights and standardization, and social accountability focuses more on the needs of patients and clients initially.

A main result in our study is that the complex and hybrid reforms all represent innovations, in different ways, but that in the dynamic accountability relationships political accountability is mostly constraining the other types. This not only reflects the high political salience of the sectors but also that the political leadership manages either to use different accountability types to its advantage or to fend off 'threatening' and competing accountability mechanisms. In particular, administrative and managerial accountability are used as hierarchical tools to keep control, while professional and legal accountability are contained. Social accountability has an interesting dynamic with political accountability, because it both potentially undermines political accountability but is also used by the political leadership to legitimate actions related to crisis. One can claim that even though our cases are overall politicized top-down reforms, the dynamics shown between accountability forms is generic and will still be there in more low-key reforms but in different combinations where political accountability probably will struggle more to trump the other types.

Of the three cases, the hospital reform innovation (the health enterprise model) is most clearly supporting our thesis of the prevailing of political accountability, in giving strong potential for political control if necessary. But there is not so much interference in daily service provision, which is catering to the professional groups. The political leadership is also using administrative accountability actively through the ownership division in the ministry and the administrative leadership in the health enterprises.

The partnership arrangement in the welfare reform shows the strongest central political control and accountability challenging the local political accountability. But it also shows strong administrative influence from the administrative leadership at the agency, regional and local level, potentially challenging political accountability, which makes us conclude that it is slightly less an example of political accountability prevailing than in the hospital sector.

Meanwhile the immigration reform (the court-like independent agency model) shows political leadership struggling the most with political accountability because of the most extreme formal delegation, making the influence of legal and professional accountability strong.

15.6   Conclusion

A main lesson from this study is that political accountability tends to both predominate and strategically link up with other forms of accountability. Another main lesson is that tasks matter and that the new and complex innovations of formal organizational models represent broad categories that allow for variation in accountability practice. The dynamics of accountability play out differently in different contexts whereby tasks have a particularly big role to play for a number of reasons. In the welfare administration reform, the political leadership has tried to interfere in various issues and individual cases rather frequently, but overall it lacks the capacity to do this consistently and is very dependent on the administrative leadership to enact control on its behalf. Nevertheless, dissatisfied clients, their interest groups, employees' unions and the media continue to hold the political and administrative leadership to account, so the dynamics are related primarily to political, administrative and social accountability.

In the hospital sector, professional medical knowledge is central, so political accountability and administrative/managerial accountability are up against professional accountability, as recently illustrated by the 2013 campaign initiated by hospital doctors to 'bring the professions back in'. But here, too, social accountability is part of the equation, in particular on the regional and local level, where societal groups are very active in the debate about the implications of NPM and the related efficiency drive for local hospitals, which are seen as vulnerable.

The reforms in immigration represent the largest formal and real change in accountability, pitting political accountability against administrative, professional and legal accountability, in particular with respect to legal expertise, but the lay representation in the IAB and external political pressure also bring social accountability into the dynamic. These reforms show the political leadership trying to control the agencies more, but succeed the least concerning IAB because of strong formal delegation and a strong legal culture that is protecting legal accountability.

The welfare state reforms represent complex organizational innovations where actors are held accountable to different forums and by different types of accountability according to the nature of the obligation and contextual constraints. We have revealed a multiple accountability regime in which the different accountability mechanisms do not substitute for each other but are redundant rather than segregated (Scott 2000; Olsen 2007). Multiple accountabilities may be an appropriate solution for an increasingly pluralistic governance system and may offer a new kind of flexibility. Accountability is about managing diverse and partly conflicting expectations (Romzek and Dubnick 1987; Willems and Van Dooren 2011).

Another lesson is that accountability often serves as a critical companion to administrative change (Schillemans 2013), and this is especially the case when organizational innovations are introduced. We have revealed that there might be a loose coupling between the new organizational forms and different accountability dimensions. The welfare state reforms introduced organizational innovations that have complicated the already broad notion of accountability in the public sector and have made accountability a more ambiguous issue (Mulgan 2003). There are many limits, barriers and obstacles for different target groups regarding accountability issues, especially during unsettled and turbulent reform periods. The more single-dimension, principal-agent approach to accountability that may fit stable and settled situations is not appropriate for complex reform periods. Organizational innovations may need to be accompanied by accountability innovations that complement more traditional forms of accountability to enhance organizational learning processes (Schillemans, van Twist and Vanhommerig 2013).

In a state with a fluid, complex, flexible, semi-autonomous and fragmented polity, we have to go beyond traditional forms of political accountability (Flinders 2012) and rethink democratic accountability in ways that resonate with the new reality of modern governance systems. We need to supplement the hierarchical approach comprising delegation and vertical channels of accountability with analyses of how multiple and hybrid accountability relations interact and change over time and across countries.

There is a lack of systematic and reliable knowledge about the outcomes and implications of organizational innovations for accountability issues, especially political accountability (Mattei 2009). From an international perspective, further research may examine variations between countries facing similar reforms. One type of focus might be on how different tasks generate different accountability dynamics, taking into consideration variations in the cultural trajectories of administrative development. Another might be to pay more attention to the demand side of accountability in reform processes and enhance organizational innovations that are less concerned with blame avoidance and less characterized by low trust and scepticism towards politics (Flinders 2014). One might thus avoid the 'reformist paradox' whereby efforts to improve accountability through reforms generate consequences that alter and complicate existing forms of accountability (Dubnick 2011). A third focus might be on the design of organizational innovations and especially on how different new organizational forms constrain and enable different accountability mechanisms and under what conditions and contexts these might work well (Bovens and Schillemans 2014).

We have focused on how reforms and organizational innovations affect accountability relations, but additional insights from our study might be achieved if one turns around the arrow and treats innovation as the dependent variable as done in the previous chapter. In practice we are facing mutually affected processes and co-evolution between accountability and innovation. One insight might be that both hybridity in governance and accountability creates a variety of preconditions for future innovation. One possibility is that the political and administrative leadership decentralize at 'let a thousand flowers bloom', even though this potentially will create control and accountability challenges. Another is that local variety in innovations, whether related to organizational or policy content, eventually can be used to establish more national standardized changes.

References

Balle Hansen, M. 2010. 'Brugerinnovation og strategisk ledelse i den offentlige sektor', ('User innovation and strategic management in the public sector'), *Ledelse & Erhvervsøkonomi* 75(1): 41–52.

Bekkers, V., Edelenbos, J. and Steijn, B. (eds.) 2011. *Innovation in the Public Sector*. Basingstoke: Palgrave Macmillan.

Bogdanor, V. 2010. 'On forms of accountability', Working Paper 03. London: 2020 Public Service Trust at the RSA.

Borins, S. 2001. 'Encouraging innovation in the public sector', *Journal of Intellectual Capital* 2(3): 310–19.

   2008. *Innovations in Government: Research, Recognition and Replication.* Washington: Brooking Institution.

Bouckaert, G., Peters, B. G. and Verhoest, K. 2010. *The Coordination of Public Sector Organizations*. Basingstoke: Palgrave Macmillan.

Bovens, M. 2007. 'Analysing and assessing public accountability. A conceptual framework', *European Law Journal* 13(4): 837–68.

Bovens, M., Curtin, D. and t'Hart, P. 2010. *The Real World of EU Accountability*. Oxford: Oxford University Press.

Bovens, M. and Schillemans, T. 2014. 'Meaningful Accountability', in M. Bovens, R. E. Goodin and T. Schillemans (eds.), *Oxford Handbook of Public Accountability*. Oxford: Oxford University Press, pp. 673–82.

Byrkjeflot, H., Christensen, T. and Lægreid, P. 2014. 'The many faces of accountability – comparing reforms in welfare, hospitals and immigration', *Scandinavian Political Studies* 37(2): 171–95.

Christensen, T., Fimreite, A. L. and Lægreid, P. 2007. 'Reform of employment and welfare administration – the challenge of coordinating diverse public organizations', *International Review of Administrative Science* 73(3): 389–408.

Christensen, T., Fimreite, A. L. and Lægreid, P. 2014. 'Joined-up government for welfare administration reform in Norway', *Public Organization Review* 14(4): 439–56.

Christensen, T. and Lægreid, P. 2002. 'New Public Management: Puzzles of democracy and the influence of citizens', *Journal of Political Philosophy* 10(3): 267–95.

2007. 'The whole-of-government approach to public sector reform', *Public Administration Review* 67(6):1059–66.

2014. 'Performance and accountability – a theoretical discussion and an empirical assessment', *Public Organization Review* 15(2): 207–25.

Christensen, T., Lægreid, P. and Norman, R. 2007. 'Organizing immigration – a comparison of New Zealand and Norway', in T. Christensen and P. Lægreid (eds.), *Transcending New Public Management*. Aldershot: Ashgate, pp. 111–34.

Christensen, T., Lægreid, P. and Stigen, I. 2006. 'Performance management and public sector reform: The Norwegian hospital reform', *International Public Management Journal* 9(2): 113–39.

Damanpour, F. 1991. 'Organizational innovation: A meta-analysis of effects of determinants and moderators', *Academy of Management Journal* 34(3): 555–90.

Damanpour, F. and Evan, W. M. 1984. 'Organizational innovation and performance: The problem of "Organizational lag"', *Administrative Science Quarterly* 29(3): 392–409.

Day, P. and Klein, R. 1987. *Accountability. Five Public Services*. London: Tavistock Publishers.

Dubnick, M. J. 2011. 'Move over Daniel: We need some "Accountability Space"', *Administration and Society* 43(6): 704–16.

Egeberg, M. 2012. 'How bureaucratic structure matters: An organizational perspective', in B. G. Peters and J. Pierre (eds.), *Handbook of Public Administration*. London: Sage, pp. 157–68.

Fagerberg, J., Mowrey, D. and Nelson, R. (eds.) 2005. *The Oxford Handbook of Innovation*. Oxford: Oxford University Press.

Fimreite, A. L. 2011. 'Partnerskapet i NAV – innovasjon eller "same procedure"?' (Partnership in NAV – innovation or 'same procedure'?), Working Paper 4/2011. Bergen: Uni Rokkan Centre.

Flinders, M. 2012. *Defending Politics. Why Democracy Matters in the Twenty-First Century*. New York: Oxford University Press.

2014. 'The future and relevance of accountability studies', in M. Bovens, R. E. Goodin and T. Schillemans (eds.), *Oxford Handbook of Public Accountability*. Oxford: Oxford University Press, pp. 661–72.

Flinders, M. and Buller, J. 2006. 'Depolitization, democracy and arena shifting', in T. Christensen and P. Lægreid (eds.), *Autonomy and Regulation. Coping with Agencies in the Modern State*. Cheltenham: Edvard Elgar, pp. 53–80.

Fredrickson, H. G. and Johnston, J. M. 1999. *Public Management Reform and Innovations*. Tuscaloosa: University of Alabama Press.

Hood, C. 2010. *The Blame Game*. Princeton: Princeton University Press.

308   *Tom Christensen and Per Lægreid*

2011. 'Blame avoidance and accountability: Positive, negative or neutral', in M. J. Dubnick and H. G. Frederickson (eds.), *Accountable Governance. Problems and Promises*. London: M.E. Sharpe, pp. 167–79.

Klijn, E. H. 2011. 'New public management and governance: A comparison', in D. Levi-Faur (ed.), *The Oxford Handbook of Governance*. Oxford: Oxford University Press, pp. 201–14.

Lodge, M. and Gill, D. 2011. 'Towards a new era of administrative reform? The myth of post-NPM in New Zealand', *Governance* 24(1): 141–66.

Lægreid, P., Opedal, S. and Stigen, I. 2005. 'The Norwegian hospital reform – balancing political control and enterprise autonomy', *Journal of Health Politics, Policy and Law* 30(6): 1035–72.

Lægreid, P., Roness, P. G. and Verhoest, K. 2011. 'Explaining the innovative culture and activity of state agencies', *Organizational Studies* 32(10): 1321–47.

Malena, C., Forster, R. and Singh, J. 2004. 'Social accountability', Social Development Papers no. 40. Washington: The World Bank.

March, J. G. and Olsen, J. P. 1989. *Rediscovering Institutions: The Organizational Basis of Politics*. New York: The Free Press.

Mattei, P. 2009. *Restructuring Welfare Organizations in Europe*. London: Palgrave Macmillan.

Moore, M. and Hartley, J. 2008. 'Innovations in governance', *Public Management Review* 10(1): 3–20.

Mulgan, R. 2000. 'Accountability: An Ever-Expanding Concept?' *Public Administration*, 78 (3): 555-573.

2003. *Holding Power to Account. Accountability in Modern Democracies*. London: Palgrave.

Mulgan, G. and Albury, D. 2003. *Innovation in the Public Sector*. London: Cabinet Office, Strategic Unit, Working Paper.

NAO 2006. *Achieving Innovation in Central Government Organisations: Detailed Research Findings*. London: National Audit Office HC 1447-II, Session 2005-2006.

Olsen, J. P. 2004. 'Innovasjon, politikk og institusjonell dynamikk' ('Innovation, policy and institutional dynamics'). Working Paper 04/2004. Oslo: ARENA Centre for European Studies.

2007. *Europe in Search for Political Order*. Oxford: Oxford University Press.

2014. 'Accountability and ambiguity', in M. Bovens, R. E. Goodin and T. Schillemans (eds.), *Oxford Handbook of Public Accountability*. Oxford: Oxford University Press, pp. 106–26.

Opedal, S. 2004. 'Statens eierstyring av helseforetakene – balansegang mellom stortingsaktivisme og foretaksautonomi' ('State owner steering of health enterprises – the balance between parliamentary activism and enterprise autonomy'). Working Paper. Stavanger: IRIS.

Osborne, S. P. (ed.) 2010. *The New Public Governance? Emerging Perspectives on the Theory and Practice of Public Governance*. Oxon: Routledge.

Pollitt, C. 2003. 'Joined-up government: A survey', *Political Studies Review* 1: 34–49.

2011. 'Innovation in the public sector: An introductory overview', in V. Bekkers, J. Edelenbos and B. Steijn (eds.), *Innovation in the Public Sector*. Basingstoke: Palgrave Macmillan, pp. 35–43.

Pollitt, C. and Bouckaert, G. 2011. *Public Management Reform: A Comparative Analysis*. 3rd edition. Oxford: Oxford University Press.

Pollitt, C. and Hupe, P. 2011. 'Talking about government: The role of magic concepts', *Public Management Review* 13(5): 641–58.

Rogers, E. M. 2003. *Diffusions of Innovations*. 5th edition. New York: The Free Press.

Romzek, B. S. 2000. 'Dynamics of public sector accountability in an era of reform', *International Review of Administrative Sciences* 66(1): 21–44.

Romzek, B. and Dubnick, M. 1987. 'Accountability in the public sector: Lessons from the Challenger tragedy', *Public Administration Review* 47(3): 227–38.

Schillemans, T. 2013. 'The public accountability review', Working Paper. Utrecht University School of Governance.

Schillemans, T., van Twist, M. and Vanhommerig, I. 2013. 'Innovations in accountability', *Public Performance & Management Review* 36(3): 407–35.

Scott, C. 2000. 'Accountability in the regulative state', *Journal of Law & Society* 38 (1): 38–66.

Stenbæk, N. and Treppendahl, M. B. 2006. *Hvad kan forklare innovation i danske virksomheder? (What Can Explain Innovation in Danish Businesses?)*. Copenhagen: Ministry of Economy and Commerce.

Sørensen, E. 2012. 'Governance and innovation in the public sector', in D. Levi-Faur (ed.), *The Oxford Handbook on Governance*. Oxford: Oxford University Press, pp. 215–27.

Vigoda-Gadot, E., Shoham, A., Ruvio, A. and Schwabski, N. 2005. *Innovation in the Public Sector. Report on the Public Surveys*. Haifa: University of Haifa, Publin Report No. D17.

Willems, T. and Van Dooren, W. 2011. 'Lost in diffusion? How collaborative arrangements lead to an accountability paradox', *International Review of Administrative Sciences* 77(3): 505–30.

Windrum, P. 2008. 'Innovation and entrepreneurship in public services', in P. Windrum and P. Koch (eds.), *Innovation in Public Sector Services. Entrepreneurship, Creativity and Management*. Cheltenham: Edward Elgar, pp. 3–21.

16   Can Public Governance Be Changed
to Enhance Innovation?

B. Guy Peters

The public sector confronts a rather complex environment concerning innovation. On the one hand, governments have been innovating for their entire existence. To some extent every time governments make new policies they are innovating. Policy reforms may be minor alterations in existing policies (see Carter 2012; Hogwood and Peters 1986) or they may be major new interventions into the economy and society (see Light 2002; Schwartz 1984), but they still represent innovations designed to improve the quality of governing. At another level the continuing reform of public sector organizations demonstrates that structural and procedural changes are also common, and many of those changes are indeed innovative.

On the other hand, the conventional characterization is one of little or no innovation, and indeed substantial resistance to change of any sort. This characterization of the public bureaucracy has appeared consistently in the popular literature and also has appeared in some academic literature on these institutions (Kaufman 1976; but see MacCarthaigh 2014). The assumption is not so much that public organizations do not change as much as it is that once created they find the means of surviving, even in political environments that may not be especially supportive of the organizations or their intended purposes.

Some of the same persistence can be observed in public policies, even though policies may change more than the organizations implementing them. Even if public policies do change, the majority of those changes will be incremental rather than fundamental, involving relatively minor changes at any one time (Hayes 2006). Those incremental changes can, however, cumulate into more significant change.[1] Therefore, any public

---

[1] This, in turn leads on to the question of the difference between an increment and more fundamental change (see Dempster and Wildavsky 1979). That said, knowing precisely what an innovation is can also be difficult. For example, was Obamacare in the United States an innovation when very similar programs were already operating in several states, and the federal-level initiative was modeled on those existing programs? Chapter 1 of this volume provides a useful definition of innovation that will inform this chapter.

policy that has been in place for a number of years, e. g., pension programs in industrial democracies, will be significantly different from the program at its initiation, with the current program typically representing numerous small changes over the lifetime of the program.

These very fundamental interpretations of stability and change within the public sector lead on to asking whether innovation is likely within the public sector. And further we should attempt to understand what factors can enhance or inhibit innovation, and change more generally, within the public sector. This chapter looks primarily at theoretical perspectives coming from institutional theory to examine the sources of resistance to change, and then utilizes the logic of those several theoretical approaches to consider ways of both making institutions more malleable and making public policies within the public sector more open to change of all sorts and perhaps particularly to innovation.

And finally by way of introduction one must ask what really constitutes innovation? There appear to be few genuine innovations in public sector institutions but a good deal of change, diffusion of innovations and copying from the private sector and from other governments (see Moore and Hartley 2008). While constructing a proposed change that an actor in the public sector favors, it may be useful to define that change as an innovation. The claims of innovation and newness may have some political power, but they also may be hyperbolic. And indeed arguing at times that a simple reform or policy diffusion is truly innovatory may not be such good poetics, as untried changes may raise concerns among more skeptical members of the organization, and also among controllers such as ministries of finance.

Thus, the question is to what extent innovations in the public sector are internally generated or reflect diffusion from other governments or the private sector. Both of these processes of change are important, and both require overcoming institutionalized patterns of policy and administration. Therefore, I examine change in a somewhat more generic manner than might be expected were this chapter totally about innovation *de novo*. I will be arguing that those processes of transformation are closely analogous, so that the differences may be of degree rather than of type.

The other question that is implicit in the study of innovation in the public sector is the extent to which there is a confirmation bias in the analysis. That is, the previous chapters give examples of innovation in the public sector (see also Tonurist, Kattel and Lember 2015). That is undeniable, but what level of innovation should we expect? How many failed attempts at innovation have there been that are not being recorded by advocates of innovation (or at least by scholars who are committed to the idea of innovation in the public sector)? And how many possibilities for innovation are not attempted because the barriers to change are obvious to potential innovators? Given that most of the innovation literature is written by apparent advocates, there seems to be inadequate consideration of the rates of success and failure in producing change.

16.1   Changing Institutions

The usual characterization, or even stereotype, of institutions is that they are stable to the point of being ossified. Indeed, much of the logic for creating strong institutions within the public sector is to ensure predictability of responses to citizens and other social actors. While we tend to think of bureaucracies as just those types of ossified institutions we need to remember that Weber was arguing in favor of creating predictability and "knowability" in how citizens would be treated by government, in contrast to the particularistic manner in which they may have been treated by other forms of public organization. One person's innovation may be another person's "arbitrary and capricious action."[2]

The common sense understanding of institutions leads us to expect stability and an absence of change, but so too do most institutional theories. While these theories do vary in the extent to which they anticipate or even permit change, they all tend to assume that institutions attempt to produce predictability and to replicate themselves across time. Given those assumptions we might expect a rather gradual transformation of institutions. Further, even when there are significant changes within an institution the assumption is that over time these structures will have a tendency to return to their fundamental type, and perhaps replicate the *status quo ante* within the institution.

Although one may expect stability, or ossification, from any institution the public bureaucracy is perhaps particularly subject to that malady. As already noted that rigidity is in part by design but in part it represents the capacity of the organizations within the bureaucracy, as well as the institution itself, to develop protections against change.[3] As I discuss the processes of innovation in public bureaucracies, I will attempt to make some differentiations among types and levels of innovation.

To this point I have been discussing innovation in a relatively undifferentiated manner, but we can think about at least three levels at which innovation may occur. These three levels will involve different degrees of

[2] This phrase comes from the Administrative Procedures Act of 1946.

[3] One of the classic concerns in institutional theory is making the distinction between organizations and institutions. I am drawing on the now familiar argument of Douglass North that institutions are the rules of game and organizations are the teams playing the game.

challenge to the existing institutional arrangements. That said, however, even the simplest level of change may challenge the institution. Even seemingly simple aspects of the repertoires of organizations may in fact be embedded in the meaning of the organization and hence may challenge the *status quo* within the organization or institution. And the varieties of change may also have differential connections to institutional theory.

As implied earlier some innovations in policy may be changes in policy instruments, or parts of administrative routines, seemingly rather minor but often possessing significant political linkages (Peters 2002). At a second level, there are programs that integrate instruments, laws and other resources to provide public services. And at a third level are the institutions or organizations themselves that may have multiple pro- grams, but also utilize routines, rule and symbols to control the actions of the participants within them.

For public bureaucracies, and even for many private bureaucracies, perhaps the major innovative challenge is to de-bureaucratize. While there has been substantial pressure for change, driven both by desires for increased efficiency (Koppenjan 2012) and increased humanity, the bureaucratic form has been a hardy perennial. Even when faced with more fluid environments and greater uncertainty the more formal mode of organization has persisted, and remains institutionalized in most public sectors. Although there are a number of ways to consider the persistence of this organizational form in the face of possible innovation, institutional theory does provide some insights.

16.1.1 Historical Institutionalism

Without discussing all the possible variations in institutional theory it is useful to look at two that appear to represent the two ends of a dimen- sion of the openness of institutions to change. On one end of that dimension *historical institutionalism* rather famously argues that policies are shaped by path dependency, and therefore policy choices made during the formative period of the organization are likely to persist during the existence of the organization (see Steinmo 2008). The excep- tion to that, at least in the original versions of the approach, was change through punctuated equilibrium, representing a major change in the policy regime being implemented, and therefore perhaps an innovation in the terms of this conference.

The logic of path dependency in historical institutionalism arose first from empirical observations, such as those mentioned in the first para- graphs of this chapter, that government organizations appear to have some bias toward stability and even permanence. That observation originally had arisen in economics (see David 2001), where presumably rational actors tended to persist in utilizing sub-optimal solutions and products even when clearly superior options were available. The economists' answer to this apparent paradox was transaction costs, based on a perception that the benefits obtained from any change to the superior solution would be less than the costs resulting from the process of change.

In political science several answers are commonly available to understand why programs persist. One is simple inertia (see Rose and Davies 1984). In other words, without any particular calculation of costs and benefits the *status quo* holds a strong sway over actors in the public sector (and perhaps also in the private sector). A second and more satisfying explanation is that the actors involved – clients as well as administrators and politicians – receive positive feedback from the existing program (Pierson 2000). These positive feedbacks may be in terms of financial rewards, prestige or success in competition with other organizations in government. Whatever the nature of the rewards, they reinforce eliciting programs and tend to reduce changes (including innovations).

A third explanation, which may move the discussion closer to the possibilities of innovation, is that the *status quo* persists because there is no real alternative to the current program. This perspective on institutions argues that for change to occur a viable alternative must be available (Peters, Pierre and King 2005). This perspective is analogous to the Advocacy-Coalition Framework in policy analysis (Sabatier and Weible 2007) that examines the manner in which conflicting views of policy are reconciled and policy change can occur. This perspective does provide more of an opportunity for innovation but still requires that the innovation overcomes the presumption of superiority of an existing program.

As already noted the original perspective on historical institutionalism was that change occurred through punctuated equilibrium, implying a significant transformation of the policy area. This original discussion did not provide much insight into where those punctuations would come from, or how they could be explained, but this did provide at least a description of change. Subsequent developments have provided models of change that more closely approximate incremental change. In particular, Streek and Thelen (2005; see also Mahoney and Thelen 2010) discuss methods such as layering, and displacement that maintain a significant part of the existing policy but add new components or reinterpret that existing policy. While these may not appear to constitute innovations, they do represent potentially important changes in policies of the institution.

16.1.2 Sociological Institutionalism

The original version of the New Institutionalism, hereafter referred to as sociological institutionalism, is perhaps the easiest to change, or at least the easiest for fostering innovation within the public sector. In this perspective institutions are defined by ongoing patterns of symbols, routines, myths, etc. The institution is maintained by socializing new members into these values, meaning that in this case the preferences of members are defined endogenously, while in other versions of institutionalism, such as the rational choice versions, the preferences of members are defined exogenously. Further, given that most members of an institution will belong to several institutions – a bureaucrat is also a member of a family, perhaps a church or some social organizations, etc. – change may occur through attempts to reconcile those values. Therefore individual members of institutions must not only learn a set of values but they must learn when to invoke each specific set of values.

The stability of institutions in this model depends upon the success of the institution in socializing its new members. Although we can think about this process in the abstract, not all institutions will have the same demands for conformity. For example, the military requires high levels of uniformity of behavior, while universities tend to revel in their diversity. Further, institutions that have values more compatible with the general values in the society will be more likely to be successful in that process of socialization.

The opportunity for change comes when the values of the institution are in conflict with those that the members bring with them from outside the institution, whether personal or those of other organizations of which the individual is also a member (see Brunson and Olsen 1993). For example, given that members of the general population represent the raw material for institutions, if differences emerge between the values of the society and those of the institution then some sort of adjustment will be required.[4] Likewise, if members of the institution can observe there are significant differences between espoused values of the institution and the behaviors of it and its members, then again conflicts will emerge. All that said, the need to constantly replace members tends to place continuing pressures on institutions for change, albeit generally gradual change.

We might consider discursive institutionalism (Schmidt 2010) as a natural extension of the sociological institutionalism. In this version of institutionalism the institution is defined through the discourses that

---

[4] For example, when the US Army was engaged in Vietnam it found that the soldiers being drafted at that time had very different values than did the soldiers during World War II and Korea. Therefore, the institution had to change to be more participative and to depend less upon authority.

define the purposes and practices of that institution. Thus, like the older sociological version within the general institutional approach the institution is largely defined through values and ideas – in this case they are defined through discourses. However, unlike the sociological institutionalism, the equilibrium in an institution is only defined temporarily, and part of the logic of this version of institutionalism is that internal discourses are in conflict and that is a source of change.

16.2   Making Institutions More Innovative

The previous discussion emphasized the static nature of institutions in the public sector – especially bureaucracies – and the difficulties in making these structures more innovative. As already noted, that is the conventional wisdom about these institutions and it is often borne out in reality. Given that tendency toward conservatism and stasis, how can institutions be designed or modified in order to facilitate greater adaptability? And as a subsidiary question, how can innovations be designed to make them more palatable to institutions that are almost inherently suspicious about change?

Some time ago Herbert Simon argued (1947) quite persuasively that much of what we know about public administration comes in the form of dichotomies, with both halves of the dichotomy having value as advice for would-be designers of organizations. For example, both centralization and decentralization were common "proverbs of administration," and choosing either half of the dichotomy would produce some benefits for an institution, but once chosen the virtues of the other half of the dichotomy would soon become apparent. Thus, much of the reform of administration has been moving back and forth between the two poles of a dichotomy, and in the end actually changing the organization relatively little.

The same dichotomization can be argued to exist for understanding the capacity of public sector organizations to innovate. In this initial part of the discussion of mechanisms for fostering innovation I discuss several possible dichotomies and demonstrate how either half of the pairs of concepts might be conducive to enhanced innovation. The presence of reasonable arguments for both sides of the dichotomy then naturally leads to the need to specify the conditions under which one or the other of those conditions may be more appropriate than the other in designing institutions and in changing existing institutions.

16.2.1   Crisis

It can be argued that crises in the public sector can be a spur to innovation. When faced with significant and unanticipated problems the public sector may have to find or invent new means of solving problems, and of organizing itself to solve those problems. These attempts to find new solutions may be in response of natural disasters, such as the Ebola outbreak in West Africa, or to human-made crises such as the Great Recession (Dodd-Frank in the United States, for example), but in either case the public sector may be motivated to examine its methods of operation and to adopt new, if perhaps untried, options for addressing the issues.

On the other hand, however, crises may provoke governments into defending and reinforcing existing patterns of behavior. Even major crises organizations, as well as individuals, tend to invoke existing protocols and run through the usual procedures even if, obviously, they are not working. The crisis management literature (see, for example, Goodhart 2008) points out the extent to which actors involved in a crisis tend to code the events in terms with which they are familiar and then also tend to follow existing procedures to attempt to "solve" the problem. In the case of the economic crisis, for example, many countries simply persisted in the same policies and procedures for economic management as had been used for decades, often thereby failing to address adequately a problem that was substantially more serious than it was understood to be.

Crisis also places strong pressures for responses onto public sector organizations that may prevent innovatory responses. Seemingly effective innovation requires some time for rethinking the *status quo* and developing new options, time that may be lacking in crisis. Persistence of established routines in the face of failure may therefore be the only available short-term option for policy makers, even within organizations that are intended to cope with, and manage, crisis, e.g., the military.[5] Thus, although innovation, and often profound innovation, ultimately may materialize from crisis, that outcome may be delayed, and Standard Operating Procedures will prevail.

16.2.2 Insulation or Involvement?

The conventional negative description of public bureaucratic organizations is that they are relatively insular, operating with their own legal foundations and their own values. This Weberian aloofness may enable

---

[5] Military history is filled with examples of generals fighting the last war, rather than innovating in the face of new challenges. The Vietnam War is but one of many examples. The military tends to be a conservative institution and hence may be unwilling to grasp new organizational and management patterns even as it grasps new material technologies.

them to maintain their particular approaches to policy and to processes of delivering policies. On the other hand, these are organizations that exist within the *public* bureaucracy and therefore are obliged to be involved to some extent with the society and with their clients and stakeholders.

The conventional assumption on the roots of innovation would be that openness to influences from the environment would be the principal sources of innovation (see Styhre 2007). Those external pressures on the organization would, within the framework provided by sociological institutionalism, produce change by having external values conflicting with the internalized values of the institution, or perhaps from the failure of those existing institutional perspectives to meet the expectations of actors in that environment. Feldman and Pentland (2005), for example, have looked at the effects of environmental change on the routines that may define institutions and described the interactions between change and routine. Thus, in this perspective, change will result from a mismatch of routines with the environmental conditions, with organizational autonomy being essential to the adaptation.

On the other hand, however, those external actors can also be a source of conservatism and an absence of change. If an existing institution is capable of supplying desired services to their clientele and protecting the interests of those clients within the policymaking system then the societal actors may well resist and innovations will be minimized. They may even resist process innovations that may seemingly increase efficiency but may potentially have negative impacts on the client group.[6] Thus, an institution that is more embedded with client groups or other dimensions of their relevant environment may find it more difficult to change than one less embedded.

As a result, more insulated institutions or organizations may be able to develop their own innovations if they lack strong pressures for conformity from their environment.[7] Thus, more turbulent environments may both demand and permit higher levels of innovation in public sector organizations (Clegg, Kornberger and Rhodes 2005; Lægreid, Roness and Verhoest 2011). And organizations with autonomy should be able to make decisions that are more creative than can those that are more

---

[6] That type of innovation may benefit the public purse and/or the organization itself, but clients may consider it as reducing the quality of services, especially services that involve direct personal services. Public sector labor unions may also resist changes that reduce levels of employment within the organization.

[7] The conventional institutionalist argument has been that environments, generally conceived of as composed of other institutions, would force conformity on institutional formats if not also on behaviors (Dimaggio and Powell 1983).

directly attached to other organization either above political organizations or below social actors.

16.2.3 Politicization

Given the involvement of organizations with their clients and other social actors, we can also make apparently contradictory arguments about the extent to which political officials control organizations. And just like the control of organizations through links with the socioeconomic environment, links with political leadership may also have somewhat ambiguous consequences. And much of the logic explaining this ambiguity is the same as for the social actors.

Political leaders may invest a good deal of energy and political capital in driving innovation in the public sector. In many instances the reforms being implemented have been based on biased assumptions about the poor performance and shirking within the bureaucracy – this was certainly true for much of the New Public Management. In other cases, however, the reforms have been more positive and seek to open the system more generally to innovation and to more creative use of public sector resources and power. Some of the more participatory reforms of the public sector in Canada and the United States (see Peters 2001), and to some extent in other countries, intended allowing public sector organizations and their employees to make truly innovative changes in the manner in which they worked.

Given the links with social actors, the capacity of public organizations to work without direct political control may aid in designing and implementing reforms to their own processes and programs than organizations that are more closely controlled. With greater autonomy it may be possible for these organizations to make extensive reforms in their more fundamental nature, as in the case of some "reinvention movement" in the United States. These reforms were particularly important in de-bureaucratizing the public sector and permitting greater freedom for civil servants, who were fostering reforms from within in their quotidian working lives in making more fundamental changes.

The perspective on innovation contained in this brief section is that political leadership may have the capacity to open doors for innovation but may be less successful in actually creating those innovations. That is, career bureaucrats are more likely to be expert and to have substantive policy ideas about how best to change policy. But those bureaucrats often encounter difficulties in moving innovations, other than perhaps in relatively simple aspects of procedure, from ideas into action. And for more significant innovations in policy and institutional structures, administrators may be rather impotent.

16.2.4   Expertise and Professionalism

The level of expertise and professionalism is yet another dimension describing public organizations and influencing their capacity to innovate. While the specialization of public organizations creates some level of expertise for virtually all of them, the technical content of their functions will make some more expert than others – the Nuclear Regulatory Commission is more expert than the General Services Administration. If we focus on higher levels of expertise and specialization in organizations, that expertise may both contribute to innovation and make innovation more difficult.

As well as having the expertise contained within an organization, these organizations can be closely connected with expert organizations within their environment. Whereas the earlier discussion of links with social actors emphasizes that the members of those groups will attempt to preserve their *droits acquises*, the impact of linkages with epistemic communities (Zito 2001) may have more variable effects on innovation. These expert groups are often more interested in changing law and policy than they are in preserving the *status quo*. These groups may be interested in implementing the best practice in the field with which they are concerned and therefore will want to innovate.

But while social actors who are recipients of government benefits may defend the *status quo* for reasons of self-interest, expert groups may defend that *status quo* if they believe the proposed innovation is potentially retrograde for their field. This was seen, for example, in a number of cases in environmental policy when proposed "innovations" (often coming from governments of the political right) in the field are perceived as harmful. These groups would also oppose policy change, although not from self-interest so much as from professional and/or ideological commitment to the *status quo*.

The professional nature of organizations in the public sector may reflect the level of specialization of the organizations, but again there may be contradictory arguments about the effects on innovation. On the one hand, highly specialized organizations may be able to insulate themselves from external pressures, claiming expertise and the need to maintain their patterns of action. On the other hand, highly specialized organizations are more likely to be linked with professional and organizational networks with other experts who will diffuse "best practice" and ideas for change.

16.2.5   Success and Failure

Aaron Wildavsky (1980: 62ff) famously argued that policy is often its own cause, meaning that policy choices made at one time may help define the choices that will be made subsequently. Further, Peters and Hogwood (1986) argued that there was relatively little true innovation in public policy, with most policy changes being merely revisions of existing policies. As discussed earlier, there are significant questions about what actually constitutes a policy innovation, but to the extent that there are such innovations they may be driven by the nature of existing policies. In particular, failed policies may be expected to produce attempts to innovate and remedy the defects in the existing policy.

Given the aforementioned, policy failure is not as easily defined or even recognized as might be assumed (McConnell 2010). Failure is often in the eye of the beholder and can be framed based upon political or ideological criteria (Zittoun 2014). That framing will not only define the possibilities for change (innovation) but also the type of change that may be introduced. In particular, policy failure is rarely so abject that fundamental change is perceived to be required. From the perspective of historical institutionalism the basic path may be sufficiently well-defined so that fundamental change is not likely.

As we have argued previously sub-optimal policies are likely to persist unless there is a viable alternative (Peters, Pierre and King 2005). Thus innovation or diffusion may be necessary for change even when performance of the existing program is weak. That is even more likely to be true when the policies in place are successful, or at least are perceived to be successful. When an existing program does indeed appear to work, then change is likely to resemble the learning and advocacy processes associated with Sabatier's model, rather than a sharp punctuated change from the past. And again we must decide whether this change constitutes a genuine innovation, and whether there are any fundamental distinctions.

Again, the level at which change is being proposed will affect the extent to which failure, or even success, is likely to engender successful innovation. Confronting failure of the program or institution as a whole may appear to require replacement even more than the failure of an instrument, but is also less likely. That level of innovation may require reconceptualization of the policy area, and may thereby upset a number of entrenched ideas and interests (Payan 2006). That level of change may occur, as expected by the original logic of historical institutionalism, but the more incremental level of change continues to dominate.

16.3 Summary and Conclusions

This chapter has provided a very preliminary discussion of why innovation can be difficult within the public sector, as well as some of the means through which innovation might be fostered. Institutional theories, as well as most institutions themselves, find it easier to cope with persistence than with change, whether that change is a genuine innovation or a more incremental adaptation to the environment. There are a number of factors that may explain higher levels of change within institutions, but few if any of these are unambiguous.

The ambiguity of the possible facilitators of innovation in public sector institutions is made even more difficult because many of these conditions are difficult to manipulate, or may – as in the case of increased organizational autonomy – represent innovations of their own. There is therefore a crucial political question as well as a question for organizational theory when considering options for innovation. The conditions for innovation may need to be constructed rather than assumed, and that will in itself require some political innovation. And even if the political battles are successful the changes that were being sought are far from guaranteed. Thus, beginning with organizations may be necessary for understanding these processes of change but it is not sufficient for explaining the success or failure of innovation efforts.

References

Brunsson, N. and Olsen, J. P. 1993. *The Reforming Organization*. London: Routledge.

Carter, P. 2012. "Policy as palimpsest," *Policy & Politics* 40(3): 423–43.

Clegg, S. R., Kornberger, M. and Rhodes, C. 2005. "Learning/Becoming/Organizing," *Organization* 12(2): 147–67.

David, P. A. 2001. "Path dependence, its critics, and the quest for 'Historical Economics,'" in P. Garrouste and S. Ionnides (eds.), *Evolution and Path Dependence in Economic Ideas*. Cheltenham: Edward Elgar, pp. 15–40.

Dempster, M. A. H. and Wildavsky, A. 1979. "On change: Or, there is no magic size for an increment," *Political Studies* 27(3): 371–89.

Dimaggio, P. and Powell, W. 1983. "The iron cage revisited: Institutional isomorphism and collective rationality in organizational fields," *American Sociological Review* 48(2): 147–60.

Feldman, M. S. and Pentland, B. 2005. "Organization routines and macro-actors," in B. Czarniawska and T. Hernes (eds.), *Actor-Network Theorizing and Action*. Malmö: Liber, pp. 91–111.

Goodhart, C, A. E. 2008. "The regulatory response to the financial crisis," *Journal of Financial Stability* 4(4): 351–68.

Hayes, M. T. 2006. *Incrementalism and Public Policy*. Lanham, MD: University Press of America.

Hogwood, B. W. and Peters, B. G. 1986. *Policy Dynamics*. Brighton: Wheatsheaf.

Kaufman, H. A. 1976. *Are Government Organizations Immortal?* Washington, DC: The Brookings Institution.

Koppenjan, J. F. M. 2012. *The New Public Governance in Public Service Delivery*. The Hague: Eleven International Publishing.

Lægreid, P., Roness, P. G. and Verhoest, K. 2011. "Explaining the innovative culture and activities of state agencies," *Organization Studies* 32(10): 1321–47.

Light, P. C. 2002. *Government's Greatest Achievements: From Civil Rights to Homeland Defense*. Washington, DC: The Brookings Institution.

MacCarthaigh, M. 2014. "Agency termination in Ireland: Culls or bonfires, or life after death?" *Public Administration* 92(4): 1017–37.

Mahoney, J. and Thelen, K. 2010. *Explaining Institutional Change: Ambiguity, Agency and Power*. Cambridge: Cambridge University Press.

McConnell, A. 2010. *Understanding Policy Success: Rethinking Public Policy*. Basingstoke: Macmillan.

March, J. G. and Olsen, J. P. 1989. *Rediscovering Institutions: The Organizational Basis of Politics*. New York: The Free Press.

Moore, M. and Hartley, J. 2008. "Innovations in governance," *Public Management Review* 10(1): 3–20.

Payan, T. 2006. *Cops, Soldiers, and Diplomats: Explaining Agency Behavior in the War on Drugs*. Lanham: Lexington Books.

Peters, B. G. 2001. *The Future of Governing*, 2nd edition. Lawrence: University Press of Kansas.

  2002. "The politics of policy instruments," in L. M. Salamon (ed.), *The Tools of Government*. New York: Oxford University Press, pp. 552–64.

Peters, B. G., Pierre, J. and King, D. S. 2005. "The politics of path dependency: political conflict in historical institutionalism," *Journal of Politics* 67(4): 1275–1300.

Pierson, P. 2000. "Increasing returns, path dependence and the study of politics," *American Political Science Review* 94(2): 251–67.

Rose, R. and Davies, P. L. 1984. *Inheritance in Public Policy: Change without Choice in Britain*. New Haven, CT: Yale University Press.

Sabatier, P. A. and Weible, C. 2007. "The advocacy-coalition: Innovations and clarifications," in P. A. Sabatier (ed.), *Theories of the Policy Process*. Boulder, CO: Westview, pp. 117–68.

Schmidt, V. A. 2010. "Taking ideas and discourse seriously: Explaining change through discursive institutionalism as the fourth new institutionalism," *European Political Science Review* 2(1): 1–25.

Schwartz, J. E. 1984. *America's Hidden Success: A Reassessment of Twenty Years of Public Policy*. New York: W. W. Norton.

Simon, H. A. 1947. *Administrative Behavior*. New York: Harper & Row.

Steinmo, S. 2008. "Historical institutionalism," in D. Della Porta and M. Keating (eds.), *Approaches and Methodologies in the Social Sciences: A Pluralist Approach*. Cambridge: Cambridge University Press, pp. 118–38.

Streek, W. and Thelen, K. 2005. *Beyond Continuity: Institutional Change in Advanced Political Economies*. Oxford: Oxford University Press.

Styhre, A. 2007. *The Innovative Bureaucracy: Bureaucracy in an Age of Fluidity*. London: Routledge.

Tonurist, P., Kattel, R. and Lember, V. 2015. "Discovering innovation labs in the public sector," Working Papers in Technology, Governance and Economic Dynamics 61. Tallinn: Tallinn University of Technology.

Wildavsky, A. 1980. "Policy as its own cause," in A. Wildavsky (ed.), *Policy: The Art and Craft of Policy Analysis*. London: Macmillan.

Zito, A. R. 2001. "Epistemic communities, collective entrepreneurship and European integration," *Journal of European Public Policy* 8(4): 586–603.

Zittoun, P. 2014. *The Political Process of Policymaking*. Basingstoke: Macmillan.

17 Conclusion
Governing Innovation and Innovating Governance

Jacob Torfing and Peter Triantafillou

17.1 The Loop between Public Innovation and Public Governance

This book has aimed to foster a theoretical and practical *rapprochement* between the rising scholarly interest in public innovation and the steadily growing research on public governance. The two bodies of literature need to speak to each other because public innovation may be enhanced through governance reforms and because, conversely, governance reforms hinge on innovation of the ways in which public organizations and private stakeholders design, produce and disseminate public services.

Economic slumps, inner-city decay, persistent high levels of unemployment, ageing populations in need of care, large waves of migration, climate challenges and gang-related crime are just a few examples of the mounting fiscal, social and political pressures on the public sector. Problems and challenges are piling up, and public resources are scarce. The standard reaction of public leaders and managers has been to find new ways of reducing public expenditure and raising public revenues in order to find the means to finance new programmes and additional services. However, after decades of performance management and economic rationalization, it has become increasingly difficult to find and cut slack in public service organizations, and the economic gains incurred from contracting out seem to be dwindling as time goes by (Petersen, Hjelmar and Vrangbæk 2015). At the same time, raising the tax burden on labour power and private corporations seems to be increasingly less appealing to elected politicians as global competition continues to become tighter. Public innovation holds the promise of helping us to find new and better solutions to wicked problems and to redesign public services in ways that give us more for less.

Innovation is currently receiving a growing attention at all levels of governance, but there is still considerable resistance to the new public

The corresponding author for this chapter is Jacob Torfing.

innovation agenda. Elected politicians and middle managers are risk averse and fear that public innovations may go wrong, failing to deliver promised results, and thus may jeopardize their political or administrative careers. Executive public managers are keen to maintain control over what goes on in their organization and may fear that innovation processes that take place close to the front line, cut across organizational boundaries or involve external for-profit and non-profit actors undermine their ability to stay on top of things. Last but not least, public employees and service users are seldom interested in having their habits, routines and services disturbed by new and innovative solutions. They know what they have, but not what they get if new and innovative solutions are introduced. As such, the seeds of innovation may fall on a hard and stony ground. Occasionally, flowers may grow and blossom when urgent problems and new ideas are conjoined by energetic entrepreneurs with strong alliances and the right timing (Kingdon 1984), but many attempts to foster innovative policies and services are aborted or killed in their infancy by political or administrative opposition rooted in pre-emptive attempts to avoid disturbance, uncertainty and risks.

The resistance to innovation from the actors in and around the public sector is supplemented by a large number of institutional and organizational barriers. Centralized control may limit the discretionary power of public employees and restrict the room for local experimentation. Political and administrative silos prevent mutual learning and exchange of ideas. Rule-based decision making may discourage public employees from searching for alternative and perhaps smarter options. Incentive systems may reward stable service production. Competition between service deliverers may prevent joint problem-solving and diffusion of new ideas and methods. The reduction of citizens and users to clients in bureaucratic welfare programmes or customers in public and private service markets prevents the public sector from tapping into their experiences, ideas and resources. The list appears to be endless, but it should not make us forget that public innovation is both possible and frequent despite the unfavourable conditions.

It is precisely because public innovation is likely to face resistance and barriers that we have to think about how governance reforms can enhance public innovation. By transforming the way that public organizations are governed, changing their structure and function and recasting the role and identity of public leaders and managers, we might succeed in breaking down some of the resistance to public innovation and removing some of the barriers. The public and intellectual demand for stability, rational decision making and impartiality was largely satisfied by the creation of a rule-based and functionally divided public bureaucracy. Starting in the

1980s, the quest for efficiency and cost savings led public decision makers all over the world to embrace the new managerialism that put public managers in charge of a thorough contractualization of the public sector that paved the way for rationalization of public service organizations and introduction of private contractors. If the public agenda is now changing and we want to stimulate public innovation, we must transform public governance once more, in order to enhance its innovative capacity while still respecting the continued demands for democratic legitimacy, impartiality and cost efficiency.

The wish to transform public governance brings us back to the demand for innovation, only this time it is not policy or service innovation, but governance innovation we are looking for (see Hartley and Torfing 2016). In other words, first-order innovation in public policy, services and the organizational support system is predicated on second-order innovation in the wider system of public governance. This is exactly what creates the loop between innovation and governance and ties the two bodies of literature together.

17.2   The Promise of New Public Governance?

As argued in the Introduction, the three governance paradigms are all, each in their specific ways, both supporting and hampering innovation. Therefore, it is not so much a question of choosing one particular governance paradigm instead of the others as it is a question about how to combine and balance elements from the different paradigms. Nevertheless, if public innovation is enhanced by multi-actor collaboration, there is good reason to expect that a further development and employment of New Public Governance will help us to stimulate public innovation. Indeed, New Public Governance is likely to spur public innovation because it introduces a more collaborative and pluricentric form of public governance and because it seems to put a larger premium on public innovation. Let us briefly consider the extent to which the various chapters support this claim.

Chapter 2 lends conditional support to the call for a more collaborative governance paradigm. Collaborative problem-solving poses high rewards in terms of finding innovative solutions to complex problems but also high risks in terms of conflicts, capture and deadlocks. Successful innovation depends on whether the stakeholders are willing to participate and engage with each other in constructive ways that develop a joint ownership over the collaborative process and its outcomes. If the stakeholders mainly participate to protect their self-interests we are not likely to see any collaboration, nor any innovation. Hence, much depends on a facilitative leadership aiming to transform the stakeholders into constructive and creative problem-solvers. Chapter 4 provides a number of examples of public innovation from around the world and finds that multi-actor collaboration is often a key lever, and Chapter 6 explains why collaboration tends to spur innovation and reflects on how participation in collaborative innovation may require a shift in the role perceptions of public and private actors that brings us closer to New Public Governance. Chapter 5 argues that New Public Governance is likely to promote and diffuse innovation because it allows innovation to come from anywhere and involves a plethora of public and private actors who can make different contributions to the innovation process. Chapter 3 highlights the potentials of collaboration in governing the risks associated with the implementation of innovative solutions. Stakeholders need to negotiate and come to agreement about the level of risk that they are prepared to accept vis-à-vis the gains they hope to achieve. Hence, a New Public Governance paradigm that spurs multi-actor collaboration is likely to strengthen all phases of the innovation process.

Chapter 3 also claims that a shift to New Public Governance is needed in order to transform the role of service users from passive recipients to co-producers and co-creators of new and better public services. Professionals in public service organizations play a crucial role in unlocking the sticky knowledge of service users and combining it with their own professional knowledge. The call for mutual interaction and constructive communication between professionals and service uses is echoed in Chapter 8, which highlights the role of unpaid volunteers in co-producing and co-creating public services, thereby stimulating innovation. Chapter 7 highlights the collaboration between groups of professionals and between professionals and public managers who need to connect and interact in more systematic ways in order to enhance innovation. Chapter 9 also calls for the creation of collaborative relations along the vertical axis of public governance. While competition between political parties and individual politicians in elected assemblies and standing committees may spur policy innovation, there is much more to be gained from creating arenas in which politicians can collaborate with each other as well as with public managers and relevant stakeholders that can help them to understand the problems or challenges at hand and provide new ideas about how they can be solved or responded to. Chapter 10 focuses on how public–private interaction can stimulate innovation and finds that both market-based contracting-out and procurement schemes and more collaborative forms of partnerships and partnering can stimulate public innovation. However, there is considerable room for improvement of the institutional design of the conditions for public–private interaction, both in relation to the emerging New Public Governance paradigm and in relation to the existing forms of interaction based on New Public Management. The common thread that ties together all these chapters is the idea that collaboration rather than hierarchical relations of command and control and competitive relations associated with distrust and rivalry will help to spur public innovation and calls for the introduction of ideas associated with New Public Governance. This paradigm cannot and should not replace the existing governance paradigms but rather supplement, engage and ultimately transform their operational practices in order to enhance innovation.

Both Chapter 11 and Chapter 12 suggest that all three governance paradigms contain important innovation drivers. Chapter 11 focuses on organizational forms of public governance and argues that both hierarchy and specialization, which are key features of old-school bureaucratic governance, and devolution, autonomy and contracting out, which are core aspects of New Public Management, can spur innovation in the public sector, but so can networks, partnerships and institutional arenas for co-creation. Chapter 12 finds that both command and incentive systems under certain conditions may enhance public innovation, but it depends on how these governance tools are perceived. Moreover, it is important for the creative performance of public employees that their public service motivation is not crowded out by the use of sticks and carrots and that they feel that they are recognized by the manager, have sufficient autonomy and enjoy considerable job safety – something that is an integral part of the kind of trust-based management recommended by New Public Governance. By comparison, Chapter 14 is much more critical of Classical Public Administration and New Public Management when it comes to fashioning an accountability system conducive for public innovation. The current indicator-based accountability systems hamper innovation and need to be reformed in order to be able to deal with complexity. Chapter 15 agrees that we need to develop new accountability systems, but these should complement rather than replace the existing accountability systems. Finally Chapter 13 argues that it is a core task for public leaders to redesign incentive and accountability systems in ways that make it favourable for public employees to innovate. More generally, the chapter calls for the development of new skills and capacities of public leaders and managers who in their attempt to spur innovation must create a supportive external and internal environment, carefully select problems and challenges, and develop a realistic strategy and facilitate its implementation. In many ways this is a new kind of innovation management that goes beyond the notion of strategic management advocated by New Public Management.

In sum, there is substantial evidence in support of the hypothesis that a shift towards New Public Governance will tend to spur innovation to the benefit of citizens and society at large. However, the support comes with two important caveats. First, the beneficial effects of a turn towards a further institutionalization of collaborative forms of governance will only occur under a particular set of conditions of which a facilitative leadership is a prerequisite. Second, the two other governance paradigms also have much to offer and should be not eliminated but integrated with New Public Governance. Accordingly, one of the fundamental political challenges facing the public administration over the next decade is to strike the right balance between different ways of governing and being governed.

17.3   How Can We Transform Governance?

The authors who have contributed to this volume have from their different vantage points offered a broad range of recommendations concerning how to transform public governance in order to enhance innovation. We have clustered the recommendations into three groups focusing on organizational design, steering instruments and the exercise of leadership and management.

17.3.1   *Organizational Design*

In order to engage politicians and stimulate innovative policies and services we must create new institutional arenas where they can interact with public employees with specialized knowledge and a range of relevant and affected citizens and private stakeholder who have different experiences, perspectives and ideas and hold resources and competences that can support implementation of new and smarter solutions. A key challenge is to craft arenas that engage politicians in collaborative processes in which centripetal, rather than centrifugal, forces predominate (Chapter 8). Another challenge is to ensure the design of organizational procedures that enable politicians to tap into the resources and ideas of lay actors while ensuring democratic legitimacy and accountability. This requires a close interaction between formal institutions of government and more informal governance institutions.

When it comes to public administration, the task is not so much to break down specialized, organizational silos but rather to drill holes in them and facilitate collaboration between different administrative departments, agencies and units (Chapter 11). There is also a persistent call for opening up public organizations through the creation of inter-organizational networks and partnerships between public and private actors at multiple levels (Chapters 2, 6 and 10). The challenge is to institutionalize networks and partnerships in order to facilitate stable interaction, while simultaneously preserving the flexibility gains that can be obtained from networking and partnering in complex and changing ways.

Public service organizations must also enhance their capacity to facilitate co-production and co-creation through an active involvement of citizens either as users or as unpaid volunteers. This requires a transformation of the organizational culture so that service users are regarded as competent and resourceful actors who can contribute to the improvement and innovation of public services. It also requires investment in public governance infrastructures: the expansion of co-production and co-creation is not free, but requires the crafting of communities of practices that include lead users, volunteers and other private stakeholders (Chapters 3 and 8). We must develop organizational designs that involve the citizens in co-production and co-creation, but the public sector must also build a capacity to support innovation initiatives coming from citizens who to a larger or lesser extent seek to involve public authorities in their projects. Citizen involvement in public innovation and public involvement in social innovation must complement and reinforce each other.

Last but not least, public sector institutions must promote organizational learning through experimentation, critical reflection and retention of novel insights and ideas. While organizational learning is always facing obstacles such as the desire for political control and risk aversion, we have seen that it is possible to promulgate organizational values favouring curiosity, openness, contestation and entrepreneurship (Chapters 6 and 15).

17.3.2   Steering Instruments

The way that we steer and regulate public service organizations and their front-line workers has a significant impact on the innovative capacity of the public sector. One of the key findings is that we need to transform the command and incentive systems associated with Classical Public Administration and New Public Management in order to make sure that performance indicators and reward schemes are perceived as supportive rather than controlling in order to prevent the crowding out of the public service motivation and intrinsic motivation of public employees in ways that may hamper innovation (Chapters 12 and 13). A movement towards a more trust-based management that ensures job safety, decentralized autonomy and professional motivation to improve and innovate services is also to be welcomed if we want to unleash the innovative potential of front-line workers. Closer collaboration between professionals and managers will prevent trust-based management from developing professional autonomy in a way that impedes collaborative innovation (Chapter 7).

New and creative ideas might be fostered in and through the daily interaction between those engaged in regulatory practices or service production, but might also come from the outside. Benefitting from innovation fostered elsewhere requires the development of procedures for scanning the external environment and using mass media and professional networks to discover innovative ideas that have been tested in other organizations, appear to have a comparative advantage and are possible to translate and adjust to one's own context (Chapter 5).

New and creative ideas may also be fostered through interaction with local stakeholders, and this calls for the construction of open and transparent rules for engaging relevant and affected actors in processes of collaborative innovation in a responsible and accountable way (Chapter 6). In close connection with this endeavour, we need to create mechanisms that bring out the innovative potential of the interaction between local authorities and private for-profit actors engaged in contracting-out, procurement and partnership arrangements. The contractual arrangements are currently only designed to enhance efficiency and quality but may also become vehicles of public innovation, especially if the proximity between the actors in spatial, cognitive, social and institutional terms is enhanced. The increased use of relational contracting, for example, instead of long and detailed lists of targets and demands with procedures for ongoing negotiations about means and ends, will provide such proximity and provide a setting more conducive to innovation (Chapter 10). Collaboration with private for-profit and non-profit actors may not only help public authorities to foster new and creative ideas and solutions but also enable them to deal with the risks associated with public innovation. For that to happen we need to develop procedures – formal or informal – for risk governance that involves multiple stakeholders in negotiation of risks and rewards (Chapters 2 and 3). Traditional risk management focuses on how to eliminate risks or mitigate their impact and that tends to hamper innovation. Instead we must compare and assess alternative packages of risks and rewards in order to collectively decide which risks we are willing to accept in order to achieve a potential benefit.

In the last two decades we have witnessed an auditing revolution in the public sectors. Some have proved useful, but others with a narrow focus on short-term, easy-to-measure performance indicators have often served to hamper innovation. Hence, we must develop ways of evaluating innovations that go beyond the performance indicators attuned to measure short-term outputs and instead create evaluation and accountability systems that are more focused on learning and are able to deal with complexity and capture a variety of imagined and unimagined effects and the way that these are constructed and perceived by multiple actors (Chapters 3, 14 and 15). The new accountability systems should take into account and accommodate the need for political control and accountability if and when public innovation is co-created with a broad range of public and private stakeholders (Chapter 15). At the same time, we should be aware of the limits to politicians' ability to steer and control public innovation due to the high level of professional and administrative autonomy that is important for mobilizing the ideas of front-line personnel (Chapter 16).

17.3.3   The Exercise of Leadership and Management

The last decades have seen a growing belief in leadership and management as a universal problem-solver. When something does not work properly, more and better leadership is called for. The recommendations in this book seem to continue this trend, although they also challenge the traditional idea of leadership and management as a relation between superiors and subordinates. The large number of recommendations concerning the exercise of leadership and management calls for the introduction of three sub-categories.

17.3.3.1   Political Leadership and Its Interaction with Public Management
Political leadership of public innovation is important because it helps to set the agenda, raise the level of ambition and secure support and resources. Political leadership of collaborative innovation processes can be strengthened by getting politicians to focus on the wicked problems that people within their jurisdiction are facing and to use political power to convene relevant actors who can help them solve the wicked problems in new and creative ways (Chapters 6 and 9). This will often require that politicians be freed from the many administrative tasks and questions that take up much of their time and prevent them from dealing with the real political issues. This may be done by reducing the time spent in routine politics in standing political committees, by working more in thematic ad hoc committees aiming to define and solve bigger political issues and by involving relevant and affected actors. Leading collaborative innovation will require some kind of political metagovernance through which politicians create, frame and participate in collaborative forums and use them as vehicles for policy innovation (Chapter 8). By default, public managers

often take charge of such metagovernance interactive governance arenas, and politicians will therefore have to be aware and fight for the role as metagovernor of the questions that call for the exercise of political authority backed by democratic legitimacy. Ideally, some kind of teamwork between political leaders and administrative managers must be established in order to coordinate their joint efforts to metagovern collaborative innovation processes. The task of creating a well-functioning teamwork falls on the public managers.

Public managers must also create, and involve politicians in creating, a political and organizational climate that is conducive for change and innovation (Chapter 13), that supports and rewards innovation regardless of whether it is a result of invention or re-invention (Chapter 5). In other words, hands-on metagovernance of collaborative processes aiming to find innovative solutions to wicked problems should be supplemented by hands-off metagovernance aiming to create the organizational and cultural conditions for public innovation.

Interaction between political and administrative leaders is also called for in relation to concrete service innovations that are fostered bottom-up through interaction between public professionals, users and local stakeholders. Hence, public managers must pay close attention to their political authorizing environment in order to determine which forms of change and innovation are politically acceptable and which are not (Chapter 13). By the same token, in order to play the role of champions and sponsors of innovation they must work hard to secure political and financial support to innovation (Chapters 4, 5 and 8).

17.3.3.2 Public Management of Organizations and Employees Public managers play a pivotal role in stimulating public innovation. The expansion of trust-based rather than control-based management will help public managers to involve professionals with specialized knowledge and competences in developing and implementing innovative solutions and create a pace for crosscutting collaboration and involvement of other relevant actors. In the process of collaborative innovation both public managers and professionals will have to transform their traditional roles and develop their connective capacities in order to work more closely together in defining problems and creating new and better solutions (Chapters 7 and 8). Public managers must be able to explain the need for public innovation and to accept a certain level of error and failure in the innovation process and thus avoid using the existing command and incentive systems too punitively (Chapter 12).

A crucial finding is that public professionals without a formal leadership role can also act as leaders of collaborative innovation and thus help to mobilize the practical and tacit knowledge of different professionals and the tacit knowledge of users, who are transformed from passive recipients to active co-producers of public service (Chapter 3). In line with the new research on distributive leadership, the task of leading and managing collaboration and innovation should be spread out and undertaken by both formal and informal leaders. Horizontal leadership of teams will often be taken care of by professionals without formal training or leadership positions, and the same goes for integrative leadership of public–private networks and partnerships. Recognizing and rewarding these leadership efforts is crucial for stimulating public innovation.

17.3.3.3   Leading and Managing Collaboration with Civil Society Actors
The innovative capacity of the public sector is enhanced when the established practices and conventional ideas are problematized by external actors from civil society and/or private markets, but the widespread tendency towards institutional separation and insulation from private actors often prevents the public sector from reaping the fruits of public–private collaboration when it comes to innovating public policies and services. Leading and managing the interaction between public and private actors is paramount to rectifying this. The development of a more integrative leadership approach requires the development of the convener role of public leaders and managers so that they can motivate actors too (Chapter 2). Another important task is to strengthen the facilitator role of public leaders and managers so that they can help and encourage actors to engage constructively in creative problem-solving and develop a sense of joint ownership over the process (Chapter 2). As a part of their facilitating role, public managers should support private actors in initiating and driving public innovation, for example, by encouraging the formation of social enterprises (Chapters 4 and 8). They must also ensure that citizens, who are involved as users or unpaid volunteers in the co-production and co-creation of public services, are given sufficient leverage to actually shape and influence service production (Chapter 8). The ability to influence service production is in itself a motivating factor for citizens to initiate and drive public innovation. Finally, since collaboration between the usual suspects of public and private actors sometimes fails to produce novel ideas, public leaders and managers must also learn to act as catalysers who disturb the collaborative arena in order to move the actors out of their comfort zone and beyond a defensive protection of status quo (Chapters 2 and 6).

    As we have seen, the chapters in this book provide a series of implicit and explicit recommendations about how to transform public governance in order to enhance public innovations. Chapter 16 cautions us that such a transformation is difficult to bring about because it in itself requires innovations that are accompanied by risks and uncertainties. Peters also cautions us not to look for simplistic answers when aiming to enhance public innovation, since the way that the public sector is organized, governed and led often has ambiguous effects on the ability to innovate. Hence, a detailed analysis of political and administrative processes and conditions is necessary. A final word of warning is to beware of the trade-offs between the enhancement of public innovation and the wish to safeguard other important goals of the public sector that necessitates careful political debate and tough choices on the part of politicians, administrators and their external collaborators.

17.4   Challenges to Public Leaders and Managers

Public leaders and managers are the vehicles of governance reforms aiming to spur public innovation, and they face a number of challenges when seeking to transform the public sector. In this situation they will need courage to spur innovation in times where safe and reliable service production is at the top of the agenda and courage to engage in collaborative processes of creative problem-solving, and adopt new forms of governance associated with NPG that will only deliver the desired results when supported by the right institutional design and proper leadership and management. There is no road map to New Public Governance and no manual showing how the new governance paradigm is to be implemented, so experimentation and trial and error on the basis of a few guiding principles and ideas are called for. Aiming to deliver new and better public solutions while introducing and experimenting with new organizational forms, steering tools and management strategies is highly demanding and will not be without frustrations and instances of failure. In order for public managers to keep up the momentum for change, these frustrations and failures must be compensated by positive experiences of how innovative solutions give us more for less. The narrative and discursive aspects of the new governance paradigm are crucial for it to become successful.

   To further complicate things, while they are struggling to deliver results in a new and emerging governance context, public leaders and managers must also aim to retain those elements of Classical Public Administration and New Public Management that are useful in the attempt to spur innovation or required in order to achieve other legitimate goals. Developing pragmatic combinations of different governance paradigms is an important strategic task that requires a pragmatic openness, critical reflection and the ability to deal with complexity. Indeed, public leaders and managers must learn to navigate in a political and administrative terrain populated with co-existing governance paradigms that contain conflicting principles and demands but also merge into strange hybrids with different and unpredictable positive and negative effects. It must not only prove its added value vis-à-vis the existing governance paradigms but also tell us about the ways that combine sufficient amounts of pathos, ethos and logos.

We should also bear in mind that the transformation of public governance in support of innovation is not a free lunch. Transforming public organizations, adjusting and redesigning steering instruments and training managers and selected staff members in new ways of initiating and facilitating multi-actor collaboration and catalysing, testing and implementing innovation require initial investments, and the short-term costs may therefore rise. Spurring collaborative innovation also draws on the political and social capital of public leaders and managers, but fortunately these forms of capital will tend to increase when they are used.

Last but not least, it should be mentioned that public leaders and managers will have to cope with the new kinds of blame game that will develop in collaborative arenas when innovations go wrong and lead to blatant failures and negative media reports. The responsibility for such innovation failures may not rest solely with the minister, mayor or their executive managers but be shared among all the actors who participated in designing and implementing the failed innovation. Nevertheless, the press might want to find a scapegoat and the implicated actors may seek to pass the blame to some of the other actors. In this situation public leaders and managers will often get considerable credit from taking the blame and trying to reinterpret the failure as an important step in a joint learning process. The opposite situation arrives when innovations are successful. Here public leaders and managers have to share the praise and honour with the other actors that participated in the co-creation of the new and successful solution.

17.5   Researching Governance Reform to Enhance Innovation

The practical and scholarly interest in public innovation is relatively new and scientific research is underdeveloped. There is a growing number of studies aiming to define public innovation and identify the drivers and barriers, but there is a surprising lack of studies aiming to assess and measure the prevalence and impact of public innovation. The contextualization of public innovation is particularly weak. Hence, the attempt to link the discussion of governance with the discussion of public innovation and explore how different forms of governance may spur public innovation is on virgin ground that the authors in this volume have taken the first step to explore. Consequently, there is an urgent need for both theoretical and empirical research on the forms, causes and consequences of public innovation in general and the relationship between the competing public governance paradigms and public innovation in particular.

The empirical research needs to go beyond single case studies and embrace a variety of different methods. Individual case studies are important in order to grasp the complexity of the interaction between governance and innovation, but regardless of their descriptive and explorative value and the potential benefits from a purposeful selection of critical cases, they often remain anecdotal and prevent generalization. One methodological strategy is, therefore, to do comparative analyses of multiple cases. The use of Qualitative Comparative Analysis (QCA) may be helpful in identifying alternative constellations of governance factors that can produce successful innovation outcomes. The use of QCA in the study of the contextual factors driving collaborative innovation in the public sector will require a careful operationalization of governance factors, the nature and character of collaboration and the forms and impact of innovation.

An alternative methodological strategy is to conduct experiments with randomized control groups, providing stronger evidence of causal mechanisms linking governance, innovation and public value production. However, such experiments are often very difficult to use in complex settings in which many actors and many policy instruments interact in changing political-administrative contexts. Alternatively, innovation research may benefit from the use of design experiments that aim to assess the impact of series of interventions in iterative cycles of design, impact assessment and redesign in order to discover what works in complex settings. The practical relevance of design experiments is high, and their political importance for advancing reforms should not be underestimated even if they do not produce the strong evidence base that more traditional experiments foster. Whatever the form, there is a need for research-based, cost-effective experiments that can produce fast learning in close dialogue with the empirical field of study. Developing procedures for initiating, conducting and reporting the results from such experiments is a joint challenge for researchers and practitioners.

Surveys based on random sampling of respondents may also be used to assess the prevalence of different forms of governance and innovative outputs and outcomes and to analyse the correlation and statistical causality between the two. However, the problem here is that the results from survey analysis rely solely on self-reported data and that we do not have any knowledge about what the respondents focused upon when they answered the questions. Hence, the combination of survey data with other data sources, such as documents, observations and in-depth interviews, is preferred.

In short, we need more studies of governance and innovation based on mixed methods and a close dialogue between researchers and practitioners. With the rise of the public innovation agenda, this need is becoming more and more urgent.

References

Hartley, J. and Torfing, J. 2016. 'Innovation', in C. Ansell and J. Torfing (eds.), *Handbook of Theories of Governance*. Cheltenham: Edward Elgar.

Kingdon, J. W. 1984. *Agendas, Alternatives, and Public Policies*. Boston: Little Brown.

Petersen, O. H., Hjelmar, U. and Vrangbæk, K. 2015. 'Is contracting-out still the great panacea? Meta-analysis of international studies of cost and service quality', presented at the ICCP Conference, Milan, 1–4 July.

Index

absorptive capacity, 102, 201–2
accountability systems. *See also*
   administrative accountability;
   indicator-based accountability;
   organizational innovation; political
   accountability
   actor forums in, 293
   challenges for, 76, 273
   dynamics of, 300
   in governance systems, 329–30
   for organizational innovation, 298, 305
   as political, 295–6, 300
   in public sector, 332–3
   redesign of, 268, 269, 329
   reform in, 26, 294–5
   results-based, 275–6, 282
   social, 293, 303
   types of, 292–4
action, distributed nature of, 38–9
actors, in public sector innovation
   collaboration by, 131–4, 209–10
   contracting out, 202–4
   forms of governance and, 197–8
   in governance reform, 335–6
   institutional proximity and, 208–9
   knowledge-creation by, 208
   public-private partnerships and, 206–11
   public procurement and, 204–6
   risk-taking by, 206, 210
   role of, 198–202, 211–12
Acumen Fund, 75
administrative accountability. *See also*
      organizational innovation
   definition of, 293
   focus of, 303
   local variation in, 302
   professionalism and, 302
   strengthening of, 294, 295–6
administrative capacity
   bureaucracy and, 221
   organizational structures and, 232
   staff dominance in, 226

administrative innovations
   in distance learning, 78
   as innovation type, 219
   need for change and, 268
   supportive environment for, 260
administrative intensity
   bureaucracy concept and, 219
   contractual relations and, 220
   innovation and, 225
   negative interpretation of, 221
   organizational structures and, 223
administrative leadership. *See also* change
      management steps; leadership
   definition of, 256–7
   functions of, 257
   innovation in, 258–9
   theories of, 259–60
Advocacy-Coalition Framework, 314
Afghanistan, health care education in, 74
Ågren, Robert, ix, 25
Alexy, O., 245
American Government Innovation Awards,
   2, 122
Andersen, Lotte Bøgh, ix–xii, 26, 118,
   246, 249
Anheier, Ahelmut, 163
Ansell, Christopher K., ix, 23
appropriateness, logic of, 147
at-risk youth. *See also* youth/young people
   crime-prevention programs, 127–8,
      129–30
   Exit Strategy, 129
   football project, 82–4
   housing/employment project, 75–8
   Resource Centre, 128–9
   Youth Uprising, 127–8
Australia, youth housing/employment
   in, 75–8
Austria, young drivers in, 169–70
authority, vs. collaboration, 118
autonomy
   in governance paradigms, 329

340